Nobu 57.
40 W. 57 St
212-757-3000.

ZAGATSURVEY®

2005

NEW YORK CITY
RESTAURANTS

Editors: Curt Gathje and Carol Diuguid

Coordinator: Larry Cohn

Published and distributed by
ZAGAT SURVEY, LLC
4 Columbus Circle
New York, New York 10019
Tel: 212 977 6000
E-mail: newyork@zagat.com
Web site: www.zagat.com

Acknowledgments

We thank Allison Amend, Lewis Beale, Siobhan Burns, Erica Curtis, Daphne Dennis, Greta Gentile, Lynn Hazlewood, Sarah Lacamoire, Janine Nichols, Bernard Onken, Steven Shukow, Miranda Van Gelder and Laura Vogel. We also thank our associate editor, Robert Seixas, and assistant editor, Griff Foxley, as well as the following members of our staff: Betsy Andrews, Reni Chin, Anuradha Duggal, Schuyler Frazier, Jeff Freier, Shelley Gallagher, Michael Gitter, Randi Gollin, Katherine Harris, Natalie Lebert, Mike Liao, Dave Makulec, Donna Marino, Emily Parsons, Robert Poole, Benjamin Schmerler, Troy Segal, Daniel Simmons, Caren Weiner Campbell and Sharon Yates.

Contents

About This Survey

Here are the results of our *2005 New York City Restaurant Survey*, covering some 1,946 restaurants as tested, and tasted, by a record 30,277 local restaurant-goers.

This marks the 26th year that Zagat Survey has reported on the shared experiences of diners like you. What started here in 1979 as a hobby involving 200 of our friends rating local restaurants purely for fun has come a long way. Today we have over 250,000 surveyors with thousands more registered to vote worldwide, and we have branched out to publish guides to entertaining, golf, hotels, resorts, spas, movies, music, nightlife, shopping, sites and attractions as well as theater. Our *Surveys* are also available on wireless devices and by subscription at zagat.com, where you can vote and shop as well.

By regularly surveying large numbers of avid, educated customers, we hope to have achieved a uniquely current and reliable guide. More than a quarter-century of experience has verified this. This year's NYC participants dined out an average of 3.3 times per week, meaning this *Survey* is based on roughly 5.2 million meals. Of these 30,000 plus surveyors, 54% are women, 46% men; the breakdown by age is 19% in their 20s; 30%, 30s; 18%, 40s; 18%, 50s; and 15%, 60s or above. Our editors have done their best to summarize these surveyors' opinions, with their exact comments shown in quotation marks. We sincerely thank each of these people; this book is really "theirs."

To help guide you to NYC's best meals and best buys, we have prepared a number of lists. See Most Popular (page 9), Top Ratings (pages 10-19), Best Buys (page 20) and Bargain Prix Fixe Menus (pages 21-22). In addition, we have provided 48 handy indexes and have tried to be concise. Given the growth of the Internet, we have also included Web addresses.

To join any of our upcoming Surveys, just register at zagat.com. Each participant will receive a free copy of the resulting guide when published. Your comments and even criticisms of this guide are also solicited. There is always room for improvement with your help. You can contact us at newyork@zagat.com or by mail at Zagat Survey, 4 Columbus Circle, New York, NY 10019. We look forward to hearing from you.

New York, NY
October 18, 2004

Nina and Tim Zagat

What's New

A Watershed Year: For NYC dining, this was the most important year in the last quarter century. It marks the end of an era with the demise of four of the city's five oldest and most renowned classic French restaurants – La Caravelle, La Côte Basque, Lutèce and Le Cirque (the latter will close at year's end but may relocate). Only La Grenouille remains. These were all places where one dressed up to dine; now the city's dress code may be summed up in a word: "informal." Despite this, the restaurant industry has greatly improved and diversified, with 226 openings versus 93 closings. Among 2004's new arrivals, we particularly note per se and Masa. If per se had had enough votes to qualify for listing in our Top Ratings, it would have been No. 1 not just for Food, but for Decor and Service as well, with the highest ratings ever achieved by any restaurant. Likewise, with more votes, Masa would have been close on per se's heels.

Outstanding Arrivals: For quality and diversity, this year's group of newcomers was the best we've ever seen. Besides per se and Masa, standouts include Asiate (Japanese-French), The Biltmore Room (Eclectic), BLT Steak, Café Gray (French), Capital Grille (Steak), Cru (Mediterranean), davidburke & donatella (American), 5 Ninth (Eclectic), Geisha (Japanese), Hearth (American-Italian), Jack's Luxury Oyster Bar (Seafood), Kittichai (Thai), La Bottega (Italian), Landmarc (French), Mas (American), Megu (Japanese), Océo (American), Pace (Italian), Public (Eclectic), Riingo (Japanese), Solo (Mediterranean), Spice Market (SE Asian), V (Steak), Vento (Italian) and Wolfgang's (Steak).

Enter Time Warner: Never before has a single building brought together such a constellation of star chefs, to wit: Thomas Keller (per se), Gray Kunz (Café Gray), Nori Sugie (Asiate), Masayoshi Takayama (Masa, Bar Masa) and Jean-Georges Vongerichten (V Steakhouse), with more to come: Chicago's Charlie Trotter (a seafood brasserie, as yet unnamed), and another Keller venture (Bouchon Bakery).

The Rising Sun: Japanese is now the favorite cuisine of 14% of New Yorkers, up from 4% in just four years. Looking back to our 1995 *Survey,* there was only one Japanese restaurant rated as high as a 26 for its food. This year there were 11 listed by Food rating as follows: Sushi Yasuda, Nobu Next Door, Nobu, Sushi of Gari, Jewel Bako, Poke, Tomoe Sushi, Honmura An, Sugiyama, Blue Ribbon Sushi and Sushi Seki. Furthermore, any of this year's new Japanese arrivals would easily outperform the best we had in 1995.

The Pinnacle: Le Bernardin encored with the *Survey's* No. 1 Food score, edging out the revitalized Bouley (No. 2) and Daniel (No. 3). Sushi Yasuda, just five years old, jumped from No. 23 to No. 5, while Alain Ducasse moved up from No. 14 to No. 10. The most noteworthy first-timer was the East Village's tiny Tasting Room, which debuted at No. 14.

Popularity Poll: In terms of overall popularity, Danny Meyer's perennial front-runners reversed position again, with Gramercy Tavern topping Union Square Cafe as NYC's all-around favorite. Craft scored big, rising from No. 23 to No. 15, while Bouley continued its comeback, moving up to the No. 8 slot. First-timers to the list, all Italian, include 'Cesca (No. 33), L'Impero (No. 35) and Fiamma Osteria (No. 50).

Westward Ho!: The Meatpacking District and next door Way West Chelsea became *the* neighborhood success stories of this year with a profusion of trendy entries: 5 Ninth, Highline, La Bottega, Matsuri, One, Pop Burger, Spice Market and Vento. And that's not all: Poised to open at press time are Ono in the Gansevoort Hotel and Il Posto, a new Batali/Bastianich project opposite Chelsea Market.

Top Chop Shops: Steakhouses showed renewed vigor this year (perhaps boosted by Atkins followers) with some big-time debuts: BLT Steak, Capital Grille, V Steakhouse and Wolfgang's, not to mention new Manhattan beachheads for Bobby Van's and Uncle Jack's. On our Popularity list, Sparks skyrocketed from No. 45 to No. 26, while the venerable Peter Luger climbed from No. 9 to No. 6 against stiff competition.

Rating the Scene: For the first time this year, we asked reviewers to assess New York's overall dining scene using the *Survey*'s 0–30 scoring system across four key criteria. Surveyors awarded the city a 27 for Choice/Diversity and a solid 23 for Creativity. But Hospitality and Table Availability were respectively rated a so-so 14 and 13. In short, the food's great in NY – but only if you can get in and get served. Along the same lines, we asked respondents to name their favorite cuisine; the hands-down winner was Italian with twice as many votes as the runner-up, French, followed in order by Japanese, American, Thai and Chinese.

Cash Flow: The average dinner cost increased only 1%, from $37.06 last year to $37.45 this time around, making NYC the most expensive place to dine in the U.S. By comparison, the U.S. average is $31.51, while overseas capitals remain a lot more expensive: London ($64.00), Paris ($62.42) and Tokyo ($70.87). As for the city's 20 most expensive restaurants, the average cost ($91.28) was similar to last year, but that figure doesn't reflect such newcomers as Masa and per se, all of which cost well over $100, setting a new benchmark for high-end dining.

On the Horizon: In addition to this year's bumper crop, a number of ambitious projects are underway: Geoffrey Zakarian's Country, a companion to his Town; The Modern, Danny Meyer's MoMA outpost helmed by Gabriel Kreuther (ex Atelier); Morimoto, showcasing Iron Chef Masaharu Morimoto; Rue de Vent, a French entry from the Batali/Bastianich juggernaut; Fornino, a Williamsburg Italian via Michael Ayoub (ex Cucina); and BLT Fish, Laurent Tourondel's seafood counterpart to his BLT Steak.

New York, NY
October 18, 2004

Nina and Tim

Nina and Tim Zagat

Ratings & Symbols

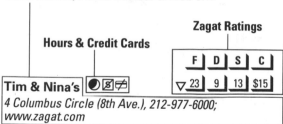

Name, Address, Phone Number & Web Site

Zagat Ratings

Hours & Credit Cards

F	D	S	C

Tim & Nina's ◐ 🚫 ⊘   ▽ 23 | 9 | 13 | $15

*4 Columbus Circle (8th Ave.), 212-977-6000;
www.zagat.com*

◪ Open 24/7, this "literal dive" in the Columbus Circle
subway station offers one-of-a-kind "Chinese-German
dining" where an "hour after you eat you're hungry for
more sweet-and-sour schnitzel"; fans ignore its "Bauhaus
meets Mao's house" look and the staff's "yin-yang"
uniforms (lederhosen for men, cheongsam for women)
and say it's "some cheap trip", even if you must "shout
to order when the trains come in."

Review, with surveyors' comments in quotes

Restaurants with the highest overall ratings and greatest
popularity and importance are printed in CAPITAL LETTERS.

Before reviews a symbol indicates whether responses
were uniform ■ or mixed ◪.

Hours: ◐ serves after 11 PM
🚫 closed on Sunday

Credit Cards: ⊘ no credit cards accepted

Ratings are on a scale of **0** to **30**. Cost **(C)** reflects our
surveyors' estimate of the price of dinner with one
drink and tip.

F	Food	D	Decor	S	Service	C	Cost
23		9		13		$15	

0–9   poor to fair   **20–25**   very good to excellent
10–15   fair to good   **26–30**   extraordinary to perfection
16–19   good to very good   ▽ low response/less reliable

For places listed without ratings, such as a newcomer or
survey write-in, the price range is indicated as follows:

I	$25 and below	E	$41 to $65
M	$26 to $40	VE	$66 or more

Most Popular

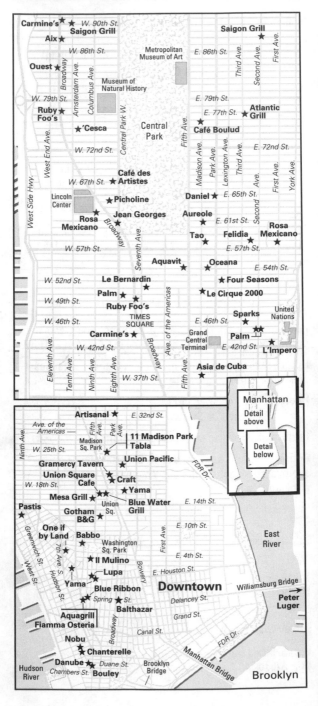

Carmine's ★ — W. 90th St.
Saigon Grill
Aix ★ — W. 88th St.
Saigon Grill ★ — E. 86th St.
Ouest ★ — W. 86th St.

Metropolitan Museum of Art
Museum of Natural History

Ruby Foo's ★ — W. 79th St.
E. 79th St.
Atlantic Grill
'Cesca ★ — E. 77th St.
Café Boulud ★
W. 72nd St. — E. 72nd St.
Central Park

Café des Artistes ★ — W. 67th St.
Lincoln Center
Picholine ★ — Daniel ★ — E. 65th St.
Jean Georges ★ — Aureole
Rosa Mexicano ★ — E. 61st St.
Tao ★ — Felidia ★ — Rosa Mexicano
W. 57th St. — E. 57th St.

Aquavit ★ — Oceana ★ — E. 54th St.
W. 52nd St.
Le Bernardin ★ — Four Seasons ★
Palm ★ — Le Cirque 2000 ★
W. 49th St.
Ruby Foo's ★ — W. 46th St.
TIMES SQUARE
Sparks ★ — United Nations
Carmine's ★ — E. 46th St.
W. 42nd St.
Grand Central Terminal
Palm ★★
L'Impero ★

Asia de Cuba ★ — W. 37th St.

Manhattan
Detail above

Detail below

Artisanal ★ — E. 32nd St.
Madison Sq. Park
W. 25th St.
11 Madison Park ★
Tabla
Union Pacific ★
Gramercy Tavern ★
Union Square Cafe ★ — Craft ★
W. 18th St.
Yama ★
Mesa Grill ★★
Blue Water Grill ★ — E. 14th St.
Pastis ★
Gotham B&G ★
Union Sq.

One if by Land ★ — Babbo ★
Washington Sq. Park
E. 10th St.
East River
Il Mulino ★
E. 4th St.
Yama ★ — Lupa ★
Blue Ribbon ★ — E. Houston St.
Downtown
Williamsburg Bridge →
Spring St. ★
Balthazar ★
Delancey St.
Peter Luger
Aquagrill ★★
Fiamma Osteria
Grand St.
Nobu ★
Canal St.
Chanterelle ★
Danube ★
Bouley ★ — Duane St.
Chambers St.
Brooklyn Bridge
Manhattan Bridge
FDR Dr.
Hudson River
Brooklyn

Most Popular

Each of our surveyors has been asked to name his or her five favorite restaurants. The following list reflects their choices, followed in parentheses by last year's ranking:

1. Gramercy Tavern (2)
2. Union Square Cafe (1)
3. Daniel (3)
4. Gotham Bar & Grill (4)
5. Blue Water Grill (6)
6. Peter Luger (9)
7. Babbo (8)
8. Bouley (12)
9. Jean Georges (7)
10. Nobu (5)
11. Le Bernardin (10)
12. Balthazar (11)
13. Eleven Madison (14)
14. Aureole (13)
15. Craft (23)
16. Chanterelle (15)
17. Four Seasons (16)
18. Aquavit (21)
19. Tabla (17)
20. Artisanal (19)
21. Atlantic Grill (20)
22. Rosa Mexicano (25)
23. Ouest (27)
24. Carmine's (26)
25. Il Mulino (22)
26. Sparks (45)
27. Aquagrill (31)
28. Asia de Cuba (29)
29. Picholine (18)
30. Café des Artistes (24)
31. Mesa Grill (30)
32. Palm (35)
33. 'Cesca (–)
34. Lupa (34)
35. L'Impero (–)
36. Café Boulud (40)
37. Le Cirque 2000 (28)
38. Danube (37)
39. Blue Ribbon (44)
40. One if by Land (39)
41. Oceana (41)
42. Tao (49)
43. Yama (38)
44. Felidia (33)
45. Saigon Grill (–)
46. Ruby Foo's (43)
47. Aix (47)
48. Pastis (–)
49. Union Pacific (32)
50. Fiamma Osteria (–)

It's obvious that many of the restaurants on the above list are among the city's most expensive, but New Yorkers also love a bargain. Fortunately, our city has an abundance of wonderful ethnic restaurants and other inexpensive spots that fill the bill. Thus, we have listed 100 Best Buys on page 20 and over 200 Prix Fixe and Pre-Theater Menus on pages 21–22. Also bear in mind that New York's outer borough restaurants include many venues at prices that are often a third or less than what you'd expect to pay in Manhattan.

Top Ratings

Excluding places with low voting, unless noted by a ▽.

Top 50 Food

28 Le Bernardin
Bouley
Daniel
Gramercy Tavern
Sushi Yasuda
Nobu, Next Door
Nobu
27 Jean Georges
Peter Luger
Alain Ducasse
Gotham Bar & Grill
Danube
Il Mulino
Tasting Room
Veritas
Café Boulud
Aureole
Sushi of Gari
Chanterelle
Trattoria L'incontro
Pearl Oyster Bar
Union Square Cafe
Babbo
Scalini Fedeli
Aquagrill

Saul
Jewel Bako
Annisa
March
26 Oceana
Tomoe Sushi
Tocqueville
Grimaldi's
La Grenouille
Roberto's
Grocery
Craft
Picholine
Atelier
Four Seasons
Wallsé
Blue Hill
Eleven Madison
Honmura An
Lombardi's
Blue Ribbon Sushi
Aquavit
L'Impero
Sushi Seki
Felidia

By Cuisine

American
28 Gramercy Tavern
27 Gotham Bar & Grill
Tasting Room
Veritas
Aureole
Union Square Cafe

American (Regional)
27 Pearl Oyster Bar/NE
25 Cooking with Jazz/Cajun
23 Mesa Grill/SW
22 Tropica/FL
20 Bayou/Creole
Jacques-Imo's/Cajun

Barbecue
23 Daisy May's
21 Virgil's
20 Blue Smoke
18 Lucy
Biscuit
17 Hog Pit

Brasseries
23 Balthazar
Artisanal
L'Absinthe
22 Brasserie 8½
21 Nice Matin
Brasserie

Cafes
27 Café Boulud
Union Square Cafe
25 River Cafe
24 Park Ave. Cafe
23 Duane Park Cafe
Café Pierre

Caribbean/West Indies
22 A/*Caribbean*
Café Habana/*Cuban*
21 Maroons/*Jamaican*
20 Ideya/*Caribbean*
El Malecon/*Dominican*
Victor's Cafe/*Cuban*

Caviar
26 La Grenouille
Four Seasons
25 Caviar Russe▽
24 Petrossian
23 Caviarteria▽
22 FireBird

Chinese
25 Oriental Garden
Shun Lee Palace
24 Mr. Chow
Tse Yang
Mr. K's
23 Chin Chin

Coffeehouses
22 Grey Dog's
Ferrara
21 Once Upon a Tart
20 Le Pain Quotidien
19 Edgar's Cafe
Cafe Lalo

Continental
26 Four Seasons
24 Petrossian
21 Kings' Carriage Hse.
19 Palm Court
16 Ye Waverly Inn
15 Sardi's

Delis
23 Barney Greengrass
Second Ave. Deli
22 Katz's Deli
20 Mill Basin Deli
Carnegie Deli
19 Sarge's Deli

Dessert
26 La Bergamote
25 ChikaLicious
24 Payard Bistro
23 Sweet Melissa
Amy's Bread
Veniero's

French
28 Le Bernardin
Bouley
Daniel
27 Jean Georges
Alain Ducasse
Café Boulud
Chanterelle
26 Tocqueville
La Grenouille
Atelier
25 Fleur de Sel
Montrachet
Le Cirque 2000

French (Bistro)
25 JoJo
db Bistro Moderne
24 Payard Bistro
Capsouto Frères
Le Tableau
Le Gigot

Greek
25 Milos
Periyali
24 Pylos
Thalassa
Taverna Kyclades
23 Molyvos

Hamburgers
24 burger joint
23 Corner Bistro
Island Burgers
21 J.G. Melon
19 Pop Burger
17 Big Nick's

Indian
26 Tabla
25 Tamarind
24 Banjara
Bread Bar at Tabla
Chola
23 Dawat

Italian
27 Il Mulino
Trattoria L'incontro
Babbo
Scalini Fedeli
26 Roberto's
L'Impero
Felidia
25 Al Di La
Lupa
Il Giglio
Piccolo Angolo
Grifone
Lusardi's

Japanese
28 Sushi Yasuda
Nobu, Next Door
Nobu
27 Sushi of Gari
Jewel Bako
26 Poke
Tomoe Sushi
Honmura An
Sugiyama
Blue Ribbon Sushi
Sushi Seki
25 Sushiden
Sushi Sen-nin

Top Food

Korean
23 Woo Lae Oak
    Hangawi
    Gam Mee Ok
    Cho Dang Gol
22 Dok Suni's
    Kum Gang San

Kosher
23 Second Ave. Deli
22 Prime Grill
    Pongal
    Chennai Garden
21 Le Marais
20 Mill Basin Deli

Mediterranean
26 Picholine
24 Convivium
    Harrison
    Red Cat
23 Il Buco
    Trio

Mexican
26 Mexicana Mama
25 Itzocan
    Pampano
24 Maya
23 Hell's Kitchen
    Rosa Mexicano

Middle Eastern
24 Mamlouk
22 Turkish Kitchen
    Zaytoons
    Moustache
21 Üsküdar
    Al Bustan

Noodle Shops
26 Honmura An
23 Sobaya
    Great NY Noodle
22 Big Wong
21 New Bo-Ky
20 Pho Bang

Pizza
27 Di Fara
26 Grimaldi's
    Lombardi's
24 Totonno Pizzeria
    Denino's
    Joe's Pizza

Seafood
28 Le Bernardin
27 Pearl Oyster Bar
    Aquagrill
26 Oceana
25 Milos
    rm

South American
23 Patria
    Chimichurri Grill
22 Churr. Plataforma
    SushiSamba
    OLA
    Calle Ocho

Southern/Soul
22 Ida Mae
    Miss Mamie's
21 Maroons
    Amy Ruth's
20 Pink Tea Cup
    Old Devil Moon

Spanish
24 Casa Mono
23 Bolo
22 Allioli
    El Faro
    Sevilla
    Azafran

Steakhouses
27 Peter Luger
25 Sparks
    MarkJoseph
    Strip House
24 Del Frisco's
    Post House
    Palm
    Wolfgang's
    BLT Steak
23 Dylan Prime
    Ruth's Chris
    Maloney & Porcelli
    Keens

Tapas
23 Bolo
22 Allioli
    Azafran
    El Cid
21 Marichu
    Solera

Thai
25 Erawan
24 Vong
23 Joya
    Wondee Siam
    Holy Basil
    Kin Khao

Vegetarian
24 Gobo
23 Hangawi
22 Vatan
    Pongal
    Chennai Garden
    Candle Cafe/79

Vietnamese
- **24** Nam
- **23** O Mai
- Saigon Grill
- Bao 111
- **22** Nha Trang
- **21** Le Colonial

Wild Cards
- **27** Danube/*Austrian*
- **26** Wallsé/*Austrian*
- Aki/*Japanese-Jamaican*
- Aquavit/*Scandinavian*
- **25** Roy's NY/*Asian-Seafood*
- **22** Spotted Pig/*Gastropub*

By Special Feature

Breakfast
- **27** Jean Georges
- **25** Norma's
- **23** Fifty Seven 57
- **22** Dumonet▽
- **21** Michael's
- **19** Regency▽

Brunch
- **27** Aquagrill
- **26** Atelier
- Wallsé
- Eleven Madison
- Aquavit
- **25** River Cafe

Buffets
- **24** Chola
- **22** Diwan
- Chennai Garden
- Salaam Bombay
- **21** Bukhara Grill
- Utsav

Business Dining
- **28** Le Bernardin
- **27** Gotham Bar & Grill
- Union Square Cafe
- **26** Four Seasons
- **25** Milos
- **23** Bayard's

Child-Friendly
- **23** L & B Spumoni
- Zum Stammtisch
- **21** Virgil's
- **20** Carmine's
- Serendipity 3
- **19** Alice's Tea Cup

Hotel Dining
- **27** Jean Georges/Trump
- Alain Ducasse/Essex Hse.
- Café Boulud/Surrey
- **26** Atelier/Ritz-Carlton CPS
- **25** Le Cirque/NY Palace
- db Bistro Moderne/City Club

Late Dining
- **26** Blue Ribbon Sushi
- **25** Blue Ribbon
- 'ino
- **24** Blue Water Grill
- **23** Corner Bistro
- Wollensky's Grill

Lunch ($20–$25)
- **27** Jean Georges
- Gotham Bar & Grill
- **26** Tocqueville
- Eleven Madison
- **25** Fleur de Sel
- Town

Meet for a Drink
- **28** Gramercy Tavern
- **27** Gotham Bar & Grill
- **25** Town
- Bond Street
- **24** Del Frisco's
- **22** Tao

Most Improved
- **27** Tasting Room
- **25** Sushiden
- 'ino
- **24** Mr. Chow
- Banjara
- Nam

Newcomers/Rated
- **25** Biltmore Room
- davidburke/donatella
- **24** Hearth
- Casa Mono
- Sumile
- Wolfgang's Steak
- BLT Steak
- **23** Megu
- Matsuri
- Public
- Spice Market
- **22** Asiate
- Spotted Pig

Other Major Arrivals▽
Café Gray
Capital Grille
Cru
5 Ninth
Kittichai
Landmarc
Mas
Masa
Océo
per se
Pure Food
Vento
V Steakhouse

Party Sites/Private Rooms
28 Le Bernardin
Daniel
Gramercy Tavern
Nobu
27 Jean Georges
26 La Grenouille
Picholine
Four Seasons
Blue Hill
25 Le Cirque 2000
One if by Land
24 Fiamma Osteria
21 21 Club

People-Watching
23 Balthazar
22 Elio's
Il Cantinori
Mercer Kitchen
21 Da Silvano
19 Angus McIndoe

Power Scenes
28 Daniel
Nobu
27 Jean Georges
Peter Luger
26 Four Seasons (lunch)
25 Le Cirque 2000

Pub Dining
23 Keens
Wollensky's Grill
21 Bridge Cafe
J.G. Melon
20 McHales
19 Moran's Chelsea

Quick Bites
22 City Bakery
Carl's Steaks
21 Once Upon a Tart
20 Fresco on the Go
19 F & B
BB Sandwich

Quiet Conversation
28 Le Bernardin
27 Chanterelle
26 Tocqueville
Picholine
Atelier
22 Asiate

Raw Bars
27 Aquagrill
24 Blue Water Grill
23 Shaffer City
Atlantic Grill
22 Ocean Grill
Blue Fin

Singles Scenes
25 Blue Ribbon
Town
24 Bread Bar at Tabla
23 Mesa Grill
Balthazar
22 Tao

Sleepers▽
28 Donguri
26 Sapori d'Ischia
Eliá
24 Fives
La Cantina
23 Ivo & Lulu

Sunday's Best
28 Bouley
Gramercy Tavern
27 Gotham Bar & Grill
Veritas
Café Boulud
25 Lupa

Tasting Menus
28 Le Bernardin ($100+)
Bouley ($75)
Daniel ($120)
Gramercy Tavern ($95)
27 Jean Georges ($118)
Alain Ducasse ($150+)

Trendy
27 Jewel Bako
26 L'Impero
25 Biltmore Room
davidburke/donatella
24 Hearth
'Cesca
Casa Mono
23 Megu
Matsuri
'inoteca
Spice Market
22 Spotted Pig
Geisha

Trips to the Country
Blue Hill/Stone Barns/NY
Freelance Café/NY
Mill River Inn/LI
Rest. du Village/CT
Ryland Inn/NJ
Xavier's/NY

24-Hour
23 Gam Mee Ok
22 Kum Gang San
20 Wo Hop
Gray's Papaya
Bereket
Kang Suh

Winning Wine Lists
28 Daniel
Gramercy Tavern
27 Jean Georges
Alain Ducasse
Gotham Bar & Grill
Danube
Tasting Room
Veritas
Chanterelle
Babbo
26 Craft
25 Montrachet
23 Bayard's

By Location

Chelsea
25 Biltmore Room
24 Red Cat
Da Umberto
23 Matsuri
O Mai
22 Gascogne

Chinatown
25 Oriental Garden
23 Canton
Great NY Noodle
New Green Bo
22 Grand Sichuan
Nha Trang

East Village
27 Tasting Room
Jewel Bako
25 Itzocan
24 Hearth
Lavagna
Jack's Luxury

East 40s
28 Sushi Yasuda
26 L'Impero
25 Sparks
Sushiden
Grifone
Pampano

East 50s
27 March
26 Oceana
La Grenouille
Four Seasons
Felidia
25 Le Cirque 2000

East 60s
28 Daniel
27 Aureole
26 Sushi Seki
25 JoJo
davidburke/donatella
rm

East 70s
27 Café Boulud
Sushi of Gari
25 Lusardi's
24 Payard Bistro
Campagnola
23 Il Monello

East 80s
26 Poke
25 Sushi Sen-nin
Erminia
Etats-Unis
24 Totonno Pizzeria
23 Primavera

East 90s & 100s
25 Itzocan
23 Nick's
22 Table d'Hôte
21 Pascalou
Vico
Sarabeth's

Financial District/Seaport
25 MarkJoseph
Roy's NY
23 Bayard's
21 Bridge Cafe
Delmonico's
Cabana

Flatiron/Union Square
- *28* Gramercy Tavern
- *27* Veritas
  Union Square Cafe
- *26* Tocqueville
  Craft
- *25* Fleur de Sel

Garment District
- *23* Keens
  Gam Mee Ok
  Cho Dang Gol
- *22* Uncle Jack's
  Ida Mae
  Kum Gang San

Gramercy/Madison Park
- *26* Eleven Madison
  Tabla
- *25* Yama
- *24* Casa Mono
  Union Pacific
  Bread Bar at Tabla

Greenwich Village
- *27* Gotham Bar & Grill
  Il Mulino
  Pearl Oyster Bar
  Babbo
  Annisa
- *26* Tomoe Sushi
  Wallsé
  Blue Hill
  Aki
  Mexicana Mama
- *25* Lupa
  Piccolo Angolo
  Strip House

Harlem
- *22* Miss Mamie's
- *21* Patsy's Pizzeria
  Amy Ruth's
- *20* Bayou
  Rao's
- *16* Sylvia's

Little Italy
- *24* Il Palazzo
- *23* Pellegrino's
  Il Cortile
  Nyonya
- *22* Angelo's/Mulberry
  Ferrara

Lower East Side
- *24* 71 Clinton
- *23* 'inoteca
  WD-50
  ápizz
  Chubo
- *22* Katz's Deli

Meatpacking District
- *23* Old Homestead
  Spice Market
- *22* Paradou
- *21* Pastis
  Macelleria
- *20* Son Cubano

Murray Hill
- *25* Sushi Sen-nin
- *24* Wolfgang's Steak
  Asia de Cuba
- *23* Hangawi
  Artisanal
  Mishima

NoHo
- *25* Bond Street
- *23* Il Buco
  Great Jones Cafe
- *22* Five Points
- *19* Sala
  Serafina

NoLita
- *26* Lombardi's
- *23* Peasant
  Public
- *22* Café Habana
- *20* Cafe Gitane
  Mexican Radio

SoHo
- *27* Aquagrill
- *26* Honmura An
  Blue Ribbon Sushi
- *25* Blue Ribbon
- *24* Fiamma Osteria
  L'Ecole

TriBeCa
- *28* Bouley
  Nobu, Next Door
  Nobu
- *27* Danube
  Chanterelle
  Scalini Fedeli

West 40s
- *25* Sushiden
  Sushi Zen
- *25* db Bistro Moderne
  Triomphe
- *24* Del Frisco's
  Esca

West 50s
- *28* Le Bernardin
- *27* Alain Ducasse
- *26* Atelier
  Sugiyama
  Aquavit
- *25* Milos

West 60s
27 Jean Georges
26 Picholine
23 Shun Lee West
   Rosa Mexicano
   Gabriel's
22 Asiate

West 70s
24 'Cesca
22 Ocean Grill
21 Pomodoro Rosso
   La Grolla
   Nice Matin
   Vinnie's Pizza

West 80s
25 Ouest
24 Celeste
23 Aix
   Barney Greengrass
   Nëo Sushi
22 Sushi Hana

West 90s & Up
24 Gennaro
23 Saigon Grill
22 A
   Terrace in the Sky
   Max
21 Métisse

Outer Boroughs

Bronx
26 Roberto's
21 Dominick's
   Mario's
20 El Malecon
19 F & J Pine
16 Lobster Box

Brooklyn: Bay Ridge
24 Tuscany Grill
   Areo
   Pearl Room
22 Chadwick's
   Embers
   Chianti

Brooklyn: Heights/Dumbo
26 Grimaldi's
25 River Cafe
   Henry's End
24 Queen
   Noodle Pudding
21 Five Front

Brooklyn: Carroll Gardens/ Boerum Hill/Cobble Hill
27 Saul
26 Grocery
23 Sweet Melissa
   Joya
22 Alma
   Zaytoons

Brooklyn: Park Slope
26 Blue Ribbon Sushi
25 Al Di La
   Blue Ribbon
24 Rose Water
   Convivium
22 Cocotte

Brooklyn: Williamsburg
27 Peter Luger
22 Allioli
   SEA
21 Bamonte's
   Planet Thailand
   Diner

Brooklyn: Other
27 Garden Cafe
   Di Fara
24 Totonno Pizzeria
   360
23 L & B Spumoni
   Gargiulo's

Queens: Astoria
27 Trattoria L'incontro
25 Piccola Venezia
24 Taverna Kyclades
23 Elias Corner
   Stamatis
22 Telly's Taverna

Queens: Other
25 Cooking with Jazz
   Erawan
24 Don Peppe
   Park Side
23 Water's Edge
   Nick's

Staten Island
24 Carol's Cafe
   Denino's
   Trattoria Romana
22 Angelina's
21 Lento's
   Aesop's Tables

Top 50 Decor

28 River Cafe
Danube
Daniel
27 Spice Market
Four Seasons
Asiate
Alain Ducasse
La Grenouille
One if by Land
Matsuri
Le Cirque 2000
Rainbow Room
Le Bernardin
Tao
FireBird
26 Café Botanica
Thalassa
Chanterelle
Bouley
Chez Es Saada
Jean Georges
Gramercy Tavern
Town
Café des Artistes
Eleven Madison

Aureole
Scalini Fedeli
Aquavit
Suba
Tabla
Biltmore Room
25 Fifty Seven 57
March
Boat House
Public
Water Club
Hangawi
Water's Edge
Terrace in the Sky
Kings' Carriage Hse.
Union Pacific
Guastavino's
Asia de Cuba
Atelier
Gotham Bar & Grill
Park, The
Craft
24 Jezebel
Bayard's
Oak Room

Gardens

A.O.C.
Barbetta
Barolo
Battery Gardens
Bottino
Bryant Park Grill
Cávo
Convivium
Da Nico
Dolphins
Five Front
Gascogne
Gavroche

Grocery
Hudson Cafeteria
I Coppi
I Trulli
Le Jardin Bistro
Miracle Grill (E. Village)
Park, The
Patois
Pure Food
Tavern on the Green
Va Tutto
ViceVersa
Vittorio Cucina

Great Rooms

Alain Ducasse
Asiate
Atelier
Balthazar
Bayard's
Biltmore Room
Brasserie
Brasserie 8½
Capital Grille
Craft
Daniel
Danube
FireBird
Four Seasons

Guastavino's
La Grenouille
March
Matsuri
Megu
Milos
Mr. K's
Scalini Fedeli
66
Spice Market
Suba
Tao
Town
Union Pacific

Romance

Alain Ducasse
Aureole
Barbetta
Blue Hill
Café des Artistes
Chanterelle
Chez es Saada
Chez Michallet
Convivium
Danube
Erminia
FireBird
Jezebel
JoJo
Kings' Carriage Hse.
La Grenouille
L'Impero
March
Mark's
Mas
One if by Land
Piccola Venezia
Place, The
Primavera
Provence
River Cafe
Scalini Fedeli
Suba
Tavern on the Green
Terrace in the Sky
Top of the Tower
Water's Edge

Views

Asiate
Battery Gardens
Boat House
Bryant Park Grill
Cipriani Dolci
Foley's Fish House
Harbour Lights
Lobster Box
Marina Cafe
Michael Jordan's
per se
Pete's Downtown
Rainbow Room
River Cafe
Riverview
Sea Grill
Tavern on the Green
Terrace in the Sky
Top of the Tower
V Steakhouse
Water Club
Water's Edge

Top 50 Service

28 Alain Ducasse
27 Le Bernardin
    Daniel
    Gramercy Tavern
    Chanterelle
    Four Seasons
26 Bouley
    Jean Georges
    March
    La Grenouille
    Danube
    Aureole
    Atelier
    Annisa
    Union Square Cafe
25 Oceana
    Gotham Bar & Grill
    Café Boulud
    Tasting Room
    Eleven Madison
    Veritas
    Picholine
    River Cafe
    Aquavit
    Le Cirque 2000

    Tabla
    Scalini Fedeli
    One if by Land
    Le Perigord
    Jewel Bako
24 Tocqueville
    Craft
    Grocery
    Bayard's
    Mr. K's
    Babbo
    Nobu
    Fifty Seven 57
    Sushi Yasuda
    Blue Hill
    Saul
    Fleur de Sel
    Honmura An
    Water's Edge
    rm
23 Le Gigot
    Erminia
    Montrachet
    L'Impero
    Hangawi

Best Buys

Full-Menu Restaurants

1. Mama's Food/*American*
2. New Bo-Ky/*Vietnamese*
3. Zaytoons/*Middle Eastern*
4. teany/*Tearoom*
5. Big Wong/*Chinese*
6. Joya/*Thai*
7. Penelope/*American*
8. Pump /*Health Food*
9. Bereket/*Turkish*
10. La Taza de Oro/*Puerto Rican*
11. Brennan & Carr/*American*
12. Olive Vine/*Middle East.*
13. Zeytuna/*Eclectic*
14. Pho Bang/*Vietnamese*
15. Rice/*Eclectic*
16. L & B Spumoni/*Italian*
17. Whole Foods/*Eclectic*
18. Nha Trang/*Vietnamese*
19. SEA/*Thai*
20. Pacifico/*Mexican*
21. Sweet-n-Tart Cafe/*Chinese*
22. Veg. Paradise/*Chinese*
23. Old Devil Moon/*Southern*
24. Chennai Garden/*Indian*
25. Great NY Noodle/*Chinese*
26. Veselka/*Ukrainian*
27. Sam's Noodle/*Chinese*
28. El Malecon/*Dominican*
29. Pho Viet Huong/*Vietnam.*
30. Wondee Siam/*Thai*
31. Wo Hop/*Chinese*
32. Mangia/*Mediterranean*
33. X.O./*Chinese*
34. Mee Noodle/*Chinese*
35. Alice's Tea/*Tearoom*
36. Pam Real/*Thai*
37. Tierras/*Colombian*
38. Pepe . . . To Go/*Italian*
39. Saigon Grill/*Vietnamese*
40. Dojo/*Health Food*
41. Zabar's Cafe/*Eclectic*
42. Nyonya/*Malaysian*
43. Le Gamin/*Bistro*
44. Biscuit/*barbecue*
45. Republic/*Asian*
46. Lamarca/*Italian*
47. New Green Bo/*Chinese*
48. Cafe Mogador/*Moroccan*
49. Moustache/*Middle East.*
50. Flor de Mayo/*Peruvian*

Specialty Shops

1. Krispy Kreme/*doughnuts*
2. Gray's Papaya/*hot dogs*
3. Emack & Bolio's/*ice cream*
4. Papaya King/*hot dogs*
5. Joe's Pizza/*pizza*
6. Little Italy Pizza/*pizza*
7. Ess-a-Bagel/*deli*
8. Chipotle/*Mexican*
9. BB Sandwich/*sandwich*
10. burger joint/*burgers*
11. Amy's Bread/*baked goods*
12. Carl's/*cheese steaks*
13. Blue 9/*burgers*
14. La Bergamote/*bakery*
15. Di Fara/*pizza*
16. Peanut Butter/*sandwich*
17. Grilled Cheese/*sandwich*
18. Pizza 33/*pizza*
19. DT.UT/*coffeehse.*
20. Grey Dog's/*coffeehse.*
21. 71 Irving Place/*coffeehse.*
22. Hale & Hearty/*soup*
23. Hampton Chutney/*Indian*
24. Veniero's/*Italian pastry*
25. Vinnie's Pizza/*pizza*
26. Sweet Melissa/*pastry*
27. ChikaLicious/*desserts*
28. Caffe Reggio/*coffee*
29. Pie/*pizza*
30. Once Upon a Tart/*sandwich*
31. Chop't Salad/*salads*
32. Better Burger/*burgers*
33. Corner Bistro/*burgers*
34. Two Boots/*pizza*
35. Burritoville/*Mexican*
36. Press 195/*sandwiches*
37. Cosí/*sandwiches*
38. 'wichcraft/*sandwiches*
39. Pinch/*pizza*
40. Mex. Sandwich/*Mexican*
41. Ferrara/*Italian pastry*
42. Denino's/*pizza*
43. A Salt & Battery/*fish 'n' chips*
44. Au Bon Pain/*baked goods*
45. Island Burgers/*burgers*
46. Dishes/*sandwich*
47. Tossed/*salads*
48. Edgar's Cafe/*coffeehse.*
49. Grimaldi's/*pizza*
50. Pintaile's/*pizza*

Bargain Prix Fixe Menus

Lunch

Amuse	20.05	Le Cirque 2000	29.00
Arqua	20.00	L'Ecole	20.05
Artisanal	20.05	Le Colonial	25.95
Asiate	35.00	Lenox Room	20.05
Atlantic Grill	20.05	Le Perigord	28.00
Aureole	20.05	L'Impero	28.00
Avra Estiatorio	24.95	Madison Bistro	21.25
Basta Pasta	15.00	Manhattan Grille	12.95
Bay Leaf	13.95	Marichu	26.00
Beacon	23.00	Mark's	30.00
Becco	16.95	Mercer Kitchen	20.00
Bistro du Nord	14.95	Milos	35.00
Bolo	20.05	Molyvos	22.50
Bombay Palace	12.95	Montparnasse	19.95
Bouley	35.00	Montrachet (Fri.)	20.05
Café Botanica	26.00	Mr. K's	25.00
Café des Artistes	25.00	Novitá	19.95
Cafe Luxembourg	24.00	Odeon	20.00
Café Pierre	36.00	Orsay	20.95
Capsouto Frères	20.05	Pampano	20.05
Chanterelle	38.00	Park Bistro	22.00
Chiam	20.50	Patria	20.05
Chin Chin	20.05	Patsy's	29.00
Chola	13.95	Payard Bistro	28.00
Churr. Plataforma	29.95	Pó	25.00
Cibo	26.95	Quatorze Bis	16.00
Cinque Terre	24.00	Queen	22.95
Circus	19.00	René Pujol	23.00
Craft	32.00	Salaam Bombay	12.95
davidburke/donatella	33.00	San Domenico	20.05
Dawat	14.00	Sapphire Indian	11.95
Delegates' Dining	22.50	Sardi's	29.95
Diwan	13.95	Seppi's	23.00
Downtown	35.00	Shaan	13.95
Duane Park Cafe	21.50	Shaffer City	19.99
Eleven Madison	25.00	Shun Lee Palace	20.05
Felidia	29.50	66	20.05
FireBird	28.95	SushiSamba	20.05
Fleur de Sel	25.00	Sushi Yasuda	20.50
Frère Jacques	22.00	Tabla	32.00
fresh.	20.05	Tamarind	20.05
Gallagher's Steak	20.05	Tavern on the Green	28.00
Gascogne	19.50	Thalia	16.95
Gigino	20.00	Tocqueville	20.05
Giorgio's/Gramercy	15.00	Town	25.00
Gotham Bar & Grill	25.00	Tse Yang	25.75
Guastavino's	25.00	Tuscan	24.00
Hangawi	24.95	21 Club	32.00
Honmura An	18.00	Ulrika's	22.00
Jean Georges	20.05	Union Pacific	20.05
Jewel of India	13.95	Utsav	13.95
JoJo	20.00	ViceVersa	20.12
Kings' Carriage Hse.	18.95	Vong	20.00
La Mediterranée	21.95	Water Club	20.05
La Metairie	25.00	Water's Edge	29.00
Le Bernardin	35.00	Zoë	20.05

Bargain Prix Fixe Menus
Dinner

Where applicable, the first price is for pre-theater, the second for normal dinner hours.

Aki†	24.00	Le Boeuf à la Mode	37.50
Alouette	22.00	L'Ecole	29.95
Amuse†	30.00	Le Colonial†	26.00
A.O.C. Bedford†	29.00	Le Gigot†	29.00
Arqua	30.00	Le Madeleine†	30.00
Artisanal	30.05	Lenox Room†	25.00
Atlantic Grill†	26.00	Le Singe Vert†	21.95
Azalea†	27.00	Le Tableau†	25.00
Bay Leaf†	20.95	Levana	29.95
Beacon	38.00	Le Veau d'Or	20.00
Becco	21.95	Luxia†	29.00
Bistro du Nord†	18.95	Madison Bistro	31.00
Boi	24.50	Mamlouk	35.00
Bombay Palace	19.95	Manhattan Grille†	24.95
Brasserie 8½†	35.00	Mark's†	36.00
Brasserie Julien†	25.00	Métisse†	25.00
Brasserie LCB†	39.00	Metro Fish	25.00
Bryant Park Grill†	25.00	Molyvos†	34.50
Café Botanica†	38.00	Montparnasse†	19.95
Cafe Nosidam†	21.95	Montrachet	35.00
Candela†	19.99	Murals on 54	39.00
Capsouto Frères	30.05	Ocean Grill†	22.95
Cascina†	24.50	Odeon†	28.00
Chez Michallet	23/30	Ouest†	26.00
Chez Napoléon	25.00	Park Bistro†	22.00
Chin Chin	30.05	Pascalou†	18.95
Cibo	29.95	Pasha†	22.95
Cinque Terre	39.00	Patois†	20.00
Del Frisco's†	34.95	Payard Bistro†	34.00
Dolphins†	20.00	Remi	30.12
Garden Cafe	28.00	Russian Samovar†	28.00
Gascogne†	27.00	San Domenico†	32.50
Gavroche†	19.00	Saul	30.00
Gigino	30.00	Seppi's†	32.00
Giovanni†	29.75	Shaan†	21.95
Halcyon†	39.00	Sharz Cafe†	18.50
Hangawi	29.95	Sumile†	35.00
Henry's End†	21.99	Sushi Yasuda	20.50
Indochine†	25.00	Table d'Hôte†	22.50
Jacques Brasserie†	22.00	Tavern on the Green†	32.00
Jarnac	29.00	Thalia†	30.05
Jewel of India†	21.95	Tocqueville†	38.00
Jules†	19.95	Torre di Pisa	26.95
Kitchen 22/82	25.00	Trata Estiatorio†	19.95
La Baraka	24/32	Trio	30.12
La Belle Vie†	21.95	21 Club†	37.00
La Boîte en Bois†	32.00	Utsav†	20.00
La Mangeoire	25/28	Vatan	22.95
La Mediterranée	25.00	ViceVersa†	30.12
La Metairie†	25.00	Village	25.00
La Petite Auberge	23.95	Vivolo†	23.95
Lavagna†	25.00	Vong†	38.00

† Pre-theater only

Restaurant Directory

A ☒⇄

22 | 10 | 20 | $23

947 Columbus Ave. (bet. 106th & 107th Sts.), 212-531-1643

☒ "Comically small" BYO French-Caribbean in Morningside Heights where "zesty", "unpretentiously inventive" chow is prepared in a "matchbox"-size kitchen that's a triumph of "nanotechnology"; given the "can't-be-beat" prices, plan to "wait on line."

Abigael's

▽ 20 | 15 | 19 | $44

1407 Broadway (bet. 38th & 39th Sts.), 212-575-1407; www.abigaels.com

☒ "You don't give up anything" to dine kosher at this Garment District New American serving "solid" food "without chichi innovation"; well, you might give up some ambiance ("a bit drab"), but "decent pricing" keeps it "packed", especially midday; N.B. the new Green Tea Lounge upstairs features a sushi bar.

Above

19 | 21 | 19 | $47

Hilton Times Sq., 234 W. 42nd St., 21st fl. (bet. 7th & 8th Aves.), 212-642-2626

☒ Usually "quiet" given its "difficult-to-find" entrance, this "unsung" hotel New American is a "haven from 42nd Street havoc" with "slightly above-average" fare and "experienced" service; sightseers split on its 21st-floor view ("cool" vs. "disappointing"), but most agree the "high" tabs live up to its name.

Acappella ☒

24 | 21 | 22 | $61

1 Hudson St. (Chambers St.), 212-240-0163; www.acappella-restaurant.com

■ "Fantastic" Northern Italian food provides the grace notes at this "dark" TriBeCa "cocoon" known for its "gratis grappa cart" and a tuxedoed staff "so attentive they'll catch your napkin before it hits the floor"; in short, expect to "feel like royalty", so long as "money is no object."

Acme Bar & Grill ●

17 | 12 | 15 | $24

9 Great Jones St. (bet. B'way & Lafayette St.), 212-420-1934; www.acmebarandgrill.com

■ "All the hot sauces known to man" line the walls of this NoHo Cajun "hoot", a "charmingly run-down" study in "Louisiana funk", where the "cheap", "white-trash comfort food" is "decent" but incidental to the "raucous" patrons swilling "Dixie beer"; "bad garage bands playing in the basement" lend extra authenticity.

Acqua

17 | 17 | 17 | $31

718 Amsterdam Ave. (bet. 94th & 95th Sts.), 212-222-2752

☒ In a "neighborhood that needs more restaurants", this Upper West Side Italian provides "great value" and is "close to Symphony Space" to boot; downsides, however, include a "routine" menu, "hit-or-miss service" and "*Trading Spaces*"-worthy decor.

Acqua Pazza

22 | 21 | 21 | $54

36 W. 52nd St. (bet. 5th & 6th Aves.), 212-582-6900; www.acquapazzanyc.com

■ Take a quick trip to the "Amalfi coast" via this "stylish" Midtown Italian seafooder, a "civilized" spot featuring "very fresh" fish, "low-carb pasta" options and "hefty" tabs; though "within walking distance of theaters", it's mostly a "power-lunch" locus, making dinner "calming" and "quiet."

Adä

23 | 22 | 22 | $47

208 E. 58th St. (bet. 2nd & 3rd Aves.), 212-371-6060

☒ Those "tired of curry-in-a-hurry" tout this "unique" nouvelle Indian oasis near the Queensboro Bridge where "sumptuous" cuisine is served with "flair" in "upscale" environs; fans say it "doesn't get the attention it deserves", but contras counter it's "frequently empty" due to "pretension" and "overpricing."

Aesop's Tables ⊠ | 21 | 20 | 19 | $42 |

1233 Bay St. (Maryland Ave.), Staten Island, 718-720-2005; www.aesopstables.net

■ A "rare find on Staten Island", this "tiny" Med–New American bistro is "surprisingly sophisticated" despite the "middle-of-nowhere" address; an "ambitious menu", "attentive" staff, "lovely garden" and not-bad pricing add up to a "charming slice of country living."

Afghan Kebab House | 18 | 10 | 16 | $21 |

2680 Broadway (102nd St.), 212-280-3500
764 Ninth Ave. (bet. 51st & 52nd Sts.), 212-307-1612
1345 Second Ave. (bet. 70th & 71st Sts.), 212-517-2776
155 W. 46th St. (bet. 6th & 7th Aves.), 212-768-3875
74-16 37th Ave. (bet. 74th & 75th Sts.), Queens, 718-565-0471

■ Your pocketbook "won't get skewered" at this "reliably exotic" Afghan chainlet supplying "fragrant" meals "on a stick" at "dirt-cheap" tabs; the BYO policy (with "no corkage" fee) helps blot out the "pretty dreary" settings.

Agave | 19 | 19 | 17 | $34 |

140 Seventh Ave. S. (bet. Charles & W. 10th Sts.), 212-989-2100; www.agaveny.com

■ This "adobe enclave" near Sheridan Square lends a "Santa Fe vibe" to the Village via an "interesting", midpriced Southwestern menu that makes for "solid, if not amazing", dining; surveyors split on service ("awfully slow" vs. "couldn't be friendlier") but no one knocks one of the "largest varieties of tequila in town."

AIX | 23 | 23 | 22 | $59 |

2398 Broadway (88th St.), 212-874-7400; www.aixnyc.com

■ West Side gastronomes are "aix-static" about this French "breath of fresh air" with "all the right moves": "adventurous", "on-point" cooking from chef Didier Virot, stylish modern surroundings (be sure to "sit upstairs"), "comfortable pro" service and plenty of "beautiful people"; ok, it's "aix-pensive", but to "save a little dough, eat at the bar."

Aja ● | – | – | – | E |

1068 First Ave. (58th St.), 212-888-8008

This new Asian bistro near the Queensboro Bridge surprises with a striking design featuring carved stone walls, mammoth Buddha statues and an indoor pond that meanders beneath a glass-paneled floor; an equally intriguing menu stresses sushi and sashimi, as well as a variety of cooked items, all at fairly steep prices.

aka Cafe ● | 19 | 15 | 18 | $28 |

49 Clinton St. (bet. Rivington & Stanton Sts.), 212-979-6096; www.akacafe.com

◪ The "portions are about as small as the prices" at this Eclectic Lower East Side sandwich 'n' snack specialist with "limited" but "inventive" offerings; its "hipster" following digs the "chic five-and-dime" decor but disses "tight" seating and a "menu that never seems to change."

Akdeniz ⊠ | – | – | – | M |

19 W. 46th St. (bet. 5th & 6th Aves.), 212-575-2307

On a stretch of West 46th with few dining options comes this new Turk drawing casual crowds with a shareable menu of hot and cold meze as well as fresh seafood, all served by a black-clad staff; bargain-seekers go bonkers over the $17.95 prix fixe dinner.

Aki
26 | 15 | 23 | $38

181 W. Fourth St. (bet. Barrow & Jones Sts.), 212-989-5440
☑ "Good things come in small packages" at this "under-the-radar" Villager with "boundary-pushing" Japanese-Jamaican cuisine that's "original", "delicious" and an "incredible value"; "service is attentive by default" since the joint's the "size of a broom closet."

Aki Sushi
18 | 11 | 16 | $27

366 W. 52nd St. (bet. 8th & 9th Aves.), 212-262-2888
1425 York Ave. (bet. 75th & 76th Sts.), 212-628-8885
☑ "Decent sushi" at "moderate" tabs is yours at this "neighborhoody" East Side/West Side Japanese duo with claustrophobe appeal since they're "rarely crowded"; still, given the "tiny" setups and "minimalist", "Home Depot" decor, many opt for "takeout or delivery."

ALAIN DUCASSE ☒
27 | 27 | 28 | $191

Essex House, 155 W. 58th St. (bet. 6th & 7th Aves.), 212-265-7300;
www.alain-ducasse.com
■ Now that Masa is officially NYC's most expensive restaurant, the prices at Alain Ducasse's "sybaritic" Central Park South showplace may seem "almost reasonable" considering what you get in return: "sumptuous" French creations from executive chef Christian Delouvrier, a "pomp-and-circumstance" setting, meticulous but "unpretentious service" (rated No. 1 in this *Survey*) and a "table that's yours for the night"; so "pretend you're Bill Gates" and trade a few shares for a "once-in-a-lifetime" indulgence in "pure hedonism."

Al Bustan
21 | 16 | 20 | $40

827 Third Ave. (bet. 50th & 51st Sts.), 212-759-5933
☑ One of NY's few Lebanese specialists, this East Midtowner is touted for its "fresh ingredients" and "authentic", "delectable" flavors, with meze standing out as a "best bet"; despite a rather "stark" setting, it's a "reliable lunch standby" and something different for dinner.

Al Di La
25 | 18 | 21 | $39

248 Fifth Ave. (Carroll St.), Brooklyn, 718-783-4565;
www.aldilatrattoria.com
■ "Fantastic", "savory" cooking at relatively "gentle prices" explains why this oh-so-"popular" Park Slope Venetian is "always packed"; "get your gondola there early" as no reserving means "interminable waits", though the arrival of their new "wine bar around the corner" ("finally!") makes "passing the time" more palatable.

Aleo
20 | 17 | 20 | $41

7 W. 20th St. (5th Ave.), 212-691-8136; www.aleorestaurant.com
■ The "food's prime-time" and the service "genuine" at this Flatiron Med-Italian "keeper" that's a "perfect summer date place" thanks to a "cute garden"; despite being parked on an "out-of-the-way block", "fair prices" help make it a "natural" neighborhood "destination."

Alfama
22 | 21 | 23 | $45

551 Hudson St. (Perry St.), 212-645-2500; www.alfamarestaurant.com
■ Have a taste of "Lisbon on the Hudson" at this "different" West Village Portuguese where the "silky" cooking is in tune with the "cool, calm and collected" atmosphere; though "prices could be cheaper", an "amazing" port list helps ease the pain while Wednesday's live "fado singer adds charm."

Al Forno Pizzeria ☒
22 | 13 | 17 | $23

1484 Second Ave. (bet. 77th & 78th Sts.), 212-249-5103
■ For "thin crusts you can count on", Upper Eastsiders head to this "underrated" pizzeria with an "awesome brick oven" that diehards

claim will give nearby Totonno a "run for their money"; "cheap" tabs and "high standards" sweeten the deal.

Alfredo of Rome
17 | 18 | 19 | $45

4 W. 49th St. (bet. 5th & 6th Aves.), 212-397-0100; www.alfredos.com

◪ Its eponymous fettuccine dish alone "justifies the existence" of this "bright, sleek" Rock Center Southern Italian festooned with "Al Hirschfeld's classic" caricatures; still, cynics nix the "inconsistent service", "noise" and "nothing-special" menu, ceding it to "tourists."

Algonquin Hotel
15 | 22 | 19 | $52

Algonquin Hotel, 59 W. 44th St. (bet. 5th & 6th Aves.), 212-840-6800; www.algonquinhotel.com

◪ The "ghost of Robert Benchley" hovers over this "venerable" Midtown hotel "survivor" where the "unexceptional", "expensive" American fare plays second fiddle to the "show-stealing" cabaret in the Oak Room; suckers for "old-time charm" opt for cocktails and "bon mots" in the wonderful wood-paneled lobby lounge.

Alias
22 | 16 | 18 | $40

76 Clinton St. (Rivington St.), 212-505-5011

■ If you can "get over the bodega facade", this "hip" Lower Eastsider (and 71 Clinton sibling) offers "innovative", "affordable" American dishes to an "interesting crowd" of regulars; granted, service can be "overly casual" and the "small space means everyone's your neighbor", but overall it's a "good option" for the area.

Alice's Tea Cup
19 | 21 | 16 | $23

102 W. 73rd St. (bet. Amsterdam & Columbus Aves.), 212-799-3006; www.alicesteacup.com

◪ For the ultimate in "mother-daughter bonding", try this "whimsical" West Side tearoom serving an "impressive selection" of brews (over 100 varieties) in what looks like "your auntie's dining room"; despite a "spacey" staff, "long waits" and "pretty-penny" prices, it earns points for "personality and originality."

Aliseo Osteria del Borgo ⌷
▽ 23 | 21 | 22 | $35

665 Vanderbilt Ave. (bet. Park & Prospect Pls.), Brooklyn, 718-783-3400

■ "Largely undiscovered", this "small" Prospect Heights Italian wine bar/eatery purveys an "excellent" albeit "limited" menu accompanied by an "outstanding" selection of "affordable" vinos from Central Italy's Marche region; the "passion of the owner" is also reflected in the "affable", "homey" ambiance.

Allioli ◐
22 | 17 | 17 | $35

291 Grand St. (bet. Havemeyer & Roebling Sts.), Brooklyn, 718-218-7338; www.allioli.net

◪ "Heavenly tapas" and "tasty sangria" sum up the appeal of this Williamsburg Spaniard seemingly lifted from the "backwaters of Barcelona"; nitpickers find portions "too small" and tabs "a bit" big, while outdoorsy types report that the "funky" garden looks "better once it's dark outside."

Alma
22 | 20 | 18 | $32

187 Columbia St., 2nd fl. (DeGraw St.), Brooklyn, 718-643-5400; www.almarestaurant.com

■ Sure, the "upscale" Mexican chow at this "festive" Carroll Gardens spot is "creative" and "well spiced", service is "friendly" and prices are "reasonable", but the "wow" award goes to the rooftop patio with "killer views" of Lower Manhattan and the Brooklyn piers; N.B. an expansion of the roof deck is underway at press time.

Alouette ◐
20 | 17 | 18 | $41

2588 Broadway (bet. 97th & 98th Sts.), 212-222-6808
■ "Gentrification" comes to the Upper Upper West Side via this "jaunty" little French duplex that "could easily hold its own anywhere"; "consistently excellent" food, "fair pricing" and a "convivial" staff compensate for digs so "tight" that a "sardine would feel crowded."

Alphabet Kitchen ◐
19 | 17 | 16 | $32

171 Ave. A (bet. 10th & 11th Sts.), 212-982-3838
◪ "Sublime sangria is the highlight" at this "bustling" Alphabet City Spaniard that also appeals with its "affordable" selection of "outstanding" tapas, not to mention the "shady back garden" complete with a "waterfall"; its weak link – "nonchalant service" – is almost forgivable given the staff's "good looks."

Alta
▽ 21 | 20 | 18 | $41

64 W. 10th St. (bet. 5th & 6th Aves.), 212-505-7777;
www.altarestaurant.com
■ There's a new twist on the "tapas scene" in the form of this "charming" Village Mediterranean with an "interesting" array of "tasty morsels" that arrive in "ultra-small" portions but "add up quickly" costwise; a "terrific" back room with balcony seating and a big brick fireplace make up for somewhat "distracted service."

Amarone ◐
18 | 14 | 18 | $36

686 Ninth Ave. (bet. 47th & 48th Sts.), 212-245-6060
◪ A "safe bet before or after the curtain", this "serviceable" Hell's Kitchen Italian "gets you to the show on time" after feeding you "wonderful homemade pasta" and other "solid" red-sauce classics; "neighborhood pricing" provides "good bang for the buck", and as for the "cramped" setup, "hey, you're in Manhattan" – get used to it.

America
14 | 15 | 14 | $29

9 E. 18th St. (bet. B'way & 5th Ave.), 212-505-2110; www.arkrestaurants.com
◪ "Comfort food rules" at this "mammoth" Flatiron American featuring an "encyclopedia-size menu" that's "not for the indecisive" but rather geared toward "tourists and kids"; though prices are "reasonable", the "underwhelming" grub and "get-out-your-megaphone" noise level strikes many as "more Las Vegas than Manhattan."

American Grill
19 | 17 | 19 | $42

420 Forest Ave. (bet. Bard Ave. & Hart Blvd.), Staten Island, 718-442-4742;
www.americangrill.org
■ The "who's who of Staten Island" patronize this "comfortable" local "power staple" for its "sharp" American cooking and "courteous" staffers who make sure "all the little things are attended to"; despite somewhat "expensive" tabs and "nothing-to-look-at" decor, there's not much else in these parts with the same "Manhattan feel."

Amici Amore I
▽ 19 | 19 | 19 | $39

29-35 Newtown Ave. (30th St.), Queens, 718-267-2771; www.amiciamore1.com
■ "Cozy, romantic" Astoria Italian "gem" that's become an "important part of the neighborhood" thanks to "dependable, well-prepared dishes", an "aim-to-please" staff and decor that's "better than expected"; those who yearn for the big city might take comfort in its "Manhattan prices."

Amma
23 | 17 | 20 | $41

246 E. 51st St. (bet. 2nd & 3rd Aves.), 212-644-8330; www.ammanyc.com
■ "Not your run-of-the-mill Indian", this "upscale" East Midtowner offers "original", "aromatic" items at slightly above-average prices in a "tasteful dining room sans Christmas lights"; but "no one knows

what will happen" since the former "chefs have left", putting the Food rating in question.

Amuse ◑
20 | 21 | 18 | $48

108 W. 18th St. (bet. 6th & 7th Aves.), 212-929-9755;
www.amusenyc.com

■ "All hunger levels" are addressed at this "modern" Chelsea New American where you can "graze lightly or eat heartily" thanks to a "Craft-y", "mix 'n' match" menu of "different-size dishes"; though the formula "takes getting used to" and prices can "add up", this experiment in "flexible dining" is usually "busy and buzzing."

Amy Ruth's
21 | 12 | 18 | $23

113 W. 116th St. (bet. Lenox & 7th Aves.), 212-280-8779;
www.amyruthsrestaurant.com

☑ "Mighty good" soul food is the excuse to "stuff yourself silly" at Carl Redding's "cholesterol-be-damned" Harlem Southerner where the "irresistible" "chicken and waffles can't be beat"; if "service is spotty" it's still "darn friendly", while "very reasonable" pricing ices the cake.

Amy's Bread
23 | 11 | 16 | $11

Chelsea Mkt., 75 Ninth Ave. (bet. 15th & 16th Sts.), 212-462-4338
972 Lexington Ave. (bet. 70th & 71st Sts.), 212-537-0270
672 Ninth Ave. (bet. 46th & 47th Sts.), 212-977-2670 ⊅
www.amysbread.com

☑ You must "forget about Atkins" at this trio of "carboholics' delights" where the "luscious displays" of "fab" breads and "world-class" baked goods look "so good they should be illegal"; despite some downsides – an "overworked staff" and "tight, limited" seating – you should still expect "prime-time long lines."

Angelica Kitchen ⊅
20 | 14 | 16 | $23

300 E. 12th St. (bet. 1st & 2nd Aves.), 212-228-2909; www.angelicakitchen.com

☑ "Health nuts abound" at this "idiosyncratic" East Village vegan, a "natural foods paradise" for the "crunchy crowd"; foes find the menu "not exactly inspiring" and say "service needs thawing" ("is smiling permitted?"), but there's no argument it's "healthy for your budget."

Angelina's
22 | 18 | 18 | $54

26 Jefferson Blvd. (Annadale Rd.), Staten Island, 718-227-7100;
www.angelinasristorante.com

■ Owner "Angelina caters to your every need" at this "Manhattan-like" Staten Island Italian, a "high-class joint" so long as you overlook the "strip-mall locale"; the cooking's "excellent", though the "Park Avenue pricing" and "wanna-be *Sopranos*" crowd can be turnoffs.

Angelo & Maxie's ◑
21 | 18 | 18 | $49

233 Park Ave. S. (19th St.), 212-220-9200; www.angelo-maxies.com

■ Often "reminiscent of a trading floor", this "guy's-night-out" chop shop turns on "young" turks with its "no-joke" array of prime beef and "rip-roaring" energy level, even if connoisseurs complain it's only in the "second tier" of steakdom; P.S. the Midtown outpost has closed, and the Flatiron survivor's cigar room is "gone à la Bloomberg."

Angelo's of Mulberry Street
22 | 15 | 19 | $40

146 Mulberry St. (bet. Grand & Hester Sts.), 212-966-1277;
www.angelomulberry.com

■ "Still going strong after all these [103] years", this Little Italy "trip down memory lane" offers "delicious" red-sauce Italian dishes, fairly "reasonable" pricing and an "old-school", been-there-forever staff; all right, the "decor needs an upgrade", but diehards insist that this "tourist heaven" is "too good for only tourists."

Angelo's Pizzeria
20 | 13 | 15 | $22

1043 Second Ave. (55th St.), 212-521-3600
117 W. 57th St. (bet. 6th & 7th Aves.), 212-333-4333

☑ "Pizza so thin they could fax it to you" is the calling card of these crosstown pizzerias where the "better-than-average" pies make up for "nondescript" decor and service, especially when you factor in the prices – you "can't get anything this cheap" in Midtown.

Angura ◑
– | – | – | M

196 Second Ave. (bet. 12th & 13th Sts.), 212-674-7060

Blond wood and bamboo are out and blood-red walls and pulsing beats are in at this hip new East Village Japanese serving a full menu in an intimate subterranean space; for smaller appetites, there's an adjacent sushi bar boasting a well-rounded sake selection.

Angus McIndoe ◑
19 | 16 | 20 | $39

258 W. 44th St. (bet. B'way & 8th Ave.), 212-221-9222;
www.angusmcindoe.com

■ Likened to "the fourth act of *The Producers*" given its star-studded cast of regulars, this triple-tiered Theater District American promises "lively people-watching" for hard-core Broadway "groupies"; predictably, the "reliable" grub and "personable" service take second billing to "seeing Nathan Lane."

Anh
19 | 15 | 16 | $27

363 Third Ave. (bet. 26th & 27th Sts.), 212-532-2858;
www.anhrestaurant.com

■ Though "not yet discovered", this "little" Gramercy Vietnamese is catching ahn as an "affordable" option for "flavorful" fare in a "relaxed" neighborhood setting; its variety of "standards" serves as a "good introduction" for greenhorns who "don't like taking risks."

Annie's
17 | 15 | 15 | $27

1381 Third Ave. (bet. 78th & 79th Sts.), 212-327-4853

☑ "Brunch is where it's at" at this "dependable" Upper East Side American, so latecomers "wait forever" on weekends while early birds dig into "massive quantities" of "home cooking" in a space that's "one step up from a coffee shop"; the "mommy crowd" may throw a tantrum, but "no strollers are allowed."

ANNISA
27 | 23 | 26 | $63

13 Barrow St. (bet. 7th Ave. S. & W. 4th St.), 212-741-6699;
www.annisarestaurant.com

■ The "amazingly inventive" Anita Lo aims high at this "intimate" Village "charmer" offering "perfectly crafted" New American food with some "memorable" twists, along with wines from female vintners; the "calm", "grown-up" vibe and "smooth" service burnish the overall "top-shelf" "epicurean pleasure" – just make sure you can afford it.

Antique Garage
∇ 21 | 24 | 22 | $36

41 Mercer St. (bet. Broome & Grand Sts.), 212-219-1019

■ If you "like your table, take it home" from this SoHo newcomer, an erstwhile auto-body shop turned "yummy" Med eatery with "cool Victorian" furniture for sale; it's a "diamond in the rough" for a meze break, but tabs can get "dangerous", especially if the table's included.

A.O.C. ◑
∇ 18 | 16 | 16 | $37

314 Bleecker St. (Grove St.), 212-675-9463; www.aocnyc.com

☑ "Basic", "reliable" French food comes at "modest" tabs at this West Village bistro blessed with a "godsend of a garden"; though picky eaters pout about an "uninspired" menu and "slightly absent service", weekenders say its "charming" brunch is hard to beat in these parts.

A.O.C. Bedford
23 | 20 | 22 | $48

14 Bedford St. (bet. Downing & Houston Sts.), 212-414-4764;
www.aocbedford.com

■ "They pay attention to details" at this Village "neighborhood boîte" where the "sophisticated" Southern European menu is "exceptionally well crafted" and "wine pairings are taken very seriously"; service is "attentive" and if the "rustic" quarters feel "tight", that adds to the "romantic" mood.

ápizz ⊠
23 | 20 | 20 | $38

217 Eldridge St. (bet. Rivington & Stanton Sts.), 212-253-9199;
www.apizz.com

■ A bona fide "find" hidden behind an "industrial" Lower East Side facade, this "welcoming" "peasant-chic" Italian appeases fans of "bold flavors" with its "earthy", not too pricey menu; the "warm, cozy" space features a "totally cool" wood-burning oven famed for producing "wonderful" "smoke-tinged pizzas."

AQ Cafe ⊠
▽ 20 | 16 | 14 | $17

Scandinavia House, 58 Park Ave. (bet. 37th & 38th Sts.), 212-847-9745;
www.aquavit.org

☑ You can "experience Aquavit on the cheap" at this lunch-only "Nordic niche" in Murray Hill where the "Scandinavian light" bites constitute "Marcus Samuelsson's answer to fast food"; expect a "spare", cafeteria-line setup that's "quick and easy" when you're "in the mood for lingonberries."

AQUAGRILL
27 | 20 | 23 | $53

210 Spring St. (6th Ave.), 212-274-0505; www.aquagrill.com

■ As "happening" as ever, this SoHo seafooder thrills deep-sea diners with "fresher-than-fresh" fish and oysters shucked at its "awesome raw bar"; the "consistent" kitchen and "spot-on" service draw a deep-pocketed crowd to the "tight", "always-packed" quarters.

AQUAVIT
26 | 26 | 25 | $68

13 W. 54th St. (bet. 5th & 6th Aves.), 212-307-7311; www.aquavit.org

■ Chef Marcus Samuelsson "soars" at this "dramatic", "one-of-a-kind" Midtowner where his "rarefied" riffs on Scandinavian fare are "expertly served" in an "enchanting" space; but admirers are sure to follow "when it moves east" to new digs in early 2005.

Areo
24 | 19 | 20 | $46

8424 Third Ave. (bet. 84th & 85th Sts.), Brooklyn, 718-238-0079

■ The "raucous" scene at this "very popular" Bay Ridge Italian works well with its "zesty", "old-world" cooking that's among "the best" in the borough; be prepared for "long waits" and "Manhattan prices", and accessorize with "gold chains", "fake fingernails" and "earplugs."

Arezzo
22 | 19 | 19 | $51

46 W. 22nd St. (bet. 5th & 6th Aves.), 212-206-0555;
www.arezzony.com

☑ This "personable" Flatiron Tuscan turns out "rich", "rewarding" food served with "no attitude" in "comfortable", "uncluttered" environs; although it's agreeably "innovative", a few fret that "prices are too high" for a "neighborhood" place.

Arqua
23 | 20 | 21 | $50

281 Church St. (White St.), 212-334-1888

■ "They make you feel welcome" at this "steady" TriBeCa "favorite" where the "dependably excellent" Northern Italian food comes complete with "gracious" service and warm Tuscan hill-town decor; locals count on it for "solid fine dining" "without pretension."

| | 18 | 17 | 18 | $39 |

21 E. Ninth St. (bet. 5th Ave. & University Pl.), 212-473-0077

📧 It's more "middle-of-the-road" than arty, but this "well-run" Village Italian aims to please with "well-prepared" standards at "affordable" tabs; the "cute fireplace" and "pretty rear garden" make it a "cozy" haven in any season, though a few still find it "unexciting."

Artie's Deli
| 17 | 10 | 15 | $21 |

2290 Broadway (bet. 82nd & 83rd Sts.), 212-579-5959; www.arties.com

📧 "Much needed" on the Upper West Side, this "ersatz old-time" deli "pushes all the nostalgia buttons" with "hearty" faves like sandwiches piled high with "mounds of pastrami"; less authentic are the "cheerful" "actor-waiters" and "Disney-esque" vibe ("lots of kids and strollers"), but at least the "price is right."

ARTISANAL
| 23 | 20 | 19 | $49 |

2 Park Ave. (enter on 32nd St., bet. Madison & Park Aves.), 212-725-8585

■ The "big cheese" on Murray Hill, Terrance Brennan's French brasserie–cum–cheese shop takes fromage to "heavenly heights" with "innumerable" "delish" choices on a "mind-blowing" menu accompanied by 160 "wines by the glass"; never mind the "clamor" and "snobby staff", it's a "must" for aficionados who also drop by to "buy some for home."

Arturo's Pizzeria ⬤
| 21 | 12 | 15 | $22 |

106 W. Houston St. (Thompson St.), 212-677-3820

📧 Pizzaphiles "taste the difference" a coal oven makes at this Village Italian "throwback" where "top-notch pies" and "cool" live jazz draw "spirited" sorts; downsides include a "divey atmosphere" and a "scrum of tourists" and "NYU students" vying for the "tight" seating.

A Salt & Battery
| 19 | 9 | 15 | $15 |

112 Greenwich Ave. (bet. 12th & 13th Sts.), 212-691-2713
80 Second Ave. (bet. 4th & 5th Sts.), 212-254-6610
www.asaltandbattery.com

📧 "Fish 'n' chips reign supreme" at these "no-frills" British "artery cloggers" that will "deep fry anything", most famously Mars bars; the BYO East Village's "sit-down" setup is "more civilised" than the strictly "carry-out" West Side operation, but pound-pinchers pronounce both "a tad" pricey.

ASIA DE CUBA ⬤
| 24 | 25 | 20 | $55 |

Morgans Hotel, 237 Madison Ave. (bet. 37th & 38th Sts.), 212-726-7755; www.chinagrillmanagement.com

📧 Jack up "your cool factor" at this "vibrant" Murray Hill Asian-Cuban where the "hipper-than-thou" "flaunt their assets" by ordering "fabulous" food at "second-mortgage" prices; Philippe Starck's "heavenly white" design "hasn't lost its luster", and if trendoids yawn "been there done that", it's "still going strong" – apparently being "just too-too" "never gets old."

ASIATE
| 22 | 27 | 23 | $79 |

Mandarin Oriental Hotel, 80 Columbus Circle, 35th fl. (60th St.), 212-805-8881; www.mandarinoriental.com/newyork/

📧 "Drop-dead views of Central Park" highlight this "dramatic" new Japanese-French aerie in the Mandarin Oriental Hotel, where chef Nori Sugie's "complex", "delectable" cuisine is framed by "soaring" "walls of windows"; for some, it's the "cutting edge" of "luxurious dining", for others it's "a bit unfocused" and service still needs polishing "considering the price tag", but optimists say "wait till this baby matures"; N.B. if you order right, lunch can be a bargain.

Assaggio
19 | 16 | 18 | $36

473 Columbus Ave. (bet. 82nd & 83rd Sts.), 212-877-0170

■ A "satisfying standby" for "lotsa pasta", this Upper West Side Italian supplies its regulars with "regular food" at a "good cost" and treats every corner "like an old friend"; add summertime "sidewalk tables" that brighten the "average-looking" layout and most dub it a "keeper."

À Table
19 | 17 | 16 | $32

171 Lafayette Ave. (bet. Adelphi St. & Clermont Ave.), Brooklyn, 718-935-9121

◪ "Not far from BAM" in "sleepy Fort Greene", this "pleasant" Gallic bistro offers "well-prepared classic" dishes in authentically "rustic" environs; if service can be "more French than desirable", "reasonable" pricing and a "swell" brunch compensate.

ATELIER
26 | 25 | 26 | $93

Ritz-Carlton Central Park, 50 Central Park S. (6th Ave.), 212-521-6125; www.ritzcarlton.com

■ "Demanding palates" agree this New French in the Ritz-Carlton Central Park is a "class act" that's "working magic" with "magnificent" cuisine served in "spacious", "quietly elegant" digs by a "superb" staff; "oh-so-smooth" and "civilized" "without being stuffy", it's a "top-shelf" "experience" – and "should be for that price"; N.B. the loss of chef Gabriel Kreuther puts the Food score in doubt.

ATLANTIC GRILL ●
23 | 19 | 20 | $47

1341 Third Ave. (bet. 76th & 77th Sts.), 212-988-9200; www.brguestrestaurants.com

■ "This formula works" say the "lively" lubbers of Steve Hanson's "loud", "happenin'" Upper Eastsider, a "hit" thanks to "excellent", "super-fresh" seafood that "won't break the bank"; it's usually "jammed to the rafters" with locals out for something "upscale" but "not overly trendy", so figure on some docktime in the "jumping" bar.

Au Bon Pain ⊬
14 | 8 | 10 | $11

684 Broadway (W. 3rd St.), 212-420-1694
58 E. Eighth St. (Mercer St.), 212-475-8546
122 E. 42nd St. (bet. Lexington & Park Aves.), 212-599-8643
Empire State Bldg., 350 Fifth Ave. (bet. 33rd & 34th Sts.), 212-502-5478
Macy's Department Store, 151 W. 34th St. (7th Ave.), 212-494-1091
Port Authority, 625 Eighth Ave. (bet. 40th & 41st Sts.), 212-502-4823
1 State St. Plaza (Water St.), 212-952-9098
6 Union Sq. E. (14th St.), 212-475-0453
125 W. 55th St. (bet. 6th & 7th Aves.), 212-246-6518
World Financial Ctr., 200 Liberty St. (West St.), 212-962-9421
Additional locations throughout the NY area
www.aubonpain.com

◪ "McDonald's for the upwardly mobile", this "self-serve" "soup 'n' sammy" chain "comes in handy" as a quick "pit stop" for "morning joe and goodies" or "economical" "carboholic" lunches; still, some cynics castigate it for "basic" eats and "wanting" service.

August ●
▽ 23 | 21 | 18 | $40

359 Bleecker St. (bet. Charles & W. 10th Sts.), 212-929-4774; www.augustny.com

■ This "rustic", "smaller-than-small" Greenwich Village newcomer "delights and surprises" with a "flavorful" regional European menu akin to a transcontinental "journey", often via "wood-burning oven"; "welcoming" service complements the "quaint" feel, while a rear garden "doubles" the size of the "cozy" space.

Au Mandarin
20 | 15 | 19 | $30

World Financial Ctr., 200-250 Vesey St. (West St.), 212-385-0313;
www.worldfinancialcenter.com/dining/

■ A "business clientele" backs this World Financial Center Chinese for its "good standard" chow, "pleasant service" and "reliable" takeout (a "banker's best friend"); widely deemed the "best in the area" of its genre "by default", it's "a bit pricey" but the "quality justifies the extra bucks."

AUREOLE ☒
27 | 26 | 26 | $79

34 E. 61st St. (bet. Madison & Park Aves.), 212-319-1660;
www.charliepalmer.com

■ A "perennial" "wow", Charlie Palmer's "classically elegant" East Side townhouse offers chef Dante Boccuzzi's "celestial" New American fare, including some "showstopping desserts"; "meticulous service" caps the "idyllic experience", but "bring your entire paycheck" or opt for the "late-lunch bargain" to "savor the moment."

Avenue A Sushi ❶
17 | 15 | 15 | $28

103 Ave. A (bet. 6th & 7th Sts.), 212-982-8109

■ This "kitschy" East Village Japanese will "satisfy your raw-fish needs" along with any lingering taste for "black lights" and "disco balls" as the DJs whip up a "noisy" "party atmosphere"; given the "decent sushi" at "decent prices", most report it's a "ton of fun."

Avra Estiatorio ❷
23 | 21 | 21 | $52

141 E. 48th St. (bet. Lexington & 3rd Aves.), 212-759-8550; www.avrany.com

■ A "little piece of Greece" alights on the East Side at this "lively" seafood specialist known for "fresh-daily" fish and other "perfectly prepared classics" served in "airy", "attractive" digs with a "terrific" interior courtyard; enthusiasts warm to the "hospitality" but warn the "prices add up" ("they get you by the pound").

Azafran
22 | 19 | 20 | $43

77 Warren St. (bet. Greenwich St. & W. B'way), 212-284-0578;
www.azafrannyc.com

■ "So many yummy choices" make this "neighborhood" TriBeCa Spaniard a "find" for "delicious" tapas and "great sangria" in a "trendy" setting that's "cool without pretension"; though most embrace this "trip to Madrid", the crowds can get "loud" and "it's not cheap."

Azalea ❶
∇ 20 | 19 | 20 | $48

224 W. 51st St. (bet. B'way & 8th Ave.), 212-262-0105; www.azaleanyc.us

■ An "outpost of Brescia" "in the thick of the Theater District", this "proficient" Northern Italian keeps patrons "happily sated" with "well-prepared" food in "pretty", "comfortable" quarters; if the performance is sometimes "just ok" for the cost, the "good buy" prix fixe is a showstopper.

Azul Bistro ❶
∇ 22 | 19 | 19 | $38

152 Stanton St. (Suffolk St.), 646-602-2004

■ "They know their meat" at this Lower East Side Argentinean where the "flavorful" cuts are "grilled perfectly" and then delivered at a "reasonable price" by an "unpretentious" staff; true-blue types call it a "great alternative" – the pampas vibe alone is "worth the trip."

Azuri Cafe ⊅
∇ 24 | 4 | 8 | $13

465 W. 51st St. (bet. 9th & 10th Aves.), 212-262-2920

◢ Maybe the "intimidating" proprietor "is to falafel what the Soup Nazi is to soup", but this West Side "hole-in-the-wall" remains a "find" for "superb, authentic" Israeli eats at "bargain" tabs; "grab it and go" is the norm, though masochists linger for the "lively banter."

BABBO ● | 27 | 23 |
110 Waverly Pl. (bet. MacDougal St. & 6th Ave.), 212-777-0303;
www.babbonyc.com
■ The Mario Batali–Joe Bastianich team makes "culinary dreams come true" at their Village Italian *"paradiso"* where "life-altering" dishes in "perfect harmony" come with "A+" wines and "savvy", "spot-on" service; the "classy" carriage-house setting hums with "high energy", but you may wear out your "speed dial and luck" trying to score a "nigh impossible" reservation.

Bacchus ● | ▽ 20 | 18 | 19 | $33 |
409 Atlantic Ave. (Bond St.), Brooklyn, 718-852-1572
■ A "welcome sight" on arid Atlantic Avenue, this "relaxed" bistro "fills a void" with "wonderful" French fare, "energetic" service and a "decent wine list"; it can get "noisy and tight", but there's a "nice garden" and bacchers claim you "can't beat the two-for-one entrees" Wednesday nights.

Baci | ▽ 21 | 17 | 19 | $38 |
7107 Third Ave. (71st St.), Brooklyn, 718-836-5536
■ What may well be "Bay Ridge's best-kept secret" is this "cozy" Italian, an aria to "old-world dining" with "quality food" and an operatic owner who wows the crowd with "beautiful love songs"; to those attuned, it's "worth the trip" to be "treated like family."

Baldoria | 19 | 17 | 18 | $52 |
249 W. 49th St. (bet. B'way & 8th Ave.), 212-582-0460; www.baldoriamo.com
☒ "Rao's – with a table" – sums up the appeal of this "enjoyable" duplex Theater District Italian where Frank Pellegrino Jr. "does his dad proud" with "hearty" "traditional" fare, "congenial" service and "Sinatra on the juke"; "brash" crowds and prices "on the high side" are in keeping with the overall "Rat Pack style."

Baldo Vino ● | ▽ 19 | 20 | 18 | $33 |
126 E. Seventh St. (bet. Ave. A & 1st Ave.), 212-979-0319
■ "A cut above the typical Italian joint", this "rustic" East Village restaurant–cum–wine bar offers "fine" food, "good value" and a "Tuscan farmhouse" ambiance; the "entertaining" staff lets you "eat at your own pace", and though you may have to "beg for your check", it's still a "winner" for a laid-back bite.

BALTHAZAR ● | 23 | 23 | 19 | $50 |
80 Spring St. (bet. B'way & Crosby St.), 212-965-1414; www.balthazarny.com
■ A "great show" that's "always in fashion", this "snazzy", "real-deal" SoHo French brasserie is a "classic" for "knockout" food (e.g. plateau de fruits de mer, steak frites) and "efficient" service in a wonderfully authentic room abuzz with wanna-bes, used-to-bes and really ares; despite "tight" seating and the "inevitable out-of-towners", the addicted deem it a "forever fabulous" "Paris fix."

Baluchi's | 18 | 14 | 16 | $25 |
283 Columbus Ave. (bet. 73rd & 74th Sts.), 212-579-3900
224 E. 53rd St. (bet. 2nd & 3rd Aves.), 212-750-5515
111 E. 29th St. (bet. Lexington Ave. & Park Ave. S.), 212-481-3861
1431 First Ave. (74th St.), 212-396-1400
1149 First Ave. (63rd St.), 212-371-3535
1724 Second Ave. (bet. 89th & 90th Sts.), 212-996-2600
104 Second Ave. (6th St.), 212-780-6000
361 Sixth Ave. (Washington Pl.), 212-929-2441
193 Spring St. (bet. Sullivan & Thompson Sts.), 212-226-2828
(continued)

(continued)

Baluchi's

240 W. 56th St. (bet. B'way & 8th Ave.), 212-397-0707
Additional locations throughout the NY area
www.baluchis.com

■ It "may be a chain", but these "accommodating" Indians supply "solid" "curry in a hurry" at "budget-conscious" tabs; they're an "easy fallback" with "no surprises", and the "50 percent–off lunch is the ticket" when you're down to "just a few rupees."

Bambou

▽ 21 | 23 | 20 | $43

243 E. 14th St. (bet. 2nd & 3rd Aves.), 212-358-0012;
www.bambounyc.com

☑ Get "back to Aruba" at this East Village "original" serving "very tasty" French-Caribbean food in an "intimate, tropical" setting that's so "authentic" "all you need is the right weather" to be completely transported; the "creative drink list" and "friendly" but "embarrassingly slow" service set the "relaxing" pace.

Bamonte's

21 | 15 | 20 | $38

32 Withers St. (bet. Lorimer St. & Union Ave.), Brooklyn,
718-384-8831

■ "Red sauce rules" at this "bustling" Williamsburg "tradition", ever a "favorite" for "delicious" Italian cooking that "comforts the soul" and "curmudgeonly but efficient" service from "been-there-for-years" waiters; with a century-plus history, it's a definite "destination" for an "authentic" dose of "old-time local color."

Banania Cafe ⊅

21 | 17 | 17 | $30

241 Smith St. (Douglass St.), Brooklyn, 718-237-9100

■ "One of the stars of Smith Street", this "funky" Cobble Hill French bistro appeals to a "huge crowd" of "thirtysomethings" who go bananas for its "imaginative", "affordable" menu; "be prepared for lines", however, when attending its "excellent weekend brunch."

Banjara ◐

24 | 17 | 19 | $29

97 First Ave. (6th St.), 212-477-5956

■ "When you're ready to graduate" from the "Christmas-tree-lighted" Curry Row competition, this East Village Indian stands "several cuts above" the rest with its "zesty" chow and "almost obsequious" service; decor that's "predictable" but "prettier" than the norm (plus a "full bar") rounds out this pleasant surprise.

Bann Thai

21 | 20 | 20 | $28

69-12 Austin St. (Yellowstone Blvd.), Queens, 718-544-9999;
www.bannthairestaurant.com

■ It's "tucked away" on a Forest Hills "road less traveled", but those in the know declare this "unassuming" Thai a banner destination for "pretty darn amazing" eats; the "authentic" flavors, "welcoming" staff and "reasonable" tabs keep the "small" room "crowded."

Bao Noodles ⊅

20 | 15 | 17 | $27

391 Second Ave. (bet. 22nd & 23rd Sts.), 212-725-6182

■ Bao 111's "lower-key" Gramercy offshoot, this "down-to-earth" Vietnamese bows in with "complex" food that "puts the 'sigh' in Saigon" at a "nice price"; "tight on space" but "big on taste", it's usually "jam-packed" with grateful neighbors.

Bao 111 ◐

23 | 20 | 18 | $40

111 Ave. C (bet. 7th & 8th Sts.), 212-254-7773; www.bao111.com

■ "New tastes" lure "young, stylish" East Villagers to this "hip twist" on Vietnamese, where the "inventive" menu meets its match in a "fabulous" sake list and "modern", "sexy" room; if its prices reflect "gentrification", it's still an "up-and-coming" "pointy-shoed" scene that "stays hopping pretty late."

Baraonda ●   18 | 18 | 15 | $43

1439 Second Ave. (75th St.), 212-288-8555; www.baraondany.com
☑ "Party" people let it all hang out at this "hectic", "Eurotrashy" Upper Eastsider that "feels like Carnival" complete with "loud club music" and late-night "table dancing"; the Italian eats are "ordinary" but "tasty", though for most the "food is not the attraction."

Barbalùc   ▽ 20 | 20 | 20 | $57

135 E. 65th St. (Lexington Ave.), 212-774-1999; www.barbaluc.com
☑ Fans of "truly Friulian" cuisine and wines are in luck since this East Side Italian serves that "sophisticated" specialty in an "elegant room" that's "beautifully styled"; the outing is bound to be "fashionable", though fence straddlers add it's "overdone" and "will cost you."

Barbès ●   ▽ 22 | 19 | 24 | $41

21 E. 36th St. (bet. 5th & Madison Aves.), 212-684-0215
■ A "sheik" "change of scenery" for Murray Hill is this "promising" French-Moroccan newcomer offering "fresh, well-prepared" food and "incredibly friendly" service; "low lighting" and "close" tables supply a "faintly exotic" vibe, but judging by the "crowded" conditions, many people already "feel at home" here.

Barbetta   20 | 23 | 20 | $56

321 W. 46th St. (bet. 8th & 9th Aves.), 212-246-9171;
www.barbettarestaurant.com
■ Nearly a "century old", this Restaurant Row Northern Italian is a pre-theater favorite in "Louis XIV" mode offering consistently rewarding "classic" cuisine and "old-world", black-tie service in a "genteel" townhouse setting; in spring and summer, the "lovely" spacious garden can be a wonderfully "romantic" escape.

Barbuto ●   ▽ 20 | 15 | 16 | $43

775 Washington St. (bet. Jane & W. 12th Sts.), 212-924-9700;
www.barbutonyc.com
☑ "Eat and be seen" at this "hip" new West Villager where owner Jonathan Waxman "hits his stride", serving a "flavorful", "market-driven" Italian menu in "airy" industrial digs defined by "wraparound garage doors" (that stay up in the summer); service may be "spaced out", but followers of fashion still count themselves in.

Barking Dog   16 | 14 | 15 | $22

150 E. 34th St. (bet. Lexington & 3rd Aves.), 212-871-3900
1678 Third Ave. (94th St.), 212-831-1800 ☞
1453 York Ave. (77th St.), 212-861-3600 ☞
☑ "Fido can tag along" to this East Side trio of "cute 'n' casual" "family" favorites serving "simple" Americana with "puppy pics" for decor; though so "big with the stroller set" that it "should be called 'Crying Baby'", most bite at the chance to wolf down "enormous" portions at such a "low cost."

Bar Masa ●⊠   ▽ 22 | 20 | 16 | $67

Time Warner Ctr., 10 Columbus Circle, 4th fl. (60th St. at B'way),
212-823-9800
☑ For those "mortals" yet to gain entry to the Time Warner Center's Japanese powerhouse Masa, this "minimalist" sibling provides "superb sushi" and other "adventurous" delicacies sans reservations; sure, it may be "high priced" for "small servings" and "less-than-stellar" service, but it's a lot cheaper than its next-door sire.

Barney Greengrass ⊅
23 | 7 | 13 | $24

*541 Amsterdam Ave. (bet. 86th & 87th Sts.), 212-724-4707;
www.barneygreengrass.com*

☑ "Old-fashioned tastes" meet "over-the-top" prices at this Upper West Side "icon", a "must" for "superlative lox", bagels, bialys and other "quintessential", "kvell"-worthy deli items; "crusty" service and "prehistoric" surroundings don't deter "weekend mobs" who say that's all "part of the charm."

Barolo ●
17 | 20 | 16 | $49

*398 W. Broadway (bet. Broome & Spring Sts.), 212-226-1102;
www.nybarolo.com*

☑ In fair weather, the "splendid" garden of this "big, airy" SoHo Italian is *the* place to be" for "good-looking" types out to "enjoy la dolce vita"; foes protest "so-so" food, "haughty attitude" and "high-end" prices, but the setting's "romantic" enough to make everything seem "a tad better than it is."

Bar Pitti ●⊅
21 | 14 | 17 | $35

268 Sixth Ave. (bet. Bleecker & Houston Sts.), 212-982-3300

■ The "early bird catches the table" at this "fab" Village Italian that's perpetually "crammed" with "cool" cats and "minor celebs" digging the "delish" food, "Euro feel" and sidewalk-table "street scene"; just don't pity the folks in line – the "marathon waits" are "totally worth it."

BarTabac ●
17 | 19 | 17 | $28

128 Smith St. (Dean St.), Brooklyn, 718-923-0918

■ "You're in France (without the smoke)" at this Boerum Hill bistro, a *très* "popular haven" for "casual" socializing over "reliable", basic French food served with "low attitude"; it's "nothing fancy", but locals say "*oui oui*" to touches like sidewalk tables and barside foosball.

Bar Tonno ●
– | – | – | M

17 Cleveland Pl. (bet. Kenmare & Spring Sts.), 212-966-7334

Chef Scott Conant (L'Impero) strikes again with this new NoHo venture, a self-styled 'modern Italian raw bar' featuring a daily changing, all-fish-all-the-time menu served in vaguely aquatic digs; late-night hours and a deep white wine list make the 22-seat setup more palatable.

Basil, The
20 | 19 | 19 | $36

206 W. 23rd St. (bet. 7th & 8th Aves.), 212-242-1014

■ "Not all neighborhoods can have Holy Basil", but Chelsea has its "quiet cousin", an "oasis" for "authentic", "piquant" Thai chow plus some "innovative" options with more "Westernized" ways; citing "sooo pleasant" service and "comfortable" blond-wood digs, well-wishers wonder "why it hasn't been discovered" yet.

Basso Est ●
∇ 22 | 14 | 21 | $35

198 Orchard St. (Stanton St.), 212-358-9469; www.bassoest.com

■ Gaining an "upper edge" on the Lower East Side, this "tiny" Italian is a "culinary gem" for "homemade pastas" and other "savory" specialties made even tastier by "more-than-affordable" tabs; a "vibrant scene" overseen by "charm-soaked waiters", it's fast becoming a "destination", so "get there early."

Basta Pasta
19 | 16 | 18 | $38

37 W. 17th St. (bet. 5th & 6th Aves.), 212-366-0888

■ "Asian pasta" "really works" at this "casual" Flatiron original where a "creative" crew in a "great open kitchen" puts Japanese-style "crossover" touches into their "fresh take on standard" Italian; "beyond the novelty", the "refreshing" result is a "compliment to both" of its allegiances.

Battery Gardens
— — — M

southwest corner of Battery Park (opp. 17 State St.), 212-809-5508;
www.batterygardens.com
The former American Park has been renamed and revamped, but its
raison d'être – a bucolic setting in Battery Park with killer harbor
views – remains as glorious as ever; look for a midpriced New American
menu with Asian accents served in airy indoor digs or (preferably) on
the sprawling patio.

Bayard's ⊠
23 24 24 $60

1 Hanover Sq. (bet. Pearl & Stone Sts.), 212-514-9454; www.bayards.com
■ To "step back into a classier time", try this ultra-"civilized"
Financial District French-American triplex offering ex-Lutece and Le
Bernardin chef Eberhard Müller's "inspired" seasonal cuisine and a
"magnificent", "blue-blood" setting in the circa-1851 India House;
"white-glove service" and an "incredible wine list" are naturals in
this "very adult" milieu, so only the "hard-to-find" location and the
fact that it's a private club at lunch explain why this star is so little
known; P.S. with handsome rooms of all sizes, it's a great place to
give a party.

Bay Leaf ⊠
19 17 17 $35

49 W. 56th St. (bet. 5th & 6th Aves.), 212-957-1818
■ Midtowners count on this Indian "favorite" to rise above its rivals
with "flavorful", "real-deal" cooking and "helpful service" in a
"calming" setting; dinner prices reflect the upgrade, so for a "budget
choice", the $13.95 "lunch buffet is definitely the way to go."

Bayou
20 18 18 $33

308 Lenox Ave. (bet. 125th & 126th Sts.), 212-426-3800;
www.bayouinharlem.com
☑ "Now, this is good eating" testify fans of this Harlem Cajun-Creole
kitchen where "really fine" Louisiana manna and "friendly" service
are an invitation to "slow down and relax"; though a little on the
"pricey" side, you can always count on a "satisfying" spread – and
they do an "excellent" Sunday brunch.

BB Sandwich Bar ●
19 3 11 $7

120 W. Third St. (bet. MacDougal St. & 6th Ave.), 212-473-7500
☑ The only menu decision is "how many you want" at this "one-note"
Villager that "cranks out" "awesome", BBQ-tinged Philly cheese
steaks – and "nothing else"; while the orthodox scoff their retooled
version is "no improvement" on the Philadelphia original, for a real
"cheap" chowdown it's a "carnivore's delight."

Beacon
23 22 21 $55

25 W. 56th St. (bet. 5th & 6th Aves.), 212-332-0500;
www.beaconnyc.com
■ Signally "great grilling" guides Midtown "suits" to Waldy Malouf's
"smart" New American for "robust, wood-fired" fare from the "grand
open hearth" that anchors the "distinctive", multi-tiered space; of
course, it's more pleasing "when someone else is buying", but frugal
folks report the prix fixe lunch is a "steal."

Becco ●
21 17 19 $40

355 W. 46th St. (bet. 8th & 9th Aves.), 212-397-7597;
www.becconyc.com
■ Bring an "additional stomach" for the "toothsome", all-you-can-eat
"pasta blitz" at this Theater District Italian where "$20 bottles of
wine" add to the "great-deal" pricing; though the recently expanded
setting is certainly "accommodating", things can get a "little hectic"
and "noisy" come prime time.

Bella Blu ●
19 | 17 | 17 | $45

967 Lexington Ave. (bet. 70th & 71st Sts.), 212-988-4624

☒ Despite the name, life is "cheerful" at this "buzzy" Northern Italian Upper Eastsider thanks to "surprisingly good" pastas and "wood-fired pizzas"; even given "perfunctory service" and "noise" when the "singles scene goes into full swing", it's a "colorful" alternative that's hardly likely to give anyone the blues.

Bella Donna
17 | 11 | 15 | $25

307 E. 77th St. (bet. 1st & 2nd Aves.), 212-535-2866
1663 First Ave. (bet. 86th & 87th Sts.), 212-534-3261

☒ Ok, they're "not the fanciest", but folks "keep coming back" to these East Side "hole-in-the-wall" Italians for their "enormous portions" of bargain "homestyle" eats; "cheek-by-jowl" seating typifies the "no-frills" approach, while 77th Street's BYO policy sweetens the already "terrific deal."

Bella Luna
16 | 16 | 17 | $32

584 Columbus Ave. (bet. 88th & 89th Sts.), 212-877-2267

☒ "Not at all trendy", this Upper Westsider attracts "a lot of locals" with its "affordable" Italian "comfort food", "kid-friendly" setting and "sidewalk seating"; dissenters yawn "run-of-the-mill", but most agree this "decent drop-in" is good "in a pinch."

Bella Via
∇ 20 | 17 | 18 | $28

47-46 Vernon Blvd. (48th Ave.), Queens, 718-361-7510;
www.bellaviarestaurant.com

■ Although "terrific coal-oven pizza" is the main attraction, this "neighborhood Italian" near the Long Island City waterfront also has a way with "homemade pastas" and other "solid" standards; the "casual setting" may be "nothing special", yet it works for a "relaxed" bite.

Belleville
21 | 21 | 18 | $35

350 Fifth Ave. (5th St.), Brooklyn, 718-832-9777

■ A breath of "fresh French air" comes to Park Slope via this newcomer that's "pure bistro", from its "wonderful homespun" Gallic fare to its "attractive" tile-and-mirrors decor; despite somewhat "spotty" service, it's usually a "full" house since "you'd pay twice as much" for the same experience across the river.

Bellini ☒
22 | 20 | 22 | $52

208 E. 52nd St. (bet. 2nd & 3rd Aves.), 212-308-0830

■ This "tasteful" Midtowner is known for "top-notch" Neapolitan food "that you don't need a microscope to see" plus "professional", "personable" service; yes, it's "pricey", but for "mature" types seeking a "classy atmosphere", the splurge is always "worthwhile."

Bello ☒
19 | 15 | 19 | $40

863 Ninth Ave. (56th St.), 212-246-6773; www.bellorestaurant.com

■ No, it's not your "grandmother at the stove", but this "old-school" Hell's Kitchen Italian sure seems that way thanks to its "simple", "reliable" cooking, as well as "caring service" and good value; with free dinnertime parking as an "added bonus", this one's a pre-theater "winner."

Bello Sguardo
∇ 22 | 19 | 19 | $35

410 Amsterdam Ave. (bet. 79th & 80th Sts.), 212-873-6252

■ Though the "name may throw you off", this new Upper West Side "adventure" offers "imaginative" Mediterranean grazing with Turkey, Greece and Morocco represented alongside Italy in its "savory small plates"; given a "pretty" candlelit space and "reasonable" tabs, fans are betting it "should become very popular" very soon.

Belluno
▽ 21 | 19 | 23 | $40

340 Lexington Ave. (bet. 39th & 40th Sts.), 212-953-3282;
www.bellunoristorante.com

■ They "remember your face" at this moderately priced Murray Hill Northern Italian providing "personal attention" in spacious, split-level digs along with an "upscale" menu that's "not just pasta"; though "relatively unknown", admirers advise it's "worth looking for."

Ben Benson's
22 | 17 | 20 | $60

123 W. 52nd St. (bet. 6th & 7th Aves.), 212-581-8888

■ Forget "all pretenses" at this "prototypical" Midtown steakhouse where cholesterol-be-damned beefeaters blow major bucks on "bucket-size" martinis and "he-man" cuts of red meat; the efficiently "gruff" service and somewhat "stodgy" room don't dismay its "mover-and-shaker crowd."

Benihana
16 | 14 | 18 | $37

120 E. 56th St. (bet. Lexington & Park Aves.), 212-593-1627
47 W. 56th St. (bet. 5th & 6th Aves.), 212-581-0930
www.benihana.com

☑ "Sit back and enjoy the show" – "entertaining chefs!" "flying food!" "corny jokes!" – at these Midtown hibachi chop shops offering affordable amusement for "tourists and kids"; but those who "daydream about Nobu" sigh it's "mediocre" and add that the "knife-twirling exhibition" no longer cuts it.

Ben's Kosher Deli
17 | 10 | 13 | $22

209 W. 38th St. (bet. 7th & 8th Aves.), 212-398-2367
Bay Terrace, 211-37 26th Ave. (211th St.), Queens, 718-229-2367
www.bensdeli.net

☑ "Kosher noshers" kvell about this "good old-fashioned" duo, home to "mile-high sandwiches" and "matzo balls the size of your fists"; sure, the "decor could use an update" (ditto the "passable" menu), but with "delis becoming an endangered species", it's "better than starving."

Beppe ☒
22 | 21 | 21 | $52

45 E. 22nd St. (bet. B'way & Park Ave. S.), 212-982-8422; www.beppenyc.com

■ "Well-executed Italian favorites" via Cesare Casella (a "chef you can count on") are the draw at this "transporting" Flatiron Tuscan offering "sublime" dining "from start to finish"; a "gorgeous terra-cotta" setting, "friendly staff" and an "exquisitely untrendy" vibe help blunt the shock of those "hefty prices."

Bereket ●⌿
20 | 3 | 12 | $12

187 E. Houston St. (Orchard St.), 212-475-7700

☑ "Late-night" types swear by this 24/7 Lower East Side Turkish kebab joint that's perfect for "after-hours alcohol absorption", but even by day it's "cheap" and "delicious"; maybe "there isn't any decor" and "you'll have to carry your food to the table", but "can 50,000 taxi drivers be wrong?"

Beso
▽ 22 | 14 | 18 | $24

210 Fifth Ave. (Union St.), Brooklyn, 718-783-4902

■ "Totally underappreciated", this Park Slope Nuevo Latino is "packed at brunch, empty at dinner but amazing at all times" according to its fans; though some say the "atmosphere is a turnoff", the "great value" pricing and "aim-to-please" service are fine as is.

Better Burger
15 | 12 | 14 | $13

1614 Second Ave. (84th St.), 212-734-6644
178 Eighth Ave. (19th St.), 212-989-6688 ●

(continued)

(continued)

Better Burger
565 Third Ave. (37th St.), 212-949-7528 ●
www.betterburgernyc.com

☑ "If organic food floats your boat", the "wholesome" burgers and air-baked fries will make you "feel righteous" at these exercises in "guilt-free fast food"; still, some hold out for "better prices", while others nix "skimpy portions", "flavorless" patties and "gimmicky" condiments.

Bettola ●
— | — | — | M

412 Amsterdam Ave. (bet. 79th & 80th Sts.), 212-787-1660
Sidewalk seating makes for primo Upper West Side people-watching at this new Italian where thin-crust pizzas and rustic, multiregional dishes emerge from a wood-fired brick oven; a well-priced wine list completes the easy neighborhood dining experience.

Beyoglu ●
20 | 17 | 18 | $32

1431 Third Ave. (81st St.), 212-650-0850
■ The Upper East Side gets a "change of pace" via this "busy" "Turkish delight" that's often "as crowded as the streets of Istanbul"; given the "flexible menu" and "bargain prices", regulars "skip the entrees" altogether and "share lots of small dishes" instead.

Bianca ⊅
▽ 22 | 18 | 21 | $33

5 Bleecker St. (bet. Bowery & Elizabeth St.), 212-260-4666
■ Insiders "head straight for the lasagna" at this "quaint" NoHo newcomer featuring recipes from Emilia-Romagna seemingly prepared by your "Italian grandma"; "charming" service and fair pricing leave admirers speechless: they "don't want to say too much or everyone will want to go."

Bice ●
20 | 19 | 18 | $53

7 E. 54th St. (bet. 5th & Madison Aves.), 212-688-1999;
www.bicenewyork.com
☑ Whether "Eurochic" or "Eurotrash", the "flashy" crowd at this "high-decibel" Midtown Northern Italian relishes the "bustle and buzz" of its "power-lunch" scene, where the food's "tasty", but the "eye candy" is even tastier; for optimum enjoyment at any meal, "bring someone else's wallet."

Big Nick's Burger Joint ●
17 | 5 | 12 | $15

2175 Broadway (77th St.), 212-362-9238
☑ The "menu's as thick as a phone book" at this "glorious", "salt-of-the-earth dump", a 24/7 Upper Westsider famed for its "juicy burgers" (not its "startling array" of "basic diner" grub); the "roughshod" decor leaves you with two options: "close your eyes" or "take it to go."

Big Wong ⊅
22 | 4 | 11 | $12

67 Mott St. (bet. Bayard & Canal Sts.), 212-964-0540
☑ For "Chinatown the way you should experience it", check out this "old-school" Cantonese that's "so cheap you'll think they outsource the cooking to China"; despite "as much ambiance as a laundromat" and service that "makes toll collectors seem warm and fuzzy", it's hard to beat for "fast good value."

Bill Hong's
19 | 13 | 18 | $46

227 E. 56th St. (bet. 2nd & 3rd Aves.), 212-751-4048;
www.billhongs.com
☑ "Old-fashioned" Cantonese comes at "new-fashioned prices" at this Midtown "mainstay" now in its 50th year; despite an "outdated atmosphere" that's reflected in the menu ("egg foo yong, anyone?"), its "famous", "one-of-a-kind lobster roll" remains a "phenomenon."

BILTMORE ROOM ◐
25 | 26 | 21 | $64

290 Eighth Ave. (bet. 24th & 25th Sts.), 212-807-0111;
www.thebiltmoreroom.com
■ "You can almost inhale the hip factor" at this pricey, crowded Chelsea newcomer where chef Gary Robins' "extraordinary" Eclectic menu is served in a "*Great Gatsby*"–esque space adorned with "marble and chandeliers" salvaged from the old Biltmore Hotel; at present, it's so popular that many hope the glow will "dim a bit, so mere mortals can get reservations."

Biricchino ⌧
20 | 12 | 20 | $35

260 W. 29th St. (8th Ave.), 212-695-6690
■ "Close proximity" to Madison Square Garden is the raison d'être of this "delicious and affordable" Chelsea Northern Italian that's just the ticket for a "pre-game" fill-up; regulars commend its "terrific homemade sausages" and tolerate the "diner"-like decor.

Biscuit ◐⇱
18 | 8 | 14 | $17

367 Flatbush Ave. (Sterling Pl.), Brooklyn, 718-398-2227
☑ "Tasty Carolina-style BBQ" keeps "homesick Southerners" satisfied at this "little" Prospect Heights "hole-in-the-wall" that's "best for takeout" given the "almost nonexistent dining area"; though purists find the ribs too "bland", the "inexpensive" pricing is positively invigorating.

Bistro Cassis
▽ 22 | 22 | 20 | $37

243 W. 14th St. (bet. 7th & 8th Aves.), 212-871-6020;
www.bistrocassisnyc.com
■ "Just like being in Paris – except for 14th Street outside", this new Chelsea French bistro is refreshingly "unpretentious", featuring "good basic" grub in a "welcoming" setting; excellent "bang for the buck" helps smooth over "service that's a little rough around the edges."

Bistro du Nord
18 | 16 | 17 | $44

1312 Madison Ave. (93rd St.), 212-289-0997
☑ Spend a "delightful moment in France" at this "minuscule" Carnegie Hill bistro with a "charming" (if "elbow-to-elbow") setting; au contrairians cite "overworked waiters" and a "past-its-prime" menu, but at least the "value-loaded prix fixes" keep its neighbors happy.

Bistro Les Amis ◐
21 | 18 | 20 | $37

180 Spring St. (Thompson St.), 212-226-8645; www.bistrolesamis.com
■ "After a long day of SoHo shopping", this "unpretentious" but "charming" French bistro is just the thing "when you don't want a scene"; "solid" cooking and "welcoming" service keep the mood "convivial" – and you "won't have to take a second mortgage" to settle the check.

Bistro Le Steak ◐
18 | 14 | 16 | $42

1309 Third Ave. (75th St.), 212-517-3800
☑ "Moderately priced steaks" arrive with a "French twist" at this "unpretentious" Upper East Side bistro that "doesn't try to be much more than a neighborhood place"; all right, "it ain't Peter Luger" and the "routine" "decor is of no interest", but it's a "good standby" for "straightforward" Gallic classics.

Bistro St. Mark's
21 | 18 | 16 | $39

76 St. Mark's Ave. (Flatbush & 6th Aves.), Brooklyn, 718-857-8600
☑ "Inventive" cooking and "gentle prices" meet cute at this Park Slope French bistro with a back garden that's like a "little vacation" and a "Monday night prix fixe that's one of the best deals in Brooklyn"; still, the "sour" staff leads some to sigh "if only the service did justice to the food."

Bistro Ten 18
▽ 21 | 20 | 20 | $35

1018 Amsterdam Ave. (110th St.), 212-662-7600; www.bistroten18.com
■ "Like a cool drink of water in a parched neighborhood" describes this Morningside Heights American bistro proffering "simple, well-executed food" and a "warm welcome" for "reasonable" prices; sightseers seek a "window seat with a view of St. John the Divine."

Bistrot Margot
17 | 17 | 17 | $32

26 Prince St. (bet. Elizabeth & Mott Sts.), 212-274-1027
■ "Something of a hidden treasure", this "narrow" NoLita bistro dishes out "decent", "affordable" French fare in "homey" environs ("if you think of Paris in the '60s as home"); a "cute little garden out back" is a good place to "rest your weary bones."

Bivio
21 | 19 | 16 | $45

637 Hudson St. (Horatio St.), 212-206-0601; www.bivionyc.com
◪ There's "beaucoup buzz" about this "sceney", "stylish" new Villager drawing "young", "too-cool-for-school" types with "wonderful", "reasonably priced" Tuscan cooking; while the "squished" seating, "loud" acoustics and "disorganized" service draw brickbats, fans report lots of "fun" to be had.

Black Cat ⌧⇲
– | – | – | I

122 E. Seventh St. (bet. Ave. A & 1st Ave.), 212-253-2331
From the owners of Ivo & Lulu comes this tiny new East Villager offering an all-organic, French-accented Eclectic menu for almost single-digit prices; it makes no bones about its BYO policy, with corkscrews lashed to each table.

Black Duck
▽ 20 | 18 | 19 | $46

Park South Hotel, 122 E. 28th St. (bet. Lexington Ave. & Park Ave. S.), 212-448-0888; www.parksouthhotel.com
◪ A "special, secret place" hidden in a Gramercy hotel, this "pleasant" New American seafooder hooks fans with "nicely prepared" fish and "live weekend jazz"; despite some sniping about "overpricing" and "amateur service", admirers have high hopes for this "buried treasure."

Bleu Evolution ◗
17 | 20 | 14 | $30

808 W. 187th St. (Fort Washington Ave.), 212-928-6006
◪ For a "little bit of Downtown" way Uptown in Hudson Heights, surveyors tout this "bohemian" French-Moroccan offering "decent" enough chow in "shabby-chic", "bordello"-esque digs topped off by a "pleasant garden"; "flaky" service and an "uneven" kitchen are the bleu notes.

Blockhead's Burritos
17 | 9 | 15 | $16

1563 Second Ave. (bet. 81st & 82nd Sts.), 212-879-1999
954 Second Ave. (bet. 50th & 51st Sts.), 212-750-2020
499 Third Ave. (bet. 33rd & 34th Sts.), 212-213-3332
Worldwide Plaza, 322 W. 50th St. (bet. 8th & 9th Aves.), 212-307-7029
◪ "Monster"-size burritos at "lilliputian" tabs are a "student's dream" at these all-over-town Mexicans; no surprise, you "don't go for the decor" or service, just to "get the job done."

BLT Steak ⌧
24 | 22 | 21 | $68

106 E. 57th St. (bet. Lexington & Park Aves.), 212-752-7470; www.bltsteak.com
■ Chef Laurent Tourondel (ex Cello) resurfaces in Midtown at this popular (as in often crowded) new haute steakhouse offering "superbly prepared" beef with sides that nearly "outpace the mains for attention"; though the à la carte, à la "Craft" style of ordering can drive the bill "sky high", in the end this "terrific addition" is "exquisite in every way."

bluechili ◐ 　　21 | 21 | 17 | $38

251 W. 51st St. (bet. B'way & 8th Ave.), 212-246-3330;
www.bluechilinyc.com

☑ "Futuristic all-white decor" bathed in "morphing colored lights" sets the "exotic" tone at this "trendy" Theater District Pan-Asian that's applauded for its "artfully prepared" dishes, not the "shaky" service; "thunderous", "DJ"-spun background music suggests it might be best for "youthful" spirits.

Blue Fin ◐ 　　22 | 23 | 19 | $52

W Times Square Hotel, 1567 Broadway (47th St.), 212-918-1400;
www.brguestrestaurants.com

☑ Arguably Times Square's "coolest scene", Steve Hanson's "lively" double-decker seafood emporium impresses "even the most fin-icky eaters" with "delectable" deep-sea dining in an "architecturally stunning" space; despite "jet-engine decibel levels" and "expense account"–worthy pricing, it's "a bastion of chic in a sea of tacky."

BLUE HILL 　　26 | 22 | 24 | $61

75 Washington Pl. (bet. 6th Ave. & Washington Sq. W.), 212-539-1776;
www.bluehillnyc.com

■ "Everything works" at this Village New American that turns out "lyrical", "farm-fresh" cuisine in a "quiet", "grown-up" setting; "unobtrusive yet attentive" service and "garden seating" make it perfect for a "special occasion with your sweetheart", and if "expensive, it's not unreasonably so" given the high quality.

Blue Mill 　　– | – | – | M

50 Commerce St. (Barrow St.), 212-352-0009

The much-beloved Villager Grange Hall has been lightly renovated into this newcomer that takes its name from a prior incarnation of the same space; early visitors report reasonably priced New American vittles and brighter decor in the same deco vein as its predecessor.

Blue 9 Burger ◐♻ 　　19 | 6 | 11 | $8

92 Third Ave. (bet. 12th & 13th Sts.), 212-979-0053;
www.blue9burger.com

☑ "NYC's answer to California's In-N-Out Burger", this easily affordable East Village patty purveyor puts out "nice 'n' greasy" specimens made from "fresh", not frozen, meat; just be patient with the "fast-food atmosphere, without the speed."

BLUE RIBBON ◐ 　　25 | 19 | 23 | $48

97 Sullivan St. (bet. Prince & Spring Sts.), 212-274-0404
280 Fifth Ave. (bet. 1st St. & Garfield Pl.), Brooklyn, 718-840-0404
www.blueribbonrestaurants.com

■ "No reservations" translates into "excruciating waits" at these "hopping" New Americans via the brilliant Bromberg brothers, but no one minds given the "delectable" chow and "impeccable" service (hint: the "Brooklyn incarnation is much roomier"); extended hours of operation win them accolades for one of the "best late-night dining" scenes in town.

Blue Ribbon Bakery ◐ 　　23 | 18 | 20 | $38

33 Downing St. (Bedford St.), 212-337-0404;
www.blueribbonrestaurants.com

■ The "smorgasbord" menu at this Village New American "runs the gamut from little dishes to substantial entrees", served in a space perfumed by the "smell of just-made bread"; regulars insist a visit to the "medieval basement" is "worth the trip alone", but others claim it's all about that "excellent brunch."

BLUE RIBBON SUSHI ◑   26 | 19 | 21 | $50

119 Sullivan St. (bet. Prince & Spring Sts.), 212-343-0404
278 Fifth Ave. (bet. 1st St. & Garfield Pl.), Brooklyn, 718-840-0408 ⊠
www.blueribbonrestaurants.com
■ "Sparkling fresh sushi", "meticulously crafted", awaits at this "fail-safe" Japanese duo where no reserving spells "ridiculous waits" (though Park Slope is "easier to get into"); "late-night hours" and an "eye-candy" following make the "big bucks" tabs easier to swallow.

Blue Smoke   20 | 17 | 19 | $39

116 E. 27th St. (bet. Lexington & Park Aves.), 212-447-7733;
www.bluesmoke.com
☑ Fans go "hog wild" for the "rib-sticking" offerings and "warm service" at this "upscale" Gramercy BBQ; though a few purists find it "not as good as it should be" (especially given the "far-from-bargain pricing"), the steadfast insist it just "keeps getting better"; P.S. there's a "hot jazz club" downstairs.

Blue Star ⇥   ▽ 20 | 15 | 18 | $29

254 Court St. (bet. DeGraw & Kane Sts.), Brooklyn, 718-858-5806
■ "Swimmingly fresh seafood" is on the docket of this new Cobble Hill poisson purveyor, an "instant hit" with locals thanks to its "laid-back", "Grateful-Dead-on-the-stereo" vibe; a "socializing" chef and a staff that "remembers your name" enhance its "neighborhood" feel.

BLUE WATER GRILL ◑   24 | 22 | 21 | $49

31 Union Sq. W. (16th St.), 212-675-9500;
www.brguestrestaurants.com
■ A "sophisticated", "metropolitan attitude" and "briny-fresh seafood" keep the trade brisk at Steve Hanson's "boisterous" Union Square "institution" that's still as "trendy" as ever ("long live *Sex and the City*!"); set in a restored "beautiful old bank", it features "cool" jazz downstairs, "table terrace" seating outside and "always smiling service" throughout its handsome, white-marble quarters.

Boat Basin Cafe ◑   11 | 20 | 11 | $22

W. 79th St. (Hudson River), 212-496-5542;
www.boatbasincafe.com
☑ "Nature provides the decor" at this alfresco Westsider that's more about "Margaritaville on the Hudson" than fine dining; regulars report the "concession-stand" American chow and "junior-varsity" service are more tolerable after an eyeful of those "phenomenal" river views; N.B. open April–October only.

Boat House   17 | 25 | 17 | $48

Central Park, enter on E. 72nd St. (Central Park Dr. N.),
212-517-2233
☑ You'll "forget you're in the middle of the city" at this "idyllic" New American "wonderland" set alongside Central Park's boat pond; the food and service are "acceptable" and the tabs "pricey", but the "priceless setting" with views "straight out of a Monet painting" makes everything more palatable.

Bobby Van's Steakhouse   23 | 17 | 21 | $59

131 E. 54th St. (bet. Lexington & Park Aves.), 212-207-8050
230 Park Ave. (46th St.), 212-867-5490 ⊠
www.bobbyvans.com
☑ "Beefeaters unite" at these "manly man" Midtown chop shops where the "juicy" prime cuts are "well done" and the "standard" decor is "good ol' boys' club"; "huge portions justify the humongous prices", though some rank it in the "second tier" of steakdom.

Boca Chica
21 | 15 | 16 | $27

13 First Ave. (1st St.), 212-473-0108
■ "Loud" twentysomethings guzzling "powerful caipirinhas" make for "playful" grazing at this "vibrant" East Village South American; no surprise, the "zesty" chow takes a backseat to the "whirlwind" atmosphere, yet with prices this "cheap", "extended waits" are a given.

Bohio
▽ 21 | 19 | 19 | $27

4055 Broadway (bet. 170th & 171st St.), 212-568-5029
☑ Stylish flair revs up traditional Dominican cooking at this "small" but "charming" Washington Heights newcomer; if a "little slow" on the service end, "nice decor" and decent pricing compensate.

Boi 🈺
▽ 23 | 19 | 21 | $39

246 E. 44th St. (bet. 2nd & 3rd Aves.), 212-681-6541; www.boi-restaurant.com
■ "Not your traditional Vietnamese", this "inviting" new arrival near Grand Central offers a "hint-of-the-West" menu with "multiple layers of flavor" and even a pastry chef; though it may be a bit "pricey" for the genre, its "lovely" looks and "attentive service" make it "worth a try."

Bolo
23 | 20 | 21 | $52

23 E. 22nd St. (bet. B'way & Park Ave. S.), 212-228-2200; www.bolorestaurant.com
☑ "Stylish takes on Spanish classics" (as well as "delicious" tapas) are the draws at Bobby Flay's "consummate" Flatiron favorite, a "zesty", "buzzy" spot humming with "high energy"; while the pricing may be a tad "expensive", "consistently creative" comestibles are the payoff.

Bombay Palace
18 | 16 | 15 | $34

30 W. 52nd St. (bet. 5th & 6th Aves.), 212-541-7777
☑ The "more-than-you-can-eat" lunch buffet is the "real-deal", "don't-miss" meal at this "traditional" Midtown Indian where the "deftly executed" dishes get "pricier at dinner"; those who find it rather "boring" head upstairs to K Lounge, its kama sutra–themed nightclub.

Bond Street ●
25 | 23 | 19 | $58

6 Bond St. (bet. B'way & Lafayette St.), 212-777-2500
☑ Both the sushi and the scene are "fabulous" at this NoHo nouveau Japanese hosting skinny, "Prada bag"–toting types who are "almost too hip to eat"; a "trendier-than-thou" staff and "kiddie-size portions" at "crazy prices" are "buzzkills", but the "dark" downstairs lounge supplies certified sex appeal.

Bonita ●
▽ 22 | 16 | 18 | $21

338 Bedford Ave. (bet. S. 2nd & 3rd Sts.), Brooklyn, 718-384-9500
☑ "Good, standard fare" is on the menu of this Williamsburg Mexican "fiesta" known for its "fair prices" and "*muy bueno* margaritas"; the "cacophonous tiled room" verges on "cramped", but amigos praise its "authentic" vibe.

Borgo Antico ●
18 | 18 | 18 | $39

22 E. 13th St. (bet. 5th Ave. & University Pl.), 212-807-1313; www.borgoanticonyc.com
☑ A "grown-up atmosphere" prevails at this "casual" Village Italian with a "comfortable" downstairs bar and "elegant" dining room above; while there may be "no fireworks" in evidence, the "simple food at reasonable prices" keeps the mood "pleasant."

Bottino
18 | 18 | 16 | $41

246 10th Ave. (bet. 24th & 25th Sts.), 212-206-6766; www.bottinonyc.com
☑ "After touring the Chelsea galleries", "art stars and their dealers" turn to this "chic, understated" Northern Italian for its "tasty" vittles

and "bonus" back garden; "snooty" service and a "middle-of-nowhere" address are the weak links, though it always works for "fashionable" "people-watching and table-hopping."

BOULEY ◑

28 | 26 | 26 | $84 |

120 W. Broadway (Duane St.), 212-964-2525;
www.bouleyrestaurants.com

■ "Food god" David Bouley is back, playing at the top of his game at his "extraordinary" TriBeCa flagship which has copped the No. 2 rating for Food in this *Survey*; "everything clicks" here, from the "wonderful aroma of apples" at the entrance to the "gorgeous vaulted space", "standard-setting" service and "preposterously good", "beautifully presented" New French cuisine; of course, all this "luxury doesn't come cheap" – with the exception of the $35 prix fixe lunch.

Bourbon Street Cafe

17 | 15 | 19 | $28 |

40-12 Bell Blvd. (bet. 40th & 41st Aves.), Queens, 718-224-2200;
www.bourbonstreetny.com

☑ "New Orleans" lands in Queens at this Cajun Southerner doling out "hearty portions" of "decent" grub at "modest" tabs; foes say this "ok attempt" is "inconsistent" and "not that authentic", though the "fun bar" is popular with "loud, young" folks.

Bouterin

21 | 23 | 20 | $58 |

420 E. 59th St. (bet. 1st Ave. & Sutton Pl.), 212-758-0323

☑ "Delicious Provençal cuisine" and a "homey" air "transport you to France" at this "sedate", "flower"-bedecked Sutton Place Gallic; no question, it's "pricey" and the decor is too "froufrou" for modernists, but it works when your "parents" or mature friends are visiting.

Brasserie ◑

21 | 23 | 20 | $48 |

100 E. 53rd St. (bet. Lexington & Park Aves.), 212-751-4840;
www.restaurantassociates.com

■ It's easy to pretend you're a "supermodel" as you strut the "futuristic catwalk" entrance to this Midtown brasserie, a "slinky", "stylish" study in "ultra-modernity" backed up by an "enticing" menu and "professional" service; voyeurs get a kick out of the "closed-circuit TVs over the bar" broadcasting "who's coming and going."

Brasserie 8½

22 | 24 | 20 | $52 |

9 W. 57th St. (bet. 5th & 6th Aves.), 212-829-0812;
www.restaurantassociates.com

■ "Drop-dead gorgeous" is the word on this "spacious" subterranean Midtown brasserie accessed by a "theatrical spiral staircase" fit for "Gloria Swanson"; chef Julian Alonzo's "first-class" cooking is on par with the decor, ditto the "well-designed" cocktails poured at its "happening bar."

Brasserie Julien ◑

18 | 19 | 17 | $41 |

1422 Third Ave. (bet. 80th & 81st Sts.), 212-744-6327; www.brasseriejulien.com

■ "Perfect neighborhood bistros" don't get much better than this "little bit of Paris" in Yorkville, a not too expensive "family-run" enterprise where "delicious" French cooking is enhanced by a "deco" interior inspired by the "Chrysler Building elevators"; live jazz and outdoor seating provide the "gravy."

Brasserie LCB

– | – | – | VE |

(fka La Côte Basque)

60 W. 55th St. (bet. 5th & 6th Aves.), 212-688-6525

Those who mourn the demise of French stalwart La Côte Basque take heart in this more casual, no-jacket-required reincarnation in the same Midtown space, helmed by the same great chef, Jean-Jacques Rachou;

look for faithful (if pricey) renditions of Parisian brasserie classics served in a brighter, belle epoque setting.

Bravo Gianni ⦿
21 | 14 | 20 | $57

230 E. 63rd St. (bet. 2nd & 3rd Aves.), 212-752-7272
☒ The "quality never wavers" at this East Side Italian "blast from the past" where chef-owner Gianni turns out "consistently good" (if "pricey") food while managing to "make you feel at home" at the same time; a post-*Survey* renovation may invalidate its Decor score.

Brawta Caribbean Café
▽ 22 | 13 | 16 | $23

347 Atlantic Ave. (Hoyt St.), Brooklyn, 718-855-5515
☒ Some "like it hot" at this authentically "spicy" BYO Boerum Hill Caribbean offering "straightforward", "lick-the-plate-clean" cuisine for "reasonable" tabs; in keeping with the tropical theme, the "slow" service transports you to the "laid-back Islands."

Bread Bar at Tabla
24 | 22 | 21 | $40

11 Madison Ave. (25th St.), 212-889-0667
■ For the "flavors of Tabla without the cost", try this downstairs sibling offering "Indian-derived" small plates and "incredible" flatbreads; given the "lightning-fast" service, "innovative" cocktails and a "wonderful" patio overlooking Madison Square, some sense it's second to naan.

Bread Tribeca
19 | 16 | 14 | $30

301 Church St. (Walker St.), 212-334-8282; www.breadtribeca.com
20 Spring St. (bet. Elizabeth & Mott Sts.), 212-334-1015
■ "Huge windows" set the "open, airy" tone at this TriBeCa Italian turning out "solid Ligurian fare" from an "open kitchen"; "half-baked" service and "too-loud music" detract, but insiders say it's just right for "jury duty"; N.B. the much smaller NoLita outpost specializes in panini.

Brennan & Carr ⦿⌿
21 | 8 | 14 | $15

3432 Nostrand Ave. (Ave. U), Brooklyn, 718-646-9559
☒ For "nostalgia on a roll", it's hard to beat this "old-fashioned", 67-year-old Sheepshead Bay American renowned for its "sloppy", "double-dipped roast beef sandwich", the "stuff that dreams are made of"; not so dreamy is the decor and service, but who cares given such "inexpensive" tabs?

Bricco
18 | 17 | 19 | $39

304 W. 56th St. (bet. 8th & 9th Aves.), 212-245-7160; www.bricconyc.com
■ A "friendly owner" and "cheerful" service enhance the "warm ambiance" at this Midtown Southern Italian that's also known for its "wonderful" brick-oven pizzas; it's a tradition here to "kiss the ceiling", and the variety of lip prints planted there provide plenty to "stare at."

Brick Cafe
▽ 23 | 21 | 20 | $30

30-95 33rd St. (31st Ave.), Queens, 718-267-2735; www.brickcafe.com
■ Bringing a touch of "SoHo" to Astoria, this "Manhattan"-esque Northern Italian bistro is a more than welcome "addition to a budding neighborhood", with "excellent" food and a "rustic", "romantic" mien; sidewalk seating and an adjoining lounge ice the cake.

Brick Lane Curry House
20 | 15 | 16 | $27

306-308 E. Sixth St. (2nd Ave.), 212-979-2900; www.bricklanecurryhouse.com
■ There's "plenty of heat in the kitchen" of this "midpriced" Sixth Street Indian that's a "step above" the competition owing to its "take-your-breath-away" spicing; while service can be on the "inconsistent" side, its Decor rating may improve following a "move down the street" post-*Survey*.

Bridge Cafe
21 | 17 | 20 | $40

279 Water St. (Dover St.), 212-227-3344

■ The "charm never wears off" at this "hidden treasure of old NY" secreted under the Brooklyn Bridge in circa-1794 digs; "consistently good" New American chow, "quaint", "saloon"-like decor and an "easygoing" vibe make it "worth the trek" to this "little-traveled" area.

Bright Food Shop
19 | 10 | 15 | $26

216-218 Eighth Ave. (21st St.), 212-243-4433

☑ "Offbeat" noshers convene at this "basic" Chelsea "hole-in-the-wall" serving a "quirky" Mex-Asian mix that splits surveyors ("inspired" vs. "overrated"); there's more agreement about the "nonchalant" service, "drab diner" decor and "rock-bottom" pricing.

Brio
19 | 14 | 19 | $34

786 Lexington Ave. (61st St.), 212-980-2300

■ Convenient "after shopping at Bloomingdale's", this "casual" Italian provides "reliable", "reasonable" dining in a "comfortable", low-key setting; younger types prefer the "terrific thin-crust pizza" at its sibling, Brio Forno, "right around the corner."

Brooklyn Diner USA ◐
16 | 14 | 15 | $29

212 W. 57th St. (bet. B'way & 7th Ave.), 212-977-2280;
www.brooklyndiner.com

☑ Ok, the "name ain't accurate" – it's "neither a diner, nor in Brooklyn" – but Shelly Fireman's "upscale" Midtown take on the genre offers "huge portions" of "good" food; in fact, "if you can get by the prices and the tourists", it can be "fun for the family."

Brother Jimmy's BBQ ◐
17 | 11 | 14 | $23

428 Amsterdam Ave. (bet. 80th & 81st Sts.), 212-501-7515
1485 Second Ave. (bet. 77th & 78th Sts.), 212-288-0999
1644 Third Ave. (93rd St.), 212-426-2020
www.brotherjimmys.com

☑ To relive your "college days", try out one of these "never-ending frat parties"–cum–Southern BBQ joints where "rowdy" crowds tuck into "messy" ribs served by "scantily clad", "Hooters-lite" waitresses; in sum, it's "not a good place for a first date" – or if you're "over 30."

Bruculino
17 | 15 | 17 | $33

225 Columbus Ave. (70th St.), 212-579-3966

☑ There's "serviceable" dining to be had in the "vicinity of Lincoln Center" at this "red-sauce" Italian that's got the "neighborhood" thing down pat; though it's "quieter" and has "less of a wait" than its sibling, Pomodoro Rosso, some say it's also "not as good."

Bruno ☒
▽ 21 | 20 | 22 | $53

240 E. 58th St. (bet. 2nd & 3rd Aves.), 212-688-4190;
www.brunosnyc.com

■ "You'll feel at home" at this Midtown Italian thanks to Bruno, its "gracious owner" and overseer of the "professional" staff; if a minority finds things a bit too "old hat" (and "expensive"), far more pronounce it "excellent all around", especially that "romantic" nightly piano.

Bryant Park Grill/Cafe
16 | 21 | 16 | $42

behind NY Public Library, 25 W. 40th St. (bet. 5th & 6th Aves.), 212-840-6500;
www.arkrestaurants.com

☑ "If only the food matched the ambiance" sigh sympathists of this American duo set in "serene" Bryant Park; the "semi-fancy" Grill boasts an "incredible roof deck" and the less expensive alfresco Cafe is more of a "singles bar", but either way the "pricey" grub is eclipsed by the "priceless" view and "crazy pickup scene."

B. Smith's Restaurant Row
18 | 18 | 18 | $45

320 W. 46th St. (bet. 8th & 9th Aves.), 212-315-1100; www.bsmith.com

☑ "Accommodating" is the approach at "domestic diva" Barbara Smith's Restaurant Row Eclectic where her "creative", "lip-smackin' good" Southern cooking keeps the room "lively", especially pre-theater; still, some say it's "not like it used to B."

Bubba Gump Shrimp Co. ◑
15 | 18 | 18 | $28

1501 Broadway (bet. 43rd & 44th Sts.), 212-391-7100; www.bubbagump.com

☑ Go ahead, "act like a tourist" at this Times Square link of the *Forrest Gump*–themed seafood chain where "everything's deep fried" and the "overzealous" staff is a tad "too happy"; despite "mediocre" eats and a "NJ mall" ambiance, at least they don't "skimp on the shrimp."

Bubby's
18 | 15 | 16 | $26

120 Hudson St. (N. Moore St.), 212-219-0666
1 Main St. (bet. Plymouth & Water Sts.), Brooklyn, 718-222-0666
www.bubbys.com

☑ "Brunch is the thing" at these "comfort-food extravaganzas" famed for their "no-frills" American chow, "family-friendly" vibe and "easy-on-the-wallet" tabs (forget the "clueless" service and "horrendous" weekend waits); P.S. the new Dumbo spin-off is "just like the original" but "on steroids."

Bukhara Grill
21 | 16 | 19 | $33

217 E. 49th St. (bet. 2nd & 3rd Aves.), 212-888-2839

■ "Chock-full of flavors, spices and textures", the cooking at this Midtown Indian takes the genre to a "higher level" with "top-notch" dishes that really "pack a wallop"; regulars commend the "delectable" $13.95 lunch buffet as one of the "best values" around.

Bull & Bear ◑
20 | 19 | 20 | $53

Waldorf-Astoria, 570 Lexington Ave. (49th St.), 212-872-4900; www.waldorfastoria.com

☑ The steaks are "succulent" but the "feel is old" (ditto the waiters) at this "solid" chop shop where the pricing will "remind you that you're eating at the Waldorf"; "suits" who find the dining room too "stodgy" use it "more as a bar", even if it's "not the same without the cigars."

Bull Run ⊠
▽ 20 | 17 | 18 | $41

Club Quarters Hotel, 52 William St. (Pine St.), 212-859-2200; www.bullrunwallstreet.com

☑ "One of the few decent choices" in the "barren" Financial District, this weekday-only New American presents a "something-for-everyone" menu in "spacious", "white-tablecloth" digs; but detractors insist that the "uninspiring" food and "unexceptional" decor "could use some work."

Burger Heaven
16 | 8 | 13 | $16

9 E. 53rd St. (bet. 5th & Madison Aves.), 212-752-0340
20 E. 49th St. (bet. 5th & Madison Aves.), 212-755-2166
804 Lexington Ave. (62nd St.), 212-838-3580
536 Madison Ave. (bet. 54th & 55th Sts.), 212-753-4214
291 Madison Ave. (bet. 40th & 41st Sts.), 212-685-6250
1534 Third Ave. (86th St.), 212-722-8292
www.burgerheaven.com

☑ Even though the "big juicy" burgers at this "cholesterol-heavy" chain come "without foie gras", they're still "decent" and "affordable" – provided you can tolerate "zero decor", "rushed" service and an "overstuffed" crowd.

burger joint at Le Parker Meridien ◐⊟

24 | 11 | 14 | $11

Le Parker Meridien, 119 W. 56th St. (bet. 6th & 7th Aves.), 212-708-7414

■ The "best-kept secret that everybody knows", this "funky" patty purveyor is "hidden behind a curtain" in an otherwise "luxe" Midtown hotel; distaste over "overwhelmed" service and "long lunch lines" evaporate after a taste of the "sinfully delicious" burgers.

Burritoville

17 | 7 | 12 | $12

298 Bleecker St. (7th Ave. S.), 212-633-9249 ◐
144 Chambers St. (bet. Greenwich St. & W. B'way), 212-571-1144
625 Ninth Ave. (44th St.), 212-333-5352 ◐
1487 Second Ave. (bet. 77th & 78th Sts.), 212-472-8800 ◐
141 Second Ave. (bet. 8th & 9th Sts.), 212-260-3300 ◐
866 Third Ave. (52nd St.), 212-980-4111
36 Water St. (Broad St.), 212-747-1100
166 W. 72nd St. (bet. Amsterdam & Columbus Aves.), 212-580-7700 ◐
352 W. 39th St. (9th Ave.), 212-563-9088
264 W. 23rd St. (bet. 7th & 8th Aves.), 212-367-9844 ◐
Additional locations throughout the NY area
www.burritoville.com

☑ "Fat-ass" burritos at "happy-meal prices" feed the "famished" at this "reliable" Tex-Mex chain; if the "incompetent service" and "lack of decor" offend, there's always "zippity quick" delivery.

Butter ◐⊠

20 | 24 | 18 | $52

415 Lafayette St. (bet. Astor Pl. & 4th St.), 212-253-2828;
www.butterrestaurant.com

☑ It helps to be "trendy and young" at this double-decker Village New American where "cool", "ski-lodgey" decor compensates for the "noses-in-the-air" attitude; while everything's "serene" in the upstairs dining room, it's all "scene" in the downstairs lounge.

Cabana ◐

21 | 18 | 18 | $33

South Street Seaport, 89 South St., Pier 17, 3rd fl. (bet. Fulton & John Sts.), 212-406-1155
1022 Third Ave. (bet. 60th & 61st Sts.), 212-980-5678
10710 70th Rd. (bet. Austin St. & Queens Blvd.), Queens, 718-263-3600

■ It's "fiesta time" at this "frenetic" Nuevo Latino mini-chain where the "hearty, tasty" grub and "hot, hot, hot" scene are just the thing "when you're feeling spicy" (yet the prices "won't burn a hole in your pocketbook"); P.S. the Seaport satellite comes equipped with "knockout" harbor views.

Cacio e Pepe

– | – | – | M

182 Second Ave. (bet. 11th & 12th Sts.), 212-505-5931

The name means 'cheese and pepper', and this rustic East Village Roman trattoria proffers the namesake pasta dish (tonnarelli served in a hollowed-out wheel of pecorino) along with a slate of midpriced specialties straight from the Eternal City; a picket-fenced, floral-bordered backyard adds seasonal appeal.

Cafe Asean ⊟

22 | 14 | 18 | $27

117 W. 10th St. (bet. Greenwich & 6th Aves.), 212-633-0348

■ "Creative" SE Asian dishes draw diners to this "unpretentious" Villager that's "nothing to look at" inside so savvy sorts head for its "super garden"; either way, be prepared for some "knee-knocking intimacy", but if the "tables are small, so is the bill."

CAFÉ BOTANICA
21 | 26 | 22 | $56

*Essex House, 160 Central Park S. (bet. 6th & 7th Aves.),
212-484-5120*

■ "Views don't get much better" than the Central Park South vistas at this Med–New American where "delightful" food, a "civilized" hotel setting and "attentive" service make for "special-occasion" dining; since all this "elegance" comes at a price, the $38 dinner prix fixe is a particularly "terrific value."

CAFÉ BOULUD
27 | 23 | 25 | $74

*Surrey Hotel, 20 E. 76th St. (bet. 5th & Madison Aves.), 212-772-2600;
www.danielnyc.com*

■ A "less formal but no less superb" version of Daniel Boulud's eponymous flagship, this East Side French is "exquisite in every way", from its "savvy seasonal menu" to the "crisp" service and "sophisticated", "jubilant" mood; ok, you'll probably "drop a bundle", but what else would you expect for "near-perfect dining"?

Cafe Centro ⊠
20 | 18 | 19 | $44

*MetLife Bldg., 200 Park Ave. (45th St. & Vanderbilt Ave.), 212-818-1222;
www.restaurantassociates.com*

■ "In the center of everything", this Grand Central–area Mediterranean brasserie hosts a "mad rush of power-lunchers" midday, and thus might be "better for dinner" when it's "far less noisy and hurried"; at any hour, the food's "tasty", the service "friendly" and the space between tables "generous" – ditto the prices.

Cafe Con Leche
17 | 11 | 14 | $22

*424 Amsterdam Ave. (bet. 80th & 81st Sts.), 212-595-7000
726 Amsterdam Ave. (bet. 95th & 96th Sts.), 212-678-7000*

☑ The "atmosphere's warm" and the "Coronas are cold" at this West Side Cuban-Dominican duo purveying "zesty", "tasty", "cheapo" chow; "slower-than-slow" service and "keep-your-eyes-shut" decor suggest they may be "better delivery options."

Café de Bruxelles ◑
21 | 16 | 19 | $38

118 Greenwich Ave. (13th St.), 212-206-1830

■ "Even Belgian visitors get homesick" after a trip to this Greenwich Village Flemish standby where the "variety of mussels is amazing" and is matched by an equally "interesting beer list"; "more old-school" than the other "upstarts" in the field, it's also praised for "generous servings" and "reasonable prices."

CAFÉ DES ARTISTES ◑
22 | 26 | 23 | $65

*1 W. 67th St. (bet. Columbus Ave. & CPW), 212-877-3500;
www.cafenyc.com*

■ "Romance is very much alive" at George and Jenifer Lang's West Side "aphrodisiac of a restaurant" thanks to a "ravishing" setting complete with lovely Howard Christy Chandler murals and "flowers everywhere"; add in "efficient service" and "excellent" if "costly" French food, and it's just the place to "charm your new love or rekindle an old one"; regulars tout the choice of seating areas.

Cafe Español ◑
20 | 13 | 18 | $31

*172 Bleecker St. (bet. MacDougal & Sullivan Sts.), 212-505-0657
78 Carmine St. (bet. Bedford St. & 7th Ave. S.), 212-675-3312
www.cafeespanol.com*

☑ The "atom bomb"–strength sangria might make you "forget the food" at these separately owned Village Spaniards, but abstainers report the cooking's "delish" and the prices "decent"; despite "noisy", "cheesy" setups, most leave "satisfied and well fed."

Café Evergreen
20 | 13 | 18 | $30

1288 First Ave. (bet. 69th & 70th Sts.), 212-744-3266

☑ For "wonderful" dim sum "without the chaos of Chinatown", Eastsiders turn to this "upscale" Cantonese also renowned for its "Hong Kong"–style cooking and unusually "good wine list"; naturally, many ask "will it still be the same?" following the departure of owner Henry Leung ("we miss you").

Café Frida
19 | 18 | 16 | $35

368 Columbus Ave. (bet. 77th & 78th Sts.), 212-712-2929

☑ "Taking West Side Mexican food up a notch", this "above-average" cantina is known for its "brilliant", "made-to-order guacamole" and "noisy", "happy" vibe; still, dissenters say the "hit-or-miss" menu is "no longer the bargain it used to be."

Cafe Gitane ●∌
20 | 17 | 15 | $23

242 Mott St. (Prince St.), 212-334-9552

■ "Everyone's cool" in a "grungy-chic" way at this "trendy", "phone booth"–size NoLita French-Moroccan offering "inexpensive, smartly prepared" eats; ignore the "sour service" and relish a cup of "excellent coffee" (with a side of "unbeatable people-watching") instead.

Café Gray
– | – | – | E

Time Warner Ctr., 10 Columbus Circle, 3rd fl. (60th St. at B'way), 212-823-6338; www.cafegray.com

Chef Gray Kunz (ex Lespinasse) marks his return to the scene after four years via this new Time Warner showcase for his Asian-accented French brasserie cooking at more relaxed (but not *that* relaxed) pricing; while the David Rockwell–designed setup is provocative – positioning the open kitchen between the diners and the Central Park view – far more amazing is the breadth of its planned offerings: breakfast, lunch, dinner and a snack kiosk in the lobby.

Café Habana ●
22 | 13 | 14 | $21

17 Prince St. (Elizabeth St.), 212-625-2001

☑ Credit the "addictive" grilled corn on the cob (along with other "cheap", "tasty" eats) for the "looong waits" at this "nonstop" NoLita Cuban-Mexican; since "lax" service and "knocking elbows with your neighbor" are part of the package, insiders opt for the "high-speed take-out counter" around the corner.

Cafe Joul
20 | 14 | 18 | $40

1070 First Ave. (bet. 58th & 59th Sts.), 212-759-3131

☑ "Good for spontaneous dining", this Sutton Place French bistro "occasionally rises above its neighborhood niche" with "solid" cooking and a relaxed, "not fancy" ambiance; foes, however, find it "uneven" and suggest it "needs a face-lift."

Cafe Lalo ●∌
19 | 18 | 11 | $18

201 W. 83rd St. (bet. Amsterdam Ave. & B'way), 212-496-6031; www.cafelalo.com

☑ While it "looked so romantic in *You've Got Mail*", in reality you're "sitting thisclosetogether" at this "crowded" West Side dessert palace–cum–"teenybopper heaven" where the "to-die-for" offerings are tempered by "glaring lights" and "sourpuss service."

Cafe Loup ●
18 | 16 | 18 | $40

105 W. 13th St. (bet. 6th & 7th Aves.), 212-255-4746

■ "Dependable" French bistro standards and "unpretentious" service make for "convivial gatherings" at this "tried-and-true" Villager; maybe the decor's "a little worn around the edges", but it's still as "comfortable as an old shoe."

Cafe Luluc ●⊄
20 | 16 | 18 | $25

214 Smith St. (Baltic St.), Brooklyn, 718-625-3815
■ Open "early" for rise 'n' shiners and "late" for all-nighters, this "cheerful" Cobble Hill cousin of Banania Cafe dishes out "satisfying" French bistro chow at "veritable bargain" tabs; a "sweet, unintrusive staff" and "pretty backyard" ice the cake.

Cafe Luxembourg ●
20 | 18 | 19 | $48

200 W. 70th St. (bet. Amsterdam & West End Aves.), 212-873-7411
■ "Classic", "classy" and thus "always crowded", this "fail-safe" Lincoln Center–area French bistro – aka "Balthazar Uptown" – "never seems to lose its flair"; "confident" cooking and "guaranteed celeb sightings" ("Robin Williams", "Paul Newman") compensate for the "terrible acoustics" and "tin-of-sardines" setup.

Cafe Mogador ●
22 | 16 | 17 | $23

101 St. Marks Pl. (bet. Ave. A & 1st Ave.), 212-677-2226
☑ It's "always buzzing" at this East Village Moroccan where "standout tagines" and other "affordable" dishes are "served with a smile" in "casual" environs; though its "mini-tables" are strictly for the "elbowless", "sidewalk seating" allows more room as well as "optimal" St. Marks Place people-watching.

Cafe Nosidam
19 | 16 | 18 | $48

768 Madison Ave. (66th St.), 212-717-5633
■ After their "Botox injections", the "kiss-kiss Madison Avenue" set convenes at this "comfortably chic" Eastsider for "solid" Italian-American grazing; forget the "steep" prices and ever-"ringing cell phones": the people-watching is primo, even if the sidewalk seating is no longer available.

Café Pierre
23 | 26 | 25 | $67

Pierre Hotel, 2 E. 61st St. (5th Ave.), 212-940-8195;
www.fourseasons.com
■ "Fit for a king", this "posh" East Side French-Continental boasts an oh-so-"civilized" air; whether for a "quiet tête-à-tête" over breakfast, lunch or dinner, an afternoon tea "fantasy escape" or cocktails accompanied by Kathleen Landis on the piano, it's a "lovely experience" all around, so if you're not "in the right tax bracket", just "pretend you are" – it's "worth the splurge."

Cafe Ronda
20 | 15 | 15 | $29

249-251 Columbus Ave. (bet. 71st & 72nd Sts.), 212-579-9929
☑ This Upper West Side yearling "does a lot with a little space", putting forth "well-prepared" renditions of "classic" Med–South American dishes as well as an "on-target brunch"; though the atmosphere is admirably "laid-back", "don't go if you're in a rush" – service can be "slow."

Café Sabarsky
22 | 24 | 19 | $37

Neue Galerie, 1048 Fifth Ave. (86th St.), 212-288-0665;
www.wallserestaurant.com
■ For the "perfect post-Klimt experience", Kurt Gutenbrunner's "atmospheric" Viennese in the Neue Galerie promises enough "old-world charm" to make the "long lines" bearable; "desserts are king" here, so insiders take their tartes and tortes at an early, "uncrowded hour", and try not to think about the "bad foreign exchange rate."

Cafe S.F.A.
17 | 16 | 16 | $28

Saks Fifth Ave., 611 Fifth Ave., 8th fl. (bet. 49th & 50th Sts.), 212-940-4080
☑ After "shopping till you drop", Saks' American cafe is a "perfect picker-upper" – and "right next to the lingerie department, so you can

buy a girdle" after working your way through its "terrific bread basket" (or something sexier if you restrained yourself); P.S. "get a window seat" for the "view of the Rock Center rooftop gardens" and St. Pat's.

Cafe Spice
19 | 14 | 15 | $26

Grand Central, lower level (42nd St. & Vanderbilt Ave.), 646-227-1300
72 University Pl. (bet. 10th & 11th Sts.), 212-253-6999
54 W. 55th St. (bet. 5th & 6th Aves.), 212-489-7444
www.cafespice.com

☑ Maybe "you won't be treated like a maharaja", but you'll be "fed like one" at this "mod Indian" trio where "huge portions" of "subtly flavored" fare appeal to "novices and experts alike"; Grand Central's takeout-only outpost "raises food-court dining to a whole new level."

Café St. Bart's
18 | 20 | 16 | $34

109 E. 50th St. (Park Ave.), 212-888-2664; www.cafestbarts.com

☑ "Serenity" seekers hone in on the "wonderful alfresco dining" at this Park Avenue American featuring a "fabulous terrace in the shadow of St. Bart's" church; though heretics huff about the "ho-hum menu" and "not-so-attentive service", true believers "never knew Episcopalian cuisine could be so good" or so modestly priced.

Cafe Steinhof
18 | 16 | 18 | $23

422 Seventh Ave. (14th St.), Brooklyn, 718-369-7776

■ A "warming place on a cold night", this "casually boho" Austrian provides "must-have" Wiener schnitzel and other "hearty dishes you can't pronounce" to Park Slopers in the mood for "Brooklyn Bavariana"; wags say it's "really spaetzle", especially considering those "cheap" tabs.

Cafeteria ●
18 | 17 | 14 | $28

119 Seventh Ave. (17th St.), 212-414-1717

☑ "Sleek, hip and *very* Chelsea", this "busy" 24/7 American provides both "round-the-clock attitude" and "affordable" comfort food that's "like mom's home cooking" – but with "much-better-looking people sitting beside you"; maybe it's "not as trendy as it used to be", but the "heavenly mac 'n' cheese" still steals the show.

Cafe Trevi ●
▽ 21 | 16 | 23 | $47

1570 First Ave. (bet. 81st & 82nd Sts.), 212-249-0040;
www.cafetrevi.com

■ Despite a change in ownership, this "friendly" East Side Northern Italian cafe is alive and well and still serving satisfying food; granted, it's "not inexpensive", but cost calculators contend it's definitely "worth the price" for a quiet, comforting evening.

Cafe Un Deux Trois ●
15 | 14 | 16 | $39

123 W. 44th St. (bet. B'way & 6th Ave.), 212-354-4148;
www.cafeundeuxtrois.biz

■ This Times Square "warhorse" may be "yesterday's news", but it still trots out "average" French bistro fare at a "fast" clip while providing "paper tablecloths and crayons" for the kids; even though it's a "cattle drive pre-theater" with "rush-hour-traffic" acoustics, you'll always "make the curtain" well fed.

Caffe Buon Gusto ●
18 | 14 | 17 | $28

236 E. 77th St. (bet. 2nd & 3rd Aves.), 212-535-6884
1009 Second Ave. (bet. 53rd & 54th Sts.), 212-755-1476
151 Montague St. (bet. Clinton & Henry Sts.), Brooklyn, 718-624-3838
www.caffebuongustoonline.com

☑ On those "too-tired-to-cook nights", folks hankering for a "non-power dinner" head for this "neighborhood" trattoria trio for "safe",

"bargain" eats; "boring" decor and "hit-or-miss"
with the territory.

Caffe Cielo   19

881 Eighth Ave. (bet. 52nd & 53rd Sts.), 212-246-9555
■ Escape the hubbub of Hell's Kitchen at this "peaceful" Italian
whose "excellent pasta specials" are served in a "relaxing room"
complete with "cloud" frescoes on the ceiling; regulars report it's
best on warmer days when its French doors open out to the sidewalk.

Caffe Grazie   18   15   20 $44

26 E. 84th St. (bet. 5th & Madison Aves.), 212-717-4407
☑ "Gracious" service and a "genteel atmosphere" attract art lovers to
this East Side Italian, a "best bet post-Met" for a "quick lunch" from its
"tasty" if somewhat "predictable" menu; the townhouse duplex setting
may be "a bit cramped", so insiders head upstairs for "more privacy."

Caffe Linda ⊠   19   13   17 $29

145 E. 49th St. (bet. Lexington & 3rd Aves.), 646-497-1818
☑ A "diamond in the rough" in tough corporate Midtown, this "homey"
Italian serves as a "pleasant retreat" with "simple but delicious" fare
and an "unpretentious" mien; on the "small" side, it "fills up fast" given
its "inexpensive pricing for the neighborhood."

Caffé on the Green   20   22   20 $47

201-10 Cross Island Pkwy. (bet. Clearview Expwy. & Utopia Pkwy.), Queens,
718-423-7272; www.caffeonthegreen.com
☑ It's "romantic inside and out" at this "picturesque" Bayside Italian
"overlooking the Throgs Neck Bridge" and set in the "former home"
of silent movie heartthrob Rudolph Valentino; the "reliable", "pricey"
cuisine draws "older" diners who say "you get what you pay for" here.

Caffe Rafaella ◑   17   18   13 $22

134 Seventh Ave. S. (bet. Charles & W. 10th Sts.), 212-929-7247
☑ "Scrumptious desserts" are practically the "whole story" at this
Village Italian populated by bohemian types who sink into the "mix 'n'
match armchairs", "slurp a latte" and "read philosophy"; the rest of
the menu is "uninspired", and if the staff's "oblivious", at least "they
never rush you."

Caffe Reggio ◑⇩   17   19   13 $14

119 MacDougal St. (bet. Bleecker & W. 3rd Sts.), 212-475-9557;
www.caffereggio.com
■ To "see what the Village was like once upon a time", pay a visit to this
"irresistible" Italian cafe serving "espresso since forever" in a "time
machine" setting that actually dates from 1927; the cappuccino here
is the "real deal", so don't be surprised if they "look down on you for
ordering an American coffee."

California Pizza Kitchen   15   11   14 $22

201 E. 60th St. (bet. 2nd & 3rd Aves.), 212-755-7773; www.cpk.com
☑ "Weird" but "inventive" toppings – "Peking duck", anyone? – set
the "unique" tone at this East Side outpost of the Left Coast pizzeria
chain; while city slickers hiss the "sterile" decor and "welcome-to-
suburbia" vibe, parents report the "noisy" atmosphere and "free
refills on soda" make it "great for the kids."

Calle Ocho   22   23   20 $44

446 Columbus Ave. (bet. 81st & 82nd Sts.), 212-873-5025;
www.calleochonyc.com
■ "Hot babes" nurse "killer drinks" at the "cool bar" of this "happening"
West Side Nuevo Latino where the "fun never ends" for "hip, young"

_nings; surprisingly, the "terrific food" "doesn't take a back seat to the scene", though the prices lead some to wince "Calle Oucho."

CamaJe ●
▽ 21 16 17 $34

85 MacDougal St. (bet. Bleecker & Houston Sts.), 212-673-8184; www.camaje.com

■ "Outstanding" French bistro fare "made with care" keeps cost-conscious fans returning to this "quiet" Village "oasis" where a "homey" setting helps distract from the "molasses"-speed service; P.S. the chef hosts "great cooking classes" three days a week.

Campagnola ●
24 18 21 $60

1382 First Ave. (bet. 73rd & 74th Sts.), 212-861-1102

■ "Eye-candy dames", "Armani suit"–wearers and "older men with their young nieces" frequent this "top-notch" Upper East Side Italian that's a bona fide "scene every night of the week"; "*fantastico*" food and "old-world" service can add up to "scary" pricing, but otherwise it's "pretty near perfect."

Canaletto
21 17 21 $48

208 E. 60th St. (bet. 2nd & 3rd Aves.), 212-317-9192

■ Despite the prices, locals laud this Italian "hideaway" for its "consistently fine" cooking, "accommodating" vibe and convenience after "shopping or a movie on the East Side"; it helps to "get to be a regular – they'll remember what you like."

Candela
18 22 18 $40

116 E. 16th St. (bet. Irving Pl. & Park Ave. S.), 212-254-1600

☑ "Dress like Stevie Nicks to fit in" at this Union Square New American, a "dark", "goth" lair illuminated by "hundreds of candles" à la "*Interview with the Vampire*"; the "well-prepared food" might be "overshadowed by the atmosphere", but those there for a "little tryst" could care less.

Candle Cafe/Candle 79
22 16 19 $30

1307 Third Ave. (bet. 74th & 75th Sts.), 212-472-0970
154 E. 79th St. (bet. Lexington & 3rd Aves.), 212-537-7179
www.candlecafe.com

■ "Tofu is your friend" at these Upper East Side vegans where the "refreshing organic" fare "with muscle" is so darn "delicious" it could "make a vegetarian out of a Texan"; while some prefer 79's "striking" decor, others go for the "laid-back" feel (and "lower prices") at the tiny Third Avenue original.

Cantinella ●
▽ 23 20 23 $49

23 Ave. A (bet. Houston & 2nd Sts.), 212-505-2550; www.cantinella.com

■ Bringing a "trendy feel to the East Village", this new Italian proffers "very good" food and "charming" service in a white-tablecloth, "tight-squeeze" setting; early arrivals report they "know what they're doing", though they might want to rethink those "Midtown" price tags.

Canton ⊄
23 13 19 $41

45 Division St. (bet. Bowery & Market St.), 212-226-4441

■ "Upscale" preparations "justify the upscale prices" at this cash-only C-town Cantonese where regulars advise letting owner Eileen Leong "order for you"; maybe the decor's beginning to "show its age", but it's the "amazingly consistent" food that validates the "trek Downtown."

Canyon Road
20 16 16 $34

1470 First Ave. (bet. 76th & 77th Sts.), 212-734-1600; www.arkrestaurants.com

☑ Aka "Blind Date Central", this "hopping" East Side Southwesterner keeps its "young crowd on the prowl" purring with "surprisingly good" food and "send-you-to-another-land" margaritas; complaints about "spotty" service and "loud" acoustics evaporate when the "reasonable" bill arrives.

Capital Grille
— — — E

155 E. 42nd St. (bet. Lexington & 3rd Aves.), 212-953-2000; www.thecapitalgrille.com
The Atlanta-based steakhouse chain has arrived in NY in spacious new quarters adjacent to the Chrysler Building; the hearty, pricey menu is enhanced by one of the city's most unusual settings, the glass-pyramid Trylon Towers designed by architect Philip Johnson.

Capsouto Frères
24 22 23 $51

451 Washington St. (Watts St.), 212-966-4900; www.capsoutofreres.com
■ Despite its "obscure" TriBeCa address ("Capsouto where?"), this "timeless" 25-year-old bistro provides "impeccable" French cooking and "cordial" service in "spacious", brick-walled digs; a "high comfort level" with "no snobs allowed" and easy parking seal the deal; P.S. "whatever you do, get the soufflé."

Caracas Arepa Bar
∇ 21 13 16 $15

91 E. Seventh St. (1st Ave.), 212-228-5062; www.caracasarepabar.com
◪ "Venezuela's answer to fast food" comes to Alphabet City via this "colorful" outpost dishing out "authentic" arepas (stuffed corn flour cakes) that "burst with flavor"; a BYO policy and "extremely cheap" pricing compensate for the "tiny", "hole-in-the-wall" layout.

Cara Mia
21 15 17 $32

654 Ninth Ave. (bet. 45th & 46th Sts.), 212-262-6767
■ Devotees of this "cozy" Hell's Kitchen Italian wish it could "return to its undiscovered status", but the secret's out about its "taste bud–pleasing" dishes and "decent" prices; since the "tiny" space can be "cramped" pre-theater, locals turn up and "kick back after 8 PM."

Cardamomm
∇ 19 13 13 $28

100 Lexington Ave. (27th St.), 212-725-2556
◪ A "welcome addition" to Curry Hill, this "cut-above" Indian offers "well-spiced, well-prepared" victuals in "no-frills" digs perfumed by "out-of-this-world aromas"; too bad the "overwhelmed" staff doesn't live up to the rest of the "hype."

Carino
18 12 20 $32

1710 Second Ave. (bet. 88th & 89th Sts.), 212-860-0566
■ Chef Mama Carino "is still going strong" at this Upper East Side Southern Italian, whipping up her "simple, sincere" home cooking and working the room to "make sure everything's ok"; the "teeny tiny" setup is reflected in the very "affordable" price tags.

Carl's Steaks ⊘
22 5 15 $10

507 Third Ave. (34th St.), 212-696-5336
◪ They "did their homework" at this Murray Hill newcomer that replicates Philly's famed cheese steak sandwich in all its "greasy", "gargantuan" glory; purists attest its version of "messy joy" on a roll is the "real deal", but advise "get it to go" – there's "almost no seating" (and no decor) here.

CARMINE'S
20 15 17 $35

2450 Broadway (bet. 90th & 91st Sts.), 212-362-2200
200 W. 44th St. (bet. B'way & 8th Ave.), 212-221-3800
www.carminesnyc.com
◪ It's "garlic city, baby" at these family-style Italian "pig-out" palaces where the "bucket-size" portions are so "bountiful" you'll need a

"suitcase for the leftovers"; given the "rambunctious" mobs and "ear-splitting cacophony", "bring someone you'd rather not listen to."

Carne ●◑
17 | 17 | 15 | $34

2737 Broadway (105th St.), 212-663-7010

☑ The "young Columbia crowd" turns to this "sceney" Upper West Side chop shop for "reliable steaks at reasonable prices" purveyed in "Downtown-style" digs; trade-offs include "high decibels" and a "disappearing" staff, yet most agree it's an "invaluable resource" in an underserved area.

Carnegie Deli ●⊄
20 | 8 | 12 | $24

854 Seventh Ave. (55th St.), 212-757-2245; www.carnegiedeli.com

☑ "Not for the small of stomach", this crowded Midtown deli is famed for "sandwiches so big they defy logic" served by "grumpy waiters" who "function as entertainment" for an audience that's half "tourists", half *Broadway Danny Rose* types; it's a "quintessential New York experience" for its "stuff-of-legends cheesecake" alone.

Carol's Cafe ⊠
24 | 17 | 19 | $54

1571 Richmond Rd. (bet. Four Corners Rd. & Seaview Ave.), Staten Island, 718-979-5600; www.carolscafe.com

■ Everything's made with "tender loving care" at this Staten Island Eclectic "shining star" helmed by "perfectionist" Carol Frazzetta, whose "inventive" cooking "tastes as good as it looks"; Islanders call it the "crown jewel" of local dining, despite prices that can be a bit "steep for the average night out."

Carriage House ●
17 | 19 | 17 | $43

136 W. 18th St. (bet. 6th & 7th Aves.), 212-647-8889

☑ Despite the "renovated carriage house" exterior, this Chelsea New American goes the "minimalist" route inside with "desert"-inspired decor à la Palm Springs; sure, the "service could use some work", but the food's "dependable", if a "little pricey for what you get."

Carvao ⊄
∇ 18 | 20 | 18 | $35

1477 Second Ave. (77th St.), 212-879-4707

☑ Though in the "shakedown" stage, this new East Side Portuguese shows "potential" via "tasty", "good-for-the-price" dishes; however, the "uneven" service and "cash-only" policy still need tuning.

Casa ●⊠
∇ 21 | 19 | 19 | $38

72 Bedford St. (Commerce St.), 212-366-9410

■ A "sweet" staff with an "authentically distracted air" serves "honest Brazilian" food backed up by "potent caipirinhas" at this "cute little" West Villager; the setup may be "a bit tight" and the decor "simple", but at least the evening ends "without a hefty bill."

Casa La Femme North ●
∇ 17 | 18 | 19 | $57

1076 First Ave. (bet. 58th & 59th Sts.), 212-223-2322

☑ After migrating Uptown from SoHo, this "sexy" Egyptian is now pitching its tented banquettes in a new locale near the Queensboro Bridge; as much of a "great date place" as ever, it features an "interesting" menu and "multiple waiters at your service", plus a belly dancer to keep things shaking.

Casa Mia
20 | 17 | 18 | $33

225 E. 24th St. (bet. 2nd & 3rd Aves.), 212-679-5606

■ There's "nothing fancy" going on at this "relaxed" Gramercy Italian – just "good", "homestyle cooking" served in a setting reminiscent of "grandma's living room"; given the "warm" staff and "reasonable" price tags, no wonder it's "been around for so many years."

Casa Mono ◐
24 | 18 | 20 | $44

52 Irving Pl. (17th St.), 212-253-2773

■ Molto Mario "does Spanish" at this "buzzing" Gramercy newcomer featuring an "adventurous" tapas menu of "mouthwatering" Catalan morsels; an "eager" staff makes up for the "infinitesimal", "ultra-cramped" setting, but insiders suggest a seat opposite the open kitchen for some "pure gastronomic theater"; N.B. there's an ancillary wine bar/waiting room (Bar Jamón) around the corner.

Cascina ◐ ⌧
19 | 16 | 18 | $38

647 Ninth Ave. (bet. 45th & 46th Sts.), 212-245-4422; www.cascina.com

■ For "pre-theater comfort" in "rustic" environs, try this Hell's Kitchen Italian featuring "consistently good" food abetted by an "unusual wine list" that includes labels from "their own vineyard" outside Milan; "earnest" service and "neighborhood"-appropriate pricing make it a "worthwhile stop."

Caserta Vecchia
▽ 21 | 14 | 20 | $26

221 Smith St. (bet. Baltic & Butler Sts.), Brooklyn, 718-624-7549; www.casertavecchiarestaurant.com

■ "Darn good" brick-oven pizzas and "amazing focaccia" are the highlights of the "small menu" at this "inexpensive" Carroll Gardens Neapolitan; maybe the "interior could be a little cozier", but the "staff's warmth makes up for it."

Casimir ◐
20 | 20 | 15 | $33

103-105 Ave. B (bet. 6th & 7th Sts.), 212-358-9683

☑ "Fabulousness" seekers keep it "*très* cool" at this Alphabet City French bistro where the "crowd is great, the food even better" and the price tag "affordable"; a "churlish" staff with "perfectly groomed five-o'clock shadows" adds extra unwanted authenticity.

Caviar Russe ⌧
▽ 25 | 24 | 24 | $87

538 Madison Ave., 2nd fl. (bet. 54th & 55th Sts.), 212-980-5908; www.caviarrusse.com

■ "Decadent" dining is yours at this Midtown New American where sybarites "nibble caviar and sip vodka" in an "elegant", "tucked-away" setting; naturally, it costs a pretty "pricey" penny, but the "heavenly" offerings and "romantic" atmosphere make this one "well worth it."

Caviarteria
▽ 23 | 13 | 15 | $57

Trump Park Ave., 502 Park Ave. (59th St.), 212-759-7410; www.caviarteria.com

☑ When the "urge to splurge" hits, bon tons head to this Midtown caviar-and-champagne purveyor for an "exotic snack" that works well for lunch or as a prelude to dinner; since the "deli"-like setting doesn't jibe with the "break-the-bank" pricing, gourmets on the go hit the retail counter.

Cávo ◐
▽ 20 | 26 | 19 | $36

42-18 31st Ave. (42nd St.), Queens, 718-721-1001; www.cavocafelounge.com

■ So "sophisticated" that it really "belongs in Manhattan", this showy Astoria Greek boasts a "vast, rambling" setting capped by a "glorious" waterfall-equipped garden; while the well presented "fresh" Hellenica draws huzzahs, locals say it's best enjoyed "early" before the "nightclub crowd" takes over.

Celeste ⌿
24 | 13 | 17 | $33

502 Amsterdam Ave. (bet. 84th & 85th Sts.), 212-874-4559

■ "Everything's great except the wait" at this "jammed", "shoebox"-size Upper West Side Neapolitan that takes neither reservations nor credit cards; still, the "out-of-sight" pastas and "well-below-market value" pricing make the "close quarters" more bearable; P.S. ask the owner about that "amazing cheese plate."

Cellini ⊠
23 | 19 | 22 | $48

65 E. 54th St. (bet. Madison & Park Aves.), 212-751-1555; www.cellinirestaurant.com

■ "Power-lunchers" tout this Midtown Northern Italian that suits suits with "solid" cooking, "old-world" service and "civilized", "rustic" environs; those in search of something less businesslike go for dinner, when it's "quieter", though at any time an "expense account" comes in handy.

Cendrillon
▽ 22 | 20 | 20 | $38

45 Mercer St. (bet. Broome & Grand Sts.), 212-343-9012; www.cendrillon.com

■ "Unique flavors come out of the kitchen" of this SoHo Filipino-Asian, a "hidden treasure" that remains mostly "undiscovered" after 10 years on the scene; its "calm, comforting" air attracts a "great mix" of folks, including "artistic" types drawn by its revolving art exhibitions.

Centolire
20 | 21 | 19 | $56

1167 Madison Ave. (bet. 85th & 86th Sts.), 212-734-7711

☑ The "setting matches the food" at Pino Luongo's "lovely" East Side Italian duplex, a "neighborhood asset" thanks to its "cut-above-the-usual" menu and "chic" ambiance; there's some talk about "variable experiences", but no debate about the "Madison Avenue prices"; P.S. insiders say "sit upstairs for finer dining."

'CESCA
24 | 23 | 23 | $55

164 W. 75th St. (Amsterdam Ave.), 212-787-6300; www.cescanyc.com

■ "Everything works" well at chef Tom Valenti's Ouest Side "sequel", a "stellar" Southern Italian that dazzles diners with its "bold, confident" cooking, "on-the-ball" service and a "snazzy", "civilized" setting; the scene's an "unlikely combination of hip and cozy" with "every element at perfect pitch", leaving a single obstacle: "getting a reservation."

Chadwick's
22 | 17 | 21 | $38

8822 Third Ave. (89th St.), Brooklyn, 718-833-9855

■ "It may look like a pub", but the "honest" food at this venerable Bay Ridge steakhouse is "surprisingly good" and backed up by "doesn't-miss-a-beat" service; it's particularly popular with "older" "early birds" who make sure to "allow sufficient time for parking."

Chance
– | – | – | M

223 Smith St. (Butler St.), Brooklyn, 718-242-1515

Chinese, French and fusion dishes share the ambitious menu at this slick new Boerum Hill arrival complete with a wall of water bubbles and a buzzing, Manhattan-style bar; for the more traditionally inclined, there's a patio out back.

Chango
16 | 16 | 14 | $34

239 Park Ave. S. (bet. 19th & 20th Sts.), 212-477-1500

☑ Ok, the Mexican grub's an "afterthought" compared to the "happy-hour specials" at this Flatiron cantina, but its "young", "rowdy" crowd is more intent on "mucho flirting" anyway; "sound barrier"–breaking noise and "spotty" (albeit "low-cut") service are part of the package.

Chanpen Thai
19 | 13 | 17 | $23

761 Ninth Ave. (51st St.), 212-586-6808

☑ A "solid performer", this "above-average" Hell's Kitchen Thai does it "quick and cheap", and is "convenient" for theatergoers to boot; perhaps the decor could be better and the "food could be spicier", but hearty eaters report the "portions are huge for the price."

CHANTERELLE ⊠

27 | 26 | 27 | VE

2 Harrison St. (Hudson St.), 212-966-6960; www.chanterellenyc.com
■The "epitome of perfect dining", David and Karen Waltuck's "enchanting" TriBeCa haute French "lives up to its lofty reputation" with "phenomenal" cuisine, "service so flawless you won't even notice it" and a "spacious, gracious" setting enhanced by "well-spaced tables" and "gorgeous floral arrangements"; for the price-conscious, the $38 prix fixe lunch is possibly the "best deal on the planet."

Charles' Southern-Style Kitchen

∇ 21 | 5 | 15 | $15

2839 Eighth Ave. (151st St.), 212-926-4313
☑ "Finger-lickin' good" fried chicken and other "real-deal" "down-home" dishes are the bait at this Harlem soul fooder where everything's a "bargain", particularly the buffet; if the "forlorn" decor is too hard to swallow, get takeout and "go sit on a stoop."

Chat 'n Chew

17 | 14 | 15 | $21

10 E. 16th St. (bet. 5th Ave. & Union Sq. W.), 212-243-1616 ◐
470 Sixth Ave. (bet. 11th & 12th Sts.), 212-243-8226
www.chatnchewnyc.com
☑ "Down-home trailer-trash cooking" keeps "carb lovers" blissful at this "easygoing" pair of roadhouse cafes famed for their "awesome" mac 'n' cheese; "chintzy" decor and "space cadet" service to the contrary, they're "greasy spoons done right", starting with that "easy-going" pricing.

Chef Ho's Peking Duck Grill

20 | 12 | 17 | $26

1720 Second Ave. (bet. 89th & 90th Sts.), 212-348-9444
☑ "When you crave Peking duck", this East Side Hunanese is a "sure thing", replete with "linen tablecloths", "friendly service" and "reasonable prices"; in spite of "pedestrian" looks, regulars insist it's a "proper restaurant", "not the usual quick-fix resource."

Chelsea Bistro

20 | 19 | 19 | $44

358 W. 23rd St. (bet. 8th & 9th Aves.), 212-727-2026
■A "let's-pretend-we're-in-France" mood prevails at this "civilized" Chelsea "hideaway" offering "leisurely fine dining" via "dependable" French bistro vittles; a "cozy" fireplace and glassed-in "sun room" in back add "romantic" notes.

Chelsea Grill

17 | 13 | 15 | $23

135 Eighth Ave. (bet. 16th & 17th Sts.), 212-242-5336
☑ To "dodge the crowds", try this never-too-crowded "touch-of-old-Chelsea" pub known for its "sloppy burgers", "great Cobb salad" and "reasonable" tabs; a "heated, year-round" garden "adds atmosphere" to the otherwise "ordinary" scene.

Chelsea Ristorante

20 | 16 | 21 | $36

108 Eighth Ave. (bet. 15th & 16th Sts.), 212-924-7786; www.chelsear.com
■The "warm" vibe at this Chelsea Northern Italian doesn't emanate from its wood-burning oven alone: "accommodating" service, "affordable" tabs and lots of "little touches" make the "consistently good" food all the more tasty.

Chennai Garden

22 | 12 | 17 | $20

129 E. 27th St. (bet. Lexington & Park Ave. S.), 212-689-1999;
www.chennaigarden.com
☑ "People in turbans" and yarmulkes meet cute at this "authentic" Gramercy newcomer featuring "tasty" Indian vegetarian fare that's "kosher too"; though the "inconsistent" service and "no-decor" decor may need "fine tuning", the "BYO" policy and "value" pricing are fine as is.

Chestnut
▽ 22 | 18 | 19 | $39

271 Smith St. (bet. DeGraw & Sackett Sts.), Brooklyn, 718-243-0049;
www.chestnutonsmith.com

◪ "Another home run for Smith Street", this new Carroll Gardens player may be in its first innings but its "carefully thought-out", "greenmarket-inspired" New American menu suggests plenty of "potential"; detractors say it's "hit-or-miss."

Chez Brigitte ⊘
▽ 17 | 6 | 18 | $17

77 Greenwich Ave. (bet. Bank St. & 7th Ave. S.), 212-929-6736

◪ One of the "last remaining outposts of the old Village", this circa-1958 French bistro puts out "decent" "counter food on the fly" in a minuscule, 11-stool setting; it's "dingy" all right, and may be "impossible" for claustrophobes, but the "super-cheap" prices make it a must-try.

Chez Es Saada ●⊉⊠
17 | 26 | 16 | $43

42 E. First St. (bet. 1st & 2nd Aves.), 212-777-5617;
www.chezessaada.com

◪ "Rose petals", "romance and intrigue" abound at this "exotic" East Villager that many feel is more about "style than substance"; the revamped Mideastern menu still arrives in "paltry" portions for rather "high prices", but the lovelorn say it's "worth every penny" if a "night of love" is the payoff.

Chez Jacqueline
20 | 18 | 19 | $46

72 MacDougal St. (bet. Bleecker & Houston Sts.), 212-505-0727

■ This touch of "Provence on MacDougal Street" from the "old days" (i.e. 1979) plies patrons with "simple" French bistro "favorites" in a "pleasant" enough setting; there's also "lovely outdoor" sidewalk seating when the weather's fine.

Chez Josephine ●⊠
20 | 21 | 21 | $48

414 W. 42nd St. (bet. 9th & 10th Aves.), 212-594-1925;
www.chezjosephine.com

■ Brace yourself for an "effusive greeting" from the "irrepressible" Jean-Claude Baker, the owner of this colorful Theater District French bistro; it's a "slightly-over-the-top" "homage" to his mother, the renowned Josephine Baker, with food that's "hearty", an "ooh-la-la" mood and a "jazzy" live pianist.

Chez Laurence ⊠
▽ 19 | 15 | 18 | $30

245 Madison Ave. (38th St.), 212-683-0284

■ Offering three squares a day, this "casual" midpriced Murray Hill French bistro "attracts a loyal following" with "solid preparations" and a "pleasant" ambiance; "convenience to Grand Central" and a "delicious" on-premises bakery seal the deal.

Chez Michallet
23 | 19 | 21 | $49

90 Bedford St. (Grove St.), 212-242-8309

■ For a "great third date", Casanovas are fond of this "romantic" Village "hideaway" offering "sublime" French bistro dishes served with "zero attitude"; the space is "tiny", so bear in mind your "whispered sweet nothings" might be overheard.

Chez Napoléon ⊠
20 | 13 | 21 | $40

365 W. 50th St. (bet. 8th & 9th Aves.), 212-265-6980;
www.cheznapoleon.com

◪ This "been-there-forever" Theater District "dowager" supplies "wonderful, old-fashioned" French bistro fare in a "small", "kitschy" setting featuring "jigsaw puzzle–covered walls"; still, what's "tried and true" for some is "tired" for others.

Chez Oskar ◐
▽ 19 | 19 | 17 | $30

211 DeKalb Ave. (Adelphi St.), Brooklyn, 718-852-6250;
www.chezoskar.com

■ "In the heart of Fort Greene" lies this "totally dependable" French bistro where the grazing's "consistently good" and the clientele's "interesting and eclectic, like the neighborhood"; "reasonable" pricing makes the "slow" service more forgivable.

Chiam Chinese Cuisine ◐
22 | 19 | 21 | $42

160 E. 48th St. (bet. Lexington & 3rd Aves.), 212-371-2323

■ An "outstanding wine list" is just one of the "unexpected treats" at this Midtown Chinese "sleeper" offering "perfectly executed" meals; it may be "pricey" for the genre, but is "well worth it" for an experience that's the "opposite of going to Chinatown."

Chianti
22 | 18 | 19 | $35

8530 Third Ave. (86th St.), Brooklyn, 718-921-6300

■ "Down-to-earth" dishes that "taste like grandma's" arrive in "tremendous", "family-style" portions at this "casual" Bay Ridge Italian; it's particularly popular with "large groups" with "large appetites", so "be prepared for crowds and noise."

ChikaLicious ◐
25 | 22 | 25 | $21

203 E. 10th St. (bet. 1st & 2nd Aves.), 212-995-9511;
www.chikalicious.com

■ The "novel concept" of this "fabulous" East Village dessert specialist is its prix fixe–only, "three-course" menu of sweets served in "delicate portions" at "entree prices"; the staff is "sweet" too and the "tiny" space looks like a "chic" "sushi bar", but since it has just 20 seats, expect a "wait."

Chimichurri Grill ◐
23 | 16 | 21 | $45

606 Ninth Ave. (bet. 43rd & 44th Sts.), 212-586-8655;
www.chimichurrigrill.com

■ "Big taste" reigns at this "tiny" Hell's Kitchen Argentinean where "wonderful", "tasty" steaks come slathered with the "namesake sauce"; the "low-key" service makes for a "mellow" mood, despite "no-frills" decor and "cramped quarters."

China Fun ◐
16 | 9 | 13 | $20

246 Columbus Ave. (bet. 71st & 72nd Sts.), 212-580-1516
1221 Second Ave. (64th St.), 212-752-0810

■ You'll find a "staggering selection" of "basic" Chinese dishes at these "always packed" crosstown twins where the "dour" service, nothing-special decor and "assembly-line" eats are trumped by the "cheap" tabs; if you want "fun, sit by the window."

China Grill
23 | 20 | 19 | $51

CBS Bldg., 60 W. 53rd St. (bet. 5th & 6th Aves.), 212-333-7788;
www.chinagrillmgt.com

■ As "busy and theatrical" as ever, this "chic" Midtown Asian lures a "cult following" thanks to "intriguing", "beautifully presented" fusion fare served in "large, sharable portions"; despite "megadecibel" noise levels and mega-bucks pricing, its "sexy", soaring interior still hosts "pretty people" seeking a "happening scene."

Chin Chin ◐
23 | 18 | 21 | $45

216 E. 49th St. (bet. 2nd & 3rd Aves.), 212-888-4555; www.chinchinny.com

■ "Classic" and "civilized", this "designer" Midtown Chinese "never fails", offering a "top-flight" menu highlighted by its "one-of-a-kind Grand Marnier shrimp"; if pricing is similarly "top-shelf", most feel "you get a lot" in return.

Chipotle
20 | 13 | 16 | $11

2 Broadway (Whitehall St.), 212-344-0941
150 E. 44th St. (bet. Lexington & 3rd Aves.), 212-682-9860
150 E. 52nd St. (bet. Lexington & 3rd Aves.), 212-755-9754
19 St. Marks Pl. (bet. 2nd & 3rd Aves.), 212-529-4502
304 W. 34th St. (8th Ave.), 212-268-4197
185 Montague St. (Court St.), Brooklyn, 718-243-9109
www.chipotle.com
■ "Finally in NYC", this "exceptional" Mexican fast-food chain already has "lines out the door" thanks to "cheap, yummy" burritos made with "free-range" meats; its "custom" ordering and "modern, cafeteria-esque" digs help "break lunchtime monotony."

ChipShop/CurryShop ⊅
18 | 13 | 15 | $18

381-383 Fifth Ave. (bet. 6th & 7th Sts.), Brooklyn, 718-832-7701;
www.chipshopnyc.com
☑ "Deep-fried candy bars" coexist with "chicken korma" at this Park Slope "shrine to Anglo-Saxon" comfort food that's half British pub, half Indian curry house; throw in a "cool pint of lager" and a "kitschy", "*Trainspotting*"-esque vibe and you've got a "bloody good" time.

Cho Dang Gol
23 | 16 | 16 | $27

55 W. 35th St. (bet. 5th & 6th Aves.), 212-695-8222
■ Ascend to "tofu heaven" at this affordable Garment District Korean featuring a "silky", "homemade" version that turns up in a number of "surprisingly good" dishes; fans say it's a fine "starter restaurant" given the "balance between spicy and non-spicy" options.

Chola
24 | 16 | 21 | $36

232 E. 58th St. (bet. 2nd & 3rd Aves.), 212-688-4619;
www.fineindiandining.com
■ Covering a "more extensive map" than most, this "knockout" East Side Indian scores with an "eclectic" range of "subtly seasoned" dishes "from all over the subcontinent"; perhaps it's a bit "expensive" for the genre, but the $13.95 lunch buffet is "fantastic."

Cholita ⊅
∇ 18 | 24 | 20 | $28

139 Smith St. (bet. Bergen & Dean Sts.), Brooklyn, 718-254-9933
☑ This "upbeat" Boerum Hill newcomer is among the "prettiest on Smith Street", yet its Peruvian menu "with a twist" earns mixed reviews: "flavorful" vs. "needs improvement"; stalwarts are willing to give them time to "get their act together."

Chop't Creative Salad
20 | 8 | 13 | $12

24 E. 17th St. (bet. B'way & 5th Ave.), 646-336-5523
■ "Not your average point-and-shoot salad vendor", this Union Square–area venue stands apart from the competition owing to the "choice and quality of its ingredients"; "more toppings than you can possibly imagine" compensate for the "expensive-for-what-it-is" pricing.

Choshi
18 | 11 | 16 | $31

77 Irving Pl. (E. 19th St.), 212-420-1419; www.cho-shi.com
☑ "Solid, dependable" sushi that "doesn't hurt your purse" is the lure at this Gramercy "neighborhood" Japanese that many use as a "great backup" to popular Yama up the block; regulars suggest you "snag an outdoor table" and ignore the "spotty" service.

Chow Bar
21 | 19 | 17 | $37

230 W. Fourth St. (W. 10th St.), 212-633-2212
☑ "Delicious Pan-Asian" chow and "dangerous cocktails" collide at this "sceney" West Villager that some dub the "poor man's China Grill";

expect a "dim, sexy" space with a "young crowd" and a "high-energy" mood, except for the "distracted" staff.

Christos Hasapo-Taverna ● | ▽ 21 | 18 | 20 | $44 |

41-08 23rd Ave. (41st St.), Queens, 718-777-8400;
www.christossteakhouse.com
☒ A "real institution", this Astoria Greek butcher shop by day turns into a steakhouse after dark, with "wonderful" chops and "local charm" available at all times; some say it's "slipping" and "isn't worth the price", but most surveyors feel it "rivals anything in Manhattan."

Chubo | 23 | 17 | 20 | $38 |

6 Clinton St. (bet. Houston & Stanton Sts.), 212-674-6300;
www.chubo.com
■ Though the menu's "limited", with "food this good who needs more choices?" ask fans of this "small but charming" Eclectic Lower Eastsider where the "deftly prepared" dishes deliver "pure bliss" on a plate; you can't help liking its "bargain three-course prix fixe", even if the "supplemental charges" can add up.

Churrascaria Plataforma | 22 | 19 | 21 | $53 |

223 W. Broadway (bet. Franklin & White Sts.), 212-925-6969
316 W. 49th St. (bet. 8th & 9th Aves.), 212-245-0505 ●
www.churrascariaplataforma.com
■ "They feed you like there's no tomorrow" at these Brazilian "nonstop food fests" trotting out a "fantasia" of skewered meats as well as a "city-block-long salad bar"; given the "omnipresent waiters" urging you to "eat everything in sight", it's "impossible to leave hungry."

Cibo | 20 | 20 | 21 | $44 |

767 Second Ave. (bet. 41st & 42nd Sts.), 212-681-1616
■ In a "neighborhood with few decent restaurants", this "upscale" Tuscan–New American near Tudor City fills a need with "tasty" grub, "welcoming" service and an "understated" but "pleasant" air; why this "sleeper" continues to "fly under the radar" puzzles proponents.

Cilantro ● | 17 | 15 | 16 | $28 |

244 E. 79th St. (2nd Ave.), 212-537-7745
1321 First Ave. (71st St.), 212-537-4040
1712 Second Ave. (bet. 88th & 89th Sts.), 212-722-4242
www.cilantronyc.com
☒ "Dependable" for "reasonably priced" Southwestern eats, these Upper East Side triplets pair "out-of-this-world" guacamole with decor right off the "set of *The Magnificent Seven*"; though tables are "too close for comfort", its "just-graduated" following is too intent on the "bargain margaritas" to notice.

Cinquanta ● | ▽ 19 | 14 | 19 | $46 |

50 E. 50th St. (bet. Madison & Park Aves.), 212-759-5050;
www.cinquantarestaurant.com
☒ Channeling "Little Italy to Midtown", this "solid" if "not exciting" Italian offers a classic menu of "old-school" items priced for modern-day "expense accounts"; "nice-touch" service compensates for a setup that "could use some redecorating."

Cinque Terre | 20 | 17 | 19 | $45 |

Jolly Madison Towers, 22 E. 38th St. (bet. Madison & Park Aves.), 212-867-2260;
www.jollymadison.com
☒ Prospectors mining Murray Hill have dug up a "diamond in the rough" at this Italian offering a taste of "Liguria without the plane ride"; if some find it "too pricey for what you get", at least it's "so quiet you can bring grandpa and he'll hear you."

Cipriani Dolci ❷
19 19 18 $42

Grand Central, West Balcony (42nd St. & Vanderbilt Ave.), 212-973-0999; www.cipriani.com

■ "Under the stars" and "above the fray" of the Grand Central Concourse, this "easygoing" Italian boasts "views from every seat", as well as new outdoor seating in a former Vanderbilt Avenue "taxi stand"; although on the "pricey" side, the food's almost as "delightful" as the signature Bellinis.

Circus
19 17 19 $44

808 Lexington Ave. (bet. 62nd & 63rd Sts.), 212-223-2965

■ The "circus-themed" decor and "cheerful" staff at this Midtown Brazilian add some zip to an otherwise "dull" stretch near Bloomie's; while the menu's "interesting" and the prices "reasonable", spectators say the caipirinhas and the beautiful young Euros drinking them put on the "best show" here.

Cité ❷
22 20 22 $59

120 W. 51st St. (bet. 6th & 7th Aves.), 212-956-7100; www.citerestaurant.com

■ This "ultimate" Midtown steakhouse is known for the "stupendous" value of its "all-you-can-drink" wine dinner; although it can be "pricey" à la carte, its quintessential corporate crowd says it's "definitely worth the cost" for the "high-class" atmosphere and "saintly" service alone.

Cité Grill ❷
20 18 19 $48

120 W. 51st St. (bet. 6th & 7th Aves.), 212-956-7262; www.citerestaurant.com

■ "More informal" and "better priced" than its "big brother next door", this Midtown grill is nonetheless "comparable" foodwise; even better, a "busy bar scene" offers the opportunity to meet young, "chic types."

Citrus Bar & Grill
19 19 17 $35

320 Amsterdam Ave. (75th St.), 212-595-0500; www.citrusnyc.com

■ Though "banana and tuna sushi seems a stretch", it's among the recommended options at this "lively" Asian-Latin fusion outpost on the "otherwise tranquil" Upper West Side; given the "formidable" din generated by "young" types downing "killer margaritas", the "outdoor seating" is much sought after.

City Bakery
22 13 13 $18

3 W. 18th St. (bet. 5th & 6th Aves.), 212-366-1414

■ Built to "satisfy any sugar craving", Maury Rubin's "adult-oriented" Flatiron bakery satisfies the "lunch-break set" with an "exotic", "wholesome" buffet as well as "divine" pastries; less celestial are its "confusing lines", "competitive seating" and serious tabs.

City Crab & Seafood Co.
18 15 16 $41

235 Park Ave. S. (19th St.), 212-529-3800

■ Bring "earplugs" to deal with the noise and enough muscle to "crack your own crabs" at this "big" Flatiron seafooder that's "dependable" in a "formula-driven", "Disney"-esque way; it's "good for a last-minute plan", despite somewhat "apathetic" service and "tired" "suburban" decor.

City Grill ❷
16 15 16 $28

269 Columbus Ave. (bet. 72nd & 73rd Sts.), 212-873-9400

■ There's "something for everyone on the menu" of this "solid", "comfy" West Side American that ranks a "notch above a diner" and certainly "won't break the bank"; foodies find it "painfully ordinary" and shrug it's "perfectly fine for those who only eat to live."

subscribe to zagat.com

City Hall ☒
21 | 21 | 20 | $52

131 Duane St. (bet. Church St. & W. B'way), 212-227-7777
■ "Fine leather briefcases" abound at Henry Meer's TriBeCa "city slicker" where "lawyers, judges" and "Bloomberg" turn up for "elegant" American surf 'n' turf, especially those "fantastic towers of shellfish"; more to the point, the tables are "spaced far enough apart not to have secrets overheard"; N.B. now serving breakfast weekdays.

City Lobster & Crab Co.
19 | 17 | 17 | $45

121 W. 49th St. (bet. 6th & 7th Aves.), 212-354-1717;
www.citylobster.com
☒ Set in "bright", sprawling digs, this Radio City–area seafooder brings a "taste of Cape Cod to Midtown" via a "quite good" menu of "standard" items; "steakhouse pricing" and "curt" service are offset by a "very happy happy hour."

Coco Pazzo
22 | 21 | 20 | $60

23 E. 74th St. (bet. 5th & Madison Aves.), 212-794-0205
☒ Regulars report that Pino Luongo's "sophisticated" East Side Northern Italian is undergoing a "revival" since the "return of prodigal son" Mark Strausman, the former chef; despite "overpricing" and service that varies "depending on who you are", word is it's "much improved" and on the road back to its "former glory."

Coco Roco
20 | 13 | 14 | $24

392 Fifth Ave. (bet. 6th & 7th Sts.), Brooklyn, 718-965-3376
☒ "Luscious", "flavorfully marinated" rotisserie chicken puts this Peruvian on "young" Park Slopers' dining maps, but a "careless" staff and "cramped" room can make the outing "inconsistent"; good thing it's a "huge value."

Cocotte
22 | 20 | 17 | $35

337 Fifth Ave. (4th St.), Brooklyn, 718-832-6848
■ "Perfect for Park Slope palates", this "charming" French–New American offers "carefully prepared" repasts in "warm, wood-and-brick" environs recalling a country "farmhouse"; though service can also be "decidedly Gallic", "amazing value" and a more than "blissful" brunch even the score.

Coffee Shop ◖
16 | 14 | 11 | $27

29 Union Sq. W. (16th St.), 212-243-7969
☒ This "buzzing" Brazilian-American blessed with a "gold-mine location" off Union Square may dish up some "good" eats, but it's more about "scene" than cuisine; "don't feel guilty" eating in front of the "skinny", "waif"-like staff – they're more intent on "perfecting their catwalk strut than waiting on tables" anyway.

Col Legno
20 | 13 | 17 | $34

231 E. Ninth St. (bet. 2nd & 3rd Aves.), 212-777-4650
☒ For "straightforward" Tuscan food and "delightful brick-oven pizza", East Village types turn to this "inexpensive" "secret spot" that's so "easy to like"; an open kitchen provides some focus to the otherwise "ungainly" interior.

Columbus Bakery
19 | 12 | 11 | $16

474 Columbus Ave. (bet. 82nd & 83rd Sts.), 212-724-6880
957 First Ave. (bet. 52nd & 53rd Sts.), 212-421-0334
www.arkrestaurants.com
☒ These "cafeteria-style" bakery/cafes are "favorites" for a "non-Starbucks" "snack and a latte", even if the staff's "unhelpful" and the "traffic flow clumsy"; P.S. the East Side branch has "less of a stroller issue" than its sibling.

Comfort Diner
16 | 12 | 14 | $20

214 E. 45th St. (bet. 2nd & 3rd Aves.), 212-867-4555
25 W. 23rd St. (bet. 5th & 6th Aves.), 212-741-1010

☑ "Step back to the '50s at this "bustling" diner duo featuring an American comfort chow menu modernized with some "Atkins-friendly" choices; though service is "spotty" and prices a tad "expensive" for the genre, at least you "walk away stuffed."

Compass
21 | 22 | 19 | $55

208 W. 70th St. (bet. Amsterdam & West End Aves.), 212-875-8600;
www.compassrestaurant.com

☑ Still in the midst of "topsy-turvy" toque changes, this "cavernous" West Side New American is holding its own with "creative cuisine" served in "dramatic", "industrial-chic" digs at appropriately "high-tech" tabs; though service inspires debate ("stellar" vs. "substandard"), there's no question that the "fantastic" prix fixe is one "excellent value."

Convivium Osteria
24 | 24 | 22 | $42

68 Fifth Ave. (bet. Bergen St. & St. Mark's Ave.), Brooklyn, 718-857-1833

■ The "gusto" factor is high at this "charming but minuscule" Park Sloper that offers "rustic twists" on Portuguese, Italian and Spanish dishes in "enchanting" digs recalling an "inn on the Mediterranean coast"; if it's slightly "overpriced" given the "morphing neighborhood", payoffs include a "beautiful garden" and "knowledgeable service."

Cooking with Jazz ☒
25 | 13 | 19 | $36

1201 154th St. (12th Ave.), Queens, 718-767-6979; www.cookingwithjazz.com

■ While your "body remains in Whitestone, your stomach travels to Bourbon Street" at this "ragin' Cajun" dishing out "dead-on" renditions of Big Easy edibles; live jazz adds to the "crowded, noisy" conditions at this "tiny" space not much bigger than a "shoebox."

Coppola's ◑
18 | 14 | 16 | $31

378 Third Ave. (bet. 27th & 28th Sts.), 212-679-0070
206 W. 79th St. (bet. Amsterdam Ave. & B'way), 212-877-3840
www.coppolas-nyc.com

☑ "You won't leave hungry" from these Italian "red-sauce" purveyors thanks to their "substantial" portions of "satisfying", "reasonably priced" pizzas and "pastas galore"; but given "hit-or-miss" service and an elbow-room shortage, they're prime candidates for "takeout."

Cornelia Street Cafe ◑
18 | 16 | 17 | $31

29 Cornelia St. (bet. Bleecker & W. 4th Sts.), 212-989-9319;
www.corneliastreetcafe.com

■ A longtime "sentimental favorite", this "quaint" Village French-American is better known for the "avant-garde" performances in its "downstairs event space" than its just "decent" grub; still, touches like a "great fireplace" and a picturesque, "tree-lined street" make it a much-loved "mainstay."

Corner Bistro ◑⇥
23 | 9 | 12 | $14

331 W. Fourth St. (Jane St.), 212-242-9502

■ "Just what a burger joint should be" sums up this "sticky-floored" Village "dive" specializing in "juicy", "messy" specimens accompanied by "sinful" fries and "cheap beer"; naturally, it's "always jam-packed", so just "make friends with the others on line and the time will fly."

Cortina
– | – | – | M

1448 Second Ave. (bet. 75th & 76th Sts.), 212-517-2066;
www.ristorantecortina.com

Along a restaurant-heavy stretch of Second Avenue lies this midpriced Upper East Side Northern Italian that serves a full roster of Tuscan favorites and is particularly known for its homemade breads and sidewalk seating; the fact that it's been around for over 20 years suggests they're doing something right here.

Cosette

21 | 15 | 22 | $35

163 E. 33rd St. (bet. Lexington & 3rd Aves.), 212-889-5489

■ Get a double dose of "Gallic charm from the owner *and* the cassoulet" at this "tiny" "Parisian corner" dispensing "excellent" French vittles in Murray Hill; though the decor may "need a spiff-up", the "decent prices" are fine as is.

Cosí

17 | 11 | 11 | $13

2160 Broadway (76th St.), 212-595-5616
841 Broadway (13th St.), 212-614-8544
60 E. 56th St. (bet. Madison & Park Aves.), 212-588-1225
Paramount Plaza, 1633 Broadway (51st St.), 212-397-9838
257 Park Ave. S. (21st St.), 212-598-4070
498 Seventh Ave. (bet. 36th & 37th Sts.), 212-947-1005
700 Sixth Ave. (bet. 22nd & 23rd Sts.), 212-645-0223
504 Sixth Ave. (13th St.), 212-462-4188
11 W. 42nd St. (bet. 5th & 6th Aves.), 212-398-6662
World Financial Ctr., 200 Vesey St. (West Side Hwy.), 212-571-2001
Additional locations throughout the NY area
www.getcosi.com

☑ Fanatics "can't go without their fix" of the "creatively filled", flatbread-based sandwiches at these "fancy" "fast-food alternatives" spread all over town; but "conveyor-belt" service and "bloated" prices lead some to have second thoughts.

Cosmic Cantina ●≠

17 | 8 | 13 | $12

101 Third Ave. (13th St.), 212-420-0975

☑ "You don't have to feel guilty" wolfing down the "filling" burritos at this East Village Mexican since they're "all organic" and dirt "cheap" to boot; citing "less-than-glamorous" decor, "shallow attempts at service" and a "spring-break" atmosphere, many opt for takeout.

Counter ●

▽ 23 | 22 | 21 | $29

105 First Ave. (bet. 6th & 7th Sts.), 212-982-5870

■ "Innovative and sophisticated" applies to both food and decor at this East Village organic wine bar specializing in "gourmet" vegetarian items that even "carnivores can appreciate"; too much "noise" and "too-high" pricing are countered by "earth-mother service."

Country Café

21 | 18 | 21 | $36

69 Thompson St. (bet. Broome & Spring Sts.), 212-966-5417;
www.countrycafesoho.com

■ "France meets North Africa" on the menu of this "cute" SoHo cafe serving "flavorful" meals; "romantic possibilities abound" in its "quiet" space, though what's "cozy" for some is "claustrophobic" to others.

Cowgirl

16 | 18 | 16 | $25

519 Hudson St. (10th St.), 212-633-1133

☑ Cowpokes "hoot and holler" over this "festive" West Villager dispensing "hearty" portions of "decent, cheap" Southwestern grub in "kitschy", "knickknack"-laden quarters; by day, it's "great for kids" while later in the evening it "turns into a bar" – but at any hour you can expect "sleepwalking" service.

Cozy Soup & Burger ●

18 | 8 | 15 | $14

739 Broadway (Astor Pl.), 212-477-5566

☑ "Juicy", "three-napkin" burgers "fill you up for the whole day" at this "oldie but goodie" Village diner; sure, the decor's "no frills" and the service "brusque", but its "cheap" tabs and 24/7 open-door policy make it a natural for a "late-night greasefest."

CRAFT
26 | 25 | 24 | $67

43 E. 19th St. (bet. B'way & Park Ave. S.), 212-780-0880

■ "Settling in for the long run", Tom Colicchio's handsome Flatiron New American invites those entering its "coolly minimalist" quarters to "build their own menu" by selecting from a roster of "superb", "deceptively simple" dishes; even though some surveyors prefer the chef to assemble the meal and question the "pay-for-each-ingredient approach", most diners consider this a "home run."

Craftbar
23 | 20 | 20 | $41

47 E. 19th St. (bet. B'way & Park Ave. S.), 212-780-0880

■ An "excellent alternative" to its "pricier" sire next door, this "stylish" Flatiron New American (inevitably nicknamed "Craft Lite") supplies "Craft quality" from a "substantially more limited menu" at prices considerably more affordable; since "they don't take reservations", it's just the ticket when you're feeling "impromptu."

Crispo ●
23 | 18 | 18 | $41

240 W. 14th St. (bet. 7th & 8th Aves.), 212-229-1818

■ A "solid" bet in the "trendy" West Village, this "rustic" Northern Italian exudes "energy" thanks to *bellissima* cooking and a "cozy", "grottolike" setting with a newly added covered back patio; given the "fair" pricing, it's usually "crowded", so regulars would prefer to keep it to themselves.

Cru ⌧
– – – VE

(fka Washington Park)

24 Fifth Ave. (9th St.), 212-529-1700; www.cru-nyc.com

A 3,200-label wine list is paired with high-concept Mediterranean dishes at this ambitious (and ambitiously priced) new Villager; the adult-oriented rear dining room features soft lighting and well-spaced tables, while a more casual, up-front area offers small plates and doesn't require reservations.

Cuba ●
– – – M

*222 Thompson St. (bet. Bleecker & W. 3rd Sts.), 212-420-7878;
www.cubanyc.com*

Caribbean authenticity comes to the Village via this new Cuban offering standards like ropa vieja and suckling pig; the front cafe is abetted by a tented back room and a subterranean, DJ-ready lounge.

Cuba Libre ●
18 | 16 | 16 | $34

165 Eighth Ave. (bet. 18th & 19th Sts.), 212-206-0038; www.cubalibreonline.com

◪ "Designer Cuban cuisine" is the draw at this Chelsea Nuevo Latino featuring "tasty" vittles, "deadly" mojitos and fairly "cheap prices"; just "so-so" for some, it's a more than "acceptable shot" for those who liken it to "visiting Cuba without the whole Communist thing."

Cube 63 ●
▽ 23 | 15 | 19 | $38

63 Clinton St. (bet. Rivington & Stanton Sts.), 212-228-6751

■ Clinton Street gets its first Japanese eatery with the arrival of this new "ultrahip" Lower Eastsider serving "well-presented", "creative" sushi in a "tiny" chartreuse setting; bargain-hunters say the corkage fee–free BYO policy really "saves a bundle."

Cub Room
19 | 19 | 17 | $44

131 Sullivan St. (Prince St.), 212-677-4100; www.cubroom.com

◪ This "pleasant" SoHo New American provides "enjoyable" meals in a "peaceful" setting where "you can actually talk" – once you've elbowed your way past the crowd at the "lively bar"; "lost-in-space" service and slightly "expensive" tabs are drawbacks, so insiders tout the cheaper adjacent cafe as a "better bet."

Cucina di Pesce ●

18	14	18	$25

87 E. Fourth St. (bet. Bowery & 2nd Ave.), 212-260-6800;
www.cucinadipesce.com
■ It's all about the "can't-be-beat" $10.95 early-bird at this longtime East Village Italian "value leader" offering "serviceable" grub in a skylit setting that lies somewhere between "kitschy" and "lovely"; even better news: it now "accepts credit cards."

Cup ●

–	–	–	I

35-01 36th St. (35th Ave.), Queens, 718-937-2322
Astoria gets a little slicker with the addition of this roomy, retro-mod coffee shop that blends old and new touches in its stylish setting as well as on its inexpensive menu of updated comfort classics; at press time, it was phasing in sidewalk seats and 24-hour operation.

Cupping Room Café ●

18	15	16	$26

359 W. Broadway (bet. Broome & Grand Sts.), 212-925-2898;
www.cuppingroomcafe.com
◪ "Enjoy SoHo as it wakes up" at this "casual" early-riser that's a "cozy" stop weekdays but considerably more "boisterous" come weekend brunch; the American comfort chow may be "standard" and the furnishings straight out of "grandma's attic", but by any standard it's a "good value."

Curry Leaf

20	11	18	$24

99 Lexington Ave. (27th St.), 212-725-5558
151 Remsen St. (bet. Clinton & Court Sts.), Brooklyn, 718-222-3900
www.curryleafnyc.com
◪ A "bland interior" is trumped by a menu brimming with "complex flavors" and a "range of spiciness" at this Gramercy Indian from the owners of Kalustyan's market; "inexpensive" tabs and a staff that's "patient" with novices add to its allure; N.B. the Brooklyn Heights branch is new and unrated.

Cyclo

19	14	17	$27

203 First Ave. (bet. 12th & 13th Sts.), 212-673-3975
■ For "pho as tasty as on the streets of Hanoi" served in "considerably more comfortable surroundings", check out this "dark" East Village Vietnamese offering "deliciously light", relatively "low-cost" food; starved-to-perfection types note "you won't gain weight eating here" since the portions are so "tiny."

Da Andrea

23	17	23	$33

557 Hudson St. (bet. Perry & W. 11th Sts.), 212-367-1979;
www.biassanot.com
■ "Da word" on this "relaxed", "congenial" West Village Northern Italian is that the homemade pastas are "wonderful", the service "friendly", the space "cramped" and the waits to enter "long"; indeed, the "bargain" pricing alone makes it "one of da bettah Hudson Street venues."

Da Antonio Ⓢ

∇	20	16	22	$50

157 E. 55th St. (bet. Lexington & 3rd Aves.), 212-588-1545; www.daantonio.com
◪ For "fine Italian food in a warm, friendly setting", this "classy" Midtowner obliges, throwing in a nightly "piano player" as a bonus; "wonderful host" Antonio Cerra "makes you feel like a regular on your first visit", but even amici wish "he'd lower his prices" a bit so they could visit more often.

Da Ciro
22 | 17 | 20 | $37

229 Lexington Ave. (bet. 33rd & 34th Sts.), 212-532-1636; www.daciro.com

■ The "focaccia robiola is better than sex" at this "quality" Murray Hill Italian where a "wood-burning oven" also turns out "upscale pizzas"; it's "not the cheapest" and it can get "noisy", but it works wonders when you're looking for a "little Chianti and a filling meal."

Da Filippo
21 | 17 | 20 | $49

1315 Second Ave. (bet. 69th & 70th Sts.), 212-472-6688

■ This "hospitable" Upper East Side Northern Italian is at its most enjoyable if you "get to know Carlo", the "gracious" owner/maitre d'; while the "high-quality" cooking is "consistently good", some say it's "overpriced for what it is."

Daily Chow
17 | 17 | 15 | $25

2 E. Second St. (Bowery), 212-254-7887; www.dailychow.com

■ "Fresh and sassy" sums up the scene at this East Village Pan-Asian that's a magnet for "NYU undergrads" due to its "satisfying", "bargain"-priced chow; although its famed Mongolian BBQ remains on the menu, nitpickers natter it's "no longer a create-your-own" option.

Daisy May's BBQ USA ⌧
23 | 4 | 13 | $18

623 11th Ave. (46th St.), 212-977-1500; www.daisymaysbbq.com

■ Ok, it's a Hell's Kitchen "shack" offering "only takeout", but this "killer" new arrival is rated No. 1 for its "finger-lickin' good" BBQ; despite a "remote" address, the "incredible delivery range" and a growing number of pushcarts make it more accessible.

Dakshin Indian Bistro
18 | 10 | 17 | $24

1713 First Ave. (bet. 88th & 89th Sts.), 212-987-9839
741 Ninth Ave. (50th St.), 212-757-4545

☑ East Side or West, the "tasty lunch buffet" is "especially welcome" at this "inexpensive", veggie-friendly Indian duo with "more or less authentic" spicing and "fast" service; since it's "not much to look at", many rule it "best for takeout."

Dallas BBQ ●
15 | 8 | 13 | $19

3956 Broadway (166th St.), 212-568-3700
261 Eighth Ave. (23rd St.), 212-462-0001
132 Second Ave. (St. Marks Pl.), 212-777-5574
1265 Third Ave. (bet. 72nd & 73rd Sts.), 212-772-9393
21 University Pl. (8th St.), 212-674-4450
27 W. 72nd St. (bet. Columbus Ave. & CPW), 212-873-2004
www.bbqnyc.com

☑ "Lumberjack-size" portions of chicken 'n' ribs are the bait at this "downmarket" BBQ chain, a "total guilty pleasure" for "easy-on-the-wallet, hard-on-the-heart" eats; though the decor's "Early Whatever" and the atmosphere occasionally "chaotic", the "fast" staff "knows what you'll order before you do."

Danal
21 | 21 | 19 | $35

90 E. 10th St. (bet. 3rd & 4th Aves.), 212-982-6930

☑ "Long on atmosphere", this midpriced East Village French bistro boasts a "sweet garden" and a "cozy" interior recalling "grandma's house" (with correspondingly "absent-minded" service); weekend brunch "hits the right high note", but the "challenge is getting a seat."

Da Nico
21 | 17 | 19 | $34

164 Mulberry St. (bet. Broome & Grand Sts.), 212-343-1212

☑ Maybe "Little Italy isn't what it used to be", but this "old-school" Italian is still the real deal for "solid" food and a garden that's "perfect" on "warm summer nights"; the possibility of a celebrity sighting helps distract from the somewhat "slow" service pace.

DANIEL ☒
28 | 28 | 27 | $102

60 E. 65th St. (bet. Madison & Park Aves.), 212-288-0033;
www.danielnyc.com

■ There's "true joie de vivre in the air" at Daniel Boulud's East Side flagship, a "crème de la crème" experience where the "sumptuous" New French cooking (rated No. 3 in this year's *Survey*) is the "stuff of dreams", the wine list "vast", the service "flawless" and the flower-festooned room "opulent to say the least"; in sum, it's the "ultimate special-occasion restaurant", and as for the price, it's "still cheaper than a midsize car."

Daniella
18 | 12 | 18 | $39

320 Eighth Ave. (26th St.), 212-807-0977

☒ Parked in a "nowhere part of town", this "small" Chelsea Italian is nevertheless handy for "pre-MSG dinners", offering "better-than-average" fare for a "reasonable" price; the "dull ambiance" and "early closing" time are trumped by "old-school" service.

Dano
▽ 19 | 14 | 17 | $32

254 Fifth Ave. (bet. 28th & 29th Sts.), 212-725-2922;
www.restaurantdano.com

■ Though it "looks like a bar from the outside", within this Gramercy New American "favorite" you'll find a "casual" bistro where the "tasty" midpriced menu and "model/actress" staff are equally appealing; fans say it's "one of the only decent" options in an otherwise "barren" area.

DANUBE ◐☒
27 | 28 | 26 | $84

30 Hudson St. (bet. Duane & Reade Sts.), 212-791-3771; www.thedanube.net

■ You can "step back in time" via the "surreal" world of "Klimt paintings" at David Bouley's TriBeCa Viennese "epicurean delight"; the "gilded" setting recalls a "countess' salon", the French-inflected food offers a "platonic ideal of Austrian cuisine" and the "impeccable" staff treats all like "royalty"; still, you may need to bring the royal jewelry to settle the bill; P.S. the "Wiener schnitzel is compulsory."

Darbar
– | – | – | M

152 E. 46th St. (bet. Lexington & 3rd Aves.), 212-681-4500

Taking over the bi-level space that formerly housed D'Artagnan, this pleasantly appointed Midtown Indian sallies forth with a roster of tried-and-true subcontinental classics; bargain-hunters have already sniffed out the $9.95 lunch buffet, served seven days a week.

Darna
▽ 20 | 21 | 18 | $37

600 Columbus Ave. (89th St.), 212-721-9123

☒ "Something different" for the Upper West Side, this "unique" French-Moroccan is glatt kosher, though "you wouldn't know it" given the "creative" kitchen; opinion splits on service ("slow but nice" vs. "surly"), but the "airy", "exotic" ambiance makes this one a "pleasant", "inviting" option.

Da Silvano ◐
21 | 16 | 18 | $54

260 Sixth Ave. (bet. Bleecker & Houston Sts.), 212-982-2343;
www.dasilvano.com

☒ Get out your "Gucci sunglasses" to blend in with the "Page Six"–worthy crowd at Silvano Marchetto's Village Tuscan, where "Gwyneth", "Madonna" and "Donatella" jockey for "streetside tables"; the food's "delicious", the setup "cramped" and the bill "expensive", but more tolerable "if there's a movie star" within range; wanna-bes settle for Cantinetta, its more modest next-door sibling.

Da Tommaso ◐
20 | 13 | 19 | $40 |

903 Eighth Ave. (bet. 53rd & 54th Sts.), 212-265-1890; www.datommaso.com

☑ "Always there when you need it", this "entertaining relic of old Hell's Kitchen" supplies "consistently good" Northern Italiana that "never lets you down"; though the "tuckered-out" decor could stand a "face-lift", "affordable" pricing keeps regulars regular.

Da Umberto ☒
24 | 17 | 21 | $56 |

107 W. 17th St. (bet. 6th & 7th Aves.), 212-989-0303

☑ Fans "go for the food, not the atmosphere" at this longtime Chelsea Tuscan, a "pricey", "old-school" type of place drawing a "mature crowd"; though service can vary – "well-trained" vs. "not up to snuff" – there's no debate about its "flawlessly prepared" dishes.

davidburke & donatella
25 | 24 | 22 | $72 |

133 E. 61st St. (bet. Lexington & Park Aves.), 212-813-2121; www.dbdrestaurant.com

☑ "Imaginative" chef David Burke (ex Park Avenue Cafe) "strikes gold" at this "very hot" East Side New American offering "witty" "amusement park rides on a plate", finished off by "fabulous" desserts; its *Bonfire of the Vanities* crowd feels at home with the "precise" service, "stylish" rooms and hostess-with-the-mostest Donatella Arpaia (Bellini), despite the "too-noisy", "tight" setup and zip code–appropriate tabs.

Dawat
23 | 19 | 21 | $44 |

210 E. 58th St. (bet. 2nd & 3rd Aves.), 212-355-7555

☑ "When you want more than Christmas lights" to illuminate your meal, opt for this "haute Indian" Midtowner venerated for "authentic", "highly flavored" subcontinental fare with "not a trace of fusion" to it; though some say both the food and decor has "lost its pizzazz", it's still "one of the more interesting" (and "costliest") of its genre.

db Bistro Moderne
25 | 22 | 23 | $60 |

City Club Hotel, 55 W. 44th St. (bet. 5th & 6th Aves.), 212-391-2400; www.danielnyc.com

■ "More affordable and relaxed" than Daniel Boulud's other venues, this lively Theater District haute French bistro is "as incredible as you've heard", purveying "sumptuous" food in a "lovely" "modern" setting; its "famous" $29 foie gras–filled burger adds a "showbiz" touch, but most agree "you'll never again eat a burger without thinking of the one here"; adherents "stick to the $42 prix fixe for true value."

Deborah
22 | 15 | 20 | $34 |

43 Carmine St. (bet. Bedford & Bleecker Sts.), 212-242-2606

■ "So small it should be called Debbie", this "railroad"-layout Villager lures a "devoted following" thanks to chef Deborah Stanton's "fresh-tasting" New Americana that's "just like what mom should have made"; though the menu's rather "limited", prices are more than "reasonable."

Dee's Brick Oven Pizza
23 | 14 | 19 | $23 |

104-02 Metropolitan Ave. (71st Dr.), Queens, 718-793-7553; www.deesbrickovenpizza.com

■ "You'll never feel sluggish from too much dough" at this Atkins-friendly Forest Hills pizzeria where "excellent" pies emerge from the wood-fired brick oven with a "thin, crispy" "crackerlike crust"; locals "go during the week" to avoid the "packed" weekend scene.

DeGrezia ☒
22 | 21 | 23 | $55 |

231 E. 50th St. (bet. 2nd & 3rd Aves.), 212-750-5353

■ "Good renderings" of Northern Italian "standbys" fill out the menu of this "subterranean" Midtowner where the staff provides "lots of attention" to its "over-50" following; it's still "relatively undiscovered after all these years", which might have something to do with its rather "expensive" tabs.

Delegates' Dining Room ⊠

▽ 17 | 20 | 18 | $37

United Nations, 4th fl. (1st Ave. & 45th St.), 212-963-7626
■ Providing "gorgeous" views of both the "East River" and "key diplomats", this UN-based Eclectic "secret" opens its doors to civilians for a "bountiful" weekday-only lunch buffet; be sure to "reserve" ahead and "arrive early for this international departure" – it "takes time to clear security."

Del Frisco's ●

24 | 23 | 22 | $63

*McGraw Hill Bldg., 1221 Sixth Ave. (49th St.), 212-575-5129;
www.lonestarsteakhouse.com*
■ You can "cut the steaks with a fork" at this "big-city" Midtown chop shop that's "power dining personified" and consequently "chockablock with suits" wolfing down "king-size everything"; despite "first-class prices", "not enough women" and a din akin to the "NYSE floor", this "top-flight" ode to "capitalism" continues to "dazzle" carnivores with its bank-size space, elegant private rooms and big, bountiful bar.

Delhi Palace

▽ 22 | 14 | 18 | $23

37-33 74th St. (bet. Roosevelt & 37th Aves.), Queens, 718-507-0666
■ For "amazing dosas and biryanis", fans head to this Jackson Heights Indian "find" featuring a vegetarian-friendly menu and an "excellent variety buffet", all served at "can't-be-beat" prices; even better, the setting's "not as chaotic" as at Jackson Diner, its "better-known" nearby rival.

Delmonico's ⊠

21 | 22 | 21 | $53

56 Beaver St. (William St.), 212-509-1144; www.delmonicosny.com
◪ This "historic" Financial District beef palace, a reincarnation of NY's oldest steakhouse, purveys "premium" "big-guy food" in a "boys' club central" setting; some say both the menu and the decor "should be modernized", but "power-lunchers" with disposable capital swear you "can't beat the atmosphere" here.

Delta Grill

20 | 16 | 17 | $30

700 Ninth Ave. (48th St.), 212-956-0934
◪ Folks "feeling nostalgic for N'Awlins" ("without the humidity") put some "South in their mouth" at this Hell's Kitchen Cajun-Creole spice-alist; purists say the cooking's "not authentic" enough, but admit that the "truck-stop" decor and "moderate" pricing are more apropos.

Denino's Pizzeria ⊄

24 | 10 | 17 | $18

*524 Port Richmond Ave. (bet. Hooker Pl. & Walker St.), Staten Island,
718-442-9401*
■ Even some "off-Islanders" find this SI pizza "purist" "worth the trip" for "unmatched", "thin-crusted" pies "topped off by an Italian ice from Ralph's across the street"; despite the "no-frills" ambiance (think "paper plates"), they continue to "pack 'em in" 'cause "they know what they're doing."

Dervish Turkish ●

19 | 16 | 18 | $33

*146 W. 47th St. (bet. 6th & 7th Aves.), 212-997-0070;
www.dervishrestaurant.com*
■ For "offbeat" yet "laid-back" dining in "busy Times Square", try this "pleasant" Turk dispensing "consistently tasty" dishes at "TKTS prices" (notably the "bargain" $20 early-bird); fans say it's like being "on the Bosphorus" yet still "convenient to Broadway theaters."

Di Fara ⊖
| 27 | 4 | 13 | $10 |

1424 Ave. J (15th St.), Brooklyn, 718-258-1367
■ There's a "genius at work" at this circa-1963 Midwood pizzeria – chef Dominic De Marco, who "handcrafts" his "thin, crispy pies" with such "painstaking, ritualistic precision" that voters have anointed this the Top Pizza in the *Survey*; the bad news: beyond-"funky" decor, "glacially slow" service, "horrendous waits."

Dim Sum Go Go
| 19 | 11 | 14 | $21 |

5 E. Broadway (Chatham Sq.), 212-732-0797
☑ "Chichi dim sum" selected "from a menu, not a pushcart" is yours at this "unconventional" C-town Cantonese that's a "gentle introduction" to the genre for novices; though some complain about "Americanized", "higher-priced" fare, at least the goods here are "made to order" and "piping hot."

Diner ●
| 21 | 17 | 18 | $29 |

85 Broadway (Berry St.), Brooklyn, 718-486-3077
☑ "Nestled beneath the Williamsburg Bridge", this "trust-fund hipster hangout" dispenses "slightly tweaked" American cooking from a "converted" 1920s Pullman car; regulars report it's "all about the specials" (which "change as often as the staff's hair color") and the "hangover"-curing brunch.

Diner 24 ●
| – | – | – | M |

102 Eighth Ave. (15th St.), 212-242-7773; www.diner24.com
Hoping to capitalize on the area's feverish nightlife scene, this groovy 24/7 Chelsea diner is poised to lure in clubbers, nightcrawlers and just plain hungry folks up late; the hook is comfort cooking that's far more ambitious than what's usually available in the wee hours, served in a fashionably understated setting.

Dish ●
| 18 | 14 | 17 | $28 |

165 Allen St. (bet. Rivington & Stanton Sts.), 212-253-8840; www.dish165.com
■ "Reliable comfort food" is served amid "no-frills" surroundings at this "laid-back" Lower East Side New American with a "mix 'n' match" menu that "lets you experiment" with your entrees and sides; "reasonable prices" and a "hip brunch" keep business brisk.

Dishes
| 21 | 10 | 13 | $15 |

6 E 45th St. (bet. 5th & Madison Aves.), 212-687-5511 🗷
Grand Central, lower level (42nd St. & Vanderbilt Ave.), 212-808-5511 ⊖
■ "Great for grazers", this weekday-only Midtown duo offers "creative" sandwiches, "killer" soups and a "dressy" salad bar at prices that are "upscale" but "worth it"; since the lines for a table can be "daunting" and the decor is easy to dis, many "get it to go."

District
| 20 | 21 | 21 | $53 |

Muse Hotel, 130 W. 46th St. (bet. 6th & 7th Aves.), 212-485-2999;
www.themusehotel.com
☑ Ticket-holders applaud the $48 pre-theater prix fixe at this "stylish" yet "undiscovered" Times Square New American; but after the curtain rises, "you can hear a pin drop", perhaps because the à-la-carte options are so "pricey"; N.B. a recent chef change may outdate the Food score.

Divane ●
| 20 | 16 | 19 | $32 |

888 Eighth Ave. (52nd St.), 212-333-5888
■ The "menu may be limited", but this new Hell's Kitchen Turk hits its "one note well" and "inexpensively" with "excellent kebabs" and other "carefully prepared" dishes; a "chatty" (verging on "intrusive") owner supplies color to the otherwise pared-down, "modern" setting.

Divino ●
19 | 14 | 19 | $38

1556 Second Ave. (bet. 80th & 81st Sts.), 212-861-1096;
www.divinoristorante.net
■ Upper Eastsiders hankering for "hearty" Northern Italian cooking head to this "longtime" standby featuring relatively "inexpensive food that tastes expensive"; while the decor doesn't make a big impact, the ambiance is "pleasant" and enhanced by live music.

Diwan
22 | 16 | 18 | $37

Helmsley Middletowne, 148 E. 48th St. (bet. Lexington & 3rd Aves.),
212-593-5425; www.diwanrestaurant.com
■ It may be "tailored for the business crowd", but this "attractive" Midtown Indian attracts diverse folk with a "well-seasoned" $13.95 lunch buffet "steal"; come suppertime it's also "excellent", albeit significantly "pricier" than its famed sibling, Jackson Diner.

Django ⊠
20 | 24 | 20 | $51

480 Lexington Ave. (46th St.), 212-871-6600
☑ In an attempt to "turn Midtown into a hip area", this "sexy" French-Med has a "jazzed-up" downstairs lounge plus a "pretty" upstairs dining room done in "modern-day harem" style; while the food is debatable ("savory" vs. "just ok"), most feel the "expensive" tabs reflect "location and decor."

Docks Oyster Bar
19 | 16 | 17 | $44

2427 Broadway (bet. 89th & 90th Sts.), 212-724-5588
633 Third Ave. (40th St.), 212-986-8080
www.docksoysterbar.com
☑ Seafood is "prepared with all due respect" at these popular "no-frills" gills dispensers where legions "meet after work" and "gorge themselves" on a "wide array" of midpriced marine eats; "killer martinis" blunt the "harried" service and "dining-in-a-tin-can" din.

Do Hwa
21 | 19 | 17 | $36

55 Carmine St. (bet. Bedford St. & 7th Ave. S.), 212-414-1224
■ Hipsters who "don't want to travel" to K-town can experience "do-it-yourself BBQ" and other "reasonably authentic" Korean chow (washed down with "great cocktails") at this "trendy" Villager; but don't "tell grandpa what you paid for the bibimbop", 'cause he just might "faint."

Dojo ⊅
14 | 8 | 11 | $14

24-26 St. Marks Pl. (bet. 2nd & 3rd Aves.), 212-674-9821
14 W. Fourth St. (Mercer St.), 212-505-8934 ●
☑ "Dirt-cheap and dirt-simple" sums up these "lowbrow" Village health-food "institutions" that might as well be NYU "cafeterias" given their "undergrad"-heavy crowds; though the Asian-accented fare "lies easy in the tummy", the "clueless" service and "spartan" decor are harder to stomach.

Dok Suni's ⊅
22 | 15 | 16 | $28

119 First Ave. (bet. 7th St. & St. Marks Pl.), 212-477-9506
☑ "Still rocking and still very East Village", this "hip intro" to Korean cooking bats out "dynamite", "semi-authentic" grub in "chill", "date-perfect" environs; despite tabs that can get "slightly pricey" and "skimpy" service from an "all-female" staff, it's most "always packed."

Dolphins ●
17 | 18 | 18 | $34

35 Cooper Sq. (bet. 5th & 6th Sts.), 212-375-9195
■ Offering "copious portions for modest costs", this "comfortable" Cooper Square seafooder is known for its "hard-to-beat" early-bird and is particularly "handy" if you're bound for the Public Theater; regulars say the "decent" food tastes "even better in the secluded garden."

Dominick's ∅
21 | 9 | 15 | $33

2335 Arthur Ave. (bet. Crescent Ave. & E. 187th St.), Bronx, 718-733-2807

■ It's easy to conjure up the heyday of "NYC's *true* Little Italy" at this Arthur Avenue Italian where "good food" arrives at your communal table "without menus or fuss" via "bossy" waiters; despite "no atmosphere", "no reservations", "no price list" and no credit cards, our surveyors report "no disappointments."

Don Giovanni ◑
18 | 12 | 15 | $23

214 10th Ave. (bet. 22nd & 23rd Sts.), 212-242-9054
358 W. 44th St. (bet. 8th & 9th Aves.), 212-581-4939
www.dongiovanni-ny.com

☑ "Not bad in a pinch", these "busy" West Side Italians "keep it simple" with "don good" brick-oven pizzas and pasta dishes at "what-a-bargain" tabs; the trade-offs are "noisy" acoustics, "poor" service and ultra-"funky" decor.

Donguri
∇ 28 | 17 | 27 | $50

309 E. 83rd St. (bet. 1st & 2nd Aves.), 212-737-5656

■ Run by a "cute couple", this "microscopic" "piece of Tokyo" on the Upper East Side has a disproportionately "big heart" and serves a "mouthwatering" selection of sashimi and "homestyle" Japanese dishes (but no sushi); a "soothing" atmosphere and "impeccable" service compensate for the "pricey" tabs and no-takeout policy.

Don Pedro's
∇ 20 | 17 | 20 | $35

1865 Second Ave. (96th St.), 212-996-3274; www.donpedros.net

■ "Unprepossessing on the outside", this Yorkville Latin-Caribbean is "fast, friendly and reasonably priced" within, dishing out "unusual combinations" in a "hip" setting; it's a destination for "something different" in an "area that desperately needs quality restaurants."

Don Peppe ∅
24 | 8 | 16 | $40

135-58 Lefferts Blvd. (149th Ave.), Queens, 718-845-7587

■ Sated diners need to be "rolled home" after a "garlic"-laden "family-style" meal at this cash-only Ozone Park Italian that's handy "after a day at Aqueduct"; service may be "brusque", weekend waits "long" and the "decor doesn't matter", but the "interesting characters here make it fun."

Dos Caminos ◑
21 | 22 | 18 | $42

373 Park Ave. S. (bet. 26th & 27th Sts.), 212-294-1000
475 W. Broadway (Houston St.), 212-277-4300
www.brguestrestaurants.com

■ "Boisterous crowds" pack these "hip", Steve Hanson–owned Mexicans pairing a "smashing" tequila selection with "*excellente*" food (especially the "knock-your-socks-off" guacamole made tableside); the "nightclub"-esque setups are as much about "scene" as cuisine, so "spotty" service comes with the territory.

Downtown ◑
∇ 21 | 18 | 18 | $64

376 W. Broadway (bet. Broome & Spring Sts.), 212-343-0999;
www.cipriani.com

☑ "People-watching" is the daily special at this "flashy" SoHo Italian serving "classic Cipriani cuisine" to "beautiful Euros"; those who've soured on the signature Bellinis claim the "scene's played out", citing "high prices", "rude" service and the scent of "pretension in the air."

Downtown Atlantic
∇ 21 | 18 | 21 | $32

364 Atlantic Ave. (bet. Bond & Hoyt Sts.), Brooklyn, 718-852-9945

■ More proof that "times are changing" on Atlantic Avenue, this Boerum Hill New American "easily holds its own", serving a "versatile" midpriced menu of "fine" comfort items to a "convivial" crowd; "delicious goods" from an on-site bakery are a plus, while occasional live music "gets things going."

DR-K
∇ 22 | 20 | 20 | $36

114 Dyckman St. (Nagle Ave.), 212-304-1717; www.drkny.com
■ Providing quality you "don't expect to find" way up on the "new frontier", this Washington Heights Nuevo Latino provokes "excitement in every bite" from a menu that stresses seafood; the colorful space boasts a "pretty hot" bar too, so many make the trek just to "have a mojito and relax."

Druids ●
∇ 19 | 14 | 19 | $35

736 10th Ave. (bet. 50th & 51st Sts.), 212-307-6410
■ The "humble surroundings" may be par for Hell's Kitchen, but this "regular old" Celtic pub offers a "significant difference" in its "surprisingly ambitious" American kitchen; the "wonderful staff" and "warm-weather" patio are further proof that the "Irish have all the luck."

DT.UT ●
16 | 18 | 14 | $12

41 Ave. B (bet. 3rd & 4th Sts.), 212-477-1021
1626 Second Ave. (bet. 84th & 85th Sts.), 212-327-1327
www.dtut.com
☑ "*Friends* lives on" at this Central Perk-y coffee-and-dessert duo where a "laptop"-toting "sub-25" crowd camps out on "thrift-store" furniture and revs up on a variety of sugar-rush "treats"; given their popularity as a "study lounge" and "meeting" scene, "why would anyone go to Starbucks?"

Duane Park Cafe
23 | 19 | 23 | $49

157 Duane St. (bet. Hudson St. & W. B'way), 212-732-5555
■ Though "overshadowed" by its much "trendier neighbors", this "civilized" TriBeCa New American is an "undervalued wonder" with "marvelous", market-fresh cuisine, "attentive service" and a "soothing" ambiance that lets you "concentrate on the food"; cognoscenti wonder why it's still "under the radar" since it's so consistently flying high.

Due ●⇗
21 | 17 | 21 | $40

1396 Third Ave. (bet. 79th & 80th Sts.), 212-772-3331
■ Fans give this "homey" Upper East Side "staple" its due by habitually returning for the "delish" Northern Italian dishes and "cordial" service; though it ranks "well above-average" in the area, it sure "would be nice if they took credit cards."

Duke's
17 | 13 | 14 | $24

99 E. 19th St. (Park Ave. S.), 212-260-2922
■ Don your "trucker hat" and "loosen your belt" at this "tacky" Gramercy "honky-tonk" frequented by "rowdy" collegians scarfing down "finger-lickin' good" Southern grub with "PBR" chasers; though "decidedly divey", it "gets the job done" for "cheap."

Dumonet
∇ 22 | 26 | 25 | $78

Carlyle Hotel, 35 E. 76th St. (Madison Ave.), 212-744-1600;
www.thecarlyle.com
■ "In keeping with the class" of its setting (the Carlyle Hotel), this modern French is an "oh-so-elegant" exercise in "formal dining"; namesake chef Jean-Louis Dumonet produces consistently good seasonal cuisine, while "expert" service and "plush" surroundings that are suitable for "mature adults" contribute to the "luxurious", big-bucks package.

DuMont
∇ 21 | 18 | 19 | $27

432 Union Ave. (bet. Devoe St. & Metropolitan Ave.), Brooklyn, 718-486-7717; www.dumontrestaurant.com

■ Williamsburgers brag "in Manhattan you'd never get a table" at the likes of this "quaint" American where the "limited" menu of "pure comfort" chow (read: burgers) is a veritable "steal"; there's "little elbow room" inside, so come summer it's all about the "back garden."

Dylan Prime
23 | 24 | 21 | $56

62 Laight St. (Greenwich St.), 212-334-4783; www.dylanprime.com

■ As "hip" as a steakhouse can be, this "stylish" TriBeCa chop shop has a "dark, sexy" setting "without the caveman feel" plus "pricey" prime cuts embellished by "unbelievable sauces and toppings"; though far "off the beaten track", it's worth the trek to stay "way ahead" of the herd.

Earl's
∇ 16 | 16 | 14 | $23

(fka Rive Gauche)

560 Third Ave. (37th St.), 212-949-5400; www.earlsnyc.com

◪ Like its "big brother Duke's", this "rough-and-ready" new Murray Hill "hangout" does the "trailer-trash theme" proud with "basic", gut-busting Southern grub combined with "lots of TVs tuned to sports"; its see-and-be-seen sidewalk seating is further inducement to "put back a few" and get "noisy."

East
16 | 11 | 15 | $26

210 E. 44th St. (bet. 2nd & 3rd Aves.), 212-687-5075
354 E. 66th St. (bet. 1st & 2nd Aves.), 212-734-5270
366 Third Ave. (bet. 26th & 27th Sts.), 212-889-2326
253 W. 55th St. (bet. B'way & 8th Ave.), 212-581-2240 ●

◪ "Sushi without killer pricing" sums up the appeal of this Japanese chainlet, an "efficient" "mass-market" source of "decent" if "not exceptional" chow (with "conveyor-belt service" in Gramercy for "extra fun"); "don't expect ambiance" say those who go the delivery route.

East Lake ●
21 | 12 | 14 | $24

42-33 Main St. (Franklin Ave.), Queens, 718-539-8532

◪ This "authentic" Flushing Cantonese bases its "staying power" on a "full-spectrum" low-cost menu stressing "wonderfully fresh seafood" (and "amazing dim sum" that "packs 'em in" on Sundays); the "chaotic" service may seem "rushed", but it sure keeps those "long lines" moving.

East of Eighth ●
16 | 16 | 17 | $28

254 W. 23rd St. (bet. 7th & 8th Aves.), 212-352-0075; www.eastofeighth.com

◪ "Where the boys" go to "meet and greet", this "handy" Chelsea Eclectic doles out "heaping" helpings of "well-priced", "middle-of-the-road" eats; "friendly" servers, a "terrific" backyard patio and a $16 "pre-theater deal" enliven the otherwise "ordinary" proceedings.

East Post ●
18 | 16 | 16 | $29

92 Second Ave. (bet. 5th & 6th Sts.), 212-387-0065

■ An "easy" East Village option for the "budget"-minded, this "enjoyable" Italian purveys "satisfying rustic fare" in "cozy" digs reminiscent of "nonna's dining room"; impatient types who "can't stand the wait" at nearby Frank call it a "great alternative."

East West
– | – | – | M

426 Seventh Ave. (bet. 14th & 15th Sts.), Brooklyn, 718-499-3990; www.theeastwest.com

Park Slope's dining scene spreads southward along Seventh Avenue with the arrival of this midpriced vegetarian/seafood specialist with both East and West accents; a backyard garden vies with a serene, candlelit interior for those in the mood for quiet conversation.

E.A.T.
18 | 10 | 13 | $37

1064 Madison Ave. (bet. 80th & 81st Sts.), 212-772-0022; www.elizabar.com

☑ Wind down from an East Side "shopathon" at Eli Zabar's "tasty" sandwich specialist, a spot so "satisfying" that loyalistas "can't help lovin'" it; still, many marvel at the "chutzpah" of the "over-the-top" prices, considering the "casual" setup and "lackluster" service.

Eatery ◐
18 | 18 | 17 | $29

798 Ninth Ave. (53rd St.), 212-765-7080; www.eaterynyc.com

■ Hip Hell's Kitchen types hang out at this "much-needed" New American "hot spot" for "refreshing" "neo-comfort" chow served in "sleek", "minimalist" digs; the "affordability" factor makes it "wildly popular" for weekend brunch, when "outdoor seating" eases the crush.

Ecco ☒
23 | 19 | 21 | $48

124 Chambers St. (bet. Church St. & W. B'way), 212-227-7074

■ A "quieter" establishment with a rather "saloonlike" vibe, this TriBeCa vet does "lovingly prepared" Italian like "you wish your mama could" and embellishes it with "old-world" service; the "tile-floor" and old-bar setting provide enough "atmosphere" so that most "don't mind" the price tag.

Edgar's Cafe ◐⊭
19 | 18 | 15 | $19

255 W. 84th St. (bet. B'way & West End Ave.), 212-496-6126

☑ If "sinful desserts" make your telltale heart beat fast, try this West Side cafe, a "relaxing haven" with "eccentric decor" evoking the "ghost of Poe"; also serving "lightish" lunch fare, it's a "quieter alternative to Cafe Lalo", if you can take the mysteriously "slow" pace.

Edison Cafe ⊭
14 | 7 | 13 | $18

Edison Hotel, 228 W. 47th St. (bet. B'way & 8th Ave.), 212-840-5000

☑ "Nosh heartily" alongside Theater District "characters" at this "kitschy throwback", a "low-end" purveyor of "down-home" Jewish eats with a generous side of "NY attitude" from its very "colorful" staff; though the meals and the milieu are more than a little "plain", it's still a "big bargain."

Edward's ◐
17 | 15 | 18 | $30

136 W. Broadway (bet. Duane & Thomas Sts.), 212-233-6436

■ As a steady Eddie "neighborhood standby", this practical TriBeCa bistro does the trick for a "casual meal" of "typical" Americana with "minimal" frills; a "family-friendly" sensibility and sidewalk tables add to its "unassuming" appeal.

Eight Mile Creek ◐
▽ 20 | 16 | 20 | $37

240 Mulberry St. (bet. Prince & Spring Sts.), 212-431-4635; www.eightmilecreek.com

■ A "real taste" of the outback awaits at this "adventurous" Little Italy Aussie offering "good grub" from 'roo to emu along with "friendly" service that will make your "g'day"; for a more casual "cold-beer-and-hot-barbie" combo, the bar "down under" is the "place to be."

EJ's Luncheonette
16 | 11 | 14 | $20

447 Amsterdam Ave. (bet. 81st & 82nd Sts.), 212-873-3444 ⊭
432 Sixth Ave. (bet. 9th & 10th Sts.), 212-473-5555
1271 Third Ave. (73rd St.), 212-472-0600 ⊭

☑ The "stroller brigade is out in force" at this "tried-and-true" "upmarket diner" trio that "hits the spot" with "wholesome" all-

American food and "blue-plate" nostalgia; they're "affordable" "no-brainers", but be ready for lines and "slapdash service" during the "out-of-control" brunch.

Elaine's ◐　　　13 | 14 | 13 | $48

1703 Second Ave. (bet. 88th & 89th Sts.), 212-534-8103

☑ "Colorful" doyenne Elaine Kaufman owns and runs this Upper East Side Italian-American that's best known for its celebrity book parties and "literati star spottings"; "if you're not Woody Allen", you may side with "regular folks" who complain of "surly service" and just "ok" eats, but then again, some say the "food isn't why anyone goes."

El Charro Español　　　▽ 21 | 12 | 21 | $41

4 Charles St. (bet. Greenwich Ave. & 7th Ave. S.), 212-242-9547

■ Proof that "old-timers" can "still deliver", this *pequeño* West Village Spaniard is "reliable" after 80 years running for "impressive" food and a "friendly feel"; devotees declare the "service is on point" while the "faded" setting is "beside the point."

El Cid　　　22 | 12 | 18 | $33

322 W. 15th St. (bet. 8th & 9th Aves.), 212-929-9332

☑ An "instant mood-lifter" for tapas fans, this "postage stamp"–size Chelsea Spaniard purveys *"muy excellente"* small plates to all who can "shoehorn" in; maybe ambiance is "lacking" (ok, "there isn't any"), but after some "potent" sangria, "it really doesn't matter."

Elephant, The ◐　　　22 | 16 | 15 | $34

58 E. First St. (bet. 1st & 2nd Aves.), 212-505-7739;
www.elephantrestaurant.com

■ To "make instant friends", check out this "pint-size", modestly priced East Village Thai-French where "amazing" food and "addictive" tropical drinks are downed amid an "absurd din"; though service is "hard to come by", most people would simply like them to "expand."

Elephant & Castle ◐　　　17 | 14 | 16 | $24

68 Greenwich Ave. (bet. 6th & 7th Aves.), 212-243-1400;
www.elephantandcastle.com

■ "Drop in and chow down" at this "longstanding" Villager doling out high-"value" American eats "without hassle" in a "cozy" space; sure, its "plain, simple" style is "not for special occasions", but there's "a reason it's still around"; P.S. brunch is a local "tradition."

ELEVEN MADISON PARK　　　26 | 26 | 25 | $62

11 Madison Ave. (24th St.), 212-889-0905; www.elevenmadisonpark.com

■ "Exciting and so classy", this "Danny Meyer triumph" on Madison Park has "contemporary charisma" to burn thanks to chef Kerry Heffernan's "impeccable" New American cuisine, an "excellent wine list" and "terrific", "charm-school" service; a "swanky" landmark space with "sky-high ceilings" caps this "standout" experience that's worth every penny; P.S. the $25 prix fixe lunch is a "steal."

El Faro　　　22 | 10 | 17 | $36

823 Greenwich St. (Horatio St.), 212-929-8210

☑ "Old-fashioned" to a tee describes this circa-1927 Village Spaniard that "never changes", serving "classic" dishes doused with "garlic aplenty" in "crowded" quarters; it's so "cherished" for "perfect paella" and pluperfect prices that few mind the "really dowdy" decor.

Eliá　　　▽ 26 | 19 | 23 | $46

8611 Third Ave. (bet. 86th & 87th Sts.), Brooklyn, 718-748-9891

■ As close as you can get to a Greek taverna in Bay Ridge, this genial, "little-known gem" transports landlubbers to the Aegean with its "fresh fish" augmented by "superb" lamb and other "must-have" specialties; even if "a bit steep" pricewise, it's an indisputable "find in this neighborhood."

Elias Corner ●⇔
23 | 8 | 14 | $33

24-02 31st St. (24th Ave.), Queens, 718-932-1510

☑ Just try to find "fresher seafood" than the "superbly grilled" goods at this Astoria Greek, a "crowded", stripped-down room redeemed by a rear patio that's "great in summer"; despite "no menus", "no ambiance", no reservations and "not the best service", the "simply delicious" fish keeps most of our surveyors in its corner.

Elio's ●
22 | 17 | 20 | $54

1621 Second Ave. (bet. 84th & 85th Sts.), 212-772-2242

☑ "What a scene" it is at this Upper East Side "institution" favored by a "Botoxed", "who's who" crowd that "doesn't mind paying top dollar" for "top-notch" Italian fare and "polished service"; while regulars are "treated properly", the "hoi polloi" say staffers sometimes seem like they're "doing you a favor."

El Malecon
20 | 7 | 14 | $16

764 Amsterdam Ave. (bet. 97th & 98th Sts.), 212-864-5648
4141 Broadway (175th St.), 212-927-3812
5592 Broadway (231st St.), Bronx, 718-432-5155 ●

☑ They're "nothing to look at", but this Uptown Dominican threesome delivers the "real" goods "real cheap", doling out "huge portions" of "habit-forming" home cooking and cafe con leche "as it should be"; since "you don't go for the ambiance", "takeout is a pleasure."

elmo ●
15 | 19 | 14 | $32

156 Seventh Ave. (bet. 19th & 20th Sts.), 212-337-8000

☑ Chelsea's "muscley boys" make a lot of "racket" at this "hip" New American that puts out "modern comfort food" in "Boca"-"minimalist" environs; forget about the "erratic" service and "so-so" eats – "eye candy" is the "main draw" here.

El Parador Cafe
22 | 16 | 22 | $39

325 E. 34th St. (bet. 1st & 2nd Aves.), 212-679-6812

■ Murray Hill's "old Mexican standby" still works its "charm" on compadres who tout the "top-notch" "traditional" food, "excellent margaritas" and "welcoming service"; sure, the '50s-era room is "not so chic", but otherwise things stay "consistently on the mark."

El Paso Taqueria
▽ 22 | 10 | 16 | $16

64 E. 97th St. (Park Ave.), 212-996-1739
1642 Lexington Ave. (104th St.), 212-831-9831 ●

■ "Great guacamole!" – this pair of "hole-in-the-wall" Mexicans "keeps it real" with "mouthwatering" chow "made fresh" and served "fast" in bare-bones digs; "restaurant-starved" Carnegie Hill dwellers are glad that this "find" is so well priced – anyone would be.

El Pote ⑤
20 | 13 | 19 | $37

718 Second Ave. (bet. 38th & 39th Sts.), 212-889-6680

☑ "You won't leave hungry" from this "comfy little" Murray Hill Spaniard, a "locally popular" stop for "tasty" paella, sangria and other standards; the "warm" service trumps the "drab" setting, and it's a "perennial draw" for those seeking el "value."

El Quijote ●
18 | 13 | 16 | $36

226 W. 23rd St. (bet. 7th & 8th Aves.), 212-929-1855

☑ One of the best darn lobster "bargains" around draws "festive" hordes to this "*olé*"-school Spaniard, a Chelsea "mainstay" for "heavy" fare with "bountiful garlic" and a "party" mood fueled by "deadly" sangria; "impossible" waits suggest that the "tacky" "Spain-of-yore" decor is "part of its charm."

Emack & Bolio's ⊖ 23 | 7 | 15 | $6

389 Amsterdam Ave. (bet. 78th & 79th Sts.), 212-362-2747 ☾
56 Seventh Ave. (bet. 13th & 14th Sts.), 212-727-1198 ☾
21-50 31st St. (bet. Ditmars & 21st Aves.), Queens, 718-278-5380
www.emackandbolios.com

■ This Boston-based chain is famed for "lip-smacking", "imaginatively flavored" ice cream; maybe the prices would buy "gallons elsewhere", but let's face it, there's "nothing better on a summer evening."

Embers 22 | 13 | 17 | $41

9519 Third Ave. (bet. 95th & 96th Sts.), Brooklyn, 718-745-3700

◪ Expect "no frills" at this 20-year-old Bay Ridge steakhouse where "outstanding slabs of beef" attract a mature, well-heeled clientele right "out of a movie"; "tables are close" and "decor is nil", but Brooklynites still "line up" since the "food says it all" and the "price is right."

Empire Diner ☾ 15 | 15 | 13 | $23

210 10th Ave. (22nd St.), 212-243-2736

◪ "Always open", this landmark 24/7 West Chelsea diner is a "happening" resource for refueling "after the galleries" or a high-octane "all-nighter"; the "aloof" staff "won't win any popularity contests", but most customers hope the "cool deco" setting and fair-weather sidewalk cafe will "stand forever."

Empire Szechuan 15 | 8 | 14 | $20

4041 Broadway (bet. 170th & 171st Sts.), 212-568-1600
2642 Broadway (100th St.), 212-662-9404
2574 Broadway (97th St.), 212-663-6004
193 Columbus Ave. (bet. 68th & 69th Sts.), 212-496-8778
15 Greenwich Ave. (bet. Christopher & W. 10th Sts.), 212-691-1535
173 Seventh Ave. S. (bet. Perry & W. 11th Sts.), 212-243-6046
381 Third Ave. (bet. 27th & 28th Sts.), 212-685-6215
251 W. 72nd St. (bet. B'way & West End Ave.), 212-873-2151

◪ An empire built on "quick, economical" eating, this Chinese chain offers an "endless" menu of "predictable" chow that works so long as you "don't expect much"; "abrupt" service and "drab" surroundings suggest it's "better for delivery."

Ennio & Michael ▽ 23 | 16 | 24 | $42

539 La Guardia Pl. (bet. Bleecker & W. 3rd Sts.), 212-677-8577

■ NoHo locals hoping to "avoid the tourists" turn to this "homey", "old reliable" neighborhood Italian where the food is "delicious" and the "caring" staff still believes that the customer "really counts"; better yet, the price is "not too high" given the quality.

Enzo's ▽ 23 | 12 | 19 | $34

1998 Williamsbridge Rd. (Neill Ave.), Bronx, 718-409-3828

◪ "Arthur Avenue, watch out": this "truly authentic" Bronx Italian is a "family" zone for reasonable red-sauce repasts built around "enormous portions"; the "feast" distracts from the functional setting, while lines "onto the sidewalk" reflect the no-reserving policy.

Epicerie ☾ 18 | 19 | 16 | $30

170 Orchard St. (bet. Rivington & Stanton Sts.), 212-420-7520

■ Lower Eastsiders get in a "groove" at this "very French" bistro that's the "real McCoy" for "honest" cooking and "quaint" environs at "appetizing" tabs; it's also a "laid-back respite" for brunch, though a "hopping bar scene" turns up the volume on weekends.

Epices du Traiteur
21 | 16 | 19 | $37

103 W. 70th St. (Columbus Ave.), 212-579-5904

■ "Someplace different" for Westsiders and Lincoln Center–goers, this "low-key hideaway" serves an "interesting, flavorful" Med-Tunisian mix in "intimate" (some say "cramped") digs; overall, it's a "best bet" for "value."

Erawan
25 | 20 | 20 | $30

42-31 Bell Blvd. (bet. 43rd Ave. & Northern Blvd.), Queens, 718-428-2112

■ "Unusually fine" and thus "usually crowded", this "solid little" Bayside Thai makes its mark with "memorable" food and atmosphere at outer borough–size price tags; since it "compares with the best", there's naturally a demand for "larger quarters."

Erminia ☒
25 | 23 | 23 | $60

250 E. 83rd St. (bet. 2nd & 3rd Aves.), 212-879-4284

■ For a "romantic escape" where "no one will find you", try this ultra-"cozy" Upper East Side "jewel" that's "just lovely" for long gazes over "superb" Northern Italiana matched with "invisible" service and a "quiet", candlelit mood; Casanovas call it the ultimate "high-end date", so be prepared to "pay heavily."

Esca
24 | 18 | 20 | $61

402 W. 43rd St. (9th Ave.), 212-564-7272

☑ Both fish and pasta lovers salute chef David Pasternack's "savory", "super-fresh" catch and al dente dough at this Theater District Italian; a product of the Batali-Bastianich team, it showcases a first-rate menu conveyed by an "energetic" crew, and though holdouts hedge about "hefty tabs", most are "hooked."

Esperanto ◑
20 | 16 | 15 | $31

145 Ave. C (9th St.), 212-505-6559

■ "Reee-lax" and "pretend you're boho" at this "sassy" little East Village Nuevo Latino supplying "tasty" grub accompanied by "strong" specialty drinks at "decent prices" (albeit at "Brazilian speed"); anyone up for "boisterous" times and a "fantastic summer" scene is speaking their language.

Esperides ◑
∇ 24 | 16 | 21 | $36

37-01 30th Ave. (37th St.), Queens, 718-545-1494

■ Offering "uncommon quality" in "traditional" Greek fare, this "simple" Astoria taverna is notable for "grilled fish at its tastiest" and other "real-deal" classics; supporters citing the "spacious" setting and "solicitous" service wonder "what more" do you need?

ESPN Zone
13 | 19 | 14 | $28

1472 Broadway (42nd St.), 212-921-3776; www.espnzone.com

☑ You'd better love "sports and tourists" to cope with this "loud" Times Square athletic arena fielding "bar food" and "tons of TVs" that air "every possible" game (even in the bathroom); those who punt on the "formulaic" grub suggest if you come here to eat, you are "missing the point."

Ess-a-Bagel
23 | 6 | 13 | $9

359 First Ave. (21st St.), 212-260-2252
831 Third Ave. (bet. 50th & 51st Sts.), 212-980-1010
www.ess-a-bagel.com

☑ These "diet-killer" delis ply "gargantuan" bagels and "delicious schmears" to those willing to brave the "bustling" setting and "brusque repartee" from the caustic "central casting" countermen; diehards declare there's "no substitute" for the "circles of life" vended here.

Essex
18 | 18 | 15 | $30

120 Essex St. (Rivington St.), 212-533-9616; www.essexnyc.com

☑ "Too cool" as a rule, this Lower Eastsider offers "original" New Americana with "spicy" accents in a "modern, loftlike" setting; most maintain the eating and "hip bar" scene make up for the "spacey" service, while "thirsty" types testify the three-drink weekend "brunch deal" always "rocks."

Etats-Unis
25 | 16 | 21 | $54

242 E. 81st St. (bet. 2nd & 3rd Aves.), 212-517-8826

■ Upper Eastsiders are "afraid the secret's out" on this "warm" New American "gem" and its "limited" but "marvelous" menu of "inventive" mains and "varied" vinos; the "shoebox" space is "usually crowded", but "everything hums" and those with "budget problems" opt for the wine bar across the way.

Ethiopian Restaurant
20 | 11 | 20 | $24

1582 York Ave. (bet. 83rd & 84th Sts.), 212-717-7311

☑ A "reliable diversion from the usual" Upper East Side options, this economical Ethiopian "nook" supplies "authentic, robust" cooking and "lovely" service but "no tableware", so the eating's strictly hand-to-mouth; if "not much on looks", "at least it's not another Italian."

Ethos ◑
21 | 17 | 18 | $36

495 Third Ave. (bet. 33rd & 34th Sts.), 212-252-1972

■ "Fantastically fresh" fish right "off the ice" is the lure at this Murray Hill Hellenic that also features "authentic" Greek clay-pot specialties providing "home-cooked quality" at the "right price"; it may be a "tight fit", but it's already made the leap from "promising" to "popular."

Euzkadi
▽ 18 | 16 | 18 | $34

108 E. Fourth St. (1st Ave.), 212-982-9788; www.euzkadirestaurant.com

■ Bask in the "funky" atmosphere at this "welcoming" East Villager that specializes in "simple" but "surprisingly good" Basque bites, especially the seafood and "really tasty" tapas; entheuziasts say this modestly priced "find" has carved out its own "interesting niche."

Evergreen Shanghai
17 | 11 | 14 | $23

785 Broadway (10th St.), 212-473-2777
10 E. 38th St. (bet. 5th & Madison Aves.), 212-448-1199
63 Mott St. (bet. Bayard & Canal Sts.), 212-571-3339 ⊟

☑ The "juicy buns" at this "serviceable" Chinese triad are just part of an "extensive menu" featuring "dependable" Shanghai-style dishes, "fresh dim sum" and even sushi at two locations; although "typical hole-in-the-wall" operations, they're "good in a fix" for low-cost food that's a "notch above the usual."

Excellent Dumpling House ⊟
20 | 5 | 12 | $14

111 Lafayette St. (bet. Canal & Walker Sts.), 212-219-0212

☑ "Just like the name says", this Chinatown "greasy spoon" is a "longtime favorite" for "piquant" potstickers served "quick"; it may be a "dump" with "utilitarian" shared tables and "interrogation-style" lighting, but for the money it's "hard to complain."

Extra Virgin
▽ 23 | 21 | 19 | $35

259 W. Fourth St. (bet. Charles & Perry Sts.), 212-691-9359

■ Given the "wonderful" Mediterranean menu, fans need no extra urgin' to keep this "cute" new West Villager "jammed in the evenings"; thanks to "great seafood", a snug, exposed-brick setting and a "best"-bet brunch, this former "neighborhood" spot is showing all the signs of becoming a "big hit."

Faan ◐
▽ | 18 | 19 | 17 | $23 |

404 Sixth Ave. (8th St.), 212-777-6999
209 Smith St. (Baltic St.), Brooklyn, 718-694-2277
■ "One-stop shopping" awaits Pan-Asian faanciers at this "affordable" Cobble Hill/Village duo purveying a "wide selection" of "flavorful" food ranging from Thai to Vietnamese to sushi; twentysomething Brooklynites cite that site's "funky patio" and "cool downstairs bar."

Fairway Cafe/Steakhouse
| 19 | 8 | 12 | $33 |

Fairway, 2127 Broadway, 2nd fl. (74th St.), 212-595-1888
☑ Mitchel London's "informal" cafe perched above the famed West Side grocer stays "on top of things" with a "well-executed" American luncheon that gives way to "great deals" on "grade-A" beef by night; the decor's "negligible" and there's "better service at the DMV", but for overall "value", it "ain't bad" at all.

F & B
| 19 | 12 | 14 | $11 |

150 E. 52nd St. (bet. Lexington & 3rd Aves.), 212-421-8600 ☒
269 W. 23rd St. (bet. 7th & 8th Aves.), 646-486-4441
www.gudtfood.com
■ For fast food that's not from the Shea Stadium school of cooking, try this "creative alternative", a "Euro-style" street-food vendor vending "nouveau hot dogs" and other "chic" snacks plus splits of champagne; N.B. the original Chelsea site has spun off a new Midtown satellite.

F & J Pine Restaurant ⊄
| 19 | 16 | 18 | $31 |

1913 Bronxdale Ave. (bet. Morris Park Ave. & White Plains Rd.), Bronx, 718-792-5956
■ "You may see a Yankee" at this "ever-popular" Bronx Italian, a "cash-only" '70s "relic" that's "newly renovated" but still bats out "oversized portions" of "saucy", good-value family-style food; fans continue to "pack" the house, so unless you're Joe Torres, be "prepared to wait."

Fanelli's Cafe ◐
| 15 | 14 | 13 | $23 |

94 Prince St. (Mercer St.), 212-226-9412
■ A "no-nonsense alternative" to oh-so-"chic" SoHo, this "old-time staple" dates to 1922 and remains the "real deal" for "cheap", "messy" pub grub served in a "bar atmosphere"; slummers settling in for burgers 'n' beers say it's "grungy" but "genuine."

Fatoosh ⊄
▽ | 22 | 9 | 18 | $13 |

330 Hicks St. (Atlantic Ave.), Brooklyn, 718-243-0500
■ This beyond "small", 12-seat Brooklyn Heights Lebanese has a sizable rep for "cheap, high-quality" eats, especially those "addictive" pizzas made from "home-baked" pita; since the "awesome" offerings arrive "without frills", takeout and delivery find favor.

FELIDIA ☒
| 26 | 21 | 23 | $65 |

243 E. 58th St. (bet. 2nd & 3rd Aves.), 212-758-1479; www.lidiasitaly.com
■ Small-screen queen Lidia Bastianich continues to "outdo herself" at this "lovely" East Side Italian townhouse where "divine pastas" and other "exciting" dishes are paired with a "phenomenal wine list"; "never-miss-a-beat" service caps the "memorable" meals, so even though the "cost is over the top", "you get what you pay for."

Félix ◐
| 17 | 17 | 14 | $38 |

340 W. Broadway (Grand St.), 212-431-0021; www.felixnyc.com
☑ A "totally Euro" crowd populates this SoHo "scene"-athon that's a "socializing" "summer staple" when the "floor-to-ceiling" windows open to the street; the "standard" bistro chow comes with a "big side of attitude", but brunch is such a "giant party" that few notice.

Ferdinando's Focacceria ⊠∅ ▽ 22 | 15 | 17 | $22
151 Union St. (bet. Columbia & Hicks Sts.), Brooklyn, 718-855-1545
■ "Step back in time" at this century-old Carroll Gardens Sicilian, a truly "old-school" source of "super" pastas and other priced-right blessings from "starch heaven"; one of the "last vestiges" of "ancient Brooklyn", it exudes authenticity that "you don't find elsewhere"; N.B. lunch-only weekdays, dinner-only Fridays and Saturdays.

Ferrara ● 22 | 15 | 15 | $18
195 Grand St. (bet. Mott & Mulberry Sts.), 212-226-6150;
www.ferraracafe.com
☑ "Mama mia": this "historic", circa-1892 Little Italy pasticceria is a "definite classic" for "after-dinner" coffee and "top-notch treats" (e.g. cannoli that "dreams are made of"); "forget the calories", but bear in mind it's a "tourist destination" and the servers are "no cream puffs."

FIAMMA OSTERIA 24 | 24 | 23 | $61
206 Spring St. (bet. 6th Ave. & Sullivan St.), 212-653-0100;
www.brguestrestaurants.com
■ Steve Hanson's "top-shelf" SoHo "knockout" has "flair" to spare, from its handsome triplex setting to the "inspired" Italian cooking, "polished" service and "spectacular wine list"; sure, it helps to have "deep pockets" to afford this "class act", but its "well-heeled" following is "blown away" and "begging for more."

50 Carmine ⊠ 22 | 16 | 19 | $44
50 Carmine St. (bet. Bedford & Bleecker Sts.), 212-206-9134
■ This Village Northern Italian "stands out from the pack" thanks to chef Sara Jenkins' "deeply flavored" pastas and other "farmer's market"–enhanced fare; it's an "accommodating", "pseudo-rustic" spot, but its "of-the-moment popularity" makes for a "noisy" scene.

Fifty Seven Fifty Seven 23 | 25 | 24 | $64
Four Seasons Hotel, 57 E. 57th St. (bet. Madison & Park Aves.), 212-758-5757;
www.fourseasons.com
■ A "feast for the eyes" and palate, this "incredibly stylish" New American in Midtown's Four Seasons Hotel wows its "smart" crowd with "unforgettable" food, "royal" service and "neo-elegant" I.M. Pei design; expect a "top-of-the-world" experience starting with "business breakfasts" and running through lunch and dinner to late-evening "power drinks" in the bar, albeit at prices that may make you think you're seeing double.

F.illi Ponte 21 | 20 | 20 | $57
39 Desbrosses St. (West Side Hwy.), 212-226-4621; www.filliponte.com
☑ So "removed from everything" that it "might as well be in NJ", this "venerable" TriBeCa Italian tries harder with "fabulous" traditional cooking, "beautiful" Hudson views and a "romantic" vibe; "consistent" quality all around helps defuse the "expensive" bill.

Finestra – | – | – | M
1370 York Ave. (73rd St.), 212-717-8594
A "laid-back" "neighborhood feel" prevails at this Yorkville Italian that's "perfect when you need a break" from cooking; its proximity to Weill Medical Center and the Hospital for Special Surgery makes it a good place to bump into your doctor after office hours.

Fino ▽ 20 | 17 | 22 | $44
4 E. 36th St. (bet. 5th & Madison Aves.), 212-689-8040; www.finon36.com ⊠
1 Wall Street Ct. (Pearl St.), 212-825-1924; www.finowallstreet.com
☑ Both the "solid" Murray Hill archetype and its younger Financial District sibling cater to "business" types with "dependable" Italian

fare and "professional service" (for a price); indeed, the Down[...] site is impressive enough for a "corporate-card" splurge.

Fiorello's Cafe ◑

| 20 | 17 | 19 | $44 |

1900 Broadway (bet. 63rd & 64th Sts.), 212-595-5330;
www.cafefiorello.com

■ Lincoln Center–goers count on this "convenient" Italian for its "skinny" gourmet pizzas and one of the "best antipasti" bars around, as well as "courteous" service in the face of "frenetic pre-curtain" pressure; in summer, alfresco tables offer "prime people-watching" and relief from the "loud", "jam-packed" room.

Fiorentino's

| 18 | 12 | 16 | $30 |

311 Ave. U (bet. McDonald Ave. & West St.), Brooklyn,
718-372-1445

☑ "Be ready to *mangia*" at this "unfancy" Gravesend "family Italian" that slings "ample" portions of "super" Neapolitan staples at "just-right" prices; "year after year" the style "never changes" – and neither does the "wait" to get in.

FIREBIRD

| 22 | 27 | 23 | $57 |

365 W. 46th St. (bet. 8th & 9th Aves.), 212-586-0244;
www.firebirdrestaurant.com

■ One of New York's "prettiest" restaurants, this "gilded" Russian duplex on Restaurant Row suggests what "dining in the Winter Palace" must have been like, from its "delectable" food fit for "czarist indulgence" to the royally "savvy service"; *da*, it's "crazy expensive", so to "avoid going into debt between dinner and the theater", bargain-hunters opt for the $40 prix fixe ($29 at lunch) – or bring a "Fabergé egg" to settle the check.

Firenze ◑

| 20 | 19 | 23 | $42 |

1594 Second Ave. (bet. 82nd & 83rd Sts.), 212-861-9368;
www.firenzenyc.com

■ "Cozy hideaways" don't get much more "intimate" than this "romantic" Upper East Side Tuscan where a "solid" menu is served in a snug (verging on "wedge-yourself-in") setting; maybe it's a "bit overpriced for a local bistro", but "aim-to-please" service makes for a "gracious", "friendly" mood.

Fish ◑

| 20 | 12 | 17 | $38 |

280 Bleecker St. (Jones St.), 212-727-2879;
www.fishtherestaurant.com

☑ Flying "under the radar" on busy Bleecker Street is this "understated" "neighborhood" place purveying "fresh", "simply prepared" seafood that "changes daily" (there's also a "terrific raw bar"); though the "nonatmosphere" draws barbs and service can be "hit or miss", "affordable" tabs keep the trade brisk.

Five Front

| 21 | 20 | 20 | $36 |

5 Front St. (Old Fulton St.), Brooklyn, 718-625-5559

■ It's a "bit out of the way", but this New American "sleeper" under the Brooklyn Bridge offers "more than meets the eye": "consistently tasty" grub, "low prices", an "efficient" staff and what may be Dumbo's "prettiest garden"; even better, the "laid-back atmosphere is a relief in an area that's too self-consciously hip."

5 Ninth

| – | – | – | E |

5 Ninth Ave. (bet. Gansevoort & Little W. 12th Sts.), 212-929-9460;
www.5ninth.com

One of the latest arrivals in the red-hot Meatpacking District, this Eclectic newcomer set in a rustic townhouse has generated lots of

-inflected cooking of up-and-coming chef Zak
ne Cafe); be prepared for a tight squeeze, as
nd the crowds are already large.

22 | **22** | **21** | **$44**

. (bet. Bowery & Lafayette St.), 212-253-5700;
www.fivepointsrestaurant.com

■ A "stream runs through the middle" of this "Zen-like" Med-American, a "rare find" off the beaten NoHo path featuring an "affordable", "first-rate" menu and "service with class"; some say the "understatedly elegant" decor is "undone" by noise, but at least there's "good eavesdropping" potential; P.S. "brunch is a must."

Fives
▽ **24** | **25** | **25** | **$60**

Peninsula Hotel, 700 Fifth Ave. (55th St.), 212-903-3918;
www.peninsula.com

■ "Civilized is the word" for this "well-kept secret" in the Peninsula Hotel where "meticulously prepared" French–New American food is served in "subdued" digs by "knowledgeable waiters"; no surprise, it's "pricey", though an adjacent wine bar offers lighter fare at lighter tariffs.

Flea Market Cafe ●
18 | **17** | **15** | **$29**

131 Ave. A (bet. 9th St. & St. Marks Pl.), 212-358-9282

☑ Enjoy "French atmosphere without the haze" (a "benefit of the no-smoking law") at this "loud" Alphabet City bistro opposite Tompkins Square Park that really "comes to life in summer when the doors open up"; "decent" low-cost chow and "kitschy" decor distract from the "indifferent service."

Fleur de Sel
25 | **21** | **24** | **$60**

5 E. 20th St. (bet. B'way & 5th Ave.), 212-460-9100;
www.fleurdeselnyc.com

■ Cyril Renaud's "flawless", "breath-of-Brittany" cooking draws huzzahs at this "small" Flatiron French "gem box" where the "exquisite preparations" are matched by "high-caliber service" "without the formality that makes other restaurants dull"; though most agree it's "worth every penny" – make that "*very many* pennies" – the $25 prix fixe lunch is a "wonder."

Flor de Mayo ●
20 | **9** | **15** | **$19**

484 Amsterdam Ave. (bet. 83rd & 84th Sts.), 212-787-3388
2651 Broadway (101st St.), 212-663-5520

☑ "Loyal locals" say the signature "roast chicken rules the roost" at this Upper West Side Peruvian-Chinese duo with "no atmosphere" and not much service, but beyond-"reasonable" tabs (it's "hard to spend more than $20" here); many prefer the Latino side of the menu to the "utterly generic" Sino offerings.

Flor de Sol ●⊠
20 | **22** | **18** | **$41**

361 Greenwich St. (bet. Franklin & Harrison Sts.), 212-366-1640

■ "Sexy as hell", this "sultry" TriBeCa Spaniard draws "shoulder-to-shoulder" crowds of "skinny" folk with its "dark", "candlelit" setting, "hot", "flirty" waiters and mind-bendingly "potent sangria"; while the tapas-heavy menu is "wonderful" and "well priced", it's "not the point" – "you go for the atmosphere."

Florent ●⊄
19 | **14** | **15** | **$28**

69 Gansevoort St. (bet. Greenwich & Washington Sts.), 212-989-5779;
www.restaurantflorent.com

■ "Best experienced in the wee hours", this "artsy" 24/7 French bistro is "still going strong" after 20 "trailblazing" years in the Meatpacking District and remains just the ticket for those "3 AM escargot" cravings;

its "haute diner" vittles (served by a "snippy", seen-it-all staff) draw "family crowds" by day and an interestingly "freaky" crew at night.

Flor's Kitchen
20 | 10 | 15 | $20

149 First Ave. (bet. 9th & 10th Sts.), 212-387-8949
170 Waverly Pl. (bet. 6th & 7th Aves.), 212-229-9926
www.florskitchen.com

◪ "No frills" sums up this East Village Venezuelan venerated for its "awesome arepas" and "unbeatable prices", if not its "marathon waits" (it has only 18 seats); the good news: it's spawned a somewhat larger Greenwich Village sibling that's equally "mouthwatering", if still undergoing some "growing pains."

Foley's Fish House
20 | 23 | 19 | $52

Renaissance NY Hotel, 714 Seventh Ave. (bet. 47th & 48th Sts.), 212-261-5200;
www.foleysfishhouse.com

■ The "oh! factor" at this otherwise "civilized" Theater District seafooder comes courtesy of its "stupendous" Times Square view (like "sitting in the middle of a postcard") that makes the food "taste even better"; all right, it's "a bit expensive", but it's still a "must-see" when you have "tourists" in tow.

Fontana di Trevi ⌧
▽ 18 | 15 | 19 | $43

151 W. 57th St. (bet. 6th & 7th Aves.), 212-247-5683;
www.fontanaditrevi.com

■ "Convenient" if you're bound for Carnegie Hall, this across-the-street Northern Italian provides "consistent", "old-fashioned" cooking and a notable "Caesar salad prepared tableside"; though service can be "slow", relatively "reasonable prices" make it "worth discovering."

44
20 | 23 | 17 | $52

Royalton Hotel, 44 W. 44th St. (bet. 5th & 6th Aves.), 212-944-8844;
www.ianschragerhotels.com

◪ "It's all about the decor" at this Midtown hotel dining room with a "glossy" interior and "must-see bathrooms" that tend to overwhelm the "reliable" if "expensive" French–New American vittles; trendoids yawn "it's so over", but on the flip side, it's now "actually quiet enough to have a real conversation."

44 & X Hell's Kitchen ●
21 | 18 | 19 | $41

622 10th Ave. (44th St.), 212-977-1170; www.44andX.com

■ "Comfort food to the max" (including one "helluva mac 'n' cheese") revs up Hell's Kitchen at this "stylish" New American with "airy" "Hamptons-like" looks and a "*Queer Eye for the Straight Guy* vibe" thanks to its "buff", "pretty-boy" staff; despite somewhat "pricey" tabs and a "far-from-civilization" address, it's still the "shining star of the neighborhood."

FOUR SEASONS ⌧
26 | 27 | 27 | $81

99 E. 52nd St. (bet. Lexington & Park Aves.), 212-754-9494;
www.fourseasonsrestaurant.com

■ "Everything's first-class – including the price" – at this "eternally fabulous" Midtown Continental where a "moneyed crowd" convenes in a "breathtaking", Philip Johnson–designed setting to savor "superb food" and "gold-standard" service; whether in the Grill Room for the "ultimate power lunch" or the Pool Room for a "present-the-diamond" dinner, it's the perfect opportunity to "see how well the other half eats."

14 Wall Street ⌧
19 | 21 | 20 | $48

14 Wall St., 31st fl. (bet. Broad St. & B'way), 212-233-2780

■ A masters-of-the-universe magnet, this Financial District French set in J.P. Morgan's "retrofitted" former apartment offers "beautiful"

Downtown views, a "staff that greets you by name" and a "well-prepared" if "expensive" menu; something of a "power-dining" locus at lunch, it's much "quieter" for dinner.

Fragole
▽ 22 | 16 | 20 | $26

394 Court St. (bet. Carroll St. & 1st Pl.), Brooklyn, 718-522-7133
■ Though "missing some of the hip edge of its predecessor, Max", this new Carroll Gardens Italian stays on target with "delicious homemade pastas" and other "consistent" standards, abetted by "attentive service" and popular pricing; a "cozy garden" out back allows the opportunity to "enjoy some sunshine with your food."

Franchia
▽ 23 | 24 | 23 | $28

12 Park Ave. (bet. 34th & 35th Sts.), 212-213-1001; www.franchia.com
■ "Metaphysical bliss" seekers zone out at this "spa-like" Murray Hill tea palace, a "Zen-tastic" spot showcasing an all-vegetarian Korean menu that's "inventive" if "expensive" for what it is; while the "minimalist decor" and "serene" vibe may "calm the soul", the vast selection of tea will "make your head spin."

Francisco's Centro Vasco
21 | 12 | 18 | $40

159 W. 23rd St. (bet. 6th & 7th Aves.), 212-645-6224
■ "Succulent", "sea monster"–size lobsters are the catch of the day every day at this "unpretentious" Chelsea Spaniard known for prices "so cheap you almost want to pay them more"; despite "tired" looks, "mobs" show up "early" to avoid the "long waits" – they "don't take reservations" here.

Frank ●⇄
22 | 14 | 15 | $28

88 Second Ave. (bet. 5th & 6th Sts.), 212-420-0202;
www.frankrestaurant.com
☑ "Value abounds" at this "very bohemian" East Village Southern Italian known for its "robust" cooking, "cheap" tabs and "minuscule" digs; expect "flighty service", "Early American garage-sale decor" and "lines down the block" (no reserving), but some pollyannas claim the inevitable "wait makes the food taste better."

Frankie & Johnnie's Steakhouse ⑤
22 | 13 | 18 | $53

269 W. 45th St. (bet. B'way & 8th Ave.), 212-997-9494 ●
32 W. 37th St. (bet. 5th & 6th Aves.), 212-947-8940
www.frankieandjohnnies.com
☑ A Theater District "classic that never changes", this circa-1926 "time-warp" steakhouse is "still nice to have around" despite "cranky" waiters and a "tight", "don't-plan-on-any-privacy" mezzanine setting; boosters say the roomier Garment District satellite is more "elegant", though just as "pricey" as its sibling.

Frank's
20 | 15 | 19 | $53

85 10th Ave. (15th St.), 212-243-1349
■ "Hidden" away in the far reaches of the Meatpacking District, this "above-average" Italian-accented steakhouse is "solid" though not cheap and "far from tops in the area"; its "humongous steaks", "respectful staff" and "unpretentious" air draw a "mostly male" crowd, hence its rep as a "bachelor-party heaven."

Franny's
– | – | – | M

295 Flatbush Ave. (bet. Prospect Pl. & St. Mark's Ave.), Brooklyn, 718-230-0221;
www.frannysbrooklyn.com
An immediate neighborhood hit, this simply appointed but seriously intentioned Prospect Heights pizzeria bakes up artisanal, crispy-crust pies in a wood-fired, brick-walled oven; high-quality ingredients (including house-cured meats) make the difference here.

Fraunces Tavern ⊠
16 | 21 | 18 | $40

54 Pearl St. (Broad St.), 212-968-1776; www.frauncestavern.com
☑ Your entree arrives "with a side of history" at this Financial District American celebrated as the spot where "George Washington bid farewell to his officers" in 1783; despite a menu as "dated as the Revolution" and a "touristy" crowd, fans admire its "wonderful building" and give it credit for "being around this long."

Fred's
17 | 16 | 18 | $28

476 Amsterdam Ave. (83rd St.), 212-579-3076
☑ "Pooch photos" line the walls of this "canine-themed" Upper Westsider where doggone good American "comfort food" comes with "comfort service" in a "comfort setting"; though some growl that it's "borderline boring", "reasonable prices" and "generous portions" have others sitting up and begging for more.

Fred's at Barneys NY
18 | 18 | 17 | $41

Barneys NY, 660 Madison Ave., 9th fl. (60th St.), 212-833-2200
■ "Serious shoppers" and the "flashy plastic surgery" set savor "gossipy lunches" and "intense people-watching" at this "stylish" Tuscan–New American tucked inside "trendy vendor" Barneys; sure, service can be "spotty" and it's "silly expensive", but honey, "if you can afford the clothes, you can afford the food."

French Roast ●
15 | 14 | 12 | $25

2340 Broadway (85th St.), 212-799-1533
458 Sixth Ave. (11th St.), 212-533-2233
☑ Visit "Paris (in a Disney kind of way)" via this bistro duo serving "fair" "faux French" fare to "youthful" types lured in by its 24/7 open-door policy; though roasted for "glorified coffee shop" looks and "doing-you-a-favor" service, at least they're "cheap and cheerful."

Frère Jacques
▽ 20 | 16 | 20 | $42

13 E. 37th St. (bet. 5th & Madison Aves.), 212-679-9355
■ "They have their act together" at this "unassuming" Murray Hill French bistro, a "charming" neighborhood "find" in an area "in need of good restaurants"; service "sans attitude" and prices that "won't break the bank" mean it won't stay a "secret" for long.

Fresco by Scotto ⊠
23 | 19 | 21 | $55

34 E. 52nd St. (bet. Madison & Park Aves.), 212-935-3434;
www.frescobyscotto.com
■ The "food's good enough to satisfy the most finicky heavy-hitter", so everyone from "Katie and Matt" to "Giuliani and Bloomberg" turns up at this Midtown Tuscan "power room" where the "big portions are made for big egos" and priced for big wallets; the Scotto clan's "welcoming" approach makes you "feel like family", but unlike your own family, "you can't wait to see them again."

Fresco on the Go ⊠
20 | 11 | 15 | $18

40 E. 52nd St. (bet. Madison & Park Aves.), 212-754-2700;
www.frescobyscotto.com
■ "If you don't have time for the real deal next door", this Fresco "quick-lunch" satellite offers "practically the same" Italian food at "cheaper" tabs; given the "tight", "good-luck-finding-a-seat" setup, most opt for takeout that's "head and shoulders above the typical" Midtown options.

fresh. ⊠
23 | 21 | 21 | $57

105 Reade St. (bet. Church St. & W. B'way), 212-406-1900;
www.freshrestaurant.com
■ "It's all in the name" at this "hip" TriBeCa fish palace, a "sailor's delight" where "inspired" offerings "right off the boat" dazzle deep-

sea diners; true, it's "wicked expensive" with a "middle-of-nowhere" address, but its "NY-chic" faux "underwater" setting and "down-to-earth" service put it "near the top of the seafood chain."

Friendhouse ● 18 | 16 | 17 | $24
132 St. Marks Pl. (Ave. A), 212-598-1188
99 Third Ave. (bet. 12th & 13th Sts.), 212-388-1838
■ With both Chinese and Japanese items on the menu, there's "something for everyone" at this "pleasant" East Villager that makes plenty of friends with its "attentive" service and "inexpensive" tabs; N.B. its newer St. Marks sibling is solely Japanese.

Friend of a Farmer 17 | 17 | 16 | $27
77 Irving Pl. (bet. 18th & 19th Sts.), 212-477-2188
◪ Channeling a "cozy Vermont B&B", this Gramercy American offers "hearty home cooking" at "non-splurge" prices in a space right out of "*Little House on the Prairie*"; though too "cutesy" and "chick"-oriented for manly men, it's still home to a "popular brunch."

Frutti di Mare ●≠ 17 | 13 | 16 | $25
84 E. Fourth St. (bet. Bowery & 2nd Ave.), 212-979-2034
◪ "Solid if unexceptional" is the word on this "unpretentious" East Village Italian seafooder best known for a $10.95 early-bird special that's almost "cheaper than if you cooked it yourself"; still, connoisseurs contemplating the "red-sauce" menu shrug "you get what you pay for."

Fujiyama Mama ● 19 | 17 | 18 | $38
467 Columbus Ave. (bet. 82nd & 83rd Sts.), 212-769-1144
◪ Sure, "time marches on", but not at this Upper West Side "'80s relic", still slicing up "disco sushi" to the tune of "blasting dance music" in a "techno environment"; though foes deride the "weary" decor and "so-so" menu, "if you're 16 and it's your birthday", look no further.

Fuleen Seafood ● ▽ 23 | 9 | 15 | $24
11 Division St. (bet. Bowery & E. B'way), 212-941-6888
■ "Forget the slow boat to China" – this Hong Kong–style Chinatown seafooder is accessible by the A train yet is as "close to the ocean as you can get" for "top-flight" fish; there's no doubting its "authenticity", though it's more navigable if you can find a waiter who "speaks English."

Funky Broome ● 18 | 10 | 13 | $23
176 Mott St. (Broome St.), 212-941-8628
◪ "Unusual" offerings that are "off the beaten menu track" make this "hip" NoLita Cantonese "more fun than the average Chinatown place", and it's "cheap" to boot; while downsides include "seen-better-days" decor (and service), word is it's "being renovated" – so fans are "hoping for the best."

Gabriela's 17 | 12 | 15 | $26
315 Amsterdam Ave. (75th St.), 212-875-8532
685 Amsterdam Ave. (93rd St.), 212-961-0574
www.gabrielas.com
◪ For the "fastest enchilada on the West Side", check out these "cheap and cheerful" Mexicans dispensing "monstrous portions" of "tasty" vittles; despite "Tijuana bus terminal" decor and a "roaring din" that stifles any "meaningful conversation", the overall mood is "festive" and very "kid friendly."

Gabriel's ▣ 23 | 19 | 22 | $53
11 W. 60th St. (bet. B'way & Columbus Ave.), 212-956-4600
■ Handy "before the opera" or "pre–mall shopping at the Time Warner Center", Gabriel Aiello's "enviable" Italian remains very much "in the

groove" with its "fabulous" Tuscan cooking, "handsome" looks and "unhurried, professional" service; if some find it "costly", others consider it a good value for such "luxe" conditions.

Gallagher's Steak House ●   19 15 17 $57
228 W. 52nd St. (bet. B'way & 8th Ave.), 212-245-5336;
www.gallaghersnysteakhouse.com
☑ "Harkening back to '30s NY", this longtime Theater District steakhouse fully "satisfies Atkins urges" with "man-size" hunks of meat dished out in large wood-paneled digs; fans say it's "been there forever for a reason", though the reason couldn't be the "testy waiters" or "unbelievable prices."

Gam Mee Ok ●   23 14 15 $21
43 W. 32nd St. (bet. B'way & 5th Ave.), 212-695-4113
■ The signature *sullongtang* beef soup "takes away all ills" and even "cures hangovers" at this "no-frills" Garment District Korean where the "limited" but "always reliable" menu is both "good and cheap"; service and decor deficits are overlooked given its 24/7 hours of operation.

Garden Cafe ☒   27 22 26 $44
620 Vanderbilt Ave. (Prospect Pl.), Brooklyn, 718-857-8863
■ "Great things come in small packages" at this "compelling" Prospect Heights New American where the "cuisine's miraculous and everything else is merely spectacular"; chef John Policastro "creates magic" in a "tranquil" space that's a "little larger than your own dining room" and staffed by servers whose "caring" ways make the food – voted No. 1 in Brooklyn in this *Survey* – even more enjoyable.

Gargiulo's   23 18 21 $42
2911 W. 15th St. (bet. Mermaid & Surf Aves.), Brooklyn, 718-266-4891;
www.gargiulos.com
■ "Old world" is putting it mildly at this circa-1907 Coney Island Neapolitan that's reminiscent of "*The Godfather*", what with the "trustworthy" food, "grand service" and abundance of "wedding parties"; despite the "not-so-great location", it's a "sure bet" for a "cheery" meal in "spacious" environs.

Gascogne   22 20 20 $47
158 Eighth Ave. (bet. 17th & 18th Sts.), 212-675-6564;
www.gascognenyc.com
■ A "quiet" refuge in a "loud city", the "secluded" back garden of this Chelsea bistro is a "great escape", but there's "*beaucoup d'ambiance*" in its "romantic" interior as well; the "unapologetically old-fashioned" Southwestern French cooking is equally "delicious" if "a little pricey."

Gavroche   – – – M
212 W. 14th St. (bet. 7th & 8th Aves.), 212-647-8553
This new, down-to-earth country French bistro in the West Village offers traditional favorites like hanger steak and charcuterie in a faux farmhouse setting; a large, vine-walled garden is already a popular refuge for an eclectic group of patrons.

Geisha ●☒   22 22 18 $59
33 E. 61st St. (bet. Madison & Park Aves.), 212-813-1113;
www.geisharestaurant.com
☑ "Beautiful Euros galore" show off their "fake tans" at this "super-trendy" new East Side Japanese, a "chic", David Rockwell–designed boîte featuring a "humming" ground-floor bar as well as a much more sedate upstairs dining room; "serious attitude" turns off many, and if the "top-of-the-line", French-inflected menu is "to die for, so is the price."

Gennaro ⌷
24 | 14 | 17 | $35

665 Amsterdam Ave. (bet. 92nd & 93rd Sts.), 212-665-5348

■ "Totally tasty", "stick-to-your-ribs" home cooking, "affordable" pricing and no reserving account for the "terribly long waits" at this "no-frills" Upper West Side Italian where diehards line up armed with "comfy shoes" and "sleeping bags"; once inside, "loud and lively is the order of the day."

Ghenet
▽ 21 | 13 | 17 | $28

284 Mulberry St. (bet. Houston & Prince Sts.), 212-343-1888; www.ghenet.com

☑ Call it digital dining: "your fingers" sub for utensils at this "cozy" NoLita Ethiopian that works especially well for big groups into "sharing" platters of "interesting", "change-of-pace" fare; if "service could be better" (ditto the decor), painless prices quiet most complaints.

Giambelli ◗
20 | 16 | 20 | $54

46 E. 50th St. (bet. Madison & Park Aves.), 212-688-2760; www.giambelli50th.com

☑ "Totally old school" describes the "reliable" cooking and "pro" service at this "comfortable" Midtown Northern Italian vet; modernists who tag it "tired" and "too expensive" for "1950s cuisine" are outvoted by those who say "still good after many, many years."

Gigino at Wagner Park
18 | 22 | 16 | $40

20 Battery Pl. (West St.), 212-528-2228

■ "Lady Liberty" is practically your tablemate at this waterside Financial District Italian with "amazing" harbor views and a "vacation-esque" vibe that peaks on the patio ("bring sunscreen" and "watch the world rollerblade by"); factor in "solid", not-too-costly food and the "inconsistent" service hardly matters.

Gigino Trattoria
21 | 18 | 18 | $39

323 Greenwich St. (bet. Duane & Reade Sts.), 212-431-1112

■ Tuscany meets TriBeCa at this "unpretentious" trattoria where the local "hip-bourgeois" set comes for "hearty", "well-executed" meals graciously served in a "warm", "rustic" room; that the "price is right" makes it all the more "rare" for the area.

Gino ⌷
20 | 14 | 19 | $41

780 Lexington Ave. (bet. 60th & 61st Sts.), 212-758-4466

■ Devoted regulars including "celebs from A list to Z" swear by this "clubby" yet homey East Side Italian that seemingly "hasn't changed" since the '40s; sure, "it's a little frayed", but those who cherish its "gutsy" red-sauce fare, classic "NY waiters" and zebra-bedecked walls say "with luck, it will last forever."

Giorgione
24 | 20 | 20 | $47

307 Spring St. (bet. Greenwich & Hudson Sts.), 212-352-2269

■ "Even Monday nights are filled with buzz" at this "off-the-beaten-path" West SoHo Italian co-owned by Giorgio DeLuca of gourmet-store fame; credit "spot-on" (if rather "pricey") cooking, "informative" service and classy/casual digs with a "perfectly Downtown" feel.

Giorgio's of Gramercy
23 | 19 | 22 | $41

27 E. 21st St. (bet. B'way & Park Ave. S.), 212-477-0007; www.giorgiosofgramercy.com

■ This "low-key" Flatiron "gem" is "still not very well known" despite its "well-crafted" New American cuisine, "good-deal" prices, "accommodating" servers and an "intimate" setting that's ripe for romance – if you don't have a date lined up, "make one on match.com and head right over."

Giovanni
21 | 18 | 19 | $

47 W. 55th St. (bet. 5th & 6th Aves.), 212-262-2828;
www.giovanni-ristorante.com

■ "Never had a bad meal" say fans of this "refined" Northern Italian that offers a prime Midtown location without typical Midtown turnoffs: it's "polite", "quiet" and "doesn't pack them in" too tightly; if prices aren't quite as "understated" as everything else, not many seem to notice.

Giovanni Venticinque
▽ 21 | 18 | 20 | $55

25 E. 83rd St. (bet. 5th & Madison Aves.), 212-988-7300

■ "Neighbors" and "museumgoers" famished after tackling the nearby Met like this "intimate" East Side Northern Italian for its "solid", "old-fashioned" food and "courteous" ways; maybe it's "more expensive than it should be", but it "serves a great purpose" in the area.

Girasole ◐
22 | 18 | 21 | $55

151 E. 82nd St. (bet. Lexington & 3rd Aves.), 212-772-6690

■ Like "a club" for locals, this Upper East Side Italian coddles its cadre of "wealthy, mature" regulars with "high-quality meals", "excellent" service and a "homey" (if your home is a townhouse) ambiance; nobody much minds that it's "a little pricey" and "noisy."

Gnocco Caffe ⊭
24 | 19 | 21 | $32

337 E. 10th St. (bet. Aves. A & B), 212-677-1913; www.gnocco.com

■ The "food will gnock you out" at this "cute" East Village Italian (don't miss the "fantastic" namesake fried dough appetizer), and the "awesome" garden, "friendly" prices and "sweet" service add to its punch.

Gobo ◑
24 | 21 | 20 | $30

401 Sixth Ave. (bet. Waverly Pl. & W. 8th St.), 212-255-3242;
www.goborestaurant.com

■ Carnivores, "cast your skepticism aside": you "won't miss meat" at this "stylish" West Village "hipster" haven that's ranked the No. 1 vegetarian in this *Survey* thanks to "inspired", mostly vegan fare with "Asian flair"; prices are "reasonable" and there are "killer desserts" – expect to leave feeling "too full" but "virtuous."

Golden Unicorn
20 | 12 | 12 | $22

18 E. Broadway, 2nd fl. (Catherine St.), 212-941-0911

☑ A "dim sum bonanza" awaits you at this "just like Hong Kong" Chinatowner that's a "madhouse" on weekends – "go early" or wait "forever"; its sprawling upstairs digs have the "charm of a bank branch" and service is "sporadic at best", but "good value" and lots of good tastes atone for a lot.

Gonzo ◑
22 | 18 | 19 | $40

140 W. 13th St. (bet. 6th & 7th Aves.), 212-645-4606

☑ Chef Vincent Scotto's vibrant Village Italian is a "sure thing" thanks to "divine", "wafer-thin" grilled pizzas and other "satisfying", "affordable" dishes served in a "warm", roomy setting complete with a "lively" front bar; "overwhelming noise" and sometimes "spotty" service are the price of popularity.

good
21 | 16 | 18 | $32

89 Greenwich Ave. (bet. Bank & W. 12th Sts.), 212-691-8080;
www.goodrestaurantnyc.com

■ To call it "pluperfect" is a stretch, but this "laid-back" West Villager surpasses its name thanks to updated New American "comfort food", easy prices and an "accommodating" staff; in sum, there's "nothing not good" about it, except the "huge brunch line."

...to Eat

20 | 15 | 16 | $24

... (bet. 83rd & 84th Sts.), 212-496-0163;
...eat.com

... hankering for "home cooking" head to this "cozy", "kid-friendly" "slice of Vermont" for "darned good" American standards "like (some) moms used to make"; the wildly popular brunch is "not for Atkins fans" or those averse to "mega-long" waits.

Googie's ◐

15 | 10 | 13 | $21

1491 Second Ave. (78th St.), 212-717-1122

☑ It's "like a baby petting zoo" at this family-centric, decor-challenged Upper East Side Italian diner known for its "addicting" fries and "insane" brunch lines; service can be "choppy", but the "large" menu, "large" portions and "small bill" "make it easy to eat out."

GOTHAM BAR & GRILL

27 | 25 | 25 | $67

12 E. 12th St. (bet. 5th Ave. & University Pl.), 212-620-4020;
www.gothambarandgrill.com

■ This "modern NY classic" has provided some 20 years of "high-end" Village dining and still stands tall in surveyors' esteem: chef Alfred Portale's "towering" New American creations continue to "tantalize", the "soaring-ceilinged" setting remains casually "glamorous" and service is "top-notch"; if prices also induce vertigo, a sure cure is the $25 bargain lunch.

Grace ◐

17 | 18 | 17 | $32

114 Franklin St. (bet. Church St. & W. B'way), 212-343-4200

☑ Though some say the "gorgeous" up-front bar "should clue you in" to this TriBeCa New American's raison d'être – "it's cocktail hour, baby!" – its "small-plate" menu is pretty "good" and served into the wee hours, making it a magnet for noshing "night-owls."

Grace's Trattoria

18 | 16 | 17 | $38

201 E. 71st St. (bet. 2nd & 3rd Aves.), 212-452-2323

☑ "Fresh ingredients" are a given at this "low-key", "comfy" Upper East Side Italian annex to gourmet grocer Grace's Marketplace; a few critics insist it "should be better", but most find it "pleasant" for "casual" dining and a "good deal" in a pricey zip code.

Gradisca ◐

∇ 18 | 16 | 17 | $36

126 W. 13th St. (bet. 6th & 7th Aves.), 212-691-4886

☑ "Simple, satisfying" pastas and other "reasonably priced" Italian eats are the draw at this "dark" Greenwich Village "grotto" that's very "romantic", though "less so when packed"; if service is "hit or miss", at least it's by "cute Italian" waiters.

GRAMERCY TAVERN

28 | 26 | 27 | $72

42 E. 20th St. (bet. B'way & Park Ave. S.), 212-477-0777;
www.gramercytavern.com

■ The "definition of fine dining" for many NYers, Danny Meyer's Flatiron New American – ranked No. 1 for Popularity this year – "exceeds expectations" on all fronts, from chef Tom Colicchio's "masterful" food to the "rustic" yet "luxuriant" decor and "beautifully choreographed", genuinely "warm" service; plan to book way ahead, and if you're price-conscious, try the less costly, but equally lovely, drop-in front tavern.

Grand Sichuan

22 | 8 | 13 | $23

125 Canal St. (Bowery), 212-625-9212 ⊅
227 Lexington Ave. (bet. 33rd & 34th Sts.), 212-679-9770
745 Ninth Ave. (bet. 50th & 51st Sts.), 212-582-2288
229 Ninth Ave. (24th St.), 212-620-5200 ◐

(continued)
Grand Sichuan
1049 Second Ave. (bet. 55th & 56th Sts.), 212-355-5855
19-23 St. Marks Pl. (bet. 2nd & 3rd Aves.), 212-529-4800
☑ "Chile heads" champion these low-cost, not-all-related Szechuans where "just reading" the "enormous" menu is an "adventure", but the real thrills start when the "nuclear heat" detonates in your mouth; the "esoteric" dishes trump the "abrupt" service and "mundane" decor.

Gray's Papaya ◑⇥
20 4 12 $4
2090 Broadway (72nd St.), 212-799-0243
539 Eighth Ave. (37th St.), 212-904-1588
402 Sixth Ave. (8th St.), 212-260-3532
☑ The city's "top dog" is arguably the "juicy", "snappy", "perfectly spiced" specimen served at these "legendary" 24/7 stand-up shacks where wiener wonks of all stripes "inhale" their fix and achieve "nirvana for under $5" – and the fruit drinks "ain't bad either"; N.B. you haven't been to NY until you've eaten here!

Great Jones Cafe ◑
23 15 16 $24
54 Great Jones St. (bet. Bowery & Lafayette St.), 212-674-9304;
www.greatjones.com
■ "Cheap", "down-home" Cajun "soul food" and a jammin' jukebox keep this "divey but homey" NoHo "hole-in-the-wall" bursting with "boho types"; brunch gets votes for "best in the land", especially if lubed with an "extra-spicy Bloody Mary" or three.

Great NY Noodle Town ◑⇥
23 4 12 $15
28½ Bowery (Bayard St.), 212-349-0923
☑ "Great is no overstatement" say fans who would "pay twice as much" for this Chinatowner's "succulent" eats, which go way beyond noodles; "gruff service", "lousy decor" and "communal" tables aren't so great, but the fact that it can be "jam-packed at 3 AM" says it all.

Green Field Churrascaria
▽ 18 13 17 $32
108-01 Northern Blvd. (108th St.), Queens, 718-672-5202;
www.greenfieldchurrascaria.com
☑ A meatpacking district in its own right, this "cavernous", "crowded", cost-effective Corona Brazilian BBQ is where servers "come a runnin'" with a "nonstop bombardment" of meat that ends only after you've "gorged yourself silly"; there's also a "cornucopia of salads", as if carnivores care.

Grey Dog's Coffee ⇥
22 18 17 $14
33 Carmine St. (bet. Bedford & Bleecker Sts.), 212-462-0041
■ "Cute", "good-vibed" Village cafe where "budget-minded nouveau bohemians" hang out over "super-sized breakfasts", "good strong coffee" and "inventive sandwiches"; on weekends, "cozy" turns into "crazy" "crowded", but "don't stress, you'll get a table" – eventually.

Grifone ⌧
25 19 24 $55
244 E. 46th St. (bet. 2nd & 3rd Aves.), 212-490-7275
■ A "class operation", this small, "sedate" UN-area Northern Italian "hideaway" offers "expertly prepared" food and "superior" service that's "very formal" yet "warm"; it draws an "older" crowd that clearly believes "civilized" dining is "worth paying for."

Grilled Cheese NYC ◑⇥
20 10 16 $11
168 Ludlow St. (bet. Houston & Stanton Sts.), 212-982-6600;
www.grilledcheesenyc.com
☑ Not your mama's grilled cheese, the "haute", "anti-Velveeta" versions served at this "tiny" Lower East Side sandwich shop come

in an "amazing" variety and make "great comfort food" for grown-ups; cynics say "dress it up all you want – it's still grilled cheese."

GRIMALDI'S ⊅
26 | 11 | 15 | $19

19 Old Fulton St. (bet. Front & Water Sts.), Brooklyn, 718-858-4300; www.grimaldis.com

■ Others are mere "cheesy imposters" declare devotees of this Dumbo coal-oven pizza paragon that sets a "benchmark" for the "real" thing, from the crust's "perfect char" to the "fresh-made" toppings; "long lines", "tight" tables, "lightning-speed" service and "Frank on the jukebox" round out this "requisite NY experience."

GROCERY, THE ⑤
26 | 17 | 24 | $50

288 Smith St. (bet. Sackett & Union Sts.), Brooklyn, 718-596-3335

■ It's "harder to get into" now that it's been "discovered", but this Carroll Gardens New American remains "true" to the strengths that first impressed locals: "impeccably prepared" seasonal fare from chef-owners Charles Kiely and Sharon Pachter, "caring" service and "sane" (for the quality) prices; since the "simple" room is small and crowded, aim for the "lovely" garden in summer.

Grotta Azzurra ●
▽ 18 | 16 | 15 | $44

387 Broome St. (Mulberry St.), 212-925-8775

☑ Surveyors are at a standoff over this "nouveau" resurrection of a Little Italy stalwart: to some it's a "welcome return" that's "better than most" in these touristy environs; to others it's "not even close" to the original, with "unprofessional" service drawing the most barbs.

Guastavino's
18 | 25 | 17 | $52

409 E. 59th St. (bet. 1st & York Aves.), 212-980-2455; www.guastavinos.com

☑ "It's mostly about the architecture" at Terence Conran's East Side New American set in a "phenomenal" vaulted-ceiling space under the Queensboro Bridge; while the food "really isn't a match" anymore, it's at least "good" if not cheap, though meals may be marred by "sketchy" service and "echoing" noise from the bar buzzing with "appletini types."

Gus' Place
20 | 17 | 20 | $36

149 Waverly Pl. (bet. 6th & 7th Aves.), 212-645-8511

■ You "gotta love Gus", the "affable" host who presides over this "relaxed" Greek-Med Villager, and locals also love his "solid" food, "fair prices" and staff that "makes you feel at home"; it's especially "delightful" when the doors open onto the sidewalk in summer.

Hacienda de Argentina ●
20 | 22 | 19 | $50

339 E. 75th St. (bet. 1st & 2nd Aves.), 212-472-5300

■ With its "pampa baronial" decor and "excellent" beef, this "cozy" East Side Argentinean steakhouse makes you feel like a "wealthy rancher" – one with "romance" in mind, given the "candlelight" and animal skins; service is "helpful", the tab's not overly steep and those empanadas are "must-haves."

Haikara Grill
▽ 20 | 17 | 17 | $48

1016 Second Ave. (bet. 53rd & 54th Sts.), 212-355-7000

☑ In a town not exactly teeming with kosher sushi options, this Eastsider is "as good as you can find" and partisans say its other Japanese–Pan-Asian fare is also "nicely done"; but even they concede service can be "slow" and the "steep prices add up."

Hakata Grill
20 | 14 | 16 | $32

230 W. 48th St. (bet. B'way & 8th Ave.), 212-245-1020

■ Below-average tabs for "above-average sushi" and other Japanese–Pacific Rim eats make this "casual" Theater District option a hit with the

B'way-bound and the deskbound ("aka the Morgan Stanley cafeteria"); it gets "cramped" but service is "efficient" and there's "fast delivery."

Halcyon
20 | 23 | 22 | $56

Rihga Royal Hotel, 151 W. 54th St. (bet. 6th & 7th Aves.), 212-468-8888
☑ "Subdued and civilized", this "luxurious" hotel New American in Midtown offers "well-prepared" food plus "unrushed" service and "widely spaced tables" for "stress-free" dining; a few find it "stuffy" and "routine", but "you can't go wrong with the pre-theater" prix fixe.

Hale & Hearty Soups ⊅
19 | 7 | 13 | $11

55 Broad St. (Beaver St.), 212-509-4100 🖾
Chelsea Market, 75 Ninth Ave. (bet. 15th & 16th Sts.), 212-255-2400
22 E. 47th St. (bet. 5th & Madison Aves.), 212-557-1900 🖾
Grand Central, lower level (42nd St. & Vanderbilt Ave.), 212-983-2845
849 Lexington Ave. (bet. 64th & 65th Sts.), 212-517-7600
Rockefeller Plaza, 30 Rockefeller Plaza (49th St.), 212-265-2117 🖾
462 Seventh Ave. (35th St.), 212-971-0605 🖾
55 W. 56th St. (bet. 5th & 6th Aves.), 212-245-9200 🖾
49 W. 42nd St. (bet. 5th & 6th Aves.), 212-575-9090 🖾
32 Court St. (Remsen St.), Brooklyn, 718-596-5600 🖾
Additional locations throughout the NY area
☑ "Speed and variety" are hallmarks of these efficient soup counters that ladle out "some real winners" plus "good" salads and sandwiches, but frugal types find it "pricey" for "are-you-kidding-me-small" portions.

Hallo Berlin
19 | 8 | 12 | $18

626 10th Ave. (bet. 44th & 45th Sts.), 212-977-1944
402 W. 51st St. (9th Ave.), 212-541-6248
☑ "Too many sausages" is the dilemma dumbfounding diners at these Hell's Kitchen German cheapies serving the best wursts plus other "old-fashioned" "beer-chugging food" – "you'll get bloated and love it", as long as you "don't expect much" by way of service or decor.

Hampton Chutney Co.
22 | 11 | 17 | $13

68 Prince St. (bet. B'way & Lafayette St.), 212-226-9996;
www.hamptonchutney.com
■ "Didn't know what it was, now I love it" say converts to this "soothing" SoHo Indian's "scrumptious" and "inventive" dosa wraps; it's "wonderful" low-cost "fast food" but "take it home" or you might have to "fight" for one of the few seats.

Hangawi
23 | 25 | 23 | $41

12 E. 32nd St. (bet. 5th & Madison Aves.), 212-213-0077;
www.hangawirestaurant.com
■ Achieve an "immediate sense of Zen" at this "shoes-off", "utterly serene" Murray Hill Korean vegetarian with "inspiring", "high-quality" food and an "attentive" staff; the enlightened focus on the "peace" and "quiet" rather than the "costly" "small portions."

Harbour Lights ●
17 | 22 | 17 | $43

South Street Seaport, Pier 17, 3rd fl. (bet. Fulton & South Sts.), 212-227-2800;
www.harbourlightsrestaurant.com
☑ It may be a tourist "mecca", but even natives get a "natural high" gazing at the "magic" harbor views from this Seaport New American's balcony; the fish-focused menu works best if you keep it "simple" and remember what you're really paying for.

Hard Rock Cafe ●
12 | 20 | 14 | $28

221 W. 57th St. (bet. B'way & 7th Ave.), 212-489-6565; www.hardrock.com
☑ NYers like to claim they were "dragged" by the "kids" or "relatives from Ohio" to this low-cost Midtown theme vet, but once there, most

find the burgers and other American standards "decent" and "made better" by the "music museum" decor; another plus: the "loud music drowns out the tourists."

Harrison, The
24 | 21 | 23 | $53

355 Greenwich St. (Harrison St.), 212-274-9310; www.theharrison.com
■ A "marvel" of "low-key cool", this "stylish but not intimidating" TriBeCa Med-American from Jimmy Bradley and Danny Abrams has it all: "terrific" food, "smart", studied service, "realistic" prices, a "classy" setting and super "star-spotting" – it's "no wonder you can never get in."

Harry Cipriani
23 | 20 | 21 | $73

Sherry Netherland, 781 Fifth Ave. (bet. 59th & 60th Sts.), 212-753-5566; www.cipriani.com
☑ At this "tiny" East Side Venetian, "big power players" and the "dripping-in-diamonds" set can be found air-kissing their way through a meal of "perfectly prepared pastas" and superb meats plus "incredible Bellinis"; it may cost a bundle to dine at its tightly packed, low "knee-banger" tables but a seat here buys you "great theater."

Haru
22 | 17 | 17 | $37

433 Amsterdam Ave. (bet. 80th & 81st Sts.), 212-579-5655 ◐
280 Park Ave. (48th St.), 212-490-9680
1329 Third Ave. (76th St.), 212-452-2230 ◐
1327 Third Ave. (76th St.), 212-452-1028 ◐
205 W. 43rd St. (bet. B'way & 8th Ave.), 212-398-9810
www.harusushi.com
■ A "hopping" sushi "scene" unfolds at these "loud, overcrowded" Japanese outlets where "young" things line up to feed on "monster-size" slabs of "not overly expensive" fish; service is all too often "rushed" – "I've had elevator rides longer than some Haru dinners."

Hasaki ◐
24 | 15 | 19 | $38

210 E. Ninth St. (bet. 2nd & 3rd Aves.), 212-473-3327; www.hasakinyc.com
■ "Premium quality" sushi that doesn't require "taking out a loan on the house" explains the appeal of this "cozy little" East Village Japanese with an "attentive" staff; "one big minus" is no reserving, but the wait is "worth it."

Hatsuhana ⌧
24 | 15 | 18 | $47

17 E. 48th St. (bet. 5th & Madison Aves.), 212-355-3345
237 Park Ave. (46th St.), 212-661-3400
www.hatsuhana.com
☑ "Simply sublime sushi" and sashimi are the calling cards of this "old-time" Japanese duo that pioneered the genre in Midtown decades ago; modernists say they've "seen better days", citing "stale" decor and overpricing, but "huge lunchtime crowds" suggest otherwise.

Havana Central
17 | 13 | 15 | $23

22 E. 17th St. (bet. B'way & 5th Ave.), 212-414-2298
☑ There's "lots of flavor" to be found at this "great-value" Cuban off Union Square that's "buffet-style at lunch" and full service come supper; though dissenters deride "super-slow" service and "marginal" cooking, all agree the "mojitos make everything taste better."

Havana Chelsea ⊟
▽ 20 | 7 | 13 | $19

190 Eighth Ave. (bet. 19th & 20th Sts.), 212-243-9421
■ "Knowing some Spanish goes a long way" at this "no-frills" Chelsea Cubano dishing up "tasty" grub that's "deceptively simple" and "definitely affordable"; just be aware that "customer service isn't their strength" and the "decor couldn't be more plain."

Haveli ●
21 | 17 | 19 | $30

100 Second Ave. (bet. 5th & 6th Sts.), 212-982-0533
■ "Heads above" the nearby "cookie-cutter competition" on Sixth Street, this "fragrant" East Village Indian offers well-spiced items from a "varied menu"; decorwise, there's a "refreshing lack of kitsch", so while you "pay a bit more" you get a lot more "class."

Hearth
24 | 20 | 23 | $55

403 E. 12th St. (1st Ave.), 646-602-1300; www.restauranthearth.com
■ Chef Marco Canora (ex Craft) brings "hearty" Tuscan-American cooking to the East Village via this "adventurous" newcomer that's already "filled with foodies" eyeballing its open kitchen; if the "deceptively simple", "exposed-brick" setting and "unpretentious" service belie its "serious" intentions, the "size of the bill" should convince you; P.S. the "back room is Siberia."

Heartland Brewery
14 | 13 | 14 | $27

1285 Sixth Ave. (51st St.), 212-582-8244
South Street Seaport, 93 South St. (Fulton St.), 646-572-2337
35 Union Sq. W. (bet. 16th & 17th Sts.), 212-645-3400 ●
127 W. 43rd St. (bet. B'way & 6th Ave.), 646-366-0235
www.heartlandbrewery.com
☑ A "lively atmosphere" is on tap at these "bustling" microbreweries where many eschew the "routine" pub grub and "stick with the beers"; brace yourself for a "frat boy central" crowd and a scene that morphs into a low-budget "meet market after dark."

Heidelberg
17 | 15 | 16 | $32

1648 Second Ave. (bet. 85th & 86th Sts.), 212-628-2332;
www.heidelbergrestaurant.com
■ There's still some "oompah-pah" left in Yorkville courtesy of this "last outpost of German gastronomy", a "kitschy throwback" replete with "hokey" decor and "waiters from another era"; ok, it might be "so old, it creaks", but it's still "hard to beat for the money."

Heights Cafe ●
17 | 18 | 17 | $29

84 Montague St. (Hicks St.), Brooklyn, 718-625-5555
☑ "Not far from the Promenade", this Brooklyn Heights New American "standby" has "great energy and looks" as well as key "outside seating" for "Montague Street people-watching"; still, critics complain the "patchy service" and "decent if uninspired" menu need work.

Hell's Kitchen
23 | 17 | 17 | $40

679 Ninth Ave. (bet. 46th & 47th Sts.), 212-977-1588;
www.hellskitchen-nyc.com
■ "Mexico never dreamed of" the "untraditional" offerings served up at this "inventive" Hell's Kitchen "hot spot" where you can "expect much more than tacos and enchiladas" at north-of-the-border prices; "hellish waits" and "deafening acoustics" come with the territory, but so does a "scintillating", "high-energy" mood.

Hemsin
▽ 21 | 9 | 16 | $24

39-17 Queens Blvd. (39th Pl.), Queens, 718-482-7998
■ "Only a brush stroke away from MoMA Queens", this Sunnyside "Turkish delight" supplies "flavorful" fare seemingly flown in from "Istanbul"; some say the "decor is nothing to write home about" (ditto the "erratic" service), but the "fair prices" are more newsworthy.

Henry's ●
17 | 18 | 16 | $32

2745 Broadway (105th St.), 212-866-0600
☑ "Spaciousness" is the trump card of this "much-needed" Upper West Side American where "you'll never have to wait" for a table,

though service ("somewhat inattentive") is another story; "predictable" chow at "affordable" prices keeps business "steady" here.

Henry's End
25 | 14 | 23 | $41

44 Henry St. (Cranberry St.), Brooklyn, 718-834-1776; www.henrysend.com

■ "You can't beat the game menu" at this Brooklyn Heights New American known for wildlife dishes so "inventive" they almost "need a patent"; despite a "lack of decor" and seating so "tight" you'll "feel like you're caged in the zoo", it's a "find", "especially for the price."

Highline ●
– | – | – | M

835 Washington St. (Little W. 12th St.), 212-243-3339; www.nychighline.com

The booming Meatpacking District extends its tentacles to Washington Street with the arrival of this new Thai triplex done up in a mod, *Austin Powers* style; though the utilitarian menu is priced to move, this one seems to be more about scene than cuisine.

Hispaniola ●
▽ 20 | 22 | 19 | $36

839 W. 181st St. (Cabrini Blvd.), 212-740-5222

■ "Bringing a bit of upscale dining" to a "starved-for-alternatives" area, this Washington Heights hybrid features "surprisingly good" Nuevo Latino–Asian food in a "beautiful" duplex setting; upstairs, the view of the GW Bridge distracts from the "spotty but well-intentioned service."

Hκ ●
▽ 20 | 19 | 16 | $28

523 Ninth Ave. (39th St.), 212-947-4208

■ "Trendy" comes to Hell's Kitchen via this "stylish", white-on-white New American in the "wasteland" behind the Port Authority; maybe it's "still working out the kinks" on the "inconsistent food and service", but locals are thrilled to find a "real restaurant" in these parts.

Hog Pit BBQ
17 | 8 | 14 | $22

22 Ninth Ave. (13th St.), 212-604-0092; www.hogpit.com

■ Deftly sidestepping the Meatpacking District's "onslaught of hipness" is this "real greasy" BBQ joint that appears to have been cloned from a "truck stop in Abilene"; regulars pigging out on the "cheap" chow shrug "it is what it is", but nevertheless are "glad the lights are low."

Holy Basil ●
23 | 18 | 18 | $28

149 Second Ave., 2nd fl. (bet. 9th & 10th Sts.), 212-460-5557

■ Thai disciples gather to "worship at the altar of masaman curry" at this "sexy" East Villager offering "fabulous" food at "amazing" prices; the setting may be "so dark you can hardly see", but it adds additional spice for those bent on "romance."

Home
21 | 17 | 18 | $37

20 Cornelia St. (bet. Bleecker & W. 4th Sts.), 212-243-9579

■ The moniker "says it all" at this Greenwich Village "trusty rock" where "comfort without the family angst" comes via "well-cooked American essentials"; the ultra-"snug" digs are redeemed by a "charming patio", but inside or out, most agree it's "really where the heart is."

HONMURA AN
26 | 24 | 24 | $51

170 Mercer St., 2nd fl. (bet. Houston & Prince Sts.), 212-334-5253

■ "Otherworldly tranquility" alights in SoHo at this "most wondrous" Japanese noodle specialist that elevates dining to "stellar" heights with its "heavenly soba", "thoughtful service" and "cool, serene environment"; definitely in a "class of its own", it satisfies "every yen" – at least "until the bill comes."

Hope & Anchor ☻   ▽ 20 17 20 $23

347 Van Brunt St. (Wolcott St.), Brooklyn, 718-237-0276

■ A "welcome bastion of hipness" in "off-the-beaten-track" Red Hook, this American diner is a "solid" choice, particularly for brunch or its "must-try" cheese steak; its buzzing nightlife scene really starts to hum with the weekend karaoke.

Houston's   20 18 18 $34

Citicorp Ctr., 153 E. 53rd St. (enter at 54th St. & 3rd Ave.), 212-888-3828
NY Life Bldg., 378 Park Ave. S. (27th St.), 212-689-1090
www.houstons.com

■ "There's never a dull moment" or a culinary misstep at this handsome American duo that impresses even "hard-to-please NYers" who "don't care that it's a chain"; "run like a tight ship" with "shockingly good service", it's renowned for its "legendary spinach dip" as well as the "ridiculous waits" to get in.

HSF   20 11 13 $23

46 Bowery (bet. Bayard & Canal Sts.), 212-374-1319

☑ "Not for the faint of heart", this "noisy", "crazy" C-town Cantonese offers a wide variety of dim sum for "cheap" sums; downsides include a "grungy" atmosphere, "communal" tables and an "English-challenged" staff that could use a "refresher course in service."

Hudson Cafeteria ☻   18 22 17 $43

Hudson Hotel, 356 W. 58th St. (bet. 8th & 9th Aves.), 212-554-6000;
www.chinagrillmgt.com

☑ There's surprisingly good food to be had at this West Side American-Eclectic set in a dark, "gothic" version of a "high school cafeteria", replete with "communal" tables and a "see-and-be-seen patio"; it's "not as trendy as it used to be", so "if the staff acts cooler than you, maybe they are."

Hue ☻   19 23 15 $49

91 Charles St. (Bleecker St.), 212-691-4575

☑ "Be prepared to wait" – "someone prettier than you just walked into" this Village Vietnamese duplex where "skinny" types toy with "tasty" vittles and plot crash strategies for the "sexy", more exclusive downstairs lounge; "outlandish" prices and service that's "hue too slow" come with the "trendy" territory.

Hunan Park ☻   18 9 15 $21

235 Columbus Ave. (bet. 70th & 71st Sts.), 212-724-4411

■ "So much food", so "little elbow room" sums up the scene at this Upper West Side Chinese where the cooking's "above average" and the cost is "low"; aesthetes avoid the rather "dingy" digs (and its "cheesy celebrity photo" montages) by opting instead for "mind-bogglingly fast delivery."

Ian   22 19 18 $47

322 E. 86th St. (bet. 1st & 2nd Aves.), 212-861-1993; www.ianrestaurant.com

■ "SoHo comes to the Upper East Side" at this "zippy" New American parked along the 86th Street "wasteland", where "quality" cuisine and "chic" decor hint at plenty of "potential"; maybe the service and price point "need work", but adherents are willing to stick by as it works out the "kinks."

Ichiro ☻   – – – M

1694 Second Ave. (bet. 87th & 88th Sts.), 212-369-6300;
www.ichi-ro.com

Spare but spacious, this Upper East Side Japanese features a soothing motif of birch trunks along the walls that brings a breath of nature to the concrete jungle; the midpriced menu runs the gamut from sushi and sashimi to hot entrees.

Ici
_ | _ | _ | M

246 DeKalb Ave. (bet. Clermont & Vanderbilt Aves.), Brooklyn, 718-789-2778

A new arrival to the underserved Fort Greene scene, this French bistro purveys a small seasonal menu of classics made from quality ingredients like free-range meat and organic dairy products; its herb-filled courtyard adds some Gallic élan.

I Coppi
23 | 21 | 20 | $46

432 E. Ninth St. (bet. Ave. A & 1st Ave.), 212-254-2263

■ The "Tuscan sun" shines on this "rustic" East Villager where outdoorsy types swear the "lush, year-round garden" will make you "swoon" – if the "outstanding" food and "romantic" atmosphere haven't already done so; it's "like nowhere else Downtown", so be prepared to pay for the experience.

Ida Mae ⊠
22 | 18 | 17 | $50

111 W. 38th St. (bet. B'way & 6th Ave.), 212-704-0038;
www.idamae.com

■ Bringing a shot of "soul to the Garment District", this "jazzy" New American puts forth an "interesting" menu full of "Southern flair"; "big prices", a "middle-of-nowhere" address and "noise" from the "enormous bar" are downsides, but locals hope it's a portent of a "neighborhood renaissance."

Ideya
20 | 16 | 17 | $34

349 W. Broadway (bet. Broome & Grand Sts.), 212-625-1441;
www.ideya.net

■ "Hip, young" types take a "mini-vacation" at this "lively" SoHo scene where "casual Caribbean" eats at "reasonable" tabs make for a year-round "summer destination"; no one minds the "slow", islands-paced service after a couple of "fabulous mojitos."

Il Bagatto
24 | 17 | 15 | $32

192 E. Second St. (bet. Aves. A & B), 212-228-0977

☑ "Happening" East Village Italian famed for a "no-fail" menu at prices that "won't kill your wallet"; the trade-offs are "forgettable decor", "ridiculous waits" and service that "gives attitude a new meaning", yet despite the "aggravation", many just plain "worship this place."

Il Buco ◐
23 | 23 | 20 | $52

47 Bond St. (bet. Bowery & Lafayette St.), 212-533-1932;
www.ilbuco.com

■ There's ambiance to spare at this "transporting" "antique-filled" NoHo Med that "almost makes you forget you're in NY" with its "romantic" mien; an "inspired" menu and "top-notch" service are more reasons why it can be so "challenging to get a seat" here.

Il Cantinori ◐
22 | 21 | 21 | $57

32 E. 10th St. (bet. B'way & University Pl.), 212-673-6044; www.il-cantinori.com

■ "A-listers" and "regular customers" alike are "treated like stars" at this "celeb"-heavy Village Northern Italian featuring "solid" food, a "glamorous setting" and exactly the "right amount of aloof"; just bear in mind that supping with the "limousine crowd" can be a "wallet buster."

Il Corallo Trattoria ◐
22 | 14 | 19 | $23

176 Prince St. (bet. Sullivan & Thompson Sts.), 212-941-7119

■ The "space is a little tight", but the portions are "enormous" at this SoHo Italian where some surveyors are "still reading" the "endless", "all-pasta-all-the-time" menu; though the "atmosphere leaves something to be desired", "great bang for the buck" satisfies everyone.

Il Cortile ☻   23 | 20 | 19 | $48
125 Mulberry St. (bet. Canal & Hester Sts.), 212-226-6060
■ A "comforting retreat" from "Mulberry Street chaos", this 30-year-old Little Italy "standby" is among the "least touristy" in the area, boasting "excellent" Italian cooking and a "stunning", skylit Garden Room; still, some warn that the "old-country" food comes at decidedly "new-country" prices and there may be lines on weekends.

Il Covo dell'Est   20 | 18 | 18 | $37
210 Ave. A (13th St.), 212-253-0777
■ This "robust" East Village Northern Italian puts forth reliably "tasty" repasts reminiscent of "eating at a favorite relative's"; a "pleasant", "low-key" vibe and fair pricing help distract from the sometimes "forgetful" service.

Il Fornaio   19 | 12 | 18 | $29
132A Mulberry St. (bet. Grand & Hester Sts.), 212-226-8306
☑ "Red sauce worth hiking Downtown for" attracts the intrepid to this "mom-and-pop joint" in Little Italy with "inexpensive" Italian food and "no sidewalk solicitors" out front; maybe the "decor could be better", but after a "stroll through the neighborhood", it's a filling "destination."

Il Gatto & La Volpe   ▽ 21 | 14 | 20 | $40
1154 First Ave. (bet. 63rd & 64th Sts.), 212-688-8444;
www.ilgattolavolpe.com
☑ There's a "neighborhoody" feel to this "friendly" East Side Italiano, a "drop-in kind of place" where the menu makes all the "familiar nods" to "classic favorites"; its "unassuming" air allows for "pleasant dining", despite the "tiny", "tight-fit" setup.

Il Gattopardo   22 | 17 | 21 | $57
33 W. 54th St. (bet. 5th & 6th Aves.), 212-246-0412
■ This Midtown Southern Italian may be relatively "unknown", but it satisfies stalwarts who don't mind that there's "nothing flashy" on its "solid regional" menu; "amazing meatballs", an "upbeat" staff and stiff tabs supply the sizzle in the otherwise "sparse" setting.

Il Giglio ⌖   25 | 18 | 23 | $65
81 Warren St. (bet. Greenwich St. & W. B'way), 212-571-5555;
www.ilgiglionyc.com
■ "Come to feast, not just dine" at this "extravagant" TriBeCa Tuscan where "they start feeding you the moment you walk in" and don't stop "until you leave"; expect a "top-tier" menu, "over-the-top" service and prices so high "they should include a hotel room" along with the meal.

Il Menestrello ⌖   ▽ 22 | 16 | 22 | $54
14 E. 52nd St. (5th Ave.), 212-421-7588
☑ This "respectable" Midtown "throwback" has "been around forever" and still draws regulars with a "solid" (if somewhat "dated") Italian menu; similarly, the decor may be "a touch old-fashioned", but at least the "old-school" staff is as well "seasoned" as the food.

Il Monello   23 | 19 | 23 | $56
1460 Second Ave. (bet. 76th & 77th Sts.), 212-535-9310
■ It "feels like a family affair" at this Upper East Side Northern Italian, what with the "couldn't-be-nicer" service and "old-world" cooking that seems to have come straight from "mama's kitchen"; "so long as you have the bucks", you can count on an "outstanding meal" in a "romantic atmosphere."

IL MULINO ⑤

27 | 17 | 23 | $77

86 W. Third St. (bet. Sullivan & Thompson Sts.), 212-673-3783;
www.ilmulinonewyork.com

■ "Don't you have a higher rating?" ask fans of this 25-year-old Villager that reclaims its long-held ranking as the *Survey's* No. 1 Italian after a hiatus last year; for the "few lucky souls" with "fast redial fingers" who manage to snag an "impossible" reservation, it's a "fabulously executed", "garlic"-laden "food orgy" replete with "incredible" black-tie service and "empty-the-bank-account" tabs; N.B. it may be even better for lunch, and is certainly less crowded.

Il Nido ⑤

23 | 18 | 22 | $61

251 E. 53rd St. (bet. 2nd & 3rd Aves.), 212-753-8450

■ Oozing "old-world charm", this longtime East Side Northern Italian "doesn't change and doesn't need to" given its "damn good food" and "earnest service"; perhaps a "bit stuffy" for younger diners, it's a perfect fit for "expense-accounters" who barely notice the "steam coming off their credit cards."

Il Palazzo

24 | 19 | 22 | $40

151 Mulberry St. (bet. Grand & Hester Sts.), 212-343-7000

■ A "solid performer in an ever-shrinking market" describes this Mulberry Street Italian that's one of the "best on the block", offering cooking that's "better than grandma's" plus "attentive", "thought-the-waiter-was-going-to-feed-me" service; the "beautiful", newly glassed-in garden might explain the slightly "higher-than-average cost."

Il Postino ●

23 | 18 | 21 | $62

337 E. 49th St. (bet. 1st & 2nd Aves.), 212-688-0033;
www.ilpostinorestaurant.com

◨ The food's "just as good as the movie" at this East Side Italian known for waiters who recite a "dizzying laundry list of specials" rather than trouble you with a menu; but those who knock the "pushy", "hard-sell" approach say that sticking to the specials can be "*molto* expensive."

Il Riccio ●

∇ 22 | 14 | 19 | $47

152 E. 79th St. (bet. Lexington & 3rd Aves.), 212-639-9111

■ It's a "tight fit" at this Upper East Side "neighborhood" joint, but regulars "hold their breath" and squeeze in for "wonderful" if not cheap Southern Italiana; the chance that there's a "celebrity seated" nearby lends frisson to the otherwise "informal" atmosphere.

Il Tinello ⑤

∇ 22 | 19 | 25 | $59

16 W. 56th St. (bet. 5th & 6th Aves.), 212-245-4388

■ Dreamers imagine that the "sumptuous" traditional fare at this "upscale" Midtown Northern Italian is "faxed directly from Italy", along with the "superb", "white-glove" service from "waiters in full dress"; a hot "business lunch spot", it draws mature folks unfazed by the high-end pricing.

Il Vagabondo ●

17 | 14 | 17 | $38

351 E. 62nd St. (bet. 1st & 2nd Aves.), 212-832-9221

◨ Like "dinner at your favorite aunt's", this East Side Italian "time warp" dishes out "big portions of red-sauce favorites" with a dollop of "gimmick": a "unique" indoor bocce ball court; the "below-par" service and decor, however, are "nothing to write home about."

Il Valentino

∇ 19 | 18 | 18 | $52

Sutton Hotel, 330 E. 56th St. (bet. 1st & 2nd Aves.), 212-355-0001;
www.thesutton.com

◨ Ok, it's "not a hopping spot", but this "comfortable" Northern Italian draws "older Sutton Place" types with its "reliable" cooking and

"pleasant" live music; still, foes bemoan its "luxury" price ta~~
the "sketchy" food and service "need improvement."

Inagiku
23 | 21 | 20 | $3~~

Waldorf-Astoria, 111 E. 49th St. (bet. Lexington & Park Aves.), 212-355-0440; www.inagiku.com

■ "Exceptional dishes at high prices" sums things up at this "unsung" Japanese "hidden in the Waldorf"; "even the rice tastes expensive", but fans say "you get what you pay for", citing the "melt-in-your-mouth" sushi, "geishalike" service and "spare but beautiful" digs.

Indochine ●
21 | 20 | 17 | $46

430 Lafayette St. (bet. Astor Pl. & E. 4th St.), 212-505-5111

■ An "'80s glow" still shimmers at this "retro glam" French-Vietnamese near the Public Theater that wins the "hip longevity award" for conjuring up a "scene" after 21 years in business; its ever-"pretty" following credits the "renaissance" to its "delicate flavors" and "exotic" looks, not the "service with two speeds: slow and slower."

industry (food) ●☒
19 | 23 | 17 | $47

509 E. Sixth St. (bet. Aves. A & B), 212-777-5920; www.industryfood.com

☑ Despite its "major scenester" rep, this "cool", "ski lodge"–like East Villager has a "lip-smacking" New American menu that's "on par with the buzz", though it still plays second fiddle to the "packed bar"; its "look-at-me" crowd tolerates the "slow" service and "high price tags", but can't decide if it's "a club or a restaurant."

Indus Valley
▽ 23 | 17 | 19 | $29

2636 Broadway (100th St.), 212-222-9222

■ "Sorely needed" on the Upper West Side say fans of this "fabulous" Indian newcomer supplying "strong flavor without excessive hotness" via "accurate, delicate spicing"; a "welcoming staff", "quick delivery" and decent pricing make this one "way above average" for the area.

'ino ●⊭
25 | 15 | 18 | $22

21 Bedford St. (bet. Downing St. & 6th Ave.), 212-989-5769; www.cafeino.com

■ Snackers adore this "primo" Village "panini palace" purveying "perfect matrimony" via "budget"-priced, "sinfully delectable" small plates wedded to an "easy-to-navigate" wine list; "cute as a button" and about as small, it's a magnet for "fashion-conscious" folk who don't mind experiencing "how sardines feel."

'inoteca ●
23 | 19 | 21 | $32

98 Rivington St. (Ludlow St.), 212-614-0473; www.inotecanyc.com

■ Although "bigger" than its "little cousin 'ino", this "delectable" Lower East Side panini-and-vino vendor is just as "crowded" with seekers of "la dolce vita"; the "vast wine list" and rather "annoying menu in Italian" are more navigable thanks to the "knowledgeable" staff, while the "low" pricing needs no translation.

Inside
▽ 20 | 16 | 19 | $42

9 Jones St. (bet. Bleecker & W. 4th Sts.), 212-229-9999; www.insideonjones.com

■ The menu morphs "seasonally" at this "relaxing" Village New American, a "small treasure" that "still seems to be a secret" despite its "first-rate" comfort chow; a "cozy" setup, "attentive" service and fairly "reasonable" tabs add to its allure.

Intermezzo
17 | 16 | 18 | $30

202 Eighth Ave. (bet. 20th & 21st Sts.), 212-929-3433; www.intermezzony.com

☑ "Decent", "dependable" Italiana at "good-value" prices makes this Chelsea "neighborhood" spot a good option "before a performance

...bel it "ordinary", citing "inconsistent
...be.

19	11	16	$27

...31st Sts.), 212-447-5822

"...y prizes" (especially for decor), but this
"plea...ay Hill Japanese nevertheless "does the
job", slicing up ...eces of "solid", "inexpensive" sushi; foes
say its "hit-or-miss" approach needs ironing out.

Isabella's ◑

19	19	18	$38

359 Columbus Ave. (77th St.), 212-724-2100;
www.brguestrestaurants.com

■ "Active Gen-X types" still line up for Steve Hanson's "busy, busy, busy" Westsider, a "very New Yorky" "social scene" fueled by a pleasing Med–New American menu; famed for its weekend "brunch crunch", it's really "jammed" come summertime when the "great sidewalk cafe" is in full swing.

Island Burgers ⇄

23	7	12	$15

766 Ninth Ave. (bet. 51st & 52nd Sts.), 212-307-7934

■ "Amazing shakes" and "decadent burgers" compensate for the "annoying lack of french fries" at this bustling Hell's Kitchen patty palace; all right, the "remote location" and "zero decor" make "takeout advisable", but in or out, this one's all about "bang for the buck, baby."

Ithaka ◑

19	15	17	$39

308 E. 86th St. (bet. 1st & 2nd Aves.), 212-628-9100;
www.ithakarestaurant.com

☑ "Simply prepared fresh fish" surfaces in Yorkville at this Hellenic seafooder known for its "warm" proprietor and "pure Greek island" ambiance; too bad it's "never busy", but at least there's "never a problem getting a table."

I Tre Merli ◑

16	17	16	$39

463 W. Broadway (bet. Houston & Prince Sts.), 212-254-8699
183 W. 10th St. (7th Ave.), 212-929-2221
www.itremerli.com

☑ A "long, inviting bar" keeps this 20-year-old SoHo "warhorse" hopping, abetted by "stylish looks", a "central location" and "reliable" Italian cooking (forget the "ditsy staff"); its new, "cute-as-a-button" West Village sibling is "smaller and cozier" and still "trying to find its feet."

I Trulli ☒

23	21	21	$53

122 E. 27th St. (bet. Lexington Ave. & Park Ave. S.), 212-481-7372;
www.itrulli.com

■ "Romantic trysts" make sense at this "intimate" Gramercy Park Southern Italian where "superb" Apulian cuisine and a "dynamite" vino selection can be savored "in the garden or by the hearth"; it's "expensive, but worth it", though the adjacent wine bar also offers a "damn good meal" for less.

Itzocan ⇄

25	12	21	$26

438 E. Ninth St. (bet. Ave. A & 1st Ave.), 212-677-5856
1575 Lexington Ave. (101st St.), 212-423-0255

■ For "big flavors in a tiny restaurant", check out this "thimble-size" East Villager where you "won't spend many pesos" on haute Mexican cuisine brimming with "fantastic" flavor; fans wishing "there were more like it" will be happy that a somewhat larger sibling has just arrived in the Upper Upper East Side.

Ivo & Lulu ⊠⊄ ▽ 23 13 22 $22

558 Broome St. (bet. 6th Ave. & Varick St.), 212-226-4399

■ The "all-organic menu" may be "short on options" but it's long on "flavor" at this "little" SoHo French-Caribbean, a "much-needed" option in an area "that's more about fanfare than food"; the BYO policy enhances its "good value", though advocates aver it's "standout dining at any price."

Ivy's Cafe ● 18 10 17 $23

154 W. 72nd St. (bet. B'way & Columbus Ave.), 212-787-3333

☑ Something of a "best-kept secret" on the Upper West Side, this affordable "mix 'n' match" Asian "pleases all palates" with both Japanese and Chinese offerings; some say the "nothing-to-look-at" decor proves you "can't judge a book by its cover", but aesthetes still find it "best for takeout."

Ixta – – – E

48 E. 29th St. (bet. Madison Ave. & Park Ave. S.), 212-683-4833; www.ixtarestaurant.com

Despite its motto – 'fun dining, not fine dining' – this Gramercy cantina aspires to a higher standard than your local taco joint, starting with striking decor that's a mix of mirrors, votives and flower blossoms; a large selection of tequilas gives the upscale Mexican chow an Ixta boost.

Jack's Luxury Oyster Bar ⊠ 24 23 24 $74

246 E. Fifth St. (bet. 2nd & 3rd Aves.), 212-673-0338

■ A "diamond in the rough East Village", this "dollhouse"-size French-Southern from the Jewel Bako team delivers "maximum enjoyment from the tiniest of spaces"; expect "sublime" food, "top-notch" service and a "romantic", bi-level setup, but be aware that all this luxury makes for one "high-price ticket."

Jackson Diner ⊄ 23 11 16 $22

37-47 74th St. (bet. Roosevelt Ave. & 37th Rd.), Queens, 718-672-1232

■ For a "heat quotient" that will "clear your sinuses", "hot-stuff" seekers head for this Jackson Heights Indian renowned for its $8.95 prix fixe, "stuff-yourself-silly" weekend lunch buffet; despite "lackluster" service and a "high-school-cafeteria" ambiance, it's "worth hopping on the 7 train" for this taste of "modern Bombay."

Jackson Hole 17 10 14 $18

517 Columbus Ave. (85th St.), 212-362-5177 ●
232 E. 64th St. (bet. 2nd & 3rd Aves.), 212-371-7187 ●
1270 Madison Ave. (91st St.), 212-427-2820
1611 Second Ave. (bet. 83rd & 84th Sts.), 212-737-8788 ●
521 Third Ave. (35th St.), 212-679-3264
69-35 Astoria Blvd. (70th St.), Queens, 718-204-7070 ●
35-01 Bell Blvd. (35th Ave.), Queens, 718-281-0330 ●

☑ "Massive burgers" that could "feed a small nation" are the "sloppy" specialty of these all-over-town "greasy spoons"; "mosh pit" settings, "marginal" service and a "big side of noise" don't deter their myriad fans, including "discriminating seven-year-old food critics."

Jacques Brasserie 18 18 18 $40

204-206 E. 85th St. (bet. 2nd & 3rd Aves.), 212-327-2272

☑ "Solid and reliable" if a tad "uninspired", this Yorkville French brasserie tries hard with "generous portions", "friendly service" and a "faux Parisian" setting; though foes say it's "not memorable", the Tuesday night special allows bargain-hunters to flex their mussels with Belgian beer.

Jacques-Imo's NYC
20 | 18 | 18 | $37

366 Columbus Ave. (77th St.), 212-799-0150

☑ For "real N'Awlins cooking in Noo Yawk", check out this Big Easy legend transplanted to the Upper West Side complete with its "authentic" Cajun-Creole menu and "party atmosphere"; despite some "kinks", the prognosis is "promising", with insiders already clucking about that "must-have fried chicken."

Jaiya Thai ●
22 | 9 | 14 | $28

396 Third Ave. (28th St.), 212-889-1330; www.jaiya.com

☑ Brace yourself for a "spicy night" at this Gramercy Thai where they "kick things up a notch" with heat levels high enough to practically "melt your fillings"; the slightly "off" service and "bare-bones" setting aren't so hot, but the "affordable" tabs are quite cool.

Jane ●
21 | 18 | 20 | $38

100 W. Houston St. (bet. La Guardia Pl. & Thompson St.), 212-254-7000; www.janerestaurant.com

■ "Anything but plain", this "trendy" New American on the Village-SoHo border wins kudos for its "standout brunch", "decent prices" and "better service than you'd expect at a hipster joint"; just "don't plan on any audible conversation" as you peruse the "reliable" menu.

Japonica
22 | 14 | 19 | $40

100 University Pl. (12th St.), 212-243-7752

☑ "Drool-worthy sushi" in "orca"-size portions tells the story at this Village Japanese; ignore the "worn-out" looks, and "don't be on a budget": prices are "high", but "you get twice as much as other places."

Jarnac
23 | 20 | 23 | $49

328 W. 12th St. (Greenwich St.), 212-924-3413; www.jarnacny.com

■ A "tiny island" of "relaxation" in the humming West Village, this "quintessential neighborhood" French bistro features "serious" food "prepared with love and pride"; the "friendly" staff includes a "roving chef" and "hospitable host" who might even "sit with you for a while."

Jasmine
20 | 16 | 17 | $25

1619 Second Ave. (84th St.), 212-517-8854

■ This Upper East Side Thai "tantalizes taste buds" with "flavorful" fare that won't "wallop your wallet"; if the "minimal" decor and "very busy" pace don't appeal, "extremely fast delivery" is a good alternative.

Jasper ●
– | – | – | M

504 La Guardia Pl. (bet. Bleecker & Houston Sts.), 212-475-9601; www.jaspernyc.com

Civilized dining comes to a frat-friendly strip of the Village via this white-tablecloth New American featuring a well-parsed, well-cooked menu that's just the ticket for entertaining visiting parents; even better, you won't need a student loan to settle the check.

Jean Claude ⌀
23 | 15 | 19 | $39

137 Sullivan St. (bet. Houston & Prince Sts.), 212-475-9232

■ For a "true Parisian dining experience", try this "très français" SoHo bistro offering "delicious" food in petite, "elbow-to-elbow" quarters; prices are fairly "relaxing to the pocket", yet quibblers "wish they accepted credit cards."

JEAN GEORGES ☒
27 | 26 | 26 | $93

Trump Int'l Hotel, 1 Central Park W. (bet. 60th & 61st Sts.), 212-299-3900; www.jean-georges.com

■ "You'll never look at food in the same way" after a meal at Jean-Georges Vongerichten's "transcendent" Columbus Circle New French

where the "stop-you-in-your-tracks" offe[...]
good"; add in "flawless" service and Ada[...]
"contemporary" design and the "costly" ta[...]
though you can bypass them via the "amazing[...]
offered in the "less formal Nougatine Room[...]

Jean-Luc
507 Columbus Ave. (bet. 84th & 85th Sts.), 212-712-1[...];
www.jeanlucrestaurant.com
The "surprisingly good" French food takes a backseat to the
"thirtysomething" bar action at this "upmarket" bistro that aims to
bring a "Downtown vibe to the Upper West Side"; still, some snipe at
"snooty Gallic" service and "terrible noise."

Jefferson
24 | 23 | 22 | $56

121 W. 10th St. (bet. Greenwich & 6th Aves.), 212-255-3333
■ "Minimal" is putting it mildly when it comes to the "sleek" design of
this Village New American, but even if the "walls are bare, the seats
are full" thanks to a "robust" Asian-inflected menu and "genuinely
friendly" service; still, the overall "serene", "understated" spell might
be broken when the bill arrives.

Jekyll & Hyde Club
10 | 22 | 13 | $31

1409 Sixth Ave. (bet. 57th & 58th Sts.), 212-541-9517;
www.jekyllandhydeclub.com
"TGIF meets Disney" at this "silly" Midtown "haunted mansion"
themer where lots of "mechanical doodads" distract from the
"monstrous service" and "frightening prices"; P.S. don't let the
"mediocre" American grub "scare" you off – "kids will eat anything"
and are likely to enjoy this experience.

Jerry's
17 | 13 | 15 | $29

101 Prince St. (bet. Greene & Mercer Sts.), 212-966-9464;
www.jerrysnyc.com
"SoHo's version of a diner", this "very hip" American has been
"hitting the spot" for years with a "no-nonsense" menu seasoned
with "a dash of panache"; "as comfortable as your favorite old T-
shirt" (and "about as glamorous"), it's also "affordable" and
"incredibly laid-back."

JEWEL BAKO
27 | 24 | 25 | $73

239 E. Fifth St. (bet. 2nd & 3rd Aves.), 212-979-1012 🈺
101 Second Ave. (bet. 5th & 6th Sts.), 212-253-7848 🌑
■ "'Meticulous' reaches new heights" at Jack and Grace Lamb's East
Village Japanese "gem" where "each piece of sushi is a treasure"
and priced accordingly; even if the setup and portions are "tiny", the
"heavenly fresh" fare, "gracious" service and "elegant", "bamboo"-
lined digs make for a "fabulous experience from start to finish"; N.B. a
more casual, less expensive satellite (Jewel Bako Makimono) has
just arrived around the corner on Second Avenue.

Jewel of India
20 | 19 | 19 | $37

15 W. 44th St. (bet. 5th & 6th Aves.), 212-869-5544
Known for a "killer lunch buffet" that's one of Midtown's "best
bargains", this plush, high-end Indian also purveys "deliciously
spicy" items from its "extensive" regular menu; detractors detect a
"downhill" motion, however, and suggest a "makeover."

Jezebel
19 | 24 | 18 | $48

630 Ninth Ave. (45th St.), 212-582-1045; www.jezebelny.com
■ "Rhett and Scarlett would feel at home" at this "deliciously decadent"
Hell's Kitchen Southern belle with a "veranda"-esque feel right down

"ch-swing" seating; despite being "expensive" with food that
e a "bit heavy", it's "a lot of fun" for "visitors" and show-goers.

J.G. Melon ●⊄   21 | 12 | 14 | $23

1291 Third Ave. (74th St.), 212-744-0585

■ It can resemble "a J. Crew catalogue shoot" given all the "Buckley
boys" and "Lilly Pulitzer" girls jammed into this "nothing-fancy" East
Side pub famed for some of the "best burgers and cottage fries" around;
since the patties are on the "small side", guys should "order two."

Jimmy Sung's   18 | 18 | 18 | $36

219 E. 44th St. (bet. 2nd & 3rd Aves.), 212-682-5678;
www.jimmysungs.com

☑ An "extremely spacious" interior with a "Beijing" feel distinguishes
this "upscale" UN-area Chinese from the competition; even if the
cooking splits surveyors ("authentic", "delightful" vs. "ordinary"),
there's consensus that tabs are on the high side for this genre.

Jing Fong ●   19 | 12 | 11 | $19

20 Elizabeth St. (bet. Bayard & Canal Sts.), 212-964-5256

■ For a "true Chinatown experience", try this "stadium-size" dim sum
extravaganza that "awes out-of-towners" with its "wide variety"
menu and "circus"-like hubbub; "rude" service may detract, but
"cheap" tabs keep it humming; P.S. a "recent remodeling" should
help the Decor score.

Joanna's   17 | 15 | 18 | $45

132 E. 61st St. (bet. Lexington & Park Aves.), 212-980-8787 ●
30 E. 92nd St. (bet. 5th & Madison Aves.), 212-360-1103

■ A "gracious" townhouse setting and "fun back garden" make
the food "taste even better" at this Carnegie Hill Northern Italian
that's a "little expensive", but redeemed by a $24.95 early-bird that
has "older" types atwitter; N.B. a new, as yet unrated Mediterranean
sibling has opened near Bloomie's.

Joe Allen ●   16 | 15 | 17 | $38

326 W. 46th St. (bet. 8th & 9th Aves.), 212-581-6464;
www.joeallenrestaurant.com

☑ There's a warm "NY vibe in the air" at this "long-established"
Restaurant Row American where ordinary folk get "neck strain"
scoping out "B'way celebs" in the crowd; if critics find "nothing to
knock your socks off" on the menu, at least it's "steady and consistent."

Joe's Pizza   24 | 5 | 12 | $8

233 Bleecker St. (Carmine St.), 212-366-1182 ●
7 Carmine St. (bet. Bleecker St. & 6th Ave.), 212-255-3946 ●
137 Seventh Ave. (bet. Carroll St. & Garfield Pl.), Brooklyn,
718-398-9198

☑ Any way you slice it, this pie-popping trio puts out some of the "best
no-nonsense pizza" in town, with "late-night" hours thrown in as a
bonus for "post–bar hoppers"; crusty service and cheesy decor come
with the territory.

Joe's Shanghai   21 | 9 | 13 | $22

113 Mott St. (bet. Canal & Hester Sts.), 212-966-6613 ⊄
9 Pell St. (bet. Bowery & Mott St.), 212-233-8888 ●⊄
24 W. 56th St. (bet. 5th & 6th Aves.), 212-333-3868
82-74 Broadway (bet. 45th & Whitney Aves.), Queens,
718-639-6888 ⊄
136-21 37th Ave. (bet. Main & Union Sts.), Queens, 718-539-3838 ⊄

☑ "Amazing" soup dumplings are the "soup-erb" specialty of this
"cheap" Chinese quintet where the "marginal" decor may vary by

location, but the "so-so service" is universal; "long waits" to get in suggest that many opt for the "close-your-eyes-and-eat" approach.

Johnny Rockets ◐
14 | 15 | 14 | $14

42 E. Eighth St. (bet. B'way & University Pl.), 212-253-8175; www.johnnyrockets.com

☑ A "blast from the past" when "nothing was unhealthy", this "retro" Village diner fries up "guilty-pleasure" grub paired with "thick, creamy shakes"; if you don't mind "cheesy music" and "spotty service", it's a "great place to kill a hangover."

John's of 12th Street ⊟
19 | 13 | 16 | $29

302 E. 12th St. (2nd Ave.), 212-475-9531

☑ It's easy to "overdose on cheese" at this circa-1908 East Village "red-sauce heaven" "dripping with candle wax and romance"; maybe the decor's "drab" and service "scattered", but the "standard" Italiana comes in "huge portions" for small prices.

John's Pizzeria ◐
22 | 13 | 15 | $20

278 Bleecker St. (bet. 6th & 7th Aves.), 212-243-1680 ⊟
408 E. 64th St. (bet. 1st & York Aves.), 212-935-2895
260 W. 44th St. (bet. B'way & 8th Ave.), 212-391-7560

■ The beat-up Village original is a "required visit for pizza freaks", but all branches of this pizzeria chainlet feature "unbelievable" brick-oven pies, so forget about the "intimidating lines" and "no-slice" policy – "nothing else matters" after one "mouthwatering" bite.

JoJo
25 | 22 | 23 | $65

160 E. 64th St. (bet. Lexington & 3rd Aves.), 212-223-5656; www.jean-georges.com

■ Jean-Georges Vongerichten's "velvet touch" prevails at this haute French bistro turning out "exquisitely prepared" repasts on two floors of an elegant East Side townhouse; a few say it's "losing its buzz", but for most it's still a "glorious" hive so long as you're "ready to spend money"; P.S. the $20 "bargain" prix fixe lunch is a perfect way to start.

Josephina ◐
19 | 17 | 18 | $42

1900 Broadway (bet. 63rd & 64th Sts.), 212-799-1000; www.josephinanyc.com

■ "You can't beat the location" of this West Side American-Eclectic smack dab across from Lincoln Center, where "stylish", "decently priced" grub is served "super-fast" enough to "get you to the show on time"; timid types eschew the "hectic" pre-theater scene in favor of the "quieter lunch" and weekend brunch.

Josephs
– | – | – | E

(fka Citarella)

1240 Sixth Ave. (49th St.), 212-332-1515; www.josephscitarella.com

Having assumed its owner's name, the former Citarella has lightly tweaked its menu and decor – good-bye downstairs sushi bar – but you can still count on "brilliant" catches of the day given its continuing affiliation with the famed fishmonger; embellished by a multi-deck, nautically themed setting, it's a fine Rock Center destination.

Joseph's Ristorante ☒
∇ 20 | 16 | 19 | $45

3 Hanover Sq. (Pearl St.), 212-747-1300

■ "Don't mind the basement location" – this "hidden" Hanover Square "treasure" is worth seeking out for "dependable", "old-school" Italian food accompanied by "serious service"; though certainly "not trendy", it's "quiet" enough for a perfect "business lunch"; N.B. closed weekends.

Josie's
20 | 15 | 16 | $31

300 Amsterdam Ave. (74th St.), 212-769-1212 ◑
565 Third Ave. (37th St.), 212-490-1558
www.josiesnyc.com

☑ "Girls go nuts" for these "guilt-free" Eclectic "chickfests", but they're "godsends for healthy eaters" of any gender thanks to "extensive" options for vegetarians as well as nods to the "lactose intolerant"; "loud crowds" and "impersonal service" are turnoffs.

Joya ◑⌀
23 | 20 | 18 | $20

215 Court St. (Warren St.), Brooklyn, 718-222-3484

■ This "affordable" Cobble Hill "gold mine" draws "buzzing" crowds with "flavor-filled" Thai chow served in a "cosmopolitan" yet "unpretentious" setting; regulars are willing to tolerate "maddening" waits in exchange for a table in the "sublime garden."

Jubilee
22 | 15 | 19 | $44

347 E. 54th St. (bet. 1st & 2nd Aves.), 212-888-3569
329 W. 51st St. (bet. 8th & 9th Aves.), 212-265-7575
www.jubileeny.com

■ Some of the "tastiest mussels around" turn up at this pair of crosstown French bistros serving "jubilantly delicious" comfort chow; connoisseurs say the new West Side branch boasts "better decor" and a "perfect pre-theater" prix fixe.

Jules ◑
19 | 18 | 15 | $33

65 St. Marks Pl. (bet. 1st & 2nd Aves.), 212-477-5560

☑ The "vibe is sexy" at this "bohemian", "terribly East Village" bistro offering "film noir dining" via "solid" Gallic grub and "red-hot" live jazz; "reasonable prices" make the "noisy" acoustics and "typical French service" more bearable.

Julian's
18 | 17 | 17 | $35

802 Ninth Ave. (bet. 53rd & 54th Sts.), 212-262-4800

■ A "steady beacon" for pre-theater dining or a "great brunch", this Italian has been a Hell's Kitchen standby for 10 years thanks to "simple", "tasty" dishes that are "priced right"; regulars report the "romantic" garden is one of its "best features."

Junior's
18 | 10 | 14 | $20

Grand Central, lower level (42nd St. & Vanderbilt Ave.), 212-983-5257
386 Flatbush Ave. Ext. (DeKalb Ave.), Brooklyn, 718-852-5257 ◑
www.juniorscheesecake.com

☑ Dine backwards and "have dessert first" at this renowned Downtown Brooklyn "cheesecake temple" where the "huge mounds" of deli/diner chow may be "average", but the sweets are "mandatory"; aesthetes favor the Grand Central satellite for its considerably "better decor."

Justin's ◑
∇ 15 | 19 | 16 | $42

31 W. 21st St. (bet. 5th & 6th Aves.), 212-352-0599; www.justinsrestaurant.com

☑ Fans feel owner Sean 'P. Diddy' Combs gets a "bad rap" for this Flatiron Southern-Caribbean, what with its "tasty" grub and "sexy", bling bling–laden atmosphere; but foes consider this Puffy's "least successful venture", citing puffed-up tariffs and a "clueless staff."

Kai
∇ 27 | 25 | 26 | $77

Ito En, 822 Madison Ave., 2nd fl. (bet. 68th & 69th Sts.), 212-988-7277;
www.itoen.com

■ "Should one meditate or eat?" is the question at this "sublime" East Side haute Japanese where an "attentive staff" serves "exquisite", "artfully arranged" kaiseki in an "austere", "nirvana-like" setting;

though the prix fixe–only meals come at "hefty" tabs, what you get in return is "priceless."

Kalustyan's Café
— | — | — | M

115 Lexington Ave. (28th St.), 212-686-5400

Serving more refined dishes than the norm, this Curry Hill Indian has a definite edge since it's a spin-off of the famed Kalustyan's market several doors down, with their wide variety of exotic spices and flavors at its service; a sleek setting with raw silk window treatments suggests its high aspirations.

Kam Chueh ◐
▽ 23 | 8 | 15 | $23

40 Bowery (bet. Bayard & Canal Sts.), 212-791-6868

■ "Budget-conscious" folks pounce on this Cantonese seafooder where you can "pick your dinner from the fish tank" or "get a regular to tell you what to order" ("some of the best items aren't on the menu"); granted, there's "no decor" and iffy service, but "hey, it's Chinatown."

Kang Suh ◐
20 | 11 | 15 | $30

1250 Broadway (32nd St.), 212-564-6845

☑ This "round-the-clock" Garment District Korean may be a "little divey", but it "gets the job done" 24/7 with "delicious", do-it-yourself BBQ and other "authentic" eats at reasonable tabs; ok, the "smell will stay with you for days – but at least it's a good smell."

Kapadokya
▽ 20 | 18 | 19 | $27

142 Montague St., 2nd fl. (bet. Clinton & Henry Sts.), Brooklyn, 718-875-2211

■ As "traditional" as can be, this "pleasant" Brooklyn Heights Turk takes you "beyond shish kebab" with its "interesting", "earthy" selections; the "sexy" weekend belly dancing "somehow makes everything taste better", ditto the "extremely affordable" pricing.

Karyatis ◐
▽ 20 | 16 | 18 | $38

35-03 Broadway (bet. 35th & 36th Sts.), Queens, 718-204-0666

☑ The "only thing missing is Zorba" at this relatively "upscale" Greek that feels like an "island retreat" with its "unrushed service" and "authentic" cooking; while dissenters say it's "lost its touch", defenders counter it's "been around a long time" for a reason.

Katsu-Hama
▽ 22 | 9 | 15 | $25

11 E. 47th St. (bet. 5th & Madison Aves.), 212-758-5909; www.katsuhama.com

■ "Awesome Japanese-style cutlets" steal the show at this simple Midtown katsu parlor, a sushi-free zone where diners line up to ingest "luscious crispy pork" accompanied by rice, miso soup and cabbage side dishes; even better, it all comes at "bargain-basement prices."

Katz's Delicatessen *2/06*
22 | 8 | 11 | $18

205 E. Houston St. (Ludlow St.), 212-254-2246

☑ "Mountainous sandwiches" piled high with "orgasm-inducing" corned beef plus pastrami so "heavenly" it "could bring peace to the world" draw crowds to this "quintessential" Lower East Side deli; less celestial are the "dumpy" digs, "intimidating" service and "police interrogation room" lighting, but "it doesn't get any more NY than this."

Keens Steakhouse
23 | 22 | 21 | $56

72 W. 36th St. (bet. 5th & 6th Aves.), 212-947-3636; www.keenssteakhouse.com

■ The "mutton chop is the way to go" at this circa-1885 "step-back-in-time" Midtown steakhouse-cum-saloon where "antique clay pipes cover the ceilings" and "testosterone" perfumes the air; whether for "business or romance", it's an ode to "days gone by" abetted by "old-school service", a very "serious scotch selection" and handsome upstairs private party rooms festooned with enough American memorabilia to fill a museum.

Kelley & Ping
18 | 15 | 12 | $23

127 Greene St. (Prince St.), 212-228-1212

☑ "After a day of shopping in SoHo", rest your dogs at this "slightly hip" Pan-Asian noodle shop–cum–dry goods emporium where the food is "fresh", "fast" and "cheap"; expect a "cafeteria-style" setup at lunchtime, full service for supper and a "sketchy" staff whenever.

Kiev ●
15 | 9 | 13 | $17

117 Second Ave. (7th St.), 212-420-9600;
www.kievrestaurantnyc.com

☑ Though its revamped menu features Eastern European grub with some Chinese twists, this longtime East Village "best bet for a thin wallet" still works "when you have a pierogi or blintz craving"; but the "gussied up" decor leaves many wondering "where did the authentic vibe go?"

Killmeyer's Old Bavaria Inn
∇ 17 | 17 | 17 | $32

4254 Arthur Kill Rd. (Sharrotts Rd.), Staten Island, 718-984-1202;
www.killmeyers.com

☑ "Don't weigh yourself" after feasting at this "old-fashioned" Staten Island German serving filling "comfort food" in "pub"-like environs; though critics carp about "inconsistent results", brew buffs raise their stein to one of the "best biergartens this side of the Black Forest."

Kings' Carriage House
21 | 25 | 21 | $52

251 E. 82nd St. (bet. 2nd & 3rd Aves.), 212-734-5490;
www.kingscarriagehouse.com

■ "Fit for a king – and priced like it too", this "upper-crust" Upper East Side Continental set in a "cozy" carriage house cossets customers with "flavorful" food and "impeccable service"; offering "high tea" as well as prix fixe–only lunch and dinner, it feels like a "special occasion whether you're celebrating something special or not."

Kin Khao
23 | 19 | 18 | $34

171 Spring St. (bet. Thompson St. & W. B'way), 212-966-3939;
www.kinkhao.com

■ For "tasty Thai" "without the sticker shock usually associated with SoHo", check out this "tried-and-true" Asian that takes on a "romantic" glow after a few "fun cocktails"; it's "always packed", but fans feel it's "good enough to endure an elbow in your satay."

Kitchen 22/Kitchen 82
21 | 18 | 18 | $36

36 E. 22nd St. (bet. B'way & Park Ave. S.), 212-228-4399 ⊠
461 Columbus Ave. (82nd St.), 212-875-1619
www.charliepalmer.com

■ "Hip eats" at "Ikea" price tags is the recipe for success at these dinner-only New Americans from Charlie Palmer, where $25 gets you a three-course supper in "generic", "no-frills" digs; regulars warn "don't go hungry" – they "don't take reservations" and the "wait is forever."

Kitchen Club
∇ 22 | 22 | 23 | $47

30 Prince St. (Mott St.), 212-274-0025; www.thekitchenclub.com

■ There's "lots of character" to be found at this "idiosyncratic" NoLita French-Japanese, from the "wonderful" cooking and "whimsical" decor to the "cool owner" and her "jewelry-wearing pup", Chibi; a cozy, adjacent sake bar is further evidence of its "real intent to please."

Kitchenette
19 | 12 | 15 | $21

1272 Amsterdam Ave. (bet. 122nd & 123rd Sts.), 212-531-7600
80 W. Broadway (Warren St.), 212-267-6740
☑ "Great home cooking" right out of "rural Arkansas" is up for grabs at these two "tiny" Southerners parked on either end of the island; fans ignore the "variable service" and "tired decor" in favor of its easily affordable prices, while insiders say "brunch is the way to go."

Kittichai
– | – | – | E

60 Thompson Hotel, 60 Thompson St. (bet. Broome & Spring Sts.),
212-219-2000; www.kittichairestaurant.com
SoHo's latest hot spot is this sexy new hotel Thai set in a Rockwell Group–designed space with big booths situated around a reflecting pool; despite the pricey, ambitious menu showcasing contemporary tastes of Bangkok, its starved-to-perfection following seems more intent on the scene.

Knickerbocker Bar & Grill ●
19 | 18 | 18 | $42

33 University Pl. (bet. 8th & 9th Sts.), 212-228-8490;
www.knickerbockerbarandgrill.com
■ "Old NY" is alive and well at this "timeless" Village steakhouse where the "hearty" American chow "won't bankrupt you" and the "lively", "real-life *Cheers*" vibe (with live jazz some nights) will elate you; it may be as "unhip as can be", but locals say that's the best thing about it.

Kodama ●
19 | 12 | 18 | $29

301 W. 45th St. (bet. 8th & 9th Aves.), 212-582-8065
■ The "price is right" at this Hell's Kitchen Japanese where the "sumptuous sushi" trumps the "sterile decor"; there's "never a problem getting a table", service is "efficient" and the "locale is great for theatergoers", so you'll always get to the show on time.

Koi ●☒
▽ 25 | 14 | 18 | $40

175 Second Ave. (11th St.), 212-777-5266
■ "At least as good as its predecessor, Iso", this new East Village Japanese seems to be "getting better with each visit", what with fish so "incredibly fresh" some swear it arrives on the plate "still moving"; it's "expensive" for the neighborhood, but most don't mind since it's "showing so much promise."

Kombit
– | – | – | M

279 Flatbush Ave. (bet. Prospect Pl. & St. Mark's Ave.), Brooklyn, 718-399-2000
Prospect Heights' Flatbush Avenue is home to this new Haitian bistro/bar serving uniquely spiced, moderately priced dishes ranging from conch stew to crispy goat, all accompanied by rice, beans and plantains; its casually upscale atmosphere is in direct contrast to its down-home spirit.

Korean Temple Cuisine ●
(aka Temple)
▽ 22 | 15 | 22 | $26

81 St. Marks Pl. (bet. 1st & 2nd Aves.), 212-979-9300; www.ktcnyc.com
■ East Villagers are getting a "delicious" "new perspective on Korean cuisine" via this "affordable" newcomer owned and run by two sisters; just keep in mind that the "skinny", "packed" quarters mean it's "not a place to stay long or be romantic."

Korea Palace ☒
19 | 15 | 18 | $33

127 E. 54th St. (bet. Lexington & Park Aves.), 212-832-2350;
www.koreapalace.com
■ "Two chopsticks up" is the verdict on this "comfortable" Midtown Korean featuring a "wide-ranging" selection of "subtly seasoned"

dishes; if it's "not quite a palace" given the bright neon, "stuck-in-the-'70s" decor, it offsets with "efficient" service and "tasty" lunch boxes.

Ko Sushi
∇ 19 | 14 | 18 | $29

1329 Second Ave. (70th St.), 212-439-1678
1619 York Ave. (85th St.), 212-772-8838

☑ Upper Eastsiders are "happy" these "simple" neighborhood sushi parlors are in their neighborhood, supplying "surprisingly good" food at "modest prices"; though picky eaters yawn "ho-hum", at least service comes "with a smile."

Krispy Kreme
22 | 6 | 13 | $5

Penn Station, 2 Penn Plaza (33rd St. on Amtrak rotunda level), 212-947-7175
30 Rockefeller Plaza, concourse level (bet. 49th & 50th Sts.), 212-957-4707
1497 Third Ave. (bet. 84th & 85th Sts.), 212-879-9111
141 W. 72nd St. (bet. Amsterdam & Columbus Aves.), 212-724-1100
265 W. 23rd St. (bet. 7th & 8th Aves.), 212-620-0111
www.krispykreme.com

☑ "Atkins schmatkins" – gluttons "go for the glazed" at these all-over-town doughnut dispensers offering sweet, sugary "sin in an edible form"; since "one ain't enough", consider "doing penance on the treadmill" afterward; P.S. "skip their weak brew" and "BYOC."

Kuma Inn ⊐
∇ 24 | 15 | 21 | $33

113 Ludlow St., 2nd fl. (bet. Delancey & Rivington Sts.), 212-353-8866

☑ "Tasty tapas" are the name of the game at this "tiny" Lower East Side Thai-Filipino with a "hidden", second-floor address; the "studio apartment–size" setup may be "very basic", but the "scrumptious", "affordable" nibbles washed down with "fine sake" make for some mighty "nice grazing."

Kum Gang San ◐
22 | 15 | 16 | $30

49 W. 32nd St. (bet. B'way & 5th Ave.), 212-967-0909
138-28 Northern Blvd. (bet. Bowne & Union Sts.), Queens, 718-461-0909

■ "Authentic, mind-numbingly spicy" Korean BBQ transports you to "Seoul" at this K-town/Queens duo that's open round the clock; some say the outer borough outlet is "better than Manhattan", but either way, you "can't go wrong" foodwise and those waterfalls make the meal "extra trippy."

Kuruma Zushi ▨
∇ 26 | 14 | 23 | $114

7 E. 47th St., 2nd fl. (bet. 5th & Madison Aves.), 212-317-2802

■ "Like going to heaven without the dying part", this mezzanine Midtown Japanese lures purists with sushi and sashimi so "succulent" that only a "shark on the loose gets it fresher"; no question, it will take a bite out of your bank account, but it's "hard to accept anywhere else after eating here."

Kyma ◐
19 | 15 | 18 | $38

300 W. 46th St. (8th Ave.), 212-957-8830

☑ "Close to the Theater District in location (but not price")" is this "unpretentious" Midtown Greek that "almost meets Astoria standards" with its "consistent", "credible" kitchen; "perfunctory service" and "plain" looks aside, it's a "wonderful find" for a "relaxing" meal.

La Baraka
20 | 17 | 21 | $37

255-09 Northern Blvd. (Little Neck Pkwy.), Queens, 718-428-1461

■ Owner Lucette "treats you like a guest in her home" at this "little" Little Neck French where the "consistently good" food is "matched by the warm service"; "excellent value" and a "cozy" ambiance add to the overall "old-school" feel.

La Belle Vie
17 | 16 | 16 | $34

184 Eighth Ave. (bet. 19th & 20th Sts.), 212-929-4320

☑ "Decent French fare" at "reasonable prices" sums up the strengths of this Chelsea bistro that's also "convenient to the Joyce Theater"; regulars say the "sluggish" service isn't as noticeable if you snag an "outdoor table" for some primo Eighth Avenue "boy-watching."

La Bergamote ⊄
26 | 14 | 15 | $13

169 Ninth Ave. (20th St.), 212-627-9010

☑ Francophiles who "miss Paris" can take solace in this Chelsea bakery/cafe where the "heavenly" offerings taste as "scrumptious as they look"; never mind the "limited seating", "early closing" times and "no-smiles" service – after a "to-die-for pastry" here, you'll know that "life is worth living."

La Boîte en Bois ⊄
22 | 16 | 20 | $47

75 W. 68th St. (bet. Columbus Ave. & CPW), 212-874-2705

■ It's "too bad they don't take plastic" at this Lincoln Center–area French, but it's "worth stopping at the ATM" for its "good food" and even better $32 pre-theater prix fixe; since it's such a "tight fit" ("don't be more than a size eight"), claustrophobes opt to dine after the pre-curtain crush.

La Bottega ●
18 | 20 | 14 | $40

Maritime Hotel, 88 Ninth Ave. (17th St.), 212-243-8400

☑ "Oh, what a scene" unfolds at this new Italian "party restaurant" set in a "happening" Chelsea hotel, where the pizzas and "Pastis-like" decor play well against the "good-looking" crowd; to counter the "madhouse" atmosphere and "apathetic" service, there's a very "cool" outdoor patio.

L'Absinthe
23 | 23 | 20 | $61

227 E. 67th St. (bet. 2nd & 3rd Aves.), 212-794-4950

■ "If you can't go to Paris", hit this *magnifique* Eastsider that's "everything" an "authentic" French brasserie "should be", from the "top-quality" cuisine to the "romantic" art nouveau decor and, alas, the "noisy" acoustics and "haughty" (though "efficient") service; it's "not cheap", but that doesn't begin to faze the "local fur-coat crowd" that collects here.

L'Acajou ●⊠
∇ 19 | 12 | 18 | $41

53 W. 19th St. (bet. 5th & 6th Aves.), 212-645-1706; www.lacajou.com

☑ This "old Flatiron warhorse" is still "chugging along", turning out bountiful bistro basics (including some Alsatian dishes) complemented by a "remarkable wine list"; though it's congenial and "filled with regulars", the "shabby decor" has some asking "couldn't they at least get some new furniture?"

La Cantina ⊠
∇ 24 | 17 | 23 | $41

38 Eighth Ave. (Jane St.), 212-727-8787

■ Choose your meal from the "dishes listed on the blackboard" at this "charming" albeit "cramped" Village Southern Italian overseen by a very "hands-on" owner; what with the "fantastic" food and "warm" vibe, fans wonder why it's "relatively undiscovered."

La Cantina Toscana
∇ 22 | 13 | 20 | $46

1109 First Ave. (bet. 60th & 61st Sts.), 212-754-5454

■ "Imaginative wild game" dishes highlight the menu of this East Side Tuscan also touted for its "fabulous wine list"; sure, it may be "tiny, tiny, tiny", but an "ambitious" kitchen with big aspirations makes adherents feel it "deserves to be better known."

Lady Mendl's
21 26 25 $39

Inn at Irving Pl., 56 Irving Pl. (bet. 17th & 18th Sts.), 212-533-4466;
www.innatirving.com

■ You'll think "you've arrived in merrie old England" upon entering this "girlie" Gramercy tearoom, a "beautiful Victorian parlor"–like space with "delicious" treats and "excellent" service; but while the "charming" milieu "transports you to another era", the "pricey" check snaps you back to reality.

La Focaccia ●
20 19 20 $33

51 Bank St. (W. 4th St.), 212-675-3754

■ On "one of the prettiest blocks" in the Village lies this "romantic" Northern Italian, a "great date place" owing to its "amiable" staff and "smooth" airs; while the "delicious" namesake flatbread is the star of the show, admirers say the rest of the "simple" menu is equally good.

La Giara
19 15 17 $34

501 Third Ave. (bet. 33rd & 34th Sts.), 212-726-9855; www.lagiara.com

☑ This "great little neighborhood" Italian in Murray Hill does a "brisk business" thanks to its reliable cooking and "inviting" atmosphere; critics complain of "variable food and service", yet most report "relaxing", "reliable" dining.

La Gioconda
▽ 23 16 22 $37

226 E. 53rd St. (bet. 2nd & 3rd Aves.), 212-371-3536;
www.lagiocondany.com

■ "Undiscovered" despite the "middle-of-Midtown" address, this "unpretentious" Italian offers "reasonably priced", "cut-above-the-usual" dishes in "quaint" digs; as it's "small" (verging on "cramped"), "reservations are highly suggested."

La Goulue ●
21 20 19 $57

746 Madison Ave. (bet. 64th & 65th Sts.), 212-988-8169

☑ It seems like "everyone knows everyone" at this Madison Avenue French bistro popular with "Birkin bag"–toting "size twos", so it helps to "look important if you want to be treated well"; the food is "fine" and the "people-watching" from outside tables offers "better theater than Broadway", making the "expensive" price tags more palatable.

LA GRENOUILLE ☒
26 27 26 $87

3 E. 52nd St. (bet. 5th & Madison Aves.), 212-752-1495;
www.la-grenouille.com

■ One of NYC's "last great French gastronomic temples" in town, this "timeless" Midtown "legend" from the Masson family attracts the cream of society owing to its "stellar" cuisine, "exquisite" service and a "floral paradise" setting akin to the "NY Botanical Gardens"; while the prix fixe–only $49 lunch and $87.50 dinner may seem *cher,* in light of the overall "extraordinary" experience the cost is quite modest.

La Grolla
21 14 19 $41

413 Amsterdam Ave. (bet. 79th & 80th Sts.), 212-496-0890

■ A "creative" menu offering specialties from the Val d'Aosta region makes this Upper West Side Northern Italian "more interesting than most"; locals say there's "nothing else like it" in these parts, lauding the "attentive" staff and "reasonable" pricing for the "quality."

Lake Club
▽ 20 23 19 $43

1150 Clove Rd. (Victory Blvd.), Staten Island, 718-442-3600;
www.lake-club.com

☑ This Staten Island eatery "changes hands as often" as some "change socks" – indeed, the post-*Survey* arrival of a new chef has ushered in a new cuisine (Italian) and put the Food score in doubt – but its "lovely lakeside" setting remains "supremely romantic", making it indisputably "great for a first date or cocktails."

La Lanterna di Vittorio ◑ ▽ 20 | 24 | 18 | $21
129 MacDougal St. (bet. W. 3rd & W. 4th Sts.), 212-529-5945
■ Some of the "best desserts and cappuccino" around turn up at this "cozy" cafe near Washington Square, by day a place to "discuss existentialism", but by night a "dark", "sexy" nexus for "cuddling up" with someone special; several "romantic fireplaces" compensate for the "limited" menu.

La Locanda dei Vini 22 | 15 | 20 | $44
737 Ninth Ave. (bet. 49th & 50th Sts.), 212-258-2900
■ The "biggest sleeper in the West 40s" might be this "civilized" venue that's "not your typical Ninth Avenue Italian" thanks to its "authentic", "*bellisimo*" cooking and "eager-to-please" staff; it's so "perfect before the theater" that if you "order a bottle of wine, you might want to miss the show."

La Lunchonette 22 | 14 | 19 | $39
130 10th Ave. (18th St.), 212-675-0342
■ Not so "out of the way" now that the "neighborhood has grown up around it", this longtime West Chelsea French bistro "far surpasses its name" with "surprisingly good" edibles served "sans attitude"; "decent pricing", "arty people–watching" and a Sunday night accordionist ice the cake.

La Mangeoire 19 | 19 | 19 | $44
1008 Second Ave. (bet. 53rd & 54th Sts.), 212-759-7086
■ "Just reopened" following a fire and as "charming" as ever, this Eastsider serves "trusty", "not fancy" French food in a "neighborhoody" setting that "makes you feel the neighborhood is Provence"; locals are "glad it's back" – you "get your money's worth" here.

Lamarca ⊠ 20 | 9 | 16 | $19
161 E. 22nd St. (3rd Ave.), 212-674-6363
☑ "Perfect for a basic pasta fix", this "bare-bones" Gramercy Italian has long "churned out" "fresh", "no-frills" fare at "reasonable prices", and "quick-lunch" seekers swear by the "great take-out" annex next door; but "inexplicably, it's not open on weekends."

La Mediterranée 19 | 19 | 20 | $41
947 Second Ave. (bet. 50th & 51st Sts.), 212-755-4155
■ "Still *très bon*" after 25 years on the scene, this "old-world" French bistro draws a "not-young" crowd with "nicely done cuisine" and atmospheric "live piano music"; there's "no NY bustle" in evidence, so it's just the ticket for "quiet", "pleasant" dining.

La Mela ◑ 19 | 10 | 17 | $32
167 Mulberry St. (bet. Broome & Grand Sts.), 212-431-9493
☑ "There's so much food you'll have to be rolled out" after a meal at this "no-menu" Little Italy "experience" famed for its $32 prix fixe dinner served "family-style" by "pushy" waiters; the "three-ring-circus" atmosphere is "not for stuffed shirts", but rather for "large groups" or "tourists."

La Metairie 23 | 21 | 22 | $51
189 W. 10th St. (W. 4th St.), 212-989-0343; www.lametairie.com
■ Imagine a "farmhouse in Provence" to get the feel of this venerable Village bistro proffering "deftly prepared" French food in "rustic", "romantic" environs; "knee-to-knee" seating and "expensive" pricing to the contrary, for most it's "enjoyable all around."

La Mirabelle
20 | 16 | 23 | $46
102 W. 86th St. (bet. Amsterdam & Columbus Aves.), 212-496-0458
■ Like "dinner at grand-mère's house", this "old-fashioned" Westsider provides "consistent, no-surprises" French cooking in "welcoming" environs; "matronly waitresses" occasionally launching into "live renditions of 'La Vie en Rose'" keep its "older" following amused.

Lan ●
∇ 22 | 18 | 17 | $37
56 Third Ave. (bet. 10th & 11th Sts.), 212-254-1959;
www.lan-nyc.com
■ Yes, the "sushi's addictive", but that's only half the story at this East Village Japanese that also specializes in "amazing sukiyaki" and "supreme shabu-shabu"; "cool and laid-back", it's considered a "welcome break from today's fusion fever."

L & B Spumoni Gardens ⌒
23 | 11 | 16 | $19
2725 86th St. (bet. W. 10th & 11th Sts.), Brooklyn, 718-449-6921;
www.spumonigardens.com
☑ "Brooklyn landmarks" don't get much more authentic than this Bensonhurst pizzeria/ice cream parlor where traditionalists order a "corner square" of the Sicilian pie topped off by some "delicious homemade spumoni"; maybe the "atmosphere's nothing to rave about", but the "outdoor seating" and "working-class prices" are.

Landmarc ●
∇ 24 | 22 | 21 | $44
179 W. Broadway (bet. Leonard & Worth Sts.), 212-343-3883;
www.landmarc-restaurant.com
■ New but already showing "real promise" as a "TriBeCa triumph", this "delightful" bi-level bistro showcases chef-owner Marc Murphy's "innovative, delicious" French cuisine with an Italian twist; however, the real jaw-dropper here is the "fantastic" wine list "without much markup"; P.S. "the no-rezzies policy can be difficult on busy nights."

L'Annam ●
18 | 11 | 16 | $20
393 Third Ave. (28th St.), 212-686-5168
121 University Pl. (13th St.), 212-420-1414
■ "Gargantuan portions" at "tiny prices" add up to a "student's dream" at this "nothing-fancy" Vietnamese duo dispensing "piles and piles of noodles" and other "basics"; sure, it has a certain "McVietnamese" vibe, but for "fast, filling" pig-outs, it's "a big winner."

La Paella
21 | 17 | 15 | $32
214 E. Ninth St. (bet. 2nd & 3rd Aves.), 212-598-4321
■ "Everything's coming up tapas" at this East Village Spaniard where the "tasty" small plates and "good prices" make for a sometimes "deafening, crowded" scene; the "dark, sexy" mood is very "third date"–worthy, but given the "tight" setup, you may be "sharing the romance with the next table."

La Palapa ●
21 | 18 | 18 | $34
359 Sixth Ave. (Washington Pl.), 212-243-6870
77 St. Marks Pl. (bet. 1st & 2nd Aves.), 212-777-2537
www.lapalapa.com
☑ A "step up from the typical burrito slingers", these "upscale-ish" Mexicans turn out "deliciously original" "nouveau" dishes in "festive" (read: "loud") settings; maybe they're "a little pricey" and "a tad too spicy", but overall, most call them the "real" deal.

La Petite Auberge
19 | 16 | 21 | $41
116 Lexington Ave. (bet. 27th & 28th Sts.), 212-689-5003
☑ Ok, the "menu hasn't changed in ages" at this "been-there-forever" Gramercy French "stalwart", but its "older crowd" remains loyal to

the "unfussy", "good-for-its-type" cooking; "faded decor" and a "stodgy" atmosphere lead aesthetes to advocate a "spruce-up."

La Pizza Fresca Ristorante   20 | 17 | 17 | $34

31 E. 20th St. (bet. B'way & Park Ave. S.), 212-598-0141

☑ Despite the "authentic Neapolitan" pies, this "worthwhile" Flatiron Italian is "much more than pizza", rolling out a variety of "delicious" pastas and other "reminders of glorious Italy"; if "service could be better", the "vast" (if "pricey") wine list washes away most complaints.

La Ripaille ◑   ▽ 22 | 21 | 23 | $42

605 Hudson St. (bet. Bethune & W. 12th Sts.), 212-255-4406

■ "*Très* French and proud of it" sums up this "long-running" Village bistro that's been pleasing patrons for 25 years with "dependable" dishes served in "rustic", "innlike" digs; even better, its "intimate", "quiet" air actually allows you to "hear your own conversation."

La Rivista ◑☒   20 | 17 | 21 | $46

313 W. 46th St. (bet. 8th & 9th Aves.), 212-245-1707;
www.larivistanyc.com

■ "Pleasant" and "convenient", this "unassuming" Restaurant Row Italian "staple" offers "efficient", "quick-in-quick-out" dining timed for theatergoers; there's "lots of food for the money", not to mention discounted parking vouchers and a nightly pianist.

L'Asso ◑   – | – | – | M

192 Mott St. (Kenmare St.), 212-219-2353

Joining a spate of new thin-crust pie purveyors, this NoLita pizzeria lassos in passersby via a picture window showcasing the dough-and-cheese masters in action against the backdrop of a wood-fired oven; in addition, there's bruschetta, fresh pastas and salads at your disposal.

La Table O & Co.   ▽ 18 | 16 | 11 | $21

92 Prince St. (bet. B'way & Mercer St.), 212-219-8155

■ From olive-oil specialist Oliviers & Company comes this "new SoHo oasis", a market–cum–Med eatery featuring an "ambitious menu" of light bites served in a "casual", mezzanine-level setting (with takeout on the ground floor); optimists trust that the "spacey" service "will get better" in time.

La Taza de Oro ☒≠   19 | 6 | 16 | $14

96 Eighth Ave. (bet. 14th & 15th Sts.), 212-243-9946

☑ "Killer" cafe con leche and "big", "cheap" portions of "really authentic" Puerto Rican grub draw everyone from "gringos" to the "Spanish community" to this venerable Chelsea "greasy spoon"; all right, it's a "dump", but since many "taxi drivers recommend it", how can you go wrong?

La Tour   17 | 14 | 15 | $37

1319 Third Ave. (bet. 75th & 76th Sts.), 212-472-7578

☑ "You can't beat" the "unlimited moules frites" at this "low-key" East Side French bistro, and regulars rate its other "typical" standards "good enough for the price" too; however, skeptics shrug "just ok", citing "uneven" eats, slightly "tired" digs and "slow" service.

Lattanzi ◑☒   22 | 18 | 21 | $50

361 W. 46th St. (bet. 8th & 9th Aves.), 212-315-0980; www.lattanzinyc.com

■ "One of the better choices for Theater District dining" is this Restaurant Row Italian, a longtime "favorite" for "fantastic, fresh" fare (including some "Roman Jewish dishes" like "wonderful fried artichokes"); "bustling and loud" pre-curtain, it gets "quieter" as the evening wears on.

Lavagna
24 19 21 $38

545 E. Fifth St. (bet. Aves. A & B), 212-979-1005; www.lavagnanyc.com
■ "Get ready for a food hangover" (it's "worth it") after indulging in the "hearty, creative" fare at this East Village Italian "standout", where the atmosphere's "romantic" and the staff's "friendliness is contagious"; better still, the "reasonable prices" extend to its "sophisticated wine list."

La Vela
∇ 17 14 17 $33

373 Amsterdam Ave. (bet. 77th & 78th Sts.), 212-877-7818
■ A "classic setting, right down to the red-checkered tablecloths" sets the mood for "homey" Tuscan meals at this "friendly" Upper West Side Italian; it's "very reasonably priced" and "never crowded or loud" – "what else do you need from a neighborhood place?"

La Villa Pizzeria
20 15 17 $22

261 Fifth Ave. (bet. 1st St. & Garfield Pl.), Brooklyn, 718-499-9888
Key Food Shopping Ctr., 6610 Ave. U (bet. 66th & 67th Sts.), Brooklyn, 718-251-8030
Lindenwood Shopping Ctr., 82-07 153rd Ave. (bet. 82nd & 83rd Sts.), Queens, 718-641-8259
☑ "Viva La Villa" cheer "comfy clothes"–clad Park Slopers fond of this "kid-friendly" Italian offering "amazing" thin-crust wood-fired pizzas plus a "huge menu" of "red-sauce" classics; aesthetes aver the only "odd" note is the "disconnect between the food quality" and the "strip-mall" feel; N.B. there are Mill Basin and Howard Beach locations too.

Layla ⊠
18 23 19 $46

211 W. Broadway (Franklin St.), 212-431-0700;
www.myriadrestaurantgroup.com
☑ "Busty belly dancers" and "sexy boudoir" decor garner "more attention" than the "only-average" Med-Mideastern fare at this "very atmospheric" TriBeCa "party restaurant", but no matter – after a few of the bar's "creative cocktails", most are having too much "fun" to notice.

LE BERNARDIN ⊠
28 27 27 $95

155 W. 51st St. (bet. 6th & 7th Aves.), 212-554-1515; www.le-bernardin.com
■ "It simply doesn't get any better" for "transcendent seafood" than at Maguy LeCoze's Midtown French "dream", where chef Eric Ripert's "beyond-sublime" cuisine (ranked No. 1 in this *Survey*) "continues to astound", while a "formal" pro staff serves with "seemingly effortless perfection" in "hushed", "elegant" quarters; such "incredible dining experiences" are sure to "sweep you off your feet" – as may the seriously "pricey" bill, but acolytes advise just "take out a loan and go" for a life-fulfilling experience.

Le Bilboquet
21 16 16 $47

25 E. 63rd St. (bet. Madison & Park Aves.), 212-751-3036
☑ While it's "a pain to maneuver in and out" of this "noisy, cramped" East Side French bistro, the stylish "Euros" who gather here consider it more than "worth contorting for" given the "chic" "scene"; those who actually come for the "great food" should arrive "early" to beat the "crowds."

Le Boeuf à la Mode
21 19 21 $49

539 E. 81st St. (bet. East End & York Aves.), 212-249-1473
■ "Filling a real need on the Upper East Side's remote" edge, this French "throwback" remains a "standby" for "delicious" "no-surprises" bistro fare and "quiet conversation"; the "older" locals who frequent it concede it's "probably not for the hip", which suits them just fine.

Le Charlot ◐
▽ 18 14 15 $47

19 E. 69th St. (bet. Madison & Park Aves.), 212-794-1628

◪ "Kiss, kiss" – it's "Euro heaven" at this East Side French bistro that provides "decent" offerings for "beautiful" "Gauloise" types "too skinny to eat"; revelers "go late to be part of" the "fun", "loud" "scene."

LE CIRQUE 2000
25 27 25 $84

NY Palace Hotel, 455 Madison Ave. (bet. 50th & 51st Sts.), 212-303-7788; www.lecirque.com

■ "Ringling Bros." could learn a thing or two from Sirio Maccioni and his "must-see" Midtown "spectacle for the senses", where "celebrities", "rich Euros and tourists" meet under the brilliantly colored "big top" for "serious", "exquisite" French fare served with "pure graciousness"; appealing as it all is, there's nothing whimsical about the prices, but who cares – this is the "best show in town"; N.B. it is scheduled to close in December 2004, but is seeking a new location.

Le Clown
17 13 16 $44

205 E. 75th St. (bet. 2nd & 3rd Aves.), 212-517-3356

◪ Check "any childhood aversions to clowns" at the door, because this "quiet" East Side French bistro is full of their "quirky" "images and memorabilia"; those who like its "homey" cooking may wonder why it's "not crowded" – others say "just ok" eats may be the answer.

L'Ecole ⊠
24 19 22 $42

French Culinary Institute, 462 Broadway (Grand St.), 212-219-3300; www.frenchculinary.com

■ "Sample the future" at the French Culinary Institute's "student restaurant" in SoHo, where tomorrow's kitchen "stars" are "striving for excellence" and "succeeding" ("give them an A!"); the "haute" French prix fixes are "possibly NY's best bargain", and extra credit goes to the "attentive" service from "rookie" staffers.

Le Colonial
21 23 19 $50

149 E. 57th St. (bet. Lexington & 3rd Aves.), 212-752-0808

■ A "gorgeous throwback to French Indochina", this "upscale" East Side Franco-Vietnamese "never disappoints" with its "tantalizing" tastes and "lush" "colonial" decor heavy on "plantation shutters and palms"; however, jaded types who feel it's "a bit theme park–like" say the "dark, sexy" upstairs lounge is "much cooler."

Le Gamin ◐
19 16 13 $20

27 Bedford St. (Downing St.), 212-243-2846
536 E. Fifth St. (bet. Aves. A & B), 212-254-8409
183 Ninth Ave. (21st St.), 212-243-8864
www.legamin.com

◪ "Perfect for a light lunch" or just a "steaming bowl" of café au lait, these "charming French crêperies" are "always packed wall-to-wall"; for most, the "cheapo" prices more than make up for "slow service."

Le Gigot
24 18 23 $49

18 Cornelia St. (bet. Bleecker & W. 4th Sts.), 212-627-3737

■ "Every neighborhood needs a tiny bistro like" this Village "charmer", offering "excellent" (if "slightly pricey") French fare served by an "efficient" staff; romeos rate its "cozy" digs "romantic as heck" "for a first date", but more expansive types find it "a little claustrophobic."

Le Jardin Bistro
18 17 16 $38

25 Cleveland Pl. (bet. Kenmare & Spring Sts.), 212-343-9599; www.lejardinbistro.com

■ "It's all about" the "magical garden" complete with a "grape arbor" at this "quaint" NoLita French bistro, "one of the most charming spots" around in warm weather; at "other times" it's not as "memorable", though the "traditional" fare is "reliable" year-round.

Le Madeleine
20 | 18 | 19 | $43

403 W. 43rd St. (bet. 9th & 10th Aves.), 212-246-2993; www.lemadeleine.com

■ A "pre-theater" "requisite" for many, this "tiny" Hell's Kitchen French bistro is most appreciated for its "romantic enclosed garden", but show-goers gladly get "shoehorned" into its "cramped" main room too; "reliable" Gallic standards and a staff that gets you "out in time for the curtain" are other pluses.

Le Madri
21 | 21 | 20 | $53

168 W. 18th St. (7th Ave.), 212-727-8022

☑ "Holding strong" "year after year", Pino Luongo's "gracious" Chelsea "classic" remains "perfect for a date" or treating "mom and dad" given its "quality" Tuscan fare, "spacious, quiet", "luxurious" setting and "attentive staff"; still, a few find it "so-so" and most suitable on an "expense account."

Le Marais ●
21 | 14 | 16 | $47

150 W. 46th St. (bet. 6th & 7th Aves.), 212-869-0900; www.lemarais.net

☑ "You can count on" this kosher French steakhouse in the Theater District for "above-average" steaks accompanied by some of "the best pommes frites in town"; naysayers note the room's "noisy" and service "slow", but even they concede it's a "standout" among the area's "few options" for the observant.

Lemongrass Grill
17 | 13 | 15 | $22

37 Barrow St. (7th Ave. S.), 212-242-0606
2534 Broadway (bet. 94th & 95th Sts.), 212-666-0888
138 E. 34th St. (bet. Lexington & 3rd Aves.), 212-213-3317
80 University Pl. (11th St.), 212-604-9870
84 William St. (Maiden Ln.), 212-809-8038
156 Court St. (bet. Dean & Pacific Sts.), Brooklyn, 718-522-9728
61A Seventh Ave. (bet. Berkeley & Lincoln Pls.), Brooklyn, 718-399-7100
www.lemongrassgrill.com

☑ The "McDonald's of Thai" it may be, but this popular chain is nonetheless a "godsend" to seekers of "reliable", "budget"-friendly fare served up "quick"; "crowds" and somewhat "sticky" digs aren't an issue if you opt for "lightning-fast delivery."

Lenox Room
19 | 20 | 19 | $51

1278 Third Ave. (bet. 73rd & 74th Sts.), 212-772-0404; www.lenoxroom.com

☑ Always "welcoming" owner Tony Fortuna "knows what he's doing" at this "very Upper East Side" New American, a "staple" for everyone from "trust-fund babies" to "ladies who lunch and their husbands"; it's "cozy and sedate" in the dining room, but mature types kick up a "loud scene" later on, when the bar becomes a "Viagra-filled playground."

Lentini ●
∇ 19 | 17 | 19 | $55

1562 Second Ave. (81st St.), 212-628-3131; www.lentinirestaurant.com

☑ "Why doesn't it get more attention?" wonder admirers who say this Upper East Side Italian is "underappreciated" for its "enjoyable" fare and "quiet", "comfortable" ambiance; others consider it "kinda vanilla" and "way too expensive."

Lento's
21 | 11 | 17 | $22

7003 Third Ave. (Ovington Ave.), Brooklyn, 718-745-9197
289-291 New Dorp Ln. (Richmond Rd.), Staten Island, 718-980-7709

☑ Never mind that it looks like "an old-man dive bar", because the "real-deal" "paper-thin-crust pizza" produced at this nearly 80-year-old

Italian "Bay Ridge landmark" (with a Staten Island offshoot) is simply "sublime"; beyond the pies, though, most find the offerings "just ok."

L'Entrecote ☒
▽ 21 | 16 | 22 | $44

1057 First Ave. (bet. 57th & 58th Sts.), 212-755-0080

■ It's "Paris on First Avenue" at this "tiny", "reliable" Sutton Place French bistro that offers some of "the best frites in town" in a space short on elbow room but long on "old-time" "authenticity"; it "hasn't changed one iota in 30 years", which suits supporters just fine.

Le Pain Quotidien
20 | 16 | 13 | $20

ABC Carpet & Home, 38 E. 19th St. (bet. B'way & Park Ave. S.), 212-673-7900
10 Fifth Ave. (8th St.), 212-253-2324
1336 First Ave. (bet. 71st & 72nd Sts.), 212-717-4800
100 Grand St. (bet. Greene & Mercer Sts.), 212-625-9009
833 Lexington Ave. (bet. 63rd & 64th Sts.), 212-755-5810
1131 Madison Ave. (bet. 84th & 85th Sts.), 212-327-4900
922 Seventh Ave. (58th St.), 212-757-0775
50 W. 72nd St. (bet. Columbus Ave. & CPW), 212-712-9700
www.painquotidien.com

☑ With outlets all over town, this "rustic" Belgian bakery/cafe import is a "bread and pastry–lover's paradise" and also supplies "quick", "fresh, organic" salads, sandwiches and such at "long communal tables" (go elsewhere for "confessional conversations"); the only crumb is "spotty" service; N.B. closes at 7 PM.

Le Père Pinard ●
21 | 20 | 17 | $34

175 Ludlow St. (bet. Houston & Stanton Sts.), 212-777-4917

■ "Euros", "hipsters" and every "young" thing in between hit this Lower East Side French bistro for "authentic" eats served till "late-night" (2 AM on weekends); it's all *très* "sexy", with an "inviting" garden and "reasonable" prices, but watch out for occasional staff "attitude."

Le Perigord
25 | 22 | 25 | $71

405 E. 52nd St. (bet. FDR Dr. & 1st Ave.), 212-755-6244; www.leperigord.com

■ "One of the last" of NYC's "old-guard French" eateries, this Sutton Place "institution" is still "graciously" run by "founding owner" Georges Briguet, and longtime chef Joel Benjamin is now back in the kitchen too; expect "wonderful classics" "lovingly" presented amid "fresh flowers and thick linens", but know that one diner's "restaurant for grown-ups" is another's "dowager."

Le Pescadou ●
▽ 20 | 15 | 18 | $48

18 King St. (6th Ave.), 212-924-3434

■ "Say *bonjour*" to "fresh, well-cooked fish" at this "cozy" SoHo French seafooder, where the bouillabaisse hits the spot and the colorful owner "tells great stories"; locals note it's something of "a neighborhood party" at the "small" bar.

Le Quinze ●
– | – | – | M

132 W. Houston St. (bet. MacDougal & Sullivan Sts.), 212-475-1515

Replacing a link in the Le Gamin chainlet, this new French bistro brings Gallic authenticity to the West Village with its pressed-tin ceilings, hanging globe lamps and obligatory chalkboard menu; it's fast becoming a Sunday brunch destination thanks to a clutch of sunny outdoor tables.

Le Refuge
22 | 21 | 21 | $53

166 E. 82nd St. (bet. Lexington & 3rd Aves.), 212-861-4505;
www.lerefugeinn.com

■ If there were such a thing as a "French country inn near the Met", it would be this townhouse "hideout" offering "warm welcomes" and "fantastic" bistro eats in "quaint", antique-stuffed environs; if some say it's "a little expensive for an ordinary evening", there's always the "bargain pre-theater prix fixe."

Le Rivage
20 16 21 $40

340 W. 46th St. (bet. 8th & 9th Aves.), 212-765-7374; www.lerivagenyc.com
■ "One of the best buys on Broadway" may be the dinner prix fixe at this comfy, "dependable" French "standby" that partisans praise as "a cut above" the Restaurant Row throng; sure, there are "no surprises" here, but "when they tell you you'll make your curtain, they mean it."

Les Enfants Terribles ●
∇ 21 18 17 $37

37 Canal St. (Ludlow St.), 212-777-7518
■ "So perfectly out-of-place" way down on the Lower East Side, this "sexy", "super-funky" French-African has nonetheless been "crowded" from day one with "hip, good-looking" "young" things; the kitchen's "unique flavors" find favor, as do "unbeatable cocktails" that fuel the "raucously enjoyable" scene.

Les Halles ●
20 15 15 $41

411 Park Ave. S. (bet. 28th & 29th Sts.), 212-679-4111
15 John St. (bet. B'way & Nassau St.), 212-285-8585
www.leshalles.net
■ "Wallow in red meat" accompanied by "transcendent frites" at this "quintessential" French bistro on Park Avenue South (with a Financial District offshoot), where "celebrity chef" Anthony Bourdain presides when not out "on world tour"; yes, it's "crowded and noisy", but it'll gain a bit of elbow room when the butcher counter moves into the next-door space in the fall of 2004.

Le Singe Vert ●
19 17 17 $35

160 Seventh Ave. (bet. 19th & 20th Sts.), 212-366-4100
■ "Pretend you're in Paris" at this Chelsea French bistro that boasts all the "authentic" hallmarks – "close tables", "penetrating noise", "European staff" – plus "tasty" "classics" along the lines of steak frites; outside seats offer prime sidewalk "ogling" in summer.

Le Souk ●
16 20 16 $37

47 Ave. B (bet. 3rd & 4th Sts.), 212-777-5454; www.lesoukny.com
☑ The "sexy" "atmosphere reigns supreme" at this "funky Alphabet City pioneer" where you can eyeball "cute belly dancers" ("both male and female"); most agree the "semblance of Moroccan" food "isn't excellent", but then "are you really here to eat?"

Les Routiers
19 15 19 $43

568 Amsterdam Ave. (bet. 87th & 88th Sts.), 212-874-2742; www.les-routiers.com
■ The "best-kept secret on the Upper West Side" may be this "sweet", "affordable" French bistro, where those in the know "try to get a table in the back room"; if the quality of the kitchen's handiwork "is any indication", Gallic "truckers" must "eat well."

Le Tableau
24 16 20 $39

511 E. Fifth St. (bet. Aves. A & B), 212-260-1333; www.letableaunyc.com
■ "If only every neighborhood had a place like" this "cute", "colorful" East Village French bistro where "heavenly", "decently priced" cuisine is "prepared with care" and served by an "unfailingly friendly" staff; just expect to be "cheek-to-cheek with your neighbor" because its "quaint" space is "damn small."

Levana
▽ | 19 | 17 | 18 | $52

141 W. 69th St. (bet. B'way & Columbus Ave.), 212-877-8457; www.levana.com

■ "Exotic" meats (venison, bison and other game) are the specialty of this "serene" West Side glatt kosher New American that's also commended for its "great wine selection" and "helpful" service; however, "you pay" for the pleasure, and some deem it "overpriced."

Le Veau d'Or ⊠
▽ | 19 | 14 | 19 | $47

129 E. 60th St. (bet. Lexington & Park Aves.), 212-838-8133

☑ Around since the '30s and seemingly "unchanged" since the Truman era, this Gallic grande dame is still *"magnifique"* according to loyal "golden-calf worshipers"; some claim it's "seen better days", though they rather relish "being the youngest people in the room."

Lever House
| 23 | 24 | 22 | $73

390 Park Ave. (enter on 53rd St., bet. Madison & Park Aves.), 212-888-2700; www.leverhouse.com

☑ A "glittering new star" in NYC's "power-scene" constellation, this Midtown "modernist" "landmark" tricked out in "honeycomb-meets-*A Clockwork Orange*" decor just may be the "Four Seasons for the next generation"; "celebs" and budding "masters of the universe" "jam in" for chef Dan Silverman's "fresh, ingredient-driven" New American cuisine, "noisy" acoustics and "ridiculously expensive" tabs be damned.

L'Express ◑
| 17 | 15 | 13 | $29

249 Park Ave. S. (20th St.), 212-254-5858

☑ "How can you go wrong with 24-hour French food?" ask admirers of this "reliable" Flatiron "standby" that "can't be beat" for "basic" bistro eats at "any time of day or night"; just know that "pandemonium" prevails during prime hours, when it can be "loud" and "crowded", and the service "spotty."

Le Zie 2000 ◑
| 22 | 14 | 19 | $34

172 Seventh Ave. (bet. 20th & 21st Sts.), 212-206-8686

■ "Seafood reigns" supreme at this "friendly" Chelsea Italian, but devotees declare "everything's good" on its "authentic Venetian" menu; no one argues with the "very reasonable" prices, but aesthetes insist the "big plastic wave in the main room" "has got to go."

Le Zinc ◑
| 19 | 16 | 17 | $39

139 Duane St. (bet. Church St. & W. B'way), 212-513-0001; www.lezincnyc.com

☑ "Characteristically TriBeCa" ("laid-back and casual"), this "art poster"–adorned French bistro from the "Chanterelle people" turns out "enjoyable", "reasonably priced" meals that work equally well for "jury duty", "family dinner" or "late-night" bites; when busy it can get "way noisy" with service "more lead than mercury", but it's still "golden" in the eyes of regulars.

Le Zoccole ◑
▽ | 20 | 15 | 17 | $33

95 Ave. A (6th St.), 212-260-6660

■ This "delicious East Village brother to Chelsea's Le Zie" offers a first-rate Northern Italian menu but specializes in cicchetti ("Venetian tapas") that go down "perfectly with a drink"; though the bi-level space is "pleasant" enough, "it's best enjoyed" "on a warm day" out in the sidewalk seats.

Li Hua
| – | – | – | I

171 Grand St. (Baxter St.), 212-343-0090

The airy, well-windowed room of this BYO Little Italy Korean is as spare as the menu, which consists of inexpensive classics (bulgoki, short ribs, bibimbop) joined by a few noodle dishes, spicy stews and a popular platter-size scallion-shrimp-and-squid pancake.

Lil' Frankie's Pizza ●⊘ ⊅   23 14 17 $22
19-21 First Ave. (bet. 1st & 2nd Sts.), 212-420-4900
■ Kin to nearby Frank, this "favorite" of the "young and hip" specializes in "cheap", "fantastic" "thin-crust" pizzas served by a "friendly" staff of "Strokes" wanna-bes; its "shabby-cool" digs were expanded recently to add a second dining room, which "goes a long way" toward "alleviating the crowding and waits."

Lili's Noodle Shop & Grill   17 14 15 $20
Embassy Suites, 102 North End Ave. (Vesey St.), 212-786-1300 ●
1500 Third Ave. (bet. 84th & 85th Sts.), 212-639-1313
200 W. 57th St. (enter on 7th Ave., bet. 56th & 57th Sts.), 212-586-5333
◪ "The delivery man arrives" practically "before you hang up the phone" when you order from these "cheap" Chinese noodle-slingers, and service is just as "swift" on-site; the Downtown branch has gotten "even better" with the recent addition of a sushi bar, while the new Midtown location has just opened at press time.

Lima's Taste ●   ▽ 18 11 14 $29
432 E. 13th St. (bet. Ave. A & 1st Ave.), 212-228-7900; www.limastaste.com
◪ What may be the "best pisco sour in the city" is poured at this "hip", "spare" East Village Peruvian, beloved for its "friendly" vibe, "hearty", "delish" fare and "inexpensive" prices; given its virtues, most are willing to overlook the sometimes "disorganized" service.

Limoncello   ▽ 22 20 21 $52
Michelangelo Hotel, 777 Seventh Ave. (bet. 50th & 51st Sts.), 212-582-7932
◪ Partisans pucker up for this "lovely" Theater District Italian and its "excellent" cuisine served in "comfortable", "quiet" environs; however, some say it's "nondescript", with "uneven" eats and "expensive" tabs.

L'IMPERO ⊠   26 24 23 $67
45 Tudor City Pl. (bet. 42nd & 43rd Sts.), 212-599-5045; www.limpero.com
■ "Civilized" and "chic", this "upscale" Italian "tucked away" in Tudor City ranks among the "best in town" thanks to chef Scott Conant's "innovative" cuisine abetted by "superb" wines; also factoring into the meals "to remember" here are the pleasingly "minimalist" decor and a staff that makes you "feel cosseted and special"; it's "definitely not cheap", but the "brilliant" prix fixe is an "excellent value."

Liquors ●   ▽ 19 15 19 $26
219 DeKalb Ave. (bet. Adelphi St. & Clermont Ave.), Brooklyn, 718-488-7700
◪ Sit in the "sweet back garden" at this "funky" Fort Greene Caribbean-Southerner for a "slammin'" meal; locals "love" its "comfortable" vibe, "friendly service" and "good prices", even if a few find the food quality "hit-or-miss."

Little Italy Pizza   22 6 13 $8
1 E. 43rd St. (bet. 5th & Madison Aves.), 212-687-3660 ⊠
11 Park Pl. (bet. B'way & Church St.), 212-227-7077 ⊠
180 Varick St. (bet. Charlton & King Sts.), 212-366-5566 ⊠
55 W. 45th St. (bet. 5th & 6th Aves.), 212-730-7575
■ "Classic NY" pizza – "greasy and delicious" – draws droves to this "standing-room-only" quartet, where "the crust is crispy", the toppings "fresh" and the price "fair"; it's "worth waiting" in "lines out the door" considering "it's about as good as a quick slice can get."

Lobster Box

16 | 15 | 16 | $40

34 City Island Ave. (Belden St.), Bronx, 718-885-1952; www.lobsterbox.com

☑ "Take a mini-vacation" via this City Island seafood house, a circa-1946 "time warp" where a "view of the Sound" serves as backdrop to "plentiful" portions of shore classics; even if most agree the eats are just "so-so", it's a festive place, especially when you become "nostalgic for the '50s."

Locanda Vini & Olii

▽ 23 | 23 | 20 | $37

129 Gates Ave. (Cambridge Pl.), Brooklyn, 718-622-9202; www.locandavinieolii.com

■ It's "well worth the trek to deepest Brooklyn" to sample the "simple, earthy" Tuscan fare served in this "charming" Clinton Hill Italian's "cozy", "restored-apothecary" digs; let the "beyond-knowledgeable" staff guide you, but keep in mind that portion sizes "run small."

LOMBARDI'S ⊟

26 | 11 | 15 | $19

32 Spring St. (bet. Mott & Mulberry Sts.), 212-941-7994

■ The "charred", "crispy-crust", "coal-fired" pizzas at this "convivial" taste of "1905 Little Italy" are once again voted among "the best in NY"; what's more, the complaints about "long lines to get in" have been answered by a post-*Survey* expansion that added seating and a bar; as for the bland decor, at least it has charm.

Londel's Supper Club

▽ 21 | 17 | 18 | $32

2620 Frederick Douglass Blvd. (bet. 139th & 140th Sts.), 212-234-6114; www.londelsrestaurant.com

☑ Admirers say this "throwback-to-old-Harlem" Southerner is a "diamond in the rough" sparkling with "wonderful" soul food and owner Londel Davis' fine "hospitality"; a few doubters point to "average" fare and "slow" service, but Sunday brunch is "da bomb."

London Lennie's

20 | 15 | 17 | $36

63-88 Woodhaven Blvd. (bet. Fleet Ct. & Penelope Ave.), Queens, 718-894-8084; www.londonlennies.com

■ Fish "so fresh you almost have to slap it" is what this Rego Park "landmark" is famed for, though the "long weekend waits" are also notorious; no matter that it feels a bit like a "big barn" – its mature followers know "reliable" food and service when they find it.

Long Tan ●

19 | 19 | 17 | $28

196 Fifth Ave. (bet. Berkeley Pl. & Union St.), Brooklyn, 718-622-8444; www.long-tan.com

■ The "fiery open kitchen" takes center stage at this "very hip" Park Slope Thai, whose "chic" eats are served in a "super-stylish" setting (complete with "lovely garden" in summer); "creative drinks" from the dimly lit bar take the sting out of "sometimes long waits" for a table.

L'Orange Bleue ●

17 | 17 | 16 | $39

430 Broome St. (Crosby St.), 212-226-4999; www.lorangebleue.com

☑ "As wacky as its name", this "funky" SoHo French-Med offers "something different", from its food to its "festive" vibe; critics may find it "uneven", but the whole place parties when they trot out the "sparkler"-topped "birthday cakes" and the "belly dancers take over."

Lorto ⌧

▽ 21 | 22 | 22 | $55

5 Gold St. (bet. Maiden Ln. & Platt St.), 212-742-8524; www.lortonyc.com

☑ Diners are of two minds about this Financial District "dress-up" Italian: while partisans call it a "classy" choice thanks to "excellent" cuisine and a "professional" staff, detractors dismiss it as "mediocre", with "vintage-1980s decor" and "slow service"; on one point all agree: it's "pricey."

Los Dos Molinos ⊠

19 17 16 $32

119 E. 18th St. (bet. Irving Pl. & Park Ave. S.), 212-505-1574

■ "The food's as spicy as the clientele" at this "kitschy", "good-time" Gramercy Southwestern known for its "hotter-than-July" grub and "spectacular" "fishbowl"-size margaritas that help tame the "heat" and take the mind off the "jammed, noisy" conditions.

Lotus ●ⓓ⊠

16 23 16 $51

409 W. 14th St. (bet. 9th Ave. & Washington St.), 212-243-4420; www.lotusnewyork.com

☑ It's like "dining in the middle of an MTV video" at this mega– Meatpacking District "nightclub"/eatery/"celeb scene"; a few report that the Pan-Asian fare is "surprisingly good" (if "overpriced"), but a more typical reaction is "people eat here?"

Louie's Westside Cafe

▽ 16 14 17 $34

441 Amsterdam Ave. (81st St.), 212-877-1900

☑ There are "not enough places like this on the Upper West Side" say supporters of this "pleasant" if somewhat "ordinary" New American that's a local standby for brunches and "dinners at the bar"; those for whom it's a "favorite hangout" insist "it should be more crowded – but who's complaining?"

Loulou

▽ 22 17 19 $35

222 DeKalb Ave. (bet. Adelphi St. & Clermont Ave.), Brooklyn, 718-246-0633

■ The "perfect neighborhood" nook for a dose of "fine" French cooking by way of Brittany, this "friendly" Fort Greene bistro is "reliable" for "romantic" dinners in "cozy" (some say "cramped") environs; however, it's brunch that really keeps 'em "coming back", especially when the "lovely" garden is open.

Luca

21 16 20 $38

1712 First Ave. (bet. 88th & 89th Sts.), 212-987-9260; www.lucatogo.com

■ Chef Luca Marcato "seamlessly supervises the kitchen while charming the hell out of guests" at this Upper East Side Northern Italian; "don't be fooled by the lack of decor" or the "middle-of-nowhere" address, because the food here is "surprisingly sophisticated" and a "good value."

Lucien ●

21 15 17 $36

14 First Ave. (bet. 1st & 2nd Sts.), 212-260-6481

■ Conjuring up "the Left Bank", this "small" East Village bistro provides "well-prepared" standards at "reasonable prices" plus a "*très* French" vibe, from the "attitudinous" staff to the "crowded, noisy" quarters that feel so Parisian "you almost expect to see" cigarette smoke.

Lucky Strike ●

16 15 14 $30

59 Grand St. (bet. W. B'way & Wooster St.), 212-941-0479; www.luckystrikeny.com

☑ An "antidote to the scene-y, overpriced" eateries that have grown up around it, Keith McNally's original SoHo bistro remains a "classic standby" for drinks, burgers and other simple eats; if some say it "no longer has that spark", the fact that it has "survived the no-smoking law" speaks volumes.

Lucy

18 21 17 $44

ABC Carpet & Home, 35 E. 18th St. (bet. B'way & Park Ave. S.), 212-475-5829; www.abchome.com

☑ Amigos declare this "upscale" Flatiron Mexican "a hit" thanks to "haute" south-of-the-border fare (overseen by Patria chef Andrew DiCataldo) and "lovely" "white"-toned digs; others say it's "still working out kinks", e.g. sometimes-"absent" service, but all agree that "creative" cocktails make the "sexy" front lounge "a must."

Luke's Bar & Grill ●▱

17 | 13 | 18 | $25

1394 Third Ave. (bet. 79th & 80th Sts.), 212-249-7070

☑ "Not-bad pub food" is the forte of this "laid-back" American that's an unassuming "Upper East Side institution" and just the place "to meet friends for a beer" and a burger; "convivial waitresses" and a "lively" "multigenerational" crowd seal the deal.

Lumi ●

▽ 17 | 17 | 18 | $49

963 Lexington Ave. (70th St.), 212-570-2335; www.lumirestaurant.com

☑ An "upscale" Upper East Side crowd turns to this Northern Italian for "well-prepared" pastas and other eats smoothly served in "pleasant" quarters; it's "pricey" and some say "nothing truly excites", but the fireplace in winter and sidewalk seats in summer earn bonus points.

Luna Piena

18 | 16 | 18 | $35

243 E. 53rd St. (bet. 2nd & 3rd Aves.), 212-308-8882

☑ This "friendly", "informal" Midtown Italian may be "unremarkable", but it's a "reliable" standby for "predictable" pastas and the like at moderate prices; what's more, its "charming little garden" is an "oasis" amid a desert of "cheesy bars."

Lunchbox Food Co. ●

19 | 17 | 15 | $26

357 West St. (bet. Clarkson & Leroy Sts.), 646-230-9466; www.lunchboxnyc.com

☑ "Worth the trek" to the "edge of the known universe" (i.e. the Way West Village), this "retro-chic" New American in a "cute" restored diner has a following for its "flavorful" food, "amazing" homemade doughnuts and appealing back garden; however, skeptics see "real potential" but "disappointing" results.

Lundy Bros.

15 | 17 | 15 | $39

1901 Emmons Ave. (Ocean Ave.), Brooklyn, 718-743-0022; www.lundybros.com

☑ No, it's "not the Lundy's you remember", but this "reincarnated" Sheepshead Bay seafood "landmark" is a "part of Brooklyn history" nonetheless, where folks "longing for the old days" line up for "large portions" of "ok" food; cynics simply sigh "you can't go home again."

LUPA ●

25 | 19 | 21 | $46

170 Thompson St. (bet. Bleecker & Houston Sts.), 212-982-5089; www.luparestaurant.com

■ "Babbo for the common folk" courtesy of the Batali-Bastianich-Denton team, this "authentic Roman trattoria" in the Village provides "simple" yet "insanely tasty" cuisine for very "friendly prices", given the pedigree; it's *molto* "cramped" and "noisy" but "who cares?", though without a reservation you may "go Lupy" "waiting for a table."

Lusardi's ●

25 | 19 | 22 | $55

1494 Second Ave. (bet. 77th & 78th Sts.), 212-249-2020; www.lusardis.com

■ It "keeps getting better with age" declare devotees of this "upscale" Upper East Side Northern Italian lauded for its "bravo" "old-school" cuisine, "exceptional wine list" and "warm", "attentive service"; no wonder its "steady" "older" clientele doesn't flinch at the "expensive" tabs or "cheek-by-jowl" dinner hour and weekend seating.

Luxia ●

19 | 17 | 18 | $41

315 W. 48th St. (bet. 8th & 9th Aves.), 212-957-0800; www.luxianyc.com

■ Though most agree the food's good enough at this Theater District Italian, its "biggest assets" may be its "dangerous cocktails" and "charming hideaway garden"; it also gets "cheers" for the kitchen's "sustainable food" policy – dishes are mostly made of organic and free-range ingredients.

Macelleria ●

21 18 18 $44

48 Gansevoort St. (bet. Greenwich & Washington Sts.), 212-741-2555
☑ Amid "attitude heaven" in the Meatpacking District lies this "unpretentious", "family-run" Italian chophouse dishing up "delicious steaks and pastas" in "cavernous", butcher shop–like digs; downstairs there's a "straight-out-of-Chianti" "converted wine cellar" that's particularly "lovely", though "spotty" service isn't.

Madiba ●

▽ 20 22 22 $33

195 DeKalb Ave. (bet. Adelphi St. & Carlton Ave.), Brooklyn, 718-855-9190;
www.madibaweb.com
■ Possibly "the only South African restaurant in NY", this "quirky, upbeat" Fort Greene pioneer has "found its groove" as well as a "hip" following for its fine fare and "wonderful" occasional live music; tipplers "hail" its "fabulous drinks" ("a glass of *bliksum*", anyone?).

Madison Bistro

20 17 20 $44

238 Madison Ave. (bet. 37th & 38th Sts.), 212-447-1919;
www.madisonbistro.com
■ This "romantic" Murray Hill "gem" "whispers tastefully and seductively in French" to passersby, luring in "daters" ("business lunchers" too) for "reliable" bistro classics served by a "lovely" crew; wallet-watchers also tout the "interesting prix fixe menus."

Madison's

▽ 21 19 21 $37

5686 Riverdale Ave. (258th St.), Bronx, 718-543-3850
■ Candidate for "best restaurant in Riverdale" – though in truth this "relaxed" Italian doesn't have much competition; locals give thanks for its "chic" atmosphere and "quality" meals served with "style" by a "friendly" staff.

Magnifico ⊠

22 15 20 $46

200 Ninth Ave. (22nd St.), 212-633-8033
☑ "Friendly host" Adolfo Magnifico "welcomes guests like an Italian uncle" at this Chelsea "sleeper", where "simple but delicious" food from The Boot's northern reaches comes in a somewhat "plain setting"; service may need polishing, since some find it "wonderful" while others shrug "amateurish."

Magnolia

▽ 21 17 17 $29

486 Sixth Ave. (12th St.), Brooklyn, 718-369-4814;
www.magnoliabrooklyn.com
☑ "Just off the beaten path" in Park Slope, this "adorable" little New American has found its stride as a "neighborhood haunt"; if "nothing to rave about", it's appreciated for its prix fixe brunch and "live jazz" on weekends.

Maia

_ _ _ M

98 Ave. B (bet. 6th & 7th Sts.), 212-358-1166
There are no menus at this roomy, moderately priced East Village Turk, where plainly pleased patrons choose from a tray of cold meze (hot meze and entrees are also available); look for photos of 1950s Istanbul on the walls and belly dancing on Wednesdays.

Malagueta

▽ 25 13 19 $25

25-35 36th Ave. (28th St.), Queens, 718-937-4821; www.malagueta.com
■ "Artistic interpretations of classic Brazilian street" snacks and "home cooking" are the specialty of this low-budget, "family-run" Astoria

"hole-in-the-wall"; the "friendly" "real-deal" staff is another reason it shows "promise" as an "outer-borough highlight."

Malatesta Trattoria ●⇗ ∇ 21 | 17 | 17 | $28
649 Washington St. (Christopher St.), 212-741-1207
■ Travel to "West Village Siberia" for a taste of "authentic, fresh" "pasta as it should be" at this "romantically disheveled" Italian manned by "sexy" servers "straight from" The Boot; remarkably low prices for the area are another big draw, but keep in mind "it's cash-only."

Maloney & Porcelli ● 23 | 20 | 22 | $58
37 E. 50th St. (bet. Madison & Park Aves.), 212-750-2233;
www.maloneyandporcelli.com
■ "The crackling pork shank is a work of art" at this chophouse–cum–"power" magnet in Midtown, which also specializes in first-class "brontosaurus"-size steaks; though quite a "manly" scene, "women like it" too, and all can agree it's "expense-account eating at its best"; P.S. the "private dining room is great for a party."

Mamá Mexico ● 19 | 17 | 18 | $32
2672 Broadway (bet. 101st & 102nd Sts.), 212-864-2323
214 E. 49th St. (bet. 2nd & 3rd Aves.), 212-935-1316
www.mamamexico.com
☑ "Eat, drink and be mariachi!" cheer revelers at this "crowded", "raucous" Mexican twosome, where "every day's a fiesta" and the "free tequila shots" "flow like water"; oh yes, there's *delicioso* food, for those sober enough to know the difference.

Mama's Food Shop ⊠⇗ 22 | 10 | 13 | $13
200 E. Third St. (bet. Aves. A & B), 212-777-4425
222 Sullivan St. (bet. Bleecker & W. 3rd Sts.), 212-505-8123
www.mamasfoodshop.com
☑ A bad day can easily be redeemed with a "heaping portion" or two of the comfort classics dished up with "lots of butter and love" at this simple Village American duo; what's more, the "mack-daddy mac 'n' cheese", fried chicken and other "soulful" standards offer some of the best "bangs for the buck" going – if you can get served.

Mamlouk 24 | 19 | 20 | $39
211 E. Fourth St. (bet. Aves. A & B), 212-529-3477
■ "Recline and be served" on comfortable settees at this "funky" East Village Middle Eastern offering "fragrant, well-cooked" dinners via a six-course, $35 set menu featuring "a multitude of fabulous" tastes; the staff will make you feel "like family", but too bad Mayor Mike outlawed the "hookah."

Mancora ● ∇ 20 | 14 | 19 | $29
99 First Ave. (6th St.), 212-253-1011
176 Smith St. (bet. Warren & Wyckoff Sts.), Brooklyn, 718-643-2629
■ "Amazingly tasty" rotisserie chicken, seviche and such in "generous portions" is the strong suit of this "authentic" Cobble Hill Peruvian (with a new offshoot in the East Village); perhaps the rather "small" quarters could use "a decorator", however "sweet service" and "inexpensive" tabs compensate.

Mandarin Court 19 | 7 | 13 | $19
61 Mott St. (bet. Bayard & Canal Sts.), 212-608-3838
☑ Sure, the decor's "on the scary side" and service is less than stellar, but "when you taste the food" all is forgiven at this Chinatown "dim sum heaven" dispensing "filling" "cart"-borne morsels; no wonder it gets "crowded on weekends."

Mandoo Bar
19 | 14 | 16 | $24

71 University Pl. (bet. 10th & 11th Sts.), 212-358-0400
2 W. 32nd St. (bet. B'way & 5th Ave.), 212-279-3075
www.mandoobar.com

■ "The namesake dumplings are the highlight" at this "hip" Garment District Korean that just expanded into the "NYU scene" with a "sleeker" new Village branch; recidivists warn those "little bundles of joy" are "addictive" ("you can't stop popping them in your mouth"), but fortunately they're relatively "cheap."

Manducatis ⌖
22 | 12 | 17 | $41

13-27 Jackson Ave. (47th Rd.), Queens, 718-729-4602

⌖ The "old-fashioned" Italian kitchen at this "family-run" Long Island City "gem" "has love and respect for food" and it shows in its "truly special" red-sauce dishes; the decor doesn't impress, but the "leisurely" service is "warm" – especially if "they know you."

Mangia ⌖
20 | 12 | 13 | $18

16 E. 48th St. (bet. 5th & Madison Aves.), 212-754-0637
Trump Bldg., 40 Wall St. (bet. Broad & William Sts.), 212-425-4040
22 W. 23rd St. (bet. 5th & 6th Aves.), 212-647-0200
50 W. 57th St. (bet. 5th & 6th Aves.), 212-582-5554
www.mangiatogo.com

■ "The highest of the high-end take-out" shops, this "chichi cafeteria" quartet presents "working lunchers" with a "tantalizing", "something-for-everyone" "spread" of "super-fresh, inventive" Med offerings; while many say it's "pricey" for a glorified "salad bar", "corporate" types depend on it for their daily office meals.

Mangiarini
22 | 14 | 19 | $32

1593 Second Ave. (bet. 82nd & 83rd Sts.), 212-734-5500;
www.mangiarini.com

■ This "matchbox-size" Upper East Side "hidden treasure" turns out "healthy", "rustic" Italian fare that "lets the ingredients shine" through; while "reasonable" prices and "warm" staffers win approval, style sticklers say the "spartan" decor's "a turnoff."

Manhattan Grille
20 | 19 | 19 | $56

1161 First Ave. (bet. 63rd & 64th Sts.), 212-888-6556;
www.themanhattangrille.com

⌖ "Clubby", comfortable East Side steakhouse that's been a longtime local standby for "huge" slabs of beef and lobsters, with accordingly "big" price tags; if upstarts find it "a bit past its prime", its faithful "older clientele" enjoys the "walk back in time."

Manhattan Ocean Club
24 | 21 | 22 | $64

57 W. 58th St. (bet. 5th & 6th Aves.), 212-371-7777;
www.manhattanoceanclub.com

■ "Several leagues above" the usual, this Midtown "seafood lovers'" haven stands out thanks to its "fresh, fresh, fresh" fish "professionally served amid "classy", "nautically" themed digs adorned with "Picasso ceramics"; no wonder it snags diners "hook, line and wallet."

Mara's Homemade
▽ 21 | 12 | 19 | $26

342 E. Sixth St. (bet. 1st & 2nd Aves.), 212-598-1110;
www.marashomemade.com

■ Crustaceans "flown in" "from New Orleans" make for memorable "crawfish boils" (in season) at this "cozy" Cajun-Creole newcomer that stands out in contrast to the Indian eateries on Curry Row; "large portions", moderate prices and "friendly", "attentive service" more than make up for the "humble" quarters.

MARCH
27 25 26 $88

405 E. 58th St. (bet. 1st Ave. & Sutton Pl.), 212-754-6272;
www.marchrestaurant.com

■ "Oh, the romance" swoon sweethearts of this "dreamy" East Side townhouse whose "intimate", sophisticated air and "loving attention to detail" make it "the place to go" when you want "to be pampered" (or maybe even "pop the question"); the "design-your-own" tasting menu is a good way to sample chef Wayne Nish's "simply superb" New American creations, but beware of "sticker shock."

Marchi's ⊠
▽ 18 17 22 $50

251 E. 31st St. (bet. 2nd & 3rd Aves.), 212-679-2494;
www.marchirestaurant.com

☑ A Kips Bay "standby" since 1930, this "no-menu", prix fixe–only "traditional" Northern Italian is seen by some as "a hidden treasure" offering "comforting" "five-course" "feasts" plus "excellent hospitality" in a "quaint" townhouse; to others it's more of an "interesting" retro experience "than a gourmet meal."

Marco New York ❶
– – – M

142 W. 10th St. (bet. Greenwich Ave. & 7th Ave. S.), 212-243-2222

The impresario behind Marco Fire Island has come ashore with this West Village trattoria near the landmark Jefferson Market library; look for a menu mixing familiar pastas and unusual roasts (e.g. wild boar) plus lighter late-night bites, presented in a narrow, white-brick grotto decorated with rotating original art.

Marco Polo Ristorante
19 16 19 $42

345 Court St. (Union St.), Brooklyn, 718-852-5015;
www.marcopoloristorante.com

☑ "Paulie Walnuts would feel right at home" at this "classic" Carroll Gardens Italian where the food's "hearty and delicious", the staff "warm and welcoming" and there's even valet parking; still, some knock "overdecorated" digs and "Manhattan" prices.

Mardi Gras ❶
18 19 17 $30

70-20 Austin St. (bet. 70th Ave. & 70th Rd.), Queens, 718-261-8555

☑ For a "taste of Bourbon Street in Forest Hills", try this "festive" Cajun-Creole serving up jambalaya, shrimp creole and other "hot stuff" along with "potent potables" and "live jazz" (on Thursdays); for most it's pure "party", though a few poopers say it's too "noisy and crowded."

Maria Pia
20 17 20 $34

319 W. 51st St. (bet. 8th & 9th Aves.), 212-765-6463; www.mariapianyc.com

■ This "cute, quaint" Theater District Italian is a pre-curtain favorite for "fresh", "simple" pastas and the like at moderate prices; shining just as brightly as the food is the "young staff" that "tries very hard to please"; P.S. "if the garden's open", head there.

Marichu
21 17 20 $49

342 E. 46th St. (bet. 1st & 2nd Aves.), 212-370-1866; www.marichu.com

☑ "Basque in the aroma" of this UN-area Spaniard's "delicious" dishes (including some "not found elsewhere") matched with "wonderful" Iberian wines and delivered by "friendly waiters" in "comfortable" environs; most feel it's "worth the steep bill", especially if seated in the "pleasant secret garden."

Marina Cafe
▽ 17 19 18 $42

154 Mansion Ave. (Hillside Terr.), Staten Island, 718-967-3077;
www.marinacafegrand.com

☑ "It's tough to beat the view" overlooking Great Kills Harbor from this Staten Island seafooder, though its "'80s" decor can seem "rather dull" if you're "not near a window"; the food gets mixed reviews ("tasty" vs. "Red Lobster–quality"), but the "relaxed, upbeat" mood is hard to argue with.

Marinella
▽ 22 | 15 | 22 | $39

49 Carmine St. (Bedford St.), 212-807-7472

■ An "old-school Italian" that "seems to have wandered out of Little Italy", this "service-oriented" West Village vet is a "tourist"- and "family-friendly" provider of "consistently fine" red-gravy fare; the "prices aren't bad" and repeat visitors report "if you're a regular they'll do anything for you."

Marion's Continental ◐
▽ 16 | 19 | 18 | $30

354 Bowery (bet. 4th & Great Jones Sts.), 212-475-7621

☑ "There's likely to be at least one drag queen" in attendance at this "retro"-"kitsch" "Susan Hayward–style" nightclub-eatery where "knock-your-socks-off" cocktails draw more notice than the American eats; the raucous "floor shows" will amuse, if you don't mind the "crowded, loud and more-than-a-bit-hectic" vibe.

Mario's
21 | 14 | 20 | $37

2342 Arthur Ave. (bet. 184th & 186th Sts.), Bronx, 718-584-1188

■ "Italian the way it used to be" describes this Arthur Avenue "true classic", a provider of "good red-sauce" dishes "graciously" served by "old-fashioned" "tuxedoed waiters"; if the vintage-1950s interior is "getting a little tacky", "loyal" regulars wouldn't have it any other way.

MarkJoseph Steakhouse Ⓢ
25 | 18 | 22 | $62

261 Water St. (off Peck Slip), 212-277-0020;
www.markjosephsteakhouse.com

■ A "he-man" haven "unexpectedly located" on an out-of-the-way Financial District corner, this "upscale" steakhouse draws a "Wall Street power" crowd for near-"perfect" porterhouses at accordingly "steep prices"; ok, maybe "nothing compares to Peter Luger", but admirers note that this rival offers "attentive" service (no "crotchety waiters" here) and "takes plastic."

Mark's
23 | 25 | 24 | $65

Mark Hotel, 25 E. 77th St. (bet. 5th & Madison Aves.), 212-879-1864;
www.mandarinoriental.com

■ "Elegant", "high-end" English-style decor competes with "solicitous" pro service and first-rate French-American food at this popular restaurant in the Mark Hotel; particularly favored for its "wine-tasting" dinners, it's also "fantastic for high tea" or brunch; what's more, the prix fixe menus are "a bargain."

Markt ◐
19 | 18 | 16 | $40

401 W. 14th St. (9th Ave.), 212-727-3314

☑ "Real Belgian" is the name of the game at this "hopping", "noisy", "big-as-a-barn" Meatpacking District brasserie, but the "people-watching" is just as "tasty", especially from "sidewalk" seats; regulars advise "keep it simple" (hint: moules frites and a trappist ale are "the perfect combo"), and don't expect snappy service.

Maroons ◐
21 | 14 | 17 | $34

244 W. 16th St. (bet. 7th & 8th Aves.), 212-206-8640

■ The "food has a touch of love" at this "charming", "soulful" Chelsea Southern-Caribbean, and while it's "not a place to find low-cal, low-fat" fare, surveyors say surrender to the "fab fried chicken" or "live to regret it"; though it expanded not long ago, "long waits" are still the norm.

Marseille
21 | 20 | 19 | $49

630 Ninth Ave. (44th St.), 212-333-2323; www.marseillenyc.com

◪ "The perfect solution" to the pre- or post-theater dining "dilemma", this Hell's Kitchen French-Mediterranean is a "spacious", "sultry" showcase for "excellent, innovative" cooking; despite complaints about "deafening" noise levels and "pricey" tabs for "smallish portions", most consider it a "find"; N.B. the departure of chef Alex Ureña puts its Food score in question.

Mars 2112
9 | 23 | 13 | $30

1633 Broadway (51st St.), 212-582-2112; www.mars2112.com

◪ "Kids love" this "awesome", "planet"-size Midtown American theme joint for its "transcendent" "spaceship ride" (read: "motion simulator") and "space-age" setup complete with costumed "aliens"; however, if you're "over 12" you may find it "overpriced" and "as devoid of good food as Mars itself."

Maruzzella ●
∇ 21 | 15 | 22 | $37

1483 First Ave. (bet. 77th & 78th Sts.), 212-988-8877

■ "Come with a reservation or expect to wait" at this "tiny" Upper Eastsider that hyperbolic habitués call "literally the best local Italian ever"; "killer fresh pastas", a "helpful", "friendly" staff and "affordable" tabs have 'em pleading "shhh, don't tell anybody about this gem."

Mary Ann's
16 | 12 | 15 | $24

2452 Broadway (bet. 90th & 91st Sts.), 212-877-0132
116 Eighth Ave. (16th St.), 212-633-0877 ⊟
1803 Second Ave. (93rd St.), 212-426-8350
1503 Second Ave. (bet. 78th & 79th Sts.), 212-249-6165
80 Second Ave. (5th St.), 212-475-5939 ⊟
107 W. Broadway (bet. Chambers & Reade Sts.), 212-766-0911 ●

◪ It "ain't authentic", but this "festive", "colorful" mini-chain is "just what a NY Tex-Mex should be" according to addicts of its "good, greasy" "cheap" eats and "mmm margaritas"; it's also "increasingly a place to bring the baby strollers" early evenings, before the "crowded" "*ay caramba*" "scene" heats up.

Mary's Fish Camp ⊠
24 | 13 | 18 | $37

64 Charles St. (W. 4th St.), 646-486-2185; www.marysfishcamp.com

■ "You can almost feel the sand between your toes" at this "divine", "diminutive" West Village seafood "shack" that's "staffed by sassy sylphs"; its "superlative" lobster rolls and other shore classics have groupies gladly enduring "cramped", "crowded" conditions, declaring "the only problem is getting in."

Mas ●⊠
∇ 28 | 27 | 27 | $66

39 Downing St. (bet. Bedford & Varick Sts.), 212-255-1790

■ Though "named for a farmhouse", this "highly sophisticated" New American hidden on a Greenwich Village side street is "certainly unlike" anything you'd find on the grange, from chef-owner Galen Zamarra's "adventurous" seasonal cuisine featuring local ingredients to the "attentive" service and "stylish" decor mixing modern with rustic; no surprise, prices are citified as well.

MASA ⊠
∇ 28 | 25 | 26 | $366

Time Warner Ctr., 10 Columbus Circle, 4th fl. (60th St. at B'way), 212-823-9800

■ Having closed his famed Ginza Sushi-Ko to open this "transporting", "Zen-like" Japanese in the Time Warner Center, LA sushi king Masayoshi Takayama is now producing "sublime" kaiseki-style dinners of a caliber never before seen in NYC; his tasting menus come with equally "stunning price tags" ($300 "before drink"), but given such "unmatched" quality, early visitors conclude "believe it or not, it's worth it."

MATSURI ◑

23 | 27 | 20 | $53

Maritime Hotel, 369 W. 16th St. (9th Ave.), 212-243-6400

■ Further evidencing how hot West Chelsea has become, this "spectacular", "cavernous", "lantern"-filled space under the Maritime Hotel sports "star-sightings galore" as well as lots of could-bes; both the ambiance and chef Tadashi Ono's Japanese food dazzle diners, so the "only problem is getting a table"; N.B. be careful not to wash your hands in the urinal or sit in the sink.

Maurizio Trattoria ◑

– | – | – | M

35 W. 13th St. (bet. 5th & 6th Aves.), 212-206-6474

This new West Village Northern Italian has 'laid-back neighborhood place' written all over it thanks to its unassuming side-street location, airy interior and well-spaced tables; hearty dishes with Tuscan roots make locals linger, while a secluded back room is just right for a quiet dinner party.

Max ◑⇗

22 | 16 | 15 | $25

1274 Amsterdam Ave. (123rd St.), 212-531-2221
51 Ave. B (bet. 3rd & 4th Sts.), 212-539-0111
www.maxrestaurantny.com

■ These East Village–Upper West Side Italian "holes-in-the-wall" have perfected their "casual", "cash-only" formula, dishing up lotsa "dependably" "delicious" pastas and such for "cheap"; no surprise, they're usually "crowded", but "cool, young" locals sanguinely "accept the long waits" given the "excellent value."

Maya

24 | 20 | 20 | $48

1191 First Ave. (bet. 64th & 65th Sts.), 212-585-1818;
www.modernmexican.com

■ Don't expect to find "basic burrito parlor" eats (or prices) at this "hip" East Side "Nuevo Mexican" – its "innovative" dishes elevate the cuisine "to a whole new level"; still, that doesn't mean you won't find "potent margaritas", "*fantástico*" guacamole and an "energetic" (read: "loud") scene.

Mayrose

15 | 11 | 13 | $21

920 Broadway (21st St.), 212-533-3663

◪ One part "upscale diner", one part "yuppieteria" describes this "always bustling" Flatiron "favorite"; seemingly everyone in the area "squishes" in at lunch for "comfort" classics like "mighty mac 'n' cheese", so "be prepared to wait"; P.S. a recent "spiff-up" may not be reflected in the Decor score.

Maz Mezcal ◑

20 | 17 | 18 | $34

316 E. 86th St. (bet. 1st & 2nd Aves.), 212-472-1599;
www.mazmezcal.com

■ It was once a "hidden gem", but "the word is out" on this "cheery" Mexican Eastsider where the vibe is "tropical island" and the "wicked" drinks and "fresh, well-prepared" eats are "one or two cuts above" the standard; just "be sure to make a reservation" and bring earplugs on "high-decibel" weekends.

McCormick & Schmick's

– | – | – | E

1285 Sixth Ave. (enter on 52nd St., bet. 6th & 7th Aves.), 212-459-1222;
www.mccormickandschmicks.com

Formerly Angelo & Maxie's chop shop, this Midtowner shifts from turf to surf by landing NYC's first outpost of the national seafood chain; while the decor leans toward the traditionally clubby (right down to the signature snugs, or private booths), the slate of grilled and roasted items is a bit more adventuresome.

McHales ●⊅ | 20 | 8 | 15 | $20 |
750 Eighth Ave. (46th St.), 212-997-8885

■ "Juicy" burgers "big enough for two" and other "cheap" bar eats are what keep the "stagehands" "coming back" to this Theater District "institution" that's ideal "before or after a show"; diehards declare it "the perfect dive."

Med' Cafe | – | – | – | M |
99 Second Ave. (bet. 5th & 6th Sts.), 212-477-8427

Once global (i.e. Global 33, its former occupant), this simple East Villager is now dedicated to the cuisine of the Mediterranean Sea; naturally, fish dominates the midpriced menu and there's a full raw bar that's even available at brunch.

Medina ● | – | – | – | M |
315 10th Ave. (bet. 28th & 29th Sts.), 212-239-0057

Hidden on a quiet block in Way West Chelsea, this cozy casbah presents Moroccan dishes in a loungelike setting complete with plush burgundy banquettes and atmospheric lanterns and sconces; a secluded back garden is inviting in warm weather.

Mediterraneo ● | 19 | 16 | 15 | $35 |
1260 Second Ave. (66th St.), 212-734-7407

☑ A recent expansion has "doubled the size" of this East Side Italian "hot spot", which means room for more relishers of its "value"-priced pastas and such; the "Euro scene" is especially "vibrant" in warm weather, when the "cheek-kissing" takes place at outdoor tables.

Mee Noodle Shop | 17 | 4 | 13 | $14 |
219 First Ave. (13th St.), 212-995-0333
795 Ninth Ave. (53rd St.), 212-765-2929
922 Second Ave. (49th St.), 212-888-0027
547 Second Ave. (bet. 30th & 31st Sts.), 212-779-1596

☑ "You get more than you pay for" at this "Chinese-on-the-quick" noodle quartet ladling "soup for the soul" at "steal" prices; those who disdain the "no-frills" setup tout "super-fast delivery."

Meet | 16 | 20 | 15 | $44 |
71-73 Gansevoort St. (Washington St.), 212-242-0990; www.the-meet.com

☑ It may feel more like "a lounge that happens to serve food" than a restaurant, but admirers attest this "mod, chic"-looking Meatpacking District Med turns out "surprisingly decent" fare; skeptics say the eats "could be better", as could service, but there's plentiful "eye candy" for distraction.

MEGU ● | 23 | 28 | 23 | $93 |
62 Thomas St. (bet. Church St. & W. B'way), 212-964-7777; www.megunyc.com

■ Bring megu-bucks to this TriBeCa Japanese newcomer occupying an "over-the-top" "Hollywood-meets-Tokyo" space, where everything from the "fabulous Buddha ice sculpture" to the "$25 edamame" contributes to the "pure drama" of the experience; as for the food, those who can focus on it report "exquisite, inventive" dishes that may "awaken taste buds you never knew existed."

MeKong | 18 | 14 | 15 | $27 |
44 Prince St. (bet. Mott & Mulberry Sts.), 212-343-8169
259 Fifth Ave. (Garfield Pl.), Brooklyn, 718-788-1210 ●

☑ Ok, it's "dark", "loud" and the servers can "seem like they don't get it", but even so this NoLita Vietnamese is deemed a "solid performer"

.resh", "spicy" food and "fair prices"; the new Park Slope outpost has a "hipper feel" and is voted "a great addition" to the area.

Meltemi
20 | 15 | 20 | $44

905 First Ave. (51st St.), 212-355-4040
☑ Even if you "missed the Olympics", you can get a taste of the "Greek islands" at this "cheery" Sutton Place Hellenic, whose "fresh" "grilled" fish and other "classics" leave "lots of satisfied customers" in their wake; still, a few carpers crab it's "unnecessarily pricey."

Menchanko-tei ●
19 | 8 | 14 | $20

131 E. 45th St. (bet. Lexington & 3rd Aves.), 212-986-6805
43-45 W. 55th St. (bet. 5th & 6th Aves.), 212-247-1585
www.menchankotei.com
■ "It's just like Tokyo (even the clientele)" at this Midtown Japanese noodle duo, where "steaming bowls" of ramen and soba in "housemade broth" make "quick" lunches to "warm the soul"; best of all, the "inexpensive" tabs don't drain the wallet.

Mercer Kitchen ●
22 | 22 | 18 | $53

Mercer Hotel, 99 Prince St. (Mercer St.), 212-966-5454;
www.jean-georges.com
☑ "Still trendy", Jean-Georges Vongerichten's "underground" "SoHo classic" proffers "creative" French–New American "done right" amid "sleek" surroundings; however, some grumble about the "inattentive" staff and wonder whether the "steep" prices "include the cost of sitting next to a celebrity."

Merchants, N.Y. ●
15 | 17 | 15 | $32

1125 First Ave. (62nd St.), 212-832-1551
112 Seventh Ave. (bet. 16th & 17th Sts.), 212-366-7267
www.merchantsny.com
☑ These "huge", "busy" "lounges with kitchens" are always "good for a glass of wine" and "popular" with "young daters" and "B&T" types who appreciate the "basic" "something-for-everyone" New American eats; detractors say call Martha – "it's time for a makeover."

Mermaid Inn ●
23 | 18 | 20 | $41

96 Second Ave. (bet. 5th & 6th Sts.), 212-674-5870;
www.themermaidnyc.com
■ "Another hit" from the Red Cat/Harrison team, this "great catch" for the East Village reels in raves with its "wonderful" seafood "simply prepared", "smart, welcoming" staff and "New-England-clam-shack-with-class" interior; prices "that won't swim away with your wallet" also please, leaving the "no-rezzies policy" as the "only drawback."

MESA GRILL
23 | 20 | 20 | $51

102 Fifth Ave. (bet. 15th & 16th Sts.), 212-807-7400; www.mesagrill.com
■ Bobby Flay shows he's "not just a cute TV chef" at his Flatiron "flagship" where the "zesty", "Flay-vorful" Southwestern cuisine "still shines" amid a "noisy", "high-energy" atmosphere; in short, this "popular" stalwart is more than "withstanding the test of time."

Meskerem ●
20 | 9 | 14 | $23

124 MacDougal St. (bet. Bleecker & W. 3rd Sts.), 212-777-8111
468 W. 47th St. (bet. 9th & 10th Aves.), 212-664-0520
www.meskeremrestaurant.com
☑ "Ditch the utensils" and "dig in with your hands" at these "better-than-most" Ethiopians offering "spicy, well-flavored" stews and such that you "soak" up with "spongy bread"; "bargain" tabs make the "slow service" and "divey" digs easy to overlook.

Métisse — 21 | 17 | 21 | $41

239 W. 105th St. (bet. Amsterdam Ave. & B'way), 212-666-8825

■ This "quiet, unhurried" Upper West Side French is "the kind of place that's getting harder and harder to find" according to admirers of its reliably good cooking, moderate prices and "unpretentious" service; no wonder it's a "favorite" "neighborhood haunt" that could also be called "the Columbia faculty club."

MetroCafe & Wine Bar — ▽ 19 | 20 | 20 | $34

32 E. 21st St. (bet. B'way & Park Ave. S.), 212-353-0800; www.metrocafenyc.com

■ "Takes the snobbiness out of wine tasting" say budding oenophiles of this "great new find in the Flatiron" that "aims to please" with its "amazing" vino selection (including 100 by the glass, plus "fantastic flights") and "varied", "something-to-suit-everyone" American menu; the "laid-back" vibe and "fair prices" are icing on the cake.

Metro Fish ⊠ — 19 | 15 | 18 | $39

8 E. 36th St. (bet. 5th & Madison Aves.), 212-683-6444; www.metrofishrestaurant.com

☑ "Straightforward" sums up this Murray Hill seafooder, from the "fresh" fish that's "simply" prepared "any way you like" and served in portions big "enough to feed a small army" to the "competent" staff; likewise the surroundings are fairly "antiseptic", but happily the prices aren't too fancy either.

Metropolitan Cafe ◑ — 16 | 16 | 16 | $33

959 First Ave. (bet. 52nd & 53rd Sts.), 212-759-5600; www.arkrestaurants.com

■ Expect "everyday" American fare for "the right price" at this "casual", "reliable" Sutton Place "standby"; it "attracts lots of families" for "weeknight dinners" and "Sunday brunch", making it quite the neighborhood "social hall."

Metsovo ◑ — 17 | 19 | 16 | $40

65 W. 70th St. (bet. Columbus Ave. & CPW), 212-873-2300

☑ "More people should know about" this "pleasant" Lincoln Center–area Greek, whose "decent" fare and "cavernous", "uncrowded" rustic space add up to a "safe" (some say "pedestrian") pre-show choice; "sketchy service" could stand some fine tuning.

Mexicana Mama ⊅ — 26 | 13 | 18 | $28

525 Hudson St. (bet. Charles & W. 10th Sts.), 212-924-4119

☑ "Devotees" of this West Village mama's "inspired" "nouveau Mexican" cooking rate it simply "the best in Nueva York" (especially items from "the specials board") and thus "worth" putting up with the "postage stamp–size" room and "hour-long" waits; better still are the "low-end prices" for such "high-end" quality, though the "cash-only policy is a bummer."

Mexican Radio ◑ — 20 | 14 | 17 | $29

19 Cleveland Pl. (bet. Kenmare & Spring Sts.), 212-343-0140; www.mexrad.com

■ For "flavorful", modestly priced "Mehico eats" and "knockout margaritas", try this "funky" NoLita "standby" that's always "crowded" with "attractive" young things; just know that broadcasts here are a little "too loud" for the sensitive of ear.

Mexican Sandwich Co. — 20 | 10 | 15 | $16

322 Fifth Ave. (bet. 2nd & 3rd Sts.), Brooklyn, 718-369-2058

☑ The "outrageously good" concept behind this Park Slope "novelty" Mexican is "cheap" "gourmet quesadillas" bursting with "clever" combos of "fresh ingredients"; the "small", "hole-in-the-wall" digs are not entirely without charm, but many choose "delivery" nonetheless.

Mezzaluna ◐

19 | 13 | 17 | $39

1295 Third Ave. (bet. 74th & 75th Sts.), 212-535-9600;
www.mezzalunany.com

☑ Further evidence that "good things come in small packages", this "tiny" East Side Italian is locally beloved for its "delicious" pastas and thin-crust pizzas; if some find it "a little costly" for the genre, especially given "sardine" seating and decor in "need of work", that's life in this "upscale neighborhood."

Mezzogiorno ◐

19 | 17 | 18 | $38

195 Spring St. (Sullivan St.), 212-334-2112; www.mezzogiorno.com

■ A "sure bet" for "nothing-fancy" pastas and pizzas at moderate prices, this "longtime" SoHo Italian remains a neighborhood "favorite" for a "pleasant", "no-surprises" experience; it's also "particularly pleasant in warm weather" when outside tables afford "great people-watching."

Michael Jordan's The Steak House NYC

20 | 21 | 18 | $59

Grand Central, North Balcony (42nd St. & Vanderbilt Ave.), 212-655-2300;
www.theglaziergroup.com

☑ If not quite a "slam dunk", MJ's "beef bistro" is a "solid" "performer" in the upscale chophouse league thanks to "quality" steaks "huge" enough "to satisfy his Airness" and a "stellar" space overlooking the Grand Central Concourse; a "word to the wise": even "the investment banker crowd" may be "surprised by the final bill" here.

Michael's ⌧

21 | 20 | 22 | $60

24 W. 55th St. (bet. 5th & 6th Aves.), 212-767-0555;
www.michaelsnewyork.com

■ "If you're a media junkie", you'll find the "best show in town" at this Midtown Californian that's a "perennial" "place to be seen" for the "power-publishing" set; "creative" cooking and "delightful service" agree with civilians too, but star-watchers suggest that breakfast is the best – and cheapest – time to come.

Mickey Mantle's ◐

13 | 19 | 15 | $34

42 Central Park S. (bet. 5th & 6th Aves.), 212-688-7777

☑ "For a game and a brew", you could do much worse than Number 7's "memorabilia"-packed "high-end sports bar" on Central Park South; still, even fans grumble about service and edibles that tend to "strike out" and a clientele heavy on "tourists."

Mi Cocina

23 | 20 | 20 | $41

57 Jane St. (Hudson St.), 212-627-8273

☑ "Top-quality regional Mexican" cooking "gorgeously presented" is what comes out of this West Village *cocina*, which also offers a standout "premium tequila selection"; if a few longtimers find it a tad too "chichi" since a renovation/expansion, most are just glad the "cheerful, lively" quarters gained some elbow room.

Mill Basin Kosher Deli

20 | 14 | 17 | $20

5823 Ave. T (bet. 58th & 59th Sts.), Brooklyn, 718-241-4910;
www.millbasindeli.com

■ "Where else can you get pastrami and Erté?" but at this Mill Basin "institution", an "old-fashioned", "no-frills" kosher Jewish deli with a "Modernist" "gallery built in"; here patrons "nourish both the stomach and the soul" noshing "delish" corned beef and knishes while gazing at great "works of art."

Milos, Estiatorio ◐

25 | 23 | 22 | $67

125 W. 55th St. (bet. 6th & 7th Aves.), 212-245-7400; www.milos.ca

☑ The "granddaddy of Greek estiatorios" is this modern Midtown "seafood temple" where you choose the "freshest imaginable" fish from a "crushed-ice display" and "pay by the weight" to have it "simply" and "beautifully" prepared; unless you order the more affordable appetizers, the prices will be as "high" as the "quality" of the catch, but most report "it's worth it", especially since dining in this "airy", Aegean-inspired space feels like a "summer vacation."

Minado

19 | 14 | 16 | $31

6 E. 32nd St. (bet. 5th & Madison Aves.), 212-725-1333; www.minado.com

☑ "Get ready to gorge" at this "huge, banquet hall"–like Murray Hiller offering an "eye-popping", "block-long" "all-you-can-eat buffet" of Japanese and Korean fare; the "boatloads" of sushi and such may not be "adventurous" but they're "surprisingly fresh", and given the "affordable" prices, "what do you expect?"

Minetta Tavern ◐

▽ 16 | 15 | 17 | $38

113 MacDougal St. (bet. Bleecker & W. 3rd Sts.), 212-475-3850

☑ This Italian "throwback" to "'30s NY" is "like a second home" for Village locals who've long counted on it for "predictable but good food" far "off the tourist path"; those who find it "really tired" suggest an "update", but "sentimentalists" don't mind a bit that it "never changes."

Mingala Burmese

18 | 10 | 16 | $21

1393-B Second Ave. (bet. 72nd & 73rd Sts.), 212-744-8008
21-23 E. Seventh St. (bet. 2nd & 3rd Aves.), 212-529-3656

☑ Adventurous eaters longing for an "alternative to typical Asian fare" need look no further than this East Side Burmese twosome turning out "cheap" dishes "worth exploring"; considering how "sweet" the service is, it's too bad the "no-frills decor" couldn't be "spiced up."

Minnow

22 | 17 | 21 | $36

442 Ninth St. (bet. 6th & 7th Aves.), Brooklyn, 718-832-5500

■ "Loving care is given to every morsel" that emerges from the kitchen at this "inventive" Park Slope seafooder that fawning fans call "fishtastic"; as for the "little" "bistrolike" room, "what it lacks in space, it makes up" for in "warm", "quaint" atmosphere; P.S. the Monday night wine-tasting dinner is "an especially good value."

Miracle Grill

20 | 16 | 17 | $32

415 Bleecker St. (bet. Bank & W. 11th Sts.), 212-924-1900
112 First Ave. (bet. 6th & 7th Sts.), 212-254-2353 ◐

■ "Once a pioneer", this "upscale Southwestern" duo "still holds up" well thanks to "delicious" fare, "imaginative drinks" and "gentle prices" that draw a "young" demographic; the "fabulous" garden at the East Village branch is a warm-weather "charmer."

Mirchi

▽ 21 | 18 | 18 | $31

29 Seventh Ave. S. (bet. Bedford & Morton Sts.), 212-414-0931;
www.mirchiny.com

■ Its "name means 'chile'" in Hindi and this Village Indian "lives up to it", so "believe them when they tell you it's spicy"; its "terrific" "street-food" menu and attractive setting place it "a cut above" the typical subcontinental – "with prices to match."

Mishima

23 | 14 | 19 | $32

164 Lexington Ave. (bet. 30th & 31st Sts.), 212-532-9596

☑ What this Murray Hill Japanese "lacks in atmosphere", it makes up for in "superior fresh sushi" made with "respect for the tradition";

factor in "friendly" service and modest prices and it's a "special find"
indeed – no wonder "getting a table on weekends can be tough."

Miss Mamie's/Miss Maude's   22 | 11 | 15 | $21
547 Lenox Ave. (bet. 137th & 138th Sts.), 212-690-3100
366 W. 110th St. (bet. Columbus & Manhattan Aves.), 212-865-6744
www.spoonbreadinc.com
■When you can't "take a vacation to the relatives down South",
these Harlem soul food kitchens are the next best thing given their
"outstanding" fried chicken, ribs and other "affordable" "home-
cooking" classics; "don't count calories" or focus on the "nonexistent
decor", just bask in the "friendliness and warmth."

Miss Saigon   18 | 11 | 16 | $23
1425 Third Ave. (bet. 80th & 81st Sts.), 212-988-8828
◪At this "dependable" Upper East Side Vietnamese, the main attraction
is "fresh", filling fare at "reasonable" prices; but "poor decor" and a
"rush-you-in-and-out" sensibility mean delivery's "a godsend."

Miss Williamsburg ⌖   ▽ 19 | 14 | 16 | $33
206 Kent Ave. (bet. Metropolitan Ave. & N. 3rd St.), Brooklyn, 718-963-0802
228 E. 10th St. (bet. 1st & 2nd Aves.), 212-228-5355
www.miss-williamsburg.com
■Its "gritty-old-dining-car" setting in a remote corner of Williamsburg
belies the "surprisingly" "flavorful and light" food on offer at this "cozy"
Italian (with a new East Village offshoot); there's also "lovely garden"
seating in summer – no wonder "young artist" types turn out in force.

Mitali ●   19 | 13 | 16 | $26
334 E. Sixth St. (bet. 1st & 2nd Aves.), 212-533-2508
◪Its crosstown sibling has closed, but this "reliable" East Village
Indian still stands as a "safe haven" amid the "Curry Row jumble";
though many find the food a "Bombay dream", others say it's "not as
inventive" as some of its newer neighbors'.

Mix in New York   18 | 21 | 19 | $73
68 W. 58th St. (bet. 5th & 6th Aves.), 212-583-0300; www.chinagrillmgt.com
◪The haute-cuisine takes on comfort food at Alain Ducasse and
Jeffrey Chodorow's Midtown French–New American include the likes
of PB&J and "the best mac 'n' cheese you've ever had", served in
"cool", "ultramodern" digs; while many would "go back in a minute",
caustic critics dismiss it as "gimmicky" and "overpriced", concluding
that "Mix needs a fix."

Mix It ●   – | – | – | M
20 Prince St. (bet. Elizabeth & Mott Sts.), 212-966-8886
The decor of this new midpriced NoLita entry may evoke a comfortable
French bistro, but its Eclectic menu goes further afield, with hanger
steak coexisting with frittatas, cheeseburgers and fish 'n' chips; late-
night hours (till 2 AM on weekends) seal the deal.

Mizu Sushi   24 | 16 | 19 | $34
29 E. 20th St. (bet. B'way & Park Ave. S.), 212-505-6688
■"The secret's out" about this Flatiron Japanese "jewel" where
"creative" sushi is sliced and rolled for an "energetic" young crowd;
it's a lively scene "without a ridiculous tab", but "go early" or be
prepared to be "crammed" in with the "crowds."

MJ Grill   ▽ 20 | 16 | 17 | $41
110 John St. (bet. Cliff & Pearl Sts.), 212-346-9848; www.mjgrill.com
◪This "casual" "little brother to MarkJoseph Steakhouse" in the
Financial District offers a "basic" steak-and-burger American menu

that's "less expensive" and has "more variety" than its parent's; of course, some are drawn more by the "raucous" "after-work" "bar scene"; N.B. closed weekends.

Mo-Bay
▽ 22 | 16 | 16 | $22

17 W. 125th St. (bet. 5th & Lenox Aves.), 212-876-9300
112 DeKalb Ave. (bet. Ashland Pl. & St. Felix St.), Brooklyn, 718-246-2800
www.mobayrestaurant.com

☒ Your "mama's home cooking" has nothing on the "mighty" offerings at these Jamaican soul fooders in Fort Greene and Harlem, where the "amazing" favorites (jerk chicken, braised oxtails, etc.) are joined by lots of veggie options; the only rub is "service on island time" and "tiny" quarters in need of "mo-space."

Mocca ⊄
19 | 10 | 16 | $24

1588 Second Ave. (bet. 82nd & 83rd Sts.), 212-734-6470

☒ Among "the last of its kind", this Upper East Side Hungarian "antique" is "the place" to go when "the urge" strikes for a "hearty, genuine" "Mittel Europa" meal; "bargain" prices are also hard to resist, though the "stern-looking staff" and decor "barely above cafeteria" level aren't.

Mojo
▽ 22 | 16 | 22 | $35

309 E. Fifth St. (bet. 1st & 2nd Aves.), 212-539-1515

■ "A little place with a lot of mojo" sums up this "quirky", "cute" Village newcomer offering Latin-accented New American fare (think "hip comfort" dishes like fish tacos and chorizo mac 'n' cheese) to "make your taste buds dance"; the "low-key atmosphere" and "friendly" staff are also winning it amigos.

Molyvos ●
23 | 20 | 21 | $50

871 Seventh Ave. (bet. 55th & 56th Sts.), 212-582-7500;
www.molyvos.com

■ A "big fat Greek favorite" is how enthusiasts view this "spacious" West 50s taverna, a longtime "winner" thanks to "terrific" "modern" Hellenic fare that's professionally served in a "warm", "elegant" setting; concertgoers concur it's just the thing "pre-Carnegie" even if prices can add up.

Monkey Bar
18 | 22 | 19 | $50

Elysée Hotel, 60 E. 54th St. (bet. Madison & Park Aves.), 212-838-2600;
www.theglaziergroup.com

☒ Feel like you're "in an old-time movie" at this Midtown steakhouse adjacent to the famous bar, where the "well-prepared" but "not very memorable" fare plays second fiddle to the "posh" "old-NY" art deco digs; maybe "it won't make anyone's all-time favorite list", but its "surprisingly quiet" midday ambiance is a boon to "business" lunchers.

Mon Petit Cafe
▽ 19 | 13 | 16 | $33

801 Lexington Ave. (62nd St.), 212-355-2233

■ "Expect a warm welcome" at this "charming" French bistro that's "convenient to Bloomie's"; it's "pleasant" enough for a "decent", "low-priced" meal, but its "small" space can "get very crowded", especially during lunch hours.

Monsoon ●
19 | 14 | 17 | $26

435 Amsterdam Ave. (81st St.), 212-580-8686

☒ To have an "interesting" meal "without spending a fortune", check out this Upper West Side Vietnamese "standby" serving consistently good fare in "cute", "exotic" environs; "speedy" delivery comes in handy during prime hours when folks "pack in like sardines."

Monster Sushi
18 | 10 | 15 | $28

535 Hudson St. (Charles St.), 646-336-1833
22 W. 46th St. (bet. 5th & 6th Aves.), 212-398-7707 ⧄
158 W. 23rd St. (bet. 6th & 7th Aves.), 212-620-9131
www.monstersushi.com
☑ This "cramped, clamorous" sushi trio "lives up to its name" with "fresh, cheap" rolls in "gargantuan" portions fit "for a sumo wrestler"; a few surveyors note "bigger isn't always better", but all appreciate that while the rolls are "twice" the usual size, "the bill isn't."

Montparnasse
21 | 19 | 18 | $43

Pickwick Arms, 230 E. 51st St. (bet. 2nd & 3rd Aves.), 212-758-6633;
www.montparnasseny.com
■ Seemingly "lifted from a Parisian side street", this Eastsider finds favor with "Francophiles" who like its "well-executed" bistro classics, "quiet, roomy" setting and unrushed pace; add "moderate prices" and some ask "why isn't this place more popular?"

Montrachet ⧄
25 | 18 | 23 | $67

239 W. Broadway (bet. Walker & White Sts.), 212-219-2777;
www.myriadrestaurantgroup.com
☑ "Still a winner" when stacked against TriBeCa's "new-school" eateries, Drew Nieporent's "civilized" "French classic" continues to "wow" with its "phenomenal" cuisine, "outstanding" wine list and "top-notch" service; as for the decor, it's undergoing a gradual redo at press time; P.S. the Friday-only $20 prix fixe lunch is "one of the best steals in NY."

Moonstruck ◗
14 | 12 | 15 | $18

244 Madison Ave. (38th St.), 212-867-2545
88 Second Ave. (5th St.), 212-420-8050
449 Third Ave. (31st St.), 212-213-1100
400 W. 23rd St. (9th Ave.), 212-924-3709
☑ An "enormous menu" and "monster portions" of "decent" chow turn up at these "cut-above-typical" diners that typically provide "no-nonsense" service; late hours are a plus and brunch draws a "young crowd" looking to "see everyone from the night before."

Moran's Chelsea
19 | 20 | 21 | $42

146 10th Ave. (19th St.), 212-627-3030; www.moranschelsea.com
■ "Everyone feels Irish" at this "warm and friendly" Chelsea vet where the steak-and-seafood fare is "quite good", but it's the "old-time beautiful" setting aglow with "Tiffany lamps, crystal" and "blazing fireplaces" that's really special; it's a local "standby" but "strangers are welcome too."

Morrells
20 | 20 | 20 | $52

900 Broadway (bet. 19th & 20th Sts.), 212-253-0900;
www.morrellsrestaurant.com
1 Rockefeller Plaza (on 49th St., bet. 5th & 6th Aves.), 212-262-7700;
www.morrellwinebar.com
☑ "The wine's the thing" at this "chic", "airy" Flatiron New American offering a "jillion" options by the bottle or glass; most also get high on its "inventive" food and savvy service, but doubters detect "no soul" and say "yikes, the price"; the more casual Rock Center cafe earns extra points for "outside seating" and "after-work" convenience.

Morton's, The Steakhouse ◗
23 | 19 | 22 | $62

551 Fifth Ave. (45th St.), 212-972-3315; www.mortons.com
☑ "You can feel the testosterone" in the air at this "clubby", dark wood–paneled Midtown link of the Chicago chophouse chain, which

offers "old-school" "carnivores" "premium steaks at premium prices";
now if they'd only "lose the Saran Wrapped" "parade of beef" "you're
forced to endure" pre-meal.

Moustache ●⊄   22 | 13 | 15 | $21

90 Bedford St. (bet. Barrow & Grove Sts.), 212-229-2220
265 E. 10th St. (bet. Ave. A & 1st Ave.), 212-228-2022
☑ "Addictive" "puffy pitas", the "best baba ghanoush" and other
"cheap, delicious" Middle Eastern eats explain the prime-time
"lines" at this East/West Village duo; they're "cramped", "plain" and
sometimes "slow", but you can't beat the "value"; P.S. 10th Street has
a sweet "hidden garden."

Moutarde ●   18 | 20 | 15 | $36

239 Fifth Ave. (Carroll St.), Brooklyn, 718-623-3600
☑ "Evocative of the French bistro ideal" but "absent the cigs" (and
"dogs"), this Park Sloper nails the "Parisian look" and most also tip
their beret to its "capably executed" food and "divine" brunch; critics
cite "ups and downs", especially servicewise, but since it's "always
hopping", the ups obviously prevail.

Mr. Chow ●   24 | 21 | 20 | $67

324 E. 57th St. (bet. 1st & 2nd Aves.), 212-751-9030
☑ It's still a "fabulous" scene at this "glamorous" "gourmet Chinese",
an '80s "'it' place" whose polished, black-and-white art deco East
Side digs continue to draw a "head-turning" crowd ranging from "rap
stars" to "the Hilton sisters"; it's de rigueur to "let the waiters order
for you" – the food will likely be "incredible", ditto the bill.

Mr. K's   24 | 24 | 24 | $56

570 Lexington Ave. (51st St.), 212-583-1668
■ All the "celebs and honchos" who've dined here "can't be wrong"
say admirers of this "haute" East Side Chinese, a peaceful "pink
paradise" replete with "sumptuous" food, "impeccable", "formal"
service and a "posh", "roomy" setting; sure, all this "opulence" comes
at a steep price, but that makes it feel all the more "royal."

Mughlai ●   19 | 12 | 17 | $31

320 Columbus Ave. (75th St.), 212-724-6363
☑ Westsiders who analyze this Indian vet's "price-to-flavor ratio"
conclude there's naan better – at least in this neck of the woods –
hence it's "always packed"; the "uninspired" setting is a moot point.

Murals on 54   – | – | – | E

Warwick Hotel, 63 W. 54th St. (6th Ave.), 212-314-7700;
www.murals54.com
Controversial murals of Sir Walter Raleigh (commissioned by William
Randolph Hearst in 1937 and covered up for years due to some racy
details) are the focal point of this new Midtowner; a modern Continental
menu provides the counterpoint to this vintage art.

My Most Favorite Dessert Co.   18 | 13 | 15 | $35

120 W. 45th St. (bet. B'way & 6th Ave.), 212-997-5130
☑ "Delicious" desserts "are indeed" the favorites at this Theater
District kosher option – in fact, some suggest you "start and end"
with them, since the rest of the menu gets mixed reviews and even
some fans call it "overpriced"; "spotty service" also draws a few jabs.

Ñ ●⊄   ▽ 20 | 19 | 17 | $28

33 Crosby St. (bet. Broome & Grand Sts.), 212-219-8856
■ Tongue-tantalizing tapas, "strong sangria" and a "young", "Euro"-
heavy crowd get together with ñtertaining results at this "dimly lit",

affordable "little" SoHo Spaniard; insiders advise "get there early" if you want to "score a table."

Nam
24 | 20 | 19 | $38

110 Reade St. (W. B'way), 212-267-1777

■ "The next best thing to eating in Saigon" is this TriBeCa "treat" that "takes Vietnamese to a new level" with its "fresh, inspired" cuisine; add "tranquil yet modern decor" and moderate tabs and it's a "winning combo" that makes sometimes-"unpolished" service easy to forgive.

Nana ●▽⇗
▽ 22 | 19 | 18 | $27

155 Fifth Ave. (bet. Lincoln & St. John's Pls.), Brooklyn, 718-230-3749

■ "Another Park Slope bargain", this Pan-Asian "on the Fifth Avenue strip" has "fantastic fusion" food plus a sushi bar, providing lots of options at "totally reasonable prices"; "friendly" service goes well with its "upscale", "industrial" look, though a few feel the DJ's "techno" is a bit "too loud."

Nanni ☒
23 | 14 | 22 | $53

146 E. 46th St. (bet. Lexington & 3rd Aves.), 212-697-4161

☒ For "old-school" Northern Italian near Grand Central, traditionalists tout this "longtime favorite" manned by a "welcoming" staff as a "true treasure" that's "worth the price"; others suggest the "angel hair is less angelic" than in years past and the digs are "looking a bit tired."

Napa & Sonoma Steak House
▽ 19 | 17 | 17 | $47

15-01 149th St. (15th Ave.), Queens, 718-746-3446

☒ Maybe it's "not in the class of the top steakhouses", but in an area with "limited choices", locals appreciate this "solid" Whitestone standby and its "hospitable" atmosphere; the less-enthused shrug "nice place", but "nothing really strikes you."

Naples 45 ☒
18 | 16 | 16 | $31

MetLife Bldg., 200 Park Ave. (45th St.), 212-972-7001

☒ "Real Neapolitan" "paper-thin pizza" is "the main draw" at this "vast" Grand Central–area Italian "dining hall" that can be "deafening" and "rushed" midday due to "mobs" of "on-the-go" lunchers; those partial to the "killer pies" regard the other offerings as just "so-so."

Natchez ⇗
▽ 22 | 14 | 14 | $36

31 Second Ave. (bet. 1st & 2nd Sts.), 212-460-9171

☒ Even though "it ain't Emeril's", throngs are "discovering" this East Village "N'Awlins" nook serving "great-value" Cajun dishes "bursting with flavors" and washed down by "potent drinks"; just be warned its "tiny, no-decor" digs and "ridiculous" no-reserving policy add up to "long waits" for a table.

Neary's ●
16 | 12 | 20 | $38

358 E. 57th St. (1st Ave.), 212-751-1434

■ Jimmy Neary is the "quintessential Irish barkeep who cares" say "older" Sutton Place denizens who rely on this "classic", "comfortable" pub for "solid", if undistinguished, "bar food"; while the crowd's "mostly regulars", you never know when you'll find yourself eating "next to the mayor" or the cardinal.

Nebraska Steak House
▽ 24 | 15 | 21 | $50

15 Stone St. (bet. Broad St. & B'way), 212-952-0620 ☒
566 E. 187th St. (Hoffman St.), Bronx, 718-584-6167

☒ These "low-key", "no-frills" meateries "deliver a good steak", though it might be hard to see what's on your plate in the "dark" "roadhouse" environs; Wall Streeters report the Financial District locale is a welcome "low-flash alternative" to other area chophouse options.

Negril ⬤

20 | 17 | 17 | $32

70 W. Third St. (bet. La Guardia Pl. & Thompson St.), 212-477-2804
362 W. 23rd St. (bet. 8th & 9th Aves.), 212-807-6411
www.negrilvillage.com

■ "Soul-warming food from the islands" and "even better drinks" have fans of these "laid-back" oases cheering "very authentic, mon"; with its "cool" lounge and "wonderful" live music, the Village branch is "more sceney", while Chelsea is deemed "better for just dining."

Nello ⬤

20 | 17 | 17 | $65

696 Madison Ave. (bet. 62nd & 63rd Sts.), 212-980-9099

☑ You can "eat well" while searching "for that rich divorcée" at this "chic" East Side Northern Italian; while the "delicious" dishes come at "stratospheric prices", the "see-and-be-seen" "scene" and prime Madison Avenue "people-watching" from sidewalk seats are, as they say in the MasterCard ads, priceless; N.B. an East 90s location is in the works at press time.

Nëo Sushi ⬤

23 | 17 | 19 | $54

2298 Broadway (83rd St.), 212-769-1003; www.neosushi.com

☑ Upper Westsiders consider themselves blessed to have a "Nobu wanna-be" in their midst, slicing and rolling "innovative", "to-die-for" sushi in a "minimalist Japanese-chic" setting; portions are minimalist as well, but you may have to "refinance the condo" to cover the check.

Neptune Room

– | – | – | E

511 Amsterdam Ave. (bet. 84th & 85th Sts.), 212-496-4100;
www.theneptuneroom.com

From the owners of Jane comes this new Upper Westsider offering an array of Mediterranean seafood served in two distinct spaces separated by a raw bar; aesthetes appreciate its casual warmth, while signature menu items like blue crab panna cotta keep foodies amused.

New Bo-Ky ⊄

21 | 5 | 11 | $11

80 Bayard St. (bet. Mott & Mulberry Sts.), 212-406-2292

☑ "Soup and more soup" is the highlight at this "no-frills" Chinatown noodle shop that's under new ownership but still follows the same "satisfying" "quick and cheap" formula; being "a stone's throw" from the courts makes it particularly handy when "on jury duty."

New Green Bo ⬤⊄

23 | 5 | 12 | $17

66 Bayard St. (bet. Elizabeth & Mott Sts.), 212-625-2359

■ "The food speaks for itself" at this Chinatown "soup-dumpling nirvana" where the house-specialty "light and pillowy" buns are "delicious, cheap" and served "fast"; the "greasy-spoon" setting dissuades few, judging by the "lines."

New Leaf Cafe

19 | 23 | 17 | $36

Fort Tryon Park, 1 Margaret Corbin Dr. (190th St.), 212-568-5323;
www.nyrp.org/newleaf

■ "Thank you, Bette Midler" say admirers of this "charming" New American "oasis" in Fort Tryon Park, which was founded by Miss M's NY Restoration Project and whose "profits go to maintaining the park"; the food's "good", you can't beat the "beautiful" surroundings and visitors appreciate that "everyone's trying hard here."

New Pasteur ⊄

21 | 5 | 13 | $16

85 Baxter St. (bet. Bayard & Canal Sts.), 212-608-3656

☑ One of the few reasons "to smile while on jury duty" is the chance to lunch at this "courthouse"-convenient Vietnamese C-towner dishing out delectable fare served "fast" for "practically pennies"; "tired" "hole-in-the-wall" digs are par for the course.

New York Burger Co.
_|_ _|_ _|_ 1

303 Park Ave. S. (bet. 23rd & 24th Sts.), 212-254-2727
'Health-conscious fast food' is the hook at this new Flatiron entry in
the burger wars that grills up all-natural Coleman beef (along with
turkey, chicken and veggie options) supplemented by homemade
sauces and real-fruit smoothies; an unexciting if spacious setting keeps
your attention focused on the low-cost grub.

Nha Trang
22 6 14 $16

87 Baxter St. (bet. Bayard & Canal Sts.), 212-233-5948
148 Centre St. (bet. Walker & White Sts.), 212-941-9292
☑ "Flavorful", "authentic" eats are the draw, not the "generic decor"
or "100-mile-an-hour" service at this Vietnamese duo in Chinatown;
they're "usually crowded", but your "wait" is rewarded with "fresh",
"wonderful" food at "ultracheap" prices.

Nice
19 10 14 $23

35 E. Broadway (bet. Catherine & Market Sts.), 212-406-9510
☑ "Go early" and "go hungry" to this "noisy" Chinatown dim sum "hall"
where carts loaded with "wonderful" "Cantonese-style" goodies "keep
coming"; misanthropes aren't thrilled that you'll sometimes be seated
"with strangers", and critics say the eats "lack oomph."

Nice Matin ◐
21 19 18 $45

201 W. 79th St. (Amsterdam Ave.), 212-873-6423;
www.nicematinnyc.com
☑ "Atmospheric" and "classy", this French-Med brasserie yearling is a
"hugely popular" addition to the Upper West Side, serving "delightful"
classics amid a "lively buzz" (some say "din"); still, a minority maintains
the "so-so" service and slightly "pricey" tabs are "not so Nice";
N.B. there's alfresco seating in summer.

Nick & Stef's Steakhouse ⊠
20 19 20 $54

9 Penn Plaza (on 33rd St., bet. 7th & 8th Aves.), 212-563-4444
■ Proving that "a steakhouse doesn't have to be dark and macho" to
be good, this "upscale" Madison Square Garden place's "California
style" "breaks" with NY "tradition", but it nevertheless delivers
first-rate "slabs of meat"; P.S. "if there's an event" on at MSG, it's
wise to score a reservation.

Nick and Toni's Cafe
18 15 17 $44

100 W. 67th St. (bet. B'way & Columbus Ave.), 212-496-4000
☑ This Upper West Side "outpost" of the Hamptons original strikes
most as a "cozy" neighborhood choice for "wood-fired" Mediterranean
fare "convenient" to Lincoln Center; however, a "disappointed"
contingent laments "indifferent" service and a relatively "pricey" menu.

Nick's
23 13 16 $22

1814 Second Ave. (bet. 93rd & 94th Sts.), 212-987-5700 ◐
108-26 Ascan Ave. (bet. Austin & Burns Sts.), Queens, 718-263-1126 ⌖
☑ "Once you get your first taste" you're hooked say fans of the
"superior", "charred" thin-crust pizzas purveyed at these "family-
style" parlors; "offhand" service and "spartan digs" don't seem to
shorten "the lines", but at least Manhattanites no longer have to
"trek" to Forest Hills since the Upper East Side offshoot opened.

Nicola's ◐
22 17 21 $55

146 E. 84th St. (Lexington Ave.), 212-249-9850
☑ This "old-style" Italian "standby" is a "clubby" Upper East Side
favorite of "well-dressed and -coiffed" "swells" who consider it "the
gold standard" for "no-surprises" food and service; others who aren't
part of the "clique", though outvoted, suggest it's "just run-of-the-mill."

Niko's Mediterranean Grill ◑   18 | 10

2161 Broadway (76th St.), 212-873-7000

☑ "Looks tacky, tastes great" is the consensus on this "bustling" Upper West Side Greek-Med that's a staple for "families" and others looking for "huge, hearty servings" at a "good price"; devotees say "just ignore" the "cramped" conditions and "plastic grapes" on the ceiling.

92   15 | 15 | 15 | $40

45 E. 92nd St. (Madison Ave.), 212-828-5300

☑ The "Carnegie Hill set" depends on this "bright", "noisy", "kid-friendly" "neighborhood fixture" for "preppy" American "comfort food" that "takes you back" in time – but "at prices you wouldn't have believed back then"; service is amiable if sometimes "slapdash."

Nino's ◑   22 | 19 | 22 | $55

1354 First Ave. (bet. 72nd & 73rd Sts.), 212-988-0002

■ "Nino makes you feel like a star" at this "high-end" East Side Northern Italian, where a "well-dressed" "older" crowd lingers late over "terrific" "traditional" favorites; insiders say "tip the piano man and he'll play your favorite tunes."

Nino's Positano   20 | 17 | 21 | $47

890 Second Ave. (bet. 47th & 48th Sts.), 212-355-5540

■ "Almost as good as the Uptown original" but minus the piano player, this "friendly", less-formal East Side Italian is deemed "one of the better" choices near Grand Central; food that's "nothing unique, just done well" and "kind", "old-world service" keep area "business" types satisfied.

Nippon ⊠   ▽ 22 | 16 | 20 | $53

155 E. 52nd St. (bet. Lexington & 3rd Aves.), 212-758-0226;
www.restaurantnippon.com

■ The cypress-wood decor may be "showing its age" at this "classic" (since '63) Midtown Japanese, but not its signature soba salads ("the height of noodledom") and other "satisfying", "no-fad" fare served with true "hospitality"; fans who've been "frequenting it for years" report it's "still going strong."

Nisos ◑   17 | 16 | 16 | $37

176 Eighth Ave. (19th St.), 646-336-8121; www.nisos-ny.com

☑ "Chelsea boys and their admirers", plus theatergoers "dining before the Joyce", "count on" this always "pleasant" Med for satisfying seafood and other Greek-accented fare; there's also a "nifty little scene at the bar" and prime "outdoor seating when weather permits."

NOBU   28 | 23 | 24 | $76

105 Hudson St. (Franklin St.), 212-219-0500;
www.myriadrestaurantgroup.com

■ "The gold standard" for "dazzling" Japanese-Peruvian "fusion" cuisine and "celebrity whiplash" is this "transcendent" TriBeCa "perennial favorite" where the "A+" experiences are deemed "worth" the "ridiculous" tabs and "monthlong wait" for a reservation; cash-carefree cognoscenti say "omakase is the way to go" – just "sit back" and let the "top-notch" staff "take care of everything"; N.B. a new location near Carnegie Hall is scheduled to open in 2005.

NOBU, NEXT DOOR ◑⊠   28 | 22 | 22 | $63

105 Hudson St. (bet. Franklin & N. Moore Sts.), 212-334-4445;
www.myriadrestaurantgroup.com

■ "Next door, but no step down" is this "no-reservations" chip off the old block that's "lots easier to get into", so long as you don't mind waiting in line; it serves "basically the same" high-quality Japanese-

Peruvian cuisine as the mothership, but is a bit "cheaper"; P.S. the "new take-out service is addictive."

Nocello

22 | 17 | 20 | $43

257 W. 55th St. (bet. B'way & 8th Ave.), 212-703-0224

■ On "an otherwise barren block" near Carnegie Hall sits this "charming" Northern Italian offering delightful, but "not terribly expensive" standards in "intimate" surroundings; insiders suggest "wait until after the theater rush" for a "quieter meal."

NoHo Star ●

17 | 13 | 15 | $29

330 Lafayette St. (Bleecker St.), 212-925-0070; www.nohostar.com

☑ Still "snappy" after 20 years, this NoHo standby provides "hard-to-beat" burgers and other "decent" American fare, plus some "Asian-influenced" choices, in "plain" but "airy" digs; it's "dependable" for a "lively" weekend brunch, but just expect "a long wait."

Noodle Pudding ⇏

24 | 18 | 21 | $33

38 Henry St. (bet. Cranberry & Middagh Sts.), Brooklyn, 718-625-3737

■ "Hate the name", love the "fresh, delicious" Italian "home cooking" sums up reaction to this "cozy", affordable Brooklyn Heights "staple"; there's "no sign out front" yet "everyone seems to know" it – i.e. there's "always a crowd", but "service remains cheery amid the chaos"; P.S. "too bad about the cash-only" and "no-reservations" policies.

No. 1 Chinese ●⇏

∇ 16 | 26 | 16 | $27

50 Ave. B (4th St.), 212-375-0677

☑ "The man behind Frank, Lil' Frankie's" et al. does "Chinatown" with this "sexy" new East Villager whose "cool" bi-level space, complete with open kitchen, is already hosting a "bustling scene"; as for its retro fare, fans say it "captures all the virtues of Americanized Chinese" food, but others say it won't be No. 1 until it works out "the kinks."

Norma's

25 | 19 | 20 | $34

Le Parker Meridien, 118 W. 57th St. (bet. 6th & 7th Aves.), 212-708-7460; www.parkermeridien.com

■ "Surpasses the hype" declare devotees of the "breakfast of champions" dished up at this "glossy" Midtown American, where "days start off right" with a "decadent", "innovative" morning meal in "larger-than-life" portions; just remember "your platinum card" and don't be surprised if the "wait borders on the absurd"; N.B. no dinner.

North Square

24 | 20 | 22 | $42

Washington Sq. Hotel, 103 Waverly Pl. (MacDougal St.), 212-254-1200; www.northsquareny.com

■ A "wonderful surprise" off the lobby of the Washington Square Hotel, this New American offers "expertly prepared" food, "pro" service and "reasonable" prices; it's favored by "college professor types" and others who appreciate its "cozy" ambiance conducive to conversation.

Notaro

19 | 14 | 20 | $33

635 Second Ave. (bet. 34th & 35th Sts.), 212-686-3400; www.notaro.com

■ "Only the locals know" this Murray Hill Northern Italian "sleeper" whose "warm, welcoming" vibe and menu of "good standards" make it a favored "neighborhood hangout" (delivery is popular as well); insiders say "make sure you try" the "spectacular bargain" dinner prix fixe.

Novecento ●

21 | 17 | 17 | $40

343 W. Broadway (bet. Broome & Grand Sts.), 212-925-4706; www.bistronovecento.com

■ "Excellent" quality and value "Argentine-style steaks" draw a "great-looking", "very Euro" crowd to this SoHo "favorite", whose "simple" space hosts a "crowded", "lively" scene later in the evening; "*futbol* fans" find the upstairs lounge just the place to take in a "weekend match."

Novitá | 24 | 19 | 22 | $48
102 E. 22nd St. (bet. Lexington Ave. & Park Ave. S.), 212-677-2222;
www.novitanyc.com
■ "A notch above" the area competition, this Gramercy Northern Italian "hideaway" offers "high-quality" Piedmontese dishes served by an "attentive" staff in an "intimate" subterranean setting; all in all it's a "fine-dining experience" that's "perfect" for "special occasions" or "a third date."

Nyonya ●✝ | 23 | 12 | 13 | $20
194 Grand St. (bet. Mott & Mulberry Sts.), 212-334-3669
5323 Eighth Ave. (54th St.), Brooklyn, 718-633-0808
☑ "As long as you can deal with the crowds, rushed service" and "zoro atmosphere", "you can't go wrong" at this Little Italy/Sunset Park pair supplying "top-notch" Malaysian "like grandma used to make (if she's from Kuala Lumpur)"; better still, this "change of pace" comes amazingly "cheap."

Oak Room ☒ | 18 | 24 | 20 | $62
Plaza Hotel, 768 Fifth Ave. (59th St.), 212-546-5330;
www.fairmont.com
☑ "If you want a throwback" to the "dressing-for-dinner" days, the Plaza's "big, beautiful oak"-paneled dining room can be counted on to "bring back memories"; its well-prepared steak and seafood are the "least impressive part" (especially "for the cost"), so some prefer to "stick to cocktails" in the adjoining Oak Bar.

OCEANA ☒ | 26 | 24 | 25 | $73
55 E. 54th St. (bet. Madison & Park Aves.), 212-759-5941;
www.oceanarestaurant.com
■ "Fish gotta swim – right onto the plate" of this "luxe" Midtowner famed for "fresh", "out-of-this-world" fin fare served by a highly "professional" staff amid "classy" "cruise-ship decor"; if a few lament small portions at "king-size prices", far more maintain there's almost "no better seafood port" in town; N.B. prix fixe only, except at the bar.

Ocean Grill | 22 | 20 | 19 | $48
384 Columbus Ave. (bet. 78th & 79th Sts.), 212-579-2300;
www.brguestrestaurants.com
■ A "favorite even for those who aren't fish-eaters", this "big, friendly" West Side seafood house's "grand selection" of "exceedingly fresh" fish (including a "bountiful" raw bar) lures an "all-ages" crowd, from "yuppies to seniors to young families"; "outdoor seating is a big plus" for those who find it "too noisy" inside.

Ocean Palace ● | 20 | 10 | 14 | $26
1414-1418 Ave. U (bet. E. 14th & 15th Sts.), Brooklyn, 718-376-3838
☑ Savvy "Brooklynites skip the trip to Manhattan's Chinatown" and head instead to this Ocean Parkway "warehouse" for "delicious" "dim sum and Hong Kong–style seafood" that's "way filling for the price"; service can be "very laid-back" and aesthetes suggest you "don't look too closely" at the decor.

Océo | ▽ 22 | 22 | 21 | $68
Time Hotel, 224 W. 49th St. (bet. B'way & 8th Ave.), 212-262-6236;
www.oceo.com
☑ "Lespinasse alumnus" Shane McBride "makes good" at this "much-needed" Theater District newcomer featuring "imaginative" 'Global

American' cuisine served by an "eager staff" in a "slick" setting that melds "cozy warmth" and "high cool"; just "plan to drop a lot of money" and know that some feel it has "potential" but is "not there yet."

Odeon ●
19 | 18 | 17 | $40

145 W. Broadway (bet. Duane & Thomas Sts.), 212-233-0507; www.theodeonrestaurant.com

■ This "TriBeCa pioneer" "hasn't lost a beat" "after 20-plus years"; the Gallic-American food remains "consistently good", the place still hums with "unmistakable energy" (especially at the "loud", "beautiful bar") and the staff's "good-looking" – even if "you can get old waiting for" their attention.

O.G. ●
∇ 22 | 17 | 22 | $33

507 E. Sixth St. (bet. Aves. A & B), 212-477-4649

■ Regulars "kind of don't want anyone else to discover" this East Village "sleeper" offering "delicious" Asian fusion dishes with pleasingly "small price tags"; given the "serene" surroundings and "lovely" service, partisans wonder why it's "not more popular."

Ola ⌧
22 | 17 | 20 | $49

304 E. 48th St. (2nd Ave.), 212-759-0590; www.olarestaurant.com

■ "Olé to Ola" say admirers who find a "spicy" slice of "heaven" near the UN thanks to chef-owner Douglas Rodriguez's "exciting" Nuevo Latino menu, complete with low-carb options; but "you don't have to be" an Atkins acolyte to dig the "jumpin'" scene, "hot", "dark" digs and "solicitous service."

Old Devil Moon
20 | 16 | 15 | $20

511 E. 12th St. (bet. Aves. A & B), 212-475-4357

◪ "Genuinely funky", this "classic East Village dive" serves "finger-lickin', rib-stickin'" "Southern treats" that are both "abundant and cheap", especially at the "best greasy brunch in town"; but the devil may have gotten to the servers, who "veer from sassy to catatonic."

Old Homestead
23 | 16 | 19 | $59

56 Ninth Ave. (bet. 14th & 15th Sts.), 212-242-9040; www.oldhomesteadsteakhouse.com

◪ "Since 1868" – way before the Meatpacking District got hip – this steakhouse has been serving "serious" slabs of beef (and of late, an infamous $41 Kobe-beef burger); the "masculine decor" may be caught in a "time warp" and the "waiters need loosening up", but the "old-timers keep coming – and the prices keep going up."

Oliva ●
∇ 21 | 15 | 17 | $30

161 E. Houston St. (Allen St.), 212-228-4143; www.olivanyc.com

◪ "It's always a party" at this "tiny", reasonable Lower East Side Basque boasting "tantalizing tapas" served by some "smokin' Spanish waitresses"; when it "gets too crowded" (which is "always"), amigos simply "chill out with a nice pitcher of sangria."

Olives
23 | 22 | 20 | $53

W Union Sq., 201 Park Ave. S. (E. 17th St.), 212-353-8345; www.toddenglish.com

■ "Civilized hip" sums up the scene at this Union Square version of Todd English's Boston hit, where the "original" Mediterranean cooking is "pricey" but can "wow your senses" (yes, "they really can do a lot with olives"), the staff is "welcoming" and the setting is both "elegant" and "very cool"; if the "hopping bar scene" detracts from dinner, there are two sensible solutions – go over and join the celebrants or check out the "impressive weekend brunch."

Olive Vine Cafe ⊄

18 | 8 | 16 | $14

362 15th St. (7th Ave.), Brooklyn, 718-499-0555

☑ "Harried Park Slope parents" rely on the "pleasurable" pita-based pizzas and other "fresh and flavorful" Mideastern fare at this "low-cost" cafe; "quick home delivery" is a plus, especially for those who find the decor "cheesy – you keep expecting a camel to show up"; N.B. the Seventh Avenue branch was closed by fire recently.

Ollie's ●

16 | 9 | 13 | $20

2957 Broadway (116th St.), 212-932-3300
2315 Broadway (84th St.), 212-362-3111
1991 Broadway (bet. 67th & 68th Sts.), 212-595-8181
200-B W. 44th St. (bet. B'way & 8th Ave.), 212-921-5988

☑ This "cheap", "crowded" Chinese chain is a West Side "staple" for "noodle-focused", "greasy" standards ("rename it Oil-lie's") served amid "minimal" decor; while "perfect when you're in a hurry", it's "not for a leisurely dinner", as the "slapdash service" is "fast – sometimes *too* fast."

O Mai

23 | 17 | 18 | $36

158 Ninth Ave. (bet. 19th & 20th Sts.), 212-633-0550

☑ Chelsea locals "thank heaven" for this "superb" supplier of "nouvelle" Vietnamese eats "seasoned just right"; its "small", stylishly spare quarters can get "uncomfortably crowded" and the "sweet" staff "harried", but those are small prices to pay for such "wonderful", affordable food.

Omen ●

24 | 19 | 22 | $49

113 Thompson St. (bet. Prince & Spring Sts.), 212-925-8923

■ "Amen for Omen" say admirers of the "subtly complex" takes on "Japanese country" cooking ("don't expect sushi or tempura") served by "courteous professionals" at this "serene" SoHo "oasis"; some tout the set menu since "ordering à la carte can rack up the bill", but even if you "go bankrupt", it's worth it for "truly different" dining.

Omonia Cafe ●

18 | 15 | 13 | $17

7612-14 Third Ave. (bet. 76th & 77th Sts.), Brooklyn, 718-491-1435
32-20 Broadway (33rd St.), Queens, 718-274-6650

☑ You can sit and "sip for hours", from early morning to late at night, at this Bay Ridge–Astoria coffeehouse couple serving "strong" java and an "authentic" Athenian "array of delectable desserts" in a "back-to-the-homeland atmosphere"; scoffers say stick to the sweets, since the savories are "garden-variety Greek."

Once Upon a Tart

21 | 13 | 15 | $14

135 Sullivan St. (bet. Houston & Prince Sts.), 212-387-8869;
www.onceuponatart.com

■ Meals always "end happily ever after" at this "cute" counter-service cafe serving "sublime" sandwiches and pastries "off the main SoHo tourist stretch"; some opt to "take it home", as free tables and servers can be "hard to find" in the "tiny", undistinguished digs.

One ●

18 | 23 | 13 | $46

1 Little W. 12th St. (bet. Hudson St. & 9th Ave.), 212-255-9717;
www.onelw12.com

☑ "Older men, younger women" and "B&T" types create "quite a scene" at this Meatpacking District lounge/eatery with a "beautiful" candlelit atmosphere; fans find "amazing drinks" and "creative", "albeit pricey" New American eats "served tapas-style", but foes focus on "slow service (go young, leave old)" and the "ridiculous velvet-rope" routine.

O'Neals' ☻
17 | 17 | 18 | $41

49 W. 64th St. (B'way), 212-787-4663; www.oneals.us

🔲 Making a "welcome return" after renovations ("thank God – Lincoln Center needed it"), this "stalwart" still delivers "moderately priced", "tried-and-true" "American standards", though some say they now come with "increased noise" from the more open setting; at least the "skillful" service ensures "you'll make your curtain."

One C.P.S. ☻
21 | 22 | 21 | $55

Plaza Hotel, 1 Central Park S. (5th Ave. & 59th St.), 212-583-1111; www.onecps.com

■ Ensconced in a "truly grand dining room" overlooking Central Park and designed by Adam Tihany, this "posh" New American brasserie in the Plaza is "dependable" for "delightful" meals; the ultimate in "NY-ish" experiences, it's also handy for out-of-towners.

One 83
▽ 19 | 20 | 19 | $43

1608 First Ave. (bet. 83rd & 84th Sts), 212-327-4700

■ "Needed by the neighborhood", this Northern Italian newcomer offers Upper Eastsiders "a welcoming atmosphere" and "reliable", "reasonably priced" *cucina*; perhaps it's "not worth a trek from far-off lands", but nearby noshers say "if the test is whether you'd go back, it passes with flying colors."

ONE IF BY LAND, TIBS
25 | 27 | 25 | $72

17 Barrow St. (bet. 7th Ave. S. & W. 4th St.), 212-228-0822; www.oneifbyland.com

■ Romeos looking for a "surefire" "deal-closer" know to "bring the diamond" to this über-"romantic" Village New American; once Aaron Burr's carriage house, it's an "enchanting" "candle- and flower-filled" setting for "sublime" prix fixe meals delivered by "tuxedoed" servers and accompanied by lovely piano music; sure, the bill might also bring you to your knees, but if the answer's "yes", it's surely "worth" it.

101 ☻
21 | 18 | 19 | $38

10018 Fourth Ave. (bet. 100th & 101st Sts.), Brooklyn, 718-833-1313

🔲 "Whether for pizza or a full meal", this "small" Bay Ridge Italian–New American is "always a pleaser" – just ask the "cool young" crowd enduring the "long wait on weekends"; be warned that it can get "sooo loud", especially on "big game nights" when the wide-screen TV is tuned to the action.

107 West
17 | 13 | 16 | $28

2787 Broadway (bet. 107th & 108th Sts.), 212-864-1555
811 W. 187th St. (bet. Ft. Washington & Pinehurst Aves.), 212-923-3311
www.107west.com

🔲 "Anything but thrilling", but good to have in these reaches of the Upper West Side and Washington Heights, this "casual" pair serves low-cost "comfort food with a Cajun–Tex-Mex twist" ("when ordering, think blackened"); some knock decor that "looks like a Florida condo's common area", but there's always "carryout."

Ony ☻
18 | 15 | 17 | $25

357 Sixth Ave. (bet. Washington Pl. & W. 4th St.), 212-414-9885
158 W. 72nd St. (bet. B'way & Columbus Ave.), 212-362-3504;
www.ony-usa.com

■ Slurpaholics "wish for cold weather" to better savor the "steaming" bowls of "terrific", "make-your-own" menchanko soup that are the specialty of this West Village–Upper West Side noodle duo, which also slices "decent sushi"; "amiable" service and prices that "won't break the bank" are further endearments.

ORIENTAL GARDEN ◐
25 | 11 | 17 | $28

14 Elizabeth St. (bet. Bayard & Canal Sts.), 212-619-0085

☑ "Only a shark eats fresher seafood" than the "straight-from-the-tank" offerings "prepared to perfection" Hong Kong–style at this Chinatown "favorite", which also excels at "delicious dim sum"; the Ritz it ain't, but its "no-frills" digs are "comfortable", the price is right and the service "a cut above the standard" for the area.

Orsay ◐
18 | 20 | 17 | $53

1057 Lexington Ave. (75th St.), 212-517-6400;
www.orsayrestaurant.com

☑ "*Très français* in every way", this "big, noisy", "upscale" East Side bistro is where "Euros" rub elbows with the "nose-job set" over "tasty" French "classics"; "attitude reigns supreme" here and you'll pay "two-star prices for one-fork food", but the "people-watching" is hard to beat once everyone gets back from the Hamptons.

Orso ◐
22 | 18 | 20 | $50

322 W. 46th St. (bet. 8th & 9th Aves.), 212-489-7212;
www.orsorestaurant.com

■ You'll have to "call early and often for a reservation" at this "ever-popular" Theater District hangout for "Broadway movers and shakers"; the Northern Italian fare is "fabulous" and the atmosphere "pleasant", but for ordinary mortals the "best part is checking out the celebs" who you may see on stage an hour later.

Osaka
∇ 23 | 19 | 19 | $30

272 Court St. (bet. DeGraw & Kane Sts.), Brooklyn, 718-643-0044

◼ "Fresh fish, huge portions and service with a smile" explain why this Cobble Hill Japanese is embraced as a "wonderful neighborhood sushi place"; thus it's often "packed tighter than a can of sardines", but there's always the "lovely" pocket garden in warmer months.

Osso Buco
16 | 14 | 16 | $32

1662 Third Ave. (93rd St.), 212-426-5422
88 University Pl. (bet. 11th & 12th Sts.), 212-645-4525

☑ It's especially "fun for a group" at these Village–Carnegie Hill Italians since the "basic" red-sauce eats "made with care" (and "lots of garlic") come in "ample" "family-style portions" at "reasonable prices"; however, as the above ratings show, these are no pacesetters.

Osteria al Doge ◐
20 | 17 | 19 | $44

142 W. 44th St. (bet. B'way & 6th Ave.), 212-944-3643;
www.osteria-doge.com

☑ A "standout" in a "sea" of Times Square Italians, this "dependable" Venetian gives ticket-holders a taste of "quality" cuisine, then "gets 'em out in time for the show"; "unless you sit upstairs", "be prepared to scream" at your dinner partner since it gets "loud."

Osteria del Circo
22 | 23 | 21 | $57

120 W. 55th St. (bet. 6th & 7th Aves.), 212-265-3636; www.osteriadelcirco.com

◼ A "true carnival of delights" awaits at this Le Cirque spin-off where the Maccioni family presides over the "noisy, bustling" scene played out against a "whimsical" circus backdrop; though for many it's really "all about the atmosphere" here, happily Mama Maccioni's Northern Italian food is "delicious" and the service, led by the family's next generation, is extremely "gracious."

Osteria del Sole ◐
23 | 18 | 20 | $42

267 W. Fourth St. (Perry St.), 212-620-6840

◼ This West Village "corner trattoria" is "always crowded with neighbors" savoring "well-prepared" Sardinian specialties delivered by an "energetic" staff in "quaint" but "tight quarters"; Casanovas claim the adjacent "plush, intimate bar" ups its "romance" factor.

Osteria Laguna ◐
20 | 18 | 18 | $41

209 E. 42nd St. (bet. 2nd & 3rd Aves.), 212-557-0001;
www.osteria-laguna.com

☑ "Decent" Venetian meals in "comfortable" (if "noisy") environs have the "business crowd" calling this "spacious" Northern Italian a "godsend east of Grand Central"; if it's "nothing to write home about", it's certainly "reasonably priced" for this locale.

Osteria Stella ◐
▽ 22 | 21 | 21 | $43

135 W. 50th St. (bet. 6th & 7th Aves.), 212-957-5050;
www.osteria-stella.com

■ In a Midtown stretch filled with "tourist traps", this "attractive" new Northern Italian is a "welcome" addition – since the food's "consistently good" and not too pricey, plus there's "plenty of seating for everybody"; P.S. the 70-ft. marble bar hosts a "loud", "hopping" happy hour.

Ota-Ya
22 | 18 | 21 | $32

1572 Second Ave. (bet. 81st & 82nd Sts.), 212-988-1188;
www.ota-ya.com

☑ The "Upper East Side's best unknown sushi" joint may be this "friendly" Japanese that's appreciated for its "fresh", "creative" rolls and "simple", "uncrowded" space where "you can always get a table"; doubters deem it "nothing special", but even they can't disparage the "very affordable" prices.

Otto ◐
21 | 18 | 18 | $35

1 Fifth Ave. (8th St.), 212-995-9559; www.ottopizzeria.com

■ Taste the Batali-Bastianich "genius" without breaking the bank via this Village pizzeria phenom proffering "high-end" pies and an "encyclopedic" Boot-focused wine list in an "Italian train station"– esque setting; "can't-be-beat" appetizers are the menu's "hidden stars" for some, while others point to the "extraordinary gelato"; P.S. for those who "can't stand the wait" for a table, it now accepts reservations and take-out orders.

OUEST
25 | 23 | 23 | $58

2315 Broadway (bet. 83rd & 84th Sts.), 212-580-8700;
www.ouestny.com

■ Chef Tom Valenti's New American comfort cuisine "wows even the most jaded palate" at this "emerging institution" on the Upper West Side that's become something of a "living room" for the neighborhood's famous and "well-to-do"; the attractive, "clubby", banquette-filled space is matched by "impeccable" service and a "superb" wine list – now "if it were only easier to get a table."

Our Place
20 | 16 | 19 | $32

141 E. 55th St. (bet. Lexington & 3rd Aves.), 212-753-3900;
www.ourplace-teagarden.com
1444 Third Ave. (82nd St.), 212-288-4888

■ "Everything you love about C-town Chinese" but "adjusted for East Side sensibilities" is the word on this pair offering "authentic", "delicious" Shanghai specialties in "serene" settings with "gracious" service; happily, its "moderate prices" fall "somewhere between the typical neighborhood" joint "and Shun Lee."

Outback Steakhouse
15 | 12 | 16 | $32

919 Third Ave. (enter on 56th St., bet. 2nd & 3rd Aves.), 212-935-6400
60 W. 23rd St. (6th Ave.), 212-989-3122
1475 86th St. (15th Ave.), Brooklyn, 718-837-7200

(continued)

Outback Steakhouse

Bay Terrace, 23-48 Bell Blvd. (26th Ave.), Queens, 718-819-0908
Queens Pl., 88-01 Queens Blvd. (56th Ave.), Queens, 718-760-7200
www.outback.com

☑ "If you want to gorge yourself" or simply release your inner "tourist", hit these "faux-Aussie" chain steakhouses where "those bloomin' onions" will "make you forget the meat's just average"; clamorous critics say "leave it to the 'burbs", but others can't resist "coming back – like a boomerang."

Oyster Bar ☒

| 21 | 16 | 15 | $43 |

Grand Central, lower level (42nd St. & Vanderbilt Ave.), 212-490-6650;
www.oysterbarny.com

■ "Prepare to be transported back to olde NY" (or at least back to 1913) at this "tile-vaulted" "bivalve mecca" beneath Grand Central that's known for its "unrivaled" raw bar selection, "fabulous" pan roasts and straightforward "fresh fish"; just ignore the "resonating noise" and "head straight to the counter" – if you don't have to go back to work, try out their list of white wines as well.

Oyster Bar at the Plaza ●

| 19 | 19 | 17 | $47 |

Plaza Hotel, 768 Fifth Ave. (enter on 58th St., bet. 5th & 6th Aves.),
212-546-5340; www.fairmont.com

☑ A Plaza Hotel "tourist tradition", this "convivial" seafooder offers a "classy" raw bar plus "good basic burgers" and such in "terrific, clubby" environs; even admirers admit it's "too expensive" considering the somewhat "ordinary" eats, but as a "place to spend an afternoon eating oysters" it's hard to beat.

Oznot's Dish ●

| 19 | 20 | 17 | $29 |

79 Berry St. (N. 9th St.), Brooklyn, 718-599-6596

■ For "offbeat Med-Mideastern fusion" in a "whimsical", "mosaic-tiled" setting, try this "quirky" Williamsburg vet that maintains a "mostly local" fan base with its "fair prices" and "comfortable" vibe; its brunch is deemed one of the "best in town", especially if you "can get an outside table."

Pace

| – | – | – | E |

121 Hudson St. (N. Moore St.), 212-965-9500

From the Midas-touch team of Jimmy Bradley and Danny Abrams (Red Cat, The Harrison, Mermaid Inn) comes this new TriBeCa Italian offering a wide-ranging menu of rustic fare at citified prices; the sprawling, sophisticated space (enhanced by a wraparound terrace) sports a faux distressed look that's in direct contrast to the teeming, beaming crowds already piling in.

Pacific Grill

| – | – | – | M |

South Street Seaport, 89 South St., Pier 17 (bet. Fulton & John Sts.),
212-964-0707

With the day's catch practically swimming over from the nearby Fulton Fish Market, this Seaport seafooder grills its fin fare Pan-Asian style, then serves it in aquatic-themed digs; while the location is a natural for tourists, the harbor view, fruit-filled cocktails and moderate prices may reel in the after-work crowd too.

Pacifico ●⊄

| 19 | 21 | 14 | $21 |

269 Pacific St. (Smith St.), Brooklyn, 718-935-9090

☑ Just off Smith Street lies this "big" Boerum Hill Mexican supplying "crowd-pleasing" standards in "transporting", "hacienda"-like digs; a "massive outdoor seating area" and "amazingly cheap" prices make "slow" service easier to overlook.

Pad Thai
16 | 12 | 15 | $24

114 Eighth Ave. (bet. 15th & 16th Sts.), 212-691-6226
■ When in a "Thai frame of mind", Chelsea locals look to this "hole-in-the-wall" for "quick fixes" of "no-frills" classics like the "namesake" dish; the "funky pink decor" may be "kind of strange", but you can really "eat on the cheap" here.

Paladar ⊅
18 | 14 | 15 | $31

161 Ludlow St. (bet. Houston & Stanton Sts.), 212-473-3535;
www.paladar.ws
■ "Hip, lively" things "pack" this Lower East Side Nuevo Latino where "talented" chef Aarón Sanchez turns out "flavorful" food in a super-festive atmosphere; better yet, "south-of-the-border" prices mean there's money for "more than one" "awesome mojito."

PALM
24 | 16 | 20 | $60

837 Second Ave. (bet. 44th & 45th Sts.), 212-687-2953 ⌧
840 Second Ave. (bet. 44th & 45th Sts.), 212-697-5198
250 W. 50th St. (bet. B'way & 8th Ave.), 212-333-7256 ◑
www.thepalm.com
■ The "prototypical NY steak joint", this "cacophonous", celebrity caricature and "sawdust"–adorned Eastsider (and its two offshoots) supplies "old boys" and other "power" types with "top-notch" meats and lobsters in "intimidatingly" "huge" portions; just ask the "gruff but competent" waiter what to order, plan to split whatever he recommends, and "make sure someone else is paying."

Palm Court
19 | 26 | 20 | $51

Plaza Hotel, 768 Fifth Ave. (59th St.), 212-546-5350;
www.fairmont.com
■ "There's no better place" for a "decadent" Sunday brunch or "pinkie-in-the-air" high tea than this "magical" Plaza Continental that reeks of "old-fashioned luxe" complete with palm trees and gilt; prices are luxe too, but it's "a must" for Aunt Sadie from St. Louis and can make even jaded natives "feel special."

Pamir
20 | 16 | 20 | $34

1437 Second Ave. (bet. 74th & 75th Sts.), 212-734-3791
■ "Reminiscent of quieter times" in Kabul, this "relaxed" Afghan "transports" Upper Eastsiders out of the province of pasta and into the kingdom of "done to perfection" kebabs, served with "charm" in an "enter-my-tent" setting with carpet-draped walls; modest tabs are also quite welcome.

Pampa ⊅
21 | 16 | 16 | $34

768 Amsterdam Ave. (bet. 97th & 98th Sts.), 212-865-2929;
www.pamparestaurant.com
■ "Defying all the wisdom about eating light", carnivores converge at this cash-only Upper West Side Argentinean for "bargain beef" blowouts spiked with tons of "garlic"; it's way more "crowded" than the pampa and service can be "brusque", but a summer garden and sublime sangria ease the pain.

Pampano
25 | 23 | 22 | $53

209 E. 49th St. (bet. 2nd & 3rd Aves.), 212-751-4545;
www.modernmexican.com
■ Co-owner Placido Domingo "hits the high C" with this "stellar", seafood-centric Midtown Mexican, where chef Richard Sandoval's "creative" "nuevo" notions take the genre "to another level"; "light", "airy" decor, "no-attitude service", "delicious drinks" and a "lovely" terrace round out the "outstanding performance."

Pam Real Thai Food ⊭

22 | 6 | 17 | $19

404 W. 49th St. (bet. 9th & 10th Aves.), 212-333-7500

🗷 "Real, indeed" say boosters of this "friendly" little BYO Thai that's "as close as you can get to Bangkok" in Hell's Kitchen thanks to "seriously delicious, seriously spicy food" (ask for it hot and prepare to "lose the top of your head"); expect no "decorating hoopla, just darn good flavor" and "value."

Panino'teca 275

▽ 22 | 18 | 20 | $21

275 Smith St. (bet. DeGraw & Sackett Sts.), Brooklyn, 718-237-2728

■ Carroll Gardens grazers enjoy "la dolce vita" along with "melty/crispy panini", "artful cheeses" and other "affordable" Italian "light bites" at this "cute little" blend of "hipness and warmth"; reports that the "kindest" people are "regulars" must be true, since the restaurant's customers helped build its lovely new garden.

Pão!

▽ 22 | 15 | 20 | $37

322 Spring St. (Greenwich St.), 212-334-5464

■ Fans say "you're lucky if you know" this "rustic" little Portuguese on SoHo's western fringe, where a "doting" staff dishes up "authentic" eats (wines too) at moderate prices; "tables are so close you'll get to know your neighbor", but sidewalk seats let you simply watch the world walk by.

Paola's

22 | 17 | 20 | $48

245 E. 84th St. (bet. 2nd & 3rd Aves.), 212-794-1890

■ "Paola is a great host" and the food is "never less than delicious" at her "cozy", "flowery" Upper East Side Italian that works as well for a "romantic" date as a "parents' anniversary"; it's "not cheap", but you'll "really feel pampered without blowing" major bucks.

Papaya King ⊭

21 | 3 | 11 | $6

179 E. 86th St. (3rd Ave.), 212-369-0648 ●
121 W. 125th St. (bet. Lenox & 7th Aves.), 212-665-5732
www.papayaking.com

🗷 The "best dogs in the free world" plus frothy fruit drinks "for next to free" have "tube-steak" junkies "lining up" at these "elbow-room-only", strictly "standup" shacks; just "close your eyes" to the "humble", "greasy" digs and countermen "focused on volume."

Paper Moon Milano ⧇

19 | 17 | 18 | $46

39 E. 58th St. (bet. Madison & Park Aves.), 212-758-8600

🗷 A "real power crowd" plus the "Madison Avenue shopping" set make for "lively" lunches at this "upscale" Midtown Northern Italian that's quieter at night; maybe the food won't send you over the moon but it's "reliable", though tabs "clearly reflect the location."

Paradou

22 | 17 | 18 | $36

8 Little W. 12th St. (bet. Greenwich & Washington Sts.), 212-463-8345;
www.paradounyc.com

■ Bypass Meatpacking District "mayhem" at this "tiny" "French haunt" offering "genuine" "Provençal flavor" via its "high-quality" menu, broad wine selection and "awesome" garden; if service can be "very leisurely", that makes it easier to "linger, nibble" and sip.

Parish & Co. ●

21 | 17 | 18 | $40

202 Ninth Ave. (22nd St.), 212-414-4988; www.parishandco.com

■ "Locals are beginning to dig" this "unpretentious" New American "alternative" in "otherwise boisterous Chelsea"; its assets include an "eclectic, flavorful" menu with "tasting and regular-size" portions plus a "pretty", "inviting" space, but since service can be "slow", you'd best "bring good company."

Park, The ●
16 | 25 | 14 | $43

118 10th Ave. (bet. 17th & 18th Sts.), 212-352-3313;
www.theparknyc.com

☑ To "see and be seen" in "cool", "gorgeous" surroundings, park it at this "vast" West Chelsea Med boasting everything from "lovely gardens" to "hot tubs"; the "lively" crowd's a mix of the "beautiful" and the "bridge and tunnel", none of whom seem to mind much if the food is getting to be "pedestrian" and service "disinterested."

Park Avalon ●
20 | 21 | 18 | $42

225 Park Ave. S. (bet. 18th & 19th Sts.), 212-533-2500;
www.brguestrestaurants.com

■ This "big", "glamorous" Flatiron New American aglow with "loads of burning candles" "still brings in" "young-ish" crowds, who consider it "perfect for a first date"; the secret to its success is "really good food" that doesn't cost too much, plus a Sunday jazz brunch that's one of the area's "best."

Park Avenue Cafe
24 | 23 | 23 | $64

100 E. 63rd St. (bet. Lexington & Park Aves.), 212-644-1900;
www.parkavenuecafe.com

■ "Don't be fooled by the conservative clientele or location", because this "sophisticated" East Side eatery "redefines New American" cooking via Neil Murphy's "impeccable" "nouveau" creations; it's "expensive", sure, but factoring in the "eager" service and renovated decor straight out of a "folk art museum", it's "worth" what you'll pay.

Park Bistro
20 | 16 | 17 | $47

414 Park Ave. S. (bet. 28th & 29th Sts.), 212-689-1360

☑ "Park here" for "dependable bistro classics" in a setting that feels more "like Paris" than Gramercy – though "tight", "metro-at-rush-hour" seating and "noise" are hardly foreign to NY; if a few find it "faded", more consider it a favorite "old friend."

Park Place
▽ 23 | 18 | 23 | $33

5816 Mosholu Ave. (Broadway), Bronx, 718-548-0977

■ Riverdale's no longer a culinary "wasteland" given places like this "caring" Continental that offers "a lot for your money" with "huge portions" of "surprisingly good" food; "relaxed yet sophisticated" (it might even "pass for romantic"), it's a "mainstay" for locals and a welcome find for explorers.

Park Side ●
24 | 19 | 21 | $40

107-01 Corona Ave. (51st Ave.), Queens, 718-271-9321;
www.parksiderestaurant.com

■ It's no wonder "weekend reservations disappear faster than hot zeppole" at this "old-fashioned" Corona Italian "classic" – its "superb" food is served "with aplomb" by "tuxedo-clad waiters"; to cap it off, "go watch the bocce matches" across the street.

Parma ●
21 | 13 | 19 | $51

1404 Third Ave. (bet. 79th & 80th Sts.), 212-535-3520

☑ "They'll do anything for regulars" at this "clubby" Upper East Side Northern Italian, a longtime standby for well-heeled locals who swear by its "generous portions" of "solid, non-gimmicky food"; sure, it "could use a major face-lift", but don't mess with its "comfortable" feel.

Parsonage
▽ 22 | 20 | 21 | $47

74 Arthur Kill Rd. (Clarke Ave.), Staten Island, 718-351-7879

☑ As if trekking to Staten Island isn't "transporting" enough, this American-Continental set in a "quaint" circa-1855 house in Historic Richmond Town also sends you back in time; though "a bit pricey", it

strikes most as "excellent all-around" ~~~~~~~ "~~~~~~~
expected" for "a touristy" enclave.

Pascalou
1308 Madison Ave. (bet. 92nd & 93rd Sts.), ~~~~~~~~~~
■ "How do they turn out such a big selectio~ ~~~~~~~~~~
closet of a kitchen?" is the question at this "n~~~~~~~~~~ Carnegie
Hill bistro; it's "charming" if "squished", an~ ~~~~ claustrophobes
concede the "early-bird special" is worth "holding your breath" for.

Pasha
| | 21 | 19 | 19 | $38 |

70 W. 71st St. (bet. Columbus Ave. & CPW), 212-579-8751;
www.pashanewyork.com
■ Upper Westsiders indulge their inner pasha at this "trusty" Turk, a
"regal" "red-walled retreat" that's like an affordable "trip to Istanbul"
with "enticing" flavors and "charming" waiters; since it's "an easy
stroll" to Lincoln Center, it's most "relaxing" after 8 PM.

⫻PASTIS ● 2/06
| | 21 | 21 | 17 | $42 |

9 Ninth Ave. (Little W. 12th St.), 212-929-4844; www.pastisny.com
☑ Though now "the old guard in the new Meatpacking District",
Balthazar's "little brother" is "still hot", so "bring your best modeling
pose" if you hope to sample its "rock-solid" French bistro eats, "slice-
of-Paris" setting and "crane-your-neck" people-watching; yes, it's
"unbearably loud" and crowded, but the "pretty" staff's attitude must
be thawing since they're "friendly, even when denying you a table."

Pastrami Queen
| | 18 | 5 | 12 | $20 |

1269 Lexington Ave. (bet. 85th & 86th Sts.), 212-828-0007
☑ Maybe "it ain't the king", but "in an area otherwise starved for
really good pastrami" and other "old-fashioned" kosher eats, this
Yorkville deli is something of "an oasis"; given less-than-royal decor
and service, "take out and save yourself the pain."

Patois
| | 21 | 18 | 18 | $37 |

255 Smith St. (bet. DeGraw & Douglass Sts.), Brooklyn, 718-855-1535;
www.patoisrestaurant.com
☑ This Carroll Gardens "trendsetter" helped "start the revolution" on
Smith Street and still offers "dynamite" French bistro fare, easy prices
and a "warm", Paris-meets-Brooklyn setting with fireplace and garden;
if a few find it "overrated", most say it's "excellent" "in any dialect."

Patria
| | 23 | 21 | 20 | $55 |

250 Park Ave. S. (20th St.), 212-777-6211
■ "The beat goes on" at NY's "granddaddy" of Nuevo Latino, a "festive"
Flatiron fixture pumping out "adventurous" food in a "vibrant"
multilevel setting with a good buzz; prices are "steep" and it all "feels
a bit mid '90s", but the joint's still "jumping", so join the fiesta.

Patroon ⧄
| | 21 | 20 | 21 | $61 |

160 E. 46th St. (bet. Lexington & 3rd Aves.), 212-883-7373;
www.patroonrestaurant.com
■ "The go-go '90s never died" at Ken Aretsky's "clubby" East Midtown
steakhouse that has added some "delicious" New American dishes
to its menu, yet still satisfies its "old-school", "power"-player crowd
with "terrific" beef; bring your "corporate" card and don't miss the
"fabulous rooftop deck" (aka cigar-"smoker's paradise").

Patsy's
| | 21 | 16 | 20 | $47 |

236 W. 56th St. (bet. B'way & 8th Ave.), 212-247-3491; www.patsys.com
☑ "Revisit 1940s NY" at this Southern Italian "institution" near Carnegie
Hall, a place to soak up "down-home red-sauce" "comfort food" in a

"c" setting with "celeb photos on the wall"; though critics
"doesn't live up to its rep" or cost, the fact that "Frankie ate
re" does the trick for many.

Patsy's Pizzeria
21 | 12 | 15 | $22

206 E. 60th St. (bet. 2nd & 3rd Aves.), 212-688-9707
2287-91 First Ave. (bet. 117th & 118th Sts.), 212-534-9783
1312 Second Ave. (69th St.), 212-639-1000
509 Third Ave. (bet. 34th & 35th Sts.), 212-689-7500
61 W. 74th St. (bet. Columbus Ave. & CPW), 212-579-3000
318 W. 23rd St. (bet. 8th & 9th Aves.), 646-486-7400
67 University Pl. (bet. 10th & 11th Sts.), 212-533-3500
■ The "thin", "crisp, smoky" crust and "beautiful sauce" are what
make the pizza so "delectable" at this "bustling, noisy" mini-chain,
(especially the "original", separately owned, circa-1932 coal-oven
East Harlem location); given the "lines out the door", devotees are
delighted that some branches "now deliver."

Paul & Jimmy's
18 | 16 | 20 | $40

123 E. 18th St. (bet. Irving Pl. & Park Ave. S.), 212-475-9540
■ Maybe it was "better 30-plus years ago", but longevity says a
lot about this "retro" Gramercy Italian offering "straightforward"
cooking, "comfortable" quarters and a "real family feel"; longtime
regulars are "glad it's not so well known."

Payard Bistro ☒
24 | 21 | 19 | $49

1032 Lexington Ave. (bet. 73rd & 74th Sts.), 212-717-5252;
www.payard.com
■ François Payard's "museum-quality" pastries are so "insanely
good" you could eat yourself into a "sugar coma" at his East Side
bistro/patisserie, but then you'd miss out on Philippe Bertineau's
"marvelous" cooking, which easily "holds its own"; the "elegant"
bi-level space has a feel that some find reminiscent of the old
Schrafft's chain, but better.

Peanut Butter & Co.
19 | 12 | 15 | $11

240 Sullivan St. (bet. Bleecker & W. 3rd Sts.), 212-677-3995;
www.ilovepeanutbutter.com
☑ "Every peanut butter combo" you can imagine and some you can't
("PB and *what*?!?") are the specialty at this "cute" little Village
sandwich shop that "speaks to your inner child"; a few Fluffernutter
phobes call it an "overpriced" "one-trick joint" with "slow" service,
but to most it's "a hoot."

PEARL OYSTER BAR ☒
27 | 14 | 19 | $39

18 Cornelia St. (bet. Bleecker & W. 4th Sts.), 212-691-8211;
www.pearloysterbar.com
■ The "seats added" in a recent expansion "help", but this still
guppy-size Village seafood "shack" remains "packed" to the gills
with "happy-as-a-clam" fin fare fanciers feasting on Rebecca
Charles' "amazingly fresh", "New England–style" eats, including
the "best lobster roll this side of Wiscasset"; "personable" service
and reasonable tabs are more reasons why you must "get there early"
or get in line.

Pearl Room
24 | 22 | 22 | $47

8201 Third Ave. (82nd St.), Brooklyn, 718-833-6666
■ The Bay Ridge "'in' crowd" favors this "Manhattan-type" seafooder
that's "kinda pricey" but proffers "excellent" food, "eager-to-please"
service and a "swanky" setting with fireplace and garden; it's a "great
singles' spot" that also works for "romantic dates" and, should things
progress further, "family gatherings."

Pearson's Texas BBQ
17 | 9 | 13 | $25

170 E. 81st St. (bet. Lexington & 3rd Aves.), 212-288-2700
Legends Sports Bar & Grill, 71-04 35th Ave. (bet. 71st & 72nd Sts.), Queens,
718-779-7715 ⊘
www.pearsonsbbq.com

☑ Though BBQ buffs debate the "crowded" new East Side branch ("a godsend" vs. "something got lost in translation"), most are "happy" they no longer need to schlep to Jackson Heights for 'cue that, at its best, is "smoky" and "succulent"; decor? – "c'mon, it's a BBQ place."

Peasant
23 | 21 | 18 | $48

194 Elizabeth St. (bet. Prince & Spring Sts.), 212-965-9511

■ "Peasants can't possibly eat as good" (or pay as much) as patrons of this "rustic" yet "hip" NoLita Italian whose wood-burning oven turns out "simple, high-quality" fare; it's "so dark" you can't read the menu, but since it's in Italian, who cares?; there's a new "grottolike" wine bar.

Peep
21 | 21 | 18 | $30

177 Prince St. (bet. Sullivan & Thompson Sts.), 212-254-7337;
www.peepsoho.net

■ "Peekaboo" bathrooms that let you "stare at fellow diners" are the "conversation piece", but this "stylish" SoHo Thai "doesn't need the gimmick" since it has "delish" food, "fab drinks" and "sleek", "think-pink" decor; better yet, it's "cheep", "without feeling like it."

Peking Duck House
22 | 16 | 17 | $31

236 E. 53rd St. (bet. 2nd & 3rd Aves.), 212-759-8260
28 Mott St. (bet. Chatham Sq. & Pell St.), 212-227-1810

■ NY's long-reigning "duke of duck" is a "crowded" Chinatowner that carves up its "meaty", "crispy"-skinned specialty in digs more "snazzy" than the area norm; few pay much attention to the "erratic" service – or the rest of the menu; N.B. the East Side sibling used to be known as Maple Garden Duck House.

Pellegrino's ◑
23 | 18 | 21 | $38

138 Mulberry St. (bet. Grand & Hester Sts.), 212-226-3177

■ "One of the better bets in Little Italy", this Mulberry Street "mainstay" stands out in a touristy area thanks to "above-par" food and "friendly", "professional" service; though "a little cramped", it works just fine for a "romantic evening."

Penang ◑
19 | 17 | 16 | $28

240 Columbus Ave. (71st St.), 212-769-3988
1596 Second Ave. (83rd St.), 212-585-3838
109 Spring St. (bet. Greene & Mercer Sts.), 212-274-8883
38-04 Prince St. (bet. 38th & 39th Aves.), Queens, 718-321-2078 ⊘

☑ If you're cravin' Malaysian, this chainlet supplies flavorful dishes in "tropical exotic" settings that can get "crowded" and "noisy", though "under 30s" don't seem to mind; critics yawn "ho-hum", but it's hard to argue with the "great bang for the buck."

Penelope ⊘
21 | 21 | 20 | $21

159 Lexington Ave. (30th St.), 212-481-3800

■ "Cute as a button" Murray Hill American with a "homey", "country-kitchen feel", matching low-cost eats and an "engaging staff" – given all that, it seems churlish to complain about "small-ish portions" and a long "wait for brunch"; P.S. you "can't leave without a cupcake."

Pepe ... To Go
22 | 10 | 15 | $19

506 Canal St. (bet. Greenwich & Washington Sts.), 212-219-3557
(continued)

(continued)
Pepe ... To Go
Grand Central, lower level (42nd St. & Vanderbilt Ave.),
212-867-6054
559 Hudson St. (bet. Perry & W. 11th Sts.), 212-255-2221 ⊖
149 Sullivan St. (bet. Houston & Prince Sts.), 212-677-4555
253 10th Ave. (bet. 24th & 25th Sts.), 212-242-6055
☑ Providing "civilized fast food for the pasta-and-wine set", these Italian "quick stops" "do the basics well" at modest prices; depending on the locale you may find "little seating", "abrupt" service and "ramshackle" decor, so some heed the name and get it "to go."

Pepolino ⬤   25 | 17 | 22 | $44
281 W. Broadway (bet. Canal & Lispenard Sts.), 212-966-9983
■ Transport yourself "to Firenze" via this TriBeCa "gem" where "sublime" Italian food is "served with charm and enthusiasm" in a bi-level setting that's "cramped" but feels like "Tuscany"; it's a standout "in this price range" but "alas, it's not so secret anymore", so weekends require reservations.

Perbacco ⬤⊖   23 | 18 | 21 | $33
234 E. Fourth St. (bet. Aves. A & B), 212-253-2038
■ "Italian tapas – what a great idea", and it's "done right" at this "tiny" East Villager where food that's "amazingly cheap for the quality" is served by a "sweet" staff that "always hits the mark" with wine tips; "each week it gets more crowded", so get "bigger, please."

Periyali ⌧   25 | 20 | 23 | $52
35 W. 20th St. (bet. 5th & 6th Aves.), 212-463-7890; www.periyali.com
■ The Flatiron forerunner that blazed the trail for "upscale Greek" dining in Manhattan is "still Olympian", from its "sophisticated" cooking and "warm service" to its "pretty", "whitewashed" setting; think of it as a "calming" "trip to the islands" and it won't seem as costly.

PER SE   ▽ 29 | 29 | 29 | $166
Time Warner Ctr., 10 Columbus Circle, 4th fl. (60th St. at B'way),
212-823-9335
■ The chosen few who've gained entry to Thomas Keller's new Columbus Circle sanctum report that it's "as good as its hype" and might even turn out to be NYC's best restaurant; "phenomenal" New American–French tasting menus, a "simply elegant" setting by Adam Tihany, "beautiful" views and "top-notch" service add up to an "unforgettable", multi-hour "event", so "put your phone on redial" and take out the "second mortgage" – it's "a must"; N.B. but for the low number of surveyors who have succeeded in getting a reservation, per se's ratings would make it No. 1 for Food, Decor and Service in this guide.

Persepolis   20 | 13 | 17 | $31
1423 Second Ave. (bet. 74th & 75th Sts.), 212-535-1100
■ Eastsiders tired of the same old, same old "dream" of the "delectable sour cherry rice" and other "tasty delights" at this simple but "soothing" Persian; "friendly" service, "huge" portions and low prices make it "a must for a taste of the exotic."

Pershing Square   15 | 17 | 15 | $36
90 E. 42nd St. (Park Ave.), 212-286-9600; www.pershingsquare.com
☑ Its "convenience" may beat its cooking, but this big, "noisy" American brasserie across from Grand Central works for anything from a "business breakfast" to evening martinis with the "good bar crowd"; optimists say "service has improved: you no longer feel you're in a Marx Brothers comedy."

Pescatore
18 | 16 | 18 | $37

955-957 Second Ave. (bet. 50th & 51st Sts.), 212-752-7151;
www.pescatorerestaurant.com

☑ This "casual" Midtown Italian seafooder is a "popular" neighborhood stop for pleasing meals, amiably served in "large portions" for fair prices; the upstairs outdoor deck "can't be beat" for summertime "people-watching removed from street noise."

Petaluma ◑
18 | 16 | 18 | $42

1356 First Ave. (73rd St.), 212-772-8800

■ "Still comfy after all these years", this "upscale" yet "kid-friendly" East Side Italian is a "favorite" fallback thanks to its "reliable" kitchen, "accommodating" service and prices that are "very reasonable" for what you get; some would visit for the "delicious fried olives" alone.

PETER LUGER STEAK HOUSE ⊅
27 | 14 | 19 | $63

178 Broadway (Driggs Ave.), Brooklyn, 718-387-7400;
www.peterluger.com

■ "No way" does steak get better than at Williamsburg's "peerless" "porterhouse palace", the *Survey*'s chophouse "champ" for 21 years running; it may look like a "bare-bones" "beer hall" but it's a "holy shrine" for carnivores who say "menus are for wimps" – those "gruff" waiters "know what you want and it moos"; remember to "hit the cash machine" before and "have your arteries cleaned" afterwards.

Pete's Downtown
▽ 18 | 15 | 19 | $35

2 Water St. (Old Fulton St.), Brooklyn, 718-858-3510

■ A "cheaper", more casual alternative to the nearby River Cafe, this Brooklyn Italian boasts the same "dreamy, movielike view of Manhattan" plus "hearty" food and "amicable" service; most think it's "worth a trip to Dumbo", even if it involves crossing the water.

Pete's Tavern ◑
13 | 15 | 15 | $28

129 E. 18th St. (Irving Pl.), 212-473-7676; www.petestavern.com

☑ Toast "the ghost of O. Henry" at this circa-1864 Gramercy tavern known for its "historic feel" and "crowded bar scene"; the American menu could use a rewrite, but the beer and burgers are fine and sidewalk seating "hikes it up a point" in summer.

Petite Abeille
19 | 13 | 16 | $23

466 Hudson St. (Barrow St.), 212-741-6479
134 W. Broadway (Duane St.), 212-791-1360
107 W. 18th St. (bet. 6th & 7th Aves.), 212-604-9350

☑ "Light-as-air waffles" and other "budget-minded" "Belgian comfort food" keep these "crowded hives buzzing"; with "quirky" Tintin-theme trappings, they're "so cute you can forgive" sometimes "kooky" service and petite setups sans "elbow room."

Petrosino ◑
▽ 22 | 21 | 20 | $43

190 Norfolk St. (Houston St.), 212-673-3773

■ In the "too-cool-for-school" Lower East Side, this Southern Italian is a "welcome grown-up" option with "delicious" food, a "hip but attentive" staff, "good wines" and tabs that "aren't too high"; "seductive" yet "casual", it's "great for a romantic date" or maybe even dinner with "your parents"; N.B. a new next-door annex, Canapa, offers pizzas and other light bites.

Petrossian ◑
24 | 24 | 23 | $70

182 W. 58th St. (7th Ave.), 212-245-2214; www.petrossian.com

■ Champagne wishes and caviar dreams come true at this storied French-Continental near Carnegie Hall, a "sybarite's delight" with "elegant" "art deco" decor and a menu that ranges well beyond those "delectable" "rare eggs"; if you're not prepared to spend "like a czar", prix fixe menus ($20 at lunch, $42 for dinner) put this "divine decadence" within easy reach.

Philip Marie
21 18 21 $39

569 Hudson St. (W. 11th St.), 212-242-6200

■ Expect to be "greeted with smiles" and fed "imaginative" New American food "like mother never made" at this West Village "charmer" with a "warm, comfortable" ambiance to match its "civilized" prices; the downstairs wine room for two guarantees a "very romantic evening" – you may want even slower service.

Pho Bang ⇗
20 6 11 $14

6 Chatham Sq. (Mott St.), 212-587-0870
157 Mott St. (bet. Broome & Grand Sts.), 212-966-3797
3 Pike St. (bet. Division St. & E. B'way), 212-233-3947
82-90 Broadway (Elmhurst Ave.), Queens, 718-205-1500
41-07 Kissena Blvd. (Main St.), Queens, 718-939-5520

☑ These Vietnamese noodle shops are "the place to go" for "fab" pho and other "fragrant", fulfilling eats at "amazingly cheap" prices; as for the setting and service, "no frills" is an understatement, but once you taste the food that's easily pho-given.

Phoenix Garden ⇗
23 7 13 $26

242 E. 40th St. (bet. 2nd & 3rd Aves.), 212-983-6666

☑ Whether it "rivals the backstreet gems of Kowloon" is debatable, but in the culinary backwater of Tudor City this brick-walled Cantonese is "a rare find", with "sublime" food (try the salt-and-pepper shrimp) that overrides the "brusque" service and minimalist setting; "Chinatown prices" and a BYO policy seal the deal.

Pho Viet Huong
20 11 13 $18

73 Mulberry St. (bet. Bayard & Canal Sts.), 212-233-8988

☑ "Superb for jurors" is one verdict on this Chinatown Vietnamese near the courts, but you don't have to be on a case to appreciate its "hearty soups" and such at "rock-bottom prices"; little decor and "indifferent service" are misdemeanors in light of its "good value."

Piadina ●⇗
▽ 18 16 17 $32

57 W. 10th St. (bet. 5th & 6th Aves.), 212-460-8017

☑ "Like being in an Italian village" rather than Greenwich Village, this "rustic", "tucked-away" "treasure" satisfies with "solid pastas", "very reasonable" prices and a staff that "won't rush you out"; space is "tight" and the lights are low, but that adds "more than a touch of romance."

Piccola Venezia
25 16 22 $51

42-01 28th Ave. (42nd St.), Queens, 718-721-8470;
www.piccola-venezia.com

■ The "mile-long menu" is "only a suggestion" – they'll make "whatever you want" at this Astoria "class act" that's "what Italian used to be": "everyone gets treated and fed well" with "no snobbery" involved; despite jabs at "dated" decor, most diners deem it "worth the cost and the "schlep."

Piccolo Angolo
25 14 22 $35

621 Hudson St. (Jane St.), 212-229-9177

■ "Entertaining" owner Renato Migliorini "recites the specials machine-gun style" and "never steers you wrong" at his "tiny", "bustling" West Village Italian, a "wonderful bargain" for "top-quality" food and "hospitality"; expect "a wait" to be seated and "get ready to be friendly" to your neighbors since you'll be sitting in each other's laps.

PICHOLINE

26 | 23 | 25 | $77

35 W. 64th St. (bet. B'way & CPW), 212-724-8585

■ All the makings for "a meal to remember" are in place at Terrance Brennan's "classy" Lincoln Center French-Med, a "best bet" pre-concert and "marvelous" anytime thanks to "inventive" food, "finely tuned service" and "elegant" decor, not to mention "phenomenal" cheese choices orchestrated by cheese master Max McCalman; expect an unreservedly "rich experience", right down to the bill.

Picket Fence

– | – | – | M

1310 Cortelyou Rd. (bet. Argyle St. & Rugby Rd.), Brooklyn, 718-282-6661

With a look as cute as its suburbs-meets-city locale, this Traditional American is the only thing going in Midwood for upscale dining; the family-friendly vibe is enhanced by fresh popcorn on the tables and a backyard bordered naturally by a picket fence.

Pie

17 | 9 | 12 | $11

124 Fourth Ave. (bet. 12th & 13th Sts.), 212-475-4977; www.piebythepound.com

☑ Putting a "twist" on the usual pizza process, this East Villager's "scissors-wielding" staff snips off sized-to-order slices of "creative", priced-by-the-pound pies; the "NYU" set approves, but "better ambiance would help" and a few outvoted critics call it "overpriced."

Pierre au Tunnel

21 | 17 | 21 | $46

250 W. 47th St. (bet. B'way & 8th Ave.), 212-575-1220; www.pierreautunnel.com

■ "All the fads and changes" haven't disturbed this "ever so traditional" Theater District "warhorse" – for decades, it's sent show-goers off "on time" and well fed, treating them graciously "from *bonsoir* to *au revoir*"; if it's looking a tad "worn", that's no surprise after all this time.

Pietrasanta

19 | 12 | 17 | $34

683 Ninth Ave. (47th St.), 212-265-9471; www.pietrasanta47th.com

☑ "Make reservations" if you hope to snag a pre-theater seat at this "friendly" Hell's Kitchen Italian serving "simple" pastas at simple prices; "fancy it's not", nor is it big on elbow room: "you could end up eating the next table's entree", but at least it would taste good.

Pietro's ☒

22 | 13 | 22 | $57

232 E. 43rd St. (bet. 2nd & 3rd Aves.), 212-682-9760; www.pietros.com

☑ This "old-school" Italian steakhouse near Grand Central has "been around forever", as have its patrons; what keeps them loyal are "huge portions", "superior food" and "great hospitality", which compensate for "shopworn" decor ("dust off the plants") and prices that induce "minor sticker shock."

Pigalle ◗

18 | 18 | 16 | $33

Days Hotel, 790 Eighth Ave. (48th St.), 212-489-2233; www.pigallenyc.com

■ "Francophiles", show-goers and insomniacs all have reason to say "*oui*" to this pleasingly "Parisian" Theater District bistro/brasserie that's "very satisfying" and "not too fancy" in attitude or price, plus it's open 24/7 – "what more can you ask for?" except sometimes less "noise."

Pig Heaven ◗

19 | 14 | 19 | $31

1540 Second Ave. (bet. 80th & 81st Sts.), 212-744-4333

■ The name's "kitschy", but they've got pork down pat ("gotta try the ribs") at this Upper East Side "porcine paradise" that's "more upscale" than the typical Chinese; decent non-pig items and a "charismatic owner" also keep locals "coming back."

Pinch, Pizza by the Inch
| 21 | 11 | 20 | $17 |

416 Park Ave. S. (bet. 28th & 29th Sts.), 212-686-5222;
www.pizzabytheinch.com

☑ Selling "inventive" pizzas by the inch is the "clever concept" behind this "friendly" Gramercy stop; though priced kind of "high" for pie, the "good" eats (pastas and salads too) "outshine the gimmick" – just try not to blush when you say "waiter, I'd like 10 inches, please."

Ping's Seafood ◑
| 21 | 11 | 14 | $25 |

22 Mott St. (bet. Bayard & Pell Sts.), 212-602-9988
83-02 Queens Blvd. (Goldsmith St.), Queens, 718-396-1238

☑ "Some of the best" Hong Kong–style seafood in town plus "diverse dim sum" at "decent prices" explain why this Chinatown-Elmhurst duo is often "loud" and "crowded"; "don't expect much service" at peak hours, or much decor anytime.

Pink Tea Cup ◑▱
| 20 | 11 | 15 | $22 |

42 Grove St. (bet. Bedford & Bleecker Sts.), 212-807-6755;
www.thepinkteacup.com

☑ "Pure fat never tasted so good" as at this low-budget, teacup-size West Villager dispensing delish, "down-home Southern soul food" that's "not for the faint of artery"; "plan on waiting in line" for brunch and act blasé if you spot "Whoopi in the corner."

Pinocchio
| ▽ 22 | 14 | 22 | $41 |

1748 First Ave. (bet. 90th & 91st Sts.), 212-828-5810

■ Yorkville locals enamored of this Italian's "excellent" food, "quaint" vibe and "personal" service say it's just "what a trattoria should be" – except for its "shoebox size"; still, its "charm" eases the squeeze.

Pintaile's Pizza
| 19 | 6 | 13 | $14 |

26 E. 91st St. (bet. 5th & Madison Aves.), 212-722-1967
1237 Second Ave. (bet. 64th & 65th Sts.), 212-752-6222
1577 York Ave. (bet. 83rd & 84th Sts.), 212-396-3479
1443 York Ave. (bet. 76th & 77th Sts.), 212-717-4990
www.pintailespizza.com

☑ "Pizza so thin you can sail it like a frisbee" is the hallmark of these Eastsiders slinging "crispy", "wheat-crust" pies with "wacky toppings that actually work"; most find them "healthy" and "delicious", but critics are left "starving" and searching for "flavor."

Pipa
| 20 | 23 | 17 | $39 |

ABC Carpet & Home, 38 E. 19th St. (bet. B'way & Park Ave. S.), 212-677-2233;
www.abchome.com

■ The tapas are terrific, the sangria's "super" and the bar is "hopping", but the "dark, sexy", "chandelier-bedecked" setting nearly steals the show at this Flatiron Spaniard in ABC Carpet & Home; too bad tabs get "pricey", and it's not so "romantic" if you have to "scream" to converse.

Pisticci ▱
| ▽ 23 | 21 | 21 | $32 |

125 La Salle St. (B'way), 212-932-3500

■ This "laid-back" Columbia-area Italian is "crowded enough already", so locals would just as soon not talk up its "divine" pastas, "enthusiastic" service and "affordable" prices; it's a good date place "when it isn't packed, which isn't often."

Pizza 33 ◑
| 22 | 8 | 13 | $10 |

489 Third Ave. (33rd St.), 212-545-9191
268 W. 23rd St. (8th Ave.), 212-206-0999

☑ "Crisp" thin crusts, "savory" sauce and "fresh toppings" equal the "best slice in Murray Hill" according to fans of this "unassuming" brick-oven joint with a newer Chelsea sibling; some dub them "disco pizza" due to their popularity with the "late-night-munchies" crowd.

P.J. Clarke's ●

16 | 16 | 16 | $31

915 Third Ave. (55th St.), 212-317-1616; www.pjclarkes.com

■ "Though renovated" not long ago, this "bustling" circa-1884 "landmark" still feels "like walking through a time machine", and still serves some of the "best" burgers till 3 AM; "shhh" – the "upscale" upstairs eatery, the Sidecar, is "one of NY's secret treasures."

Place, The

22 | 24 | 21 | $45

310 W. Fourth St. (bet. Bank & W. 12th Sts.), 212-924-2711; www.theplaceny.com

■ The "ultimate date place" could well be this "intimate" West Village Med–New American, a "dimly lit", "grotto"-like "hideaway" that's at its "coziest by the fire" in winter; if you can get your mind off "romance", you'll find "very good" food and service too.

Planet Thailand ●⊟

21 | 19 | 15 | $24

133 N. Seventh St. (bet. Bedford Ave. & Berry St.), Brooklyn, 718-599-5758

☑ This "funky", "warehouse"-size Williamsburg "original" is still a "happening" place to "bask in hipster glory" while exploring a "never-ending" menu of "cheap, tasty" Thai-Japanese eats; "loud" DJ music adds to the "good scene", but "absent" service spoils it for some.

Plantain ⊠

▽ 22 | 17 | 21 | $31

20 W. 38th St. (bet. 5th & 6th Aves.), 212-869-8601; www.plantainrestaurant.com

■ "Pepping up" the "monotonous" Garment District with its "vibrant colors and flavors", this Caribbean "find" specializes in "wonderful" small plates served by an "accommodating" staff; it's an "out-of-the-ordinary" option and can be "cheap" to boot thanks to lunchbox specials and "great happy-hour deals."

Pó

25 | 16 | 21 | $45

31 Cornelia St. (bet. Bleecker & W. 4th Sts.), 212-645-2189

■ The "lucky" few who nab "impossible-to-get" reservations at this "tiny", "relaxed" Greenwich Village Italian (Mario Batali's first venture) are treated to "absolutely delicious" "rustic" cuisine served by a "friendly, professional" crew; while prices are "reasonable" given the "quality", "bargain"-hunters note that the six-course, $40 tasting menu is truly "an amazing deal."

Poke

26 | 5 | 20 | $32

305 E. 85th St. (bet. 1st & 2nd Aves.), 212-249-0569

☑ It sure isn't atmosphere that lures diners to this Upper East Side Japanese – "decor is lacking altogether" – rather it's "creative", "fresh" sushi to make the "taste buds sing"; the "gregarious owner" also keeps customers "coming back" and a great BYO policy boosts the "value."

Pomodoro Rosso

21 | 16 | 20 | $36

229 Columbus Ave. (bet. 70th & 71st Sts.), 212-721-3009

☑ "Packed every night", this "homey" Lincoln Center Italian has customers lining up for its "tasty, reasonably priced" dishes studded with "record quantities of garlic"; it's "quite a find" for the area – now "if only they'd take reservations."

Pongal

22 | 15 | 13 | $24

110 Lexington Ave. (bet. 27th & 28th Sts.), 212-696-9458

☑ Even "carnivores enjoy" the "amazing" "meatless" dishes at this Curry Hill South Indian, a kosher vegetarian whose "crisp dosas" are considered "some of the best NY has to offer"; service is "notoriously unreliable" and the decor minimal, but "that's ok" – everyone's here "for the food."

Pongsri Thai

19 | 11 | 16 | $24

106 Bayard St. (Baxter St.), 212-349-3132
311 Second Ave. (18th St.), 212-477-2727
244 W. 48th St. (bet. B'way & 8th Ave.), 212-582-3392 ◗

🔺 "Reliable" food, "cheap" prices and "location" sum up the appeal of this "no-frills" Thai trio handy for "pre-theater" and "jury duty" fill-ups; the decor may be "dressed-up cafeteria" and the service "fast and robotic", but "you can always find a table"; N.B. the bare-bones Chinatown branch is also known as Thailand Restaurant.

Ponticello

▽ 24 | 21 | 21 | $44

46-11 Broadway (bet. 46th & 47th Sts.), Queens, 718-278-4514;
www.ponticelloristorante.com

■ It's "looking great" after a "recent renovation", meaning this Astoria Italian's "upscale ambiance" now "matches" its "outstanding" traditional cuisine; party-throwers say the "cavelike" "private room overlooking the wine cellar" (one of three event spaces) is "perfection."

Pop ◗

▽ 18 | 16 | 14 | $33

127 Fourth Ave. (bet. 12th & 13th Sts.), 212-767-1800

■ "More lounge than restaurant" it may be, but this Village New American offers "surprisingly good" mini-burgers, pizzas and such to soak up its "fabulous" drinks; "loud music", "low couches and tables" and a "hot" (if "spacey") staff add to the nightclub feel.

Pop Burger ◗

19 | 17 | 12 | $18

58-60 Ninth Ave. (bet. 14th & 15th Sts.), 212-414-8686

■ One part "burger joint", one part "late-night" (till 4 AM) lounge/eatery, this Meatpacking District New American provides "tasty mini-burgers", shakes and more at its "mod"-looking "fast-food" counter, while the big, "trendy" bar area offers more ambitious choices; most say it's a "great concept", though "snooty" service may be a turnoff.

Popover Cafe

18 | 14 | 15 | $24

551 Amsterdam Ave. (bet. 86th & 87th Sts.), 212-595-8555;
www.popovercafe.com

🔺 "It's all about the popovers" at this Upper West Side American "brunch favorite", where the "stroller crowd" endures "endless waits" to savor the "puffy, light" namesake and maybe "cuddle a teddy bear"; the less-impressed find it all "too cute", with mostly "uninspired" eats and "variable" service.

Porters ◗

17 | 17 | 18 | $42

216 Seventh Ave. (bet. 22nd & 23rd Sts.), 212-229-2878;
www.portersnyc.com

🔺 "Dim and quasi-moody", this Chelsea Med–New American stands out with its "terrific" live jazz (Sundays and Mondays) and "secret" back patio; while its pasta-and-steak menu satisfies some, critics say "it should be better at these prices", knocking "mediocre" eats and "dull decor."

Portofino Grille

19 | 21 | 20 | $43

1162 First Ave. (bet. 63rd & 64th Sts.), 212-832-4141;
www.portofinogrille.com

■ You "dine under the stars" "twinkling on the ceiling" at this East Side Italian, whose faux "old Italy" decor is "romantic" to fans, "kitschy" to cynics; either way, most appreciate its "quality" pastas and other "comfort" favorites served by a "friendly, generous staff."

Positano ◑
21 | 15 | 20 | $34

122 Mulberry St. (bet. Canal & Hester Sts.), 212-334-9808
■ Little Italy buffs consider this standby "a real bargain" for "*molto buono*" Southern Italian cooking and matching atmosphere; sidewalk seating along Mulberry Street adds to its "positively Positano" feel.

Post House   *Gev-'04*
24 | 21 | 22 | $65

√Lowell Hotel, 28 E. 63rd St. (bet. Madison & Park Aves.), 212-935-2888; www.theposthouse.com
■ "When you really need a 30-oz. veal chop", try this "tranquil", "genteel" East Side steakhouse "with slightly less testosterone than some of the others" (i.e. "women feel more welcome"); a "pro" staff serves "stiff drinks", "fine wines" and "superb beef" with "few surprises", which suits the "business"-oriented clientele just fine.

Press 195 ⊘
20 | 12 | 15 | $15

195 Fifth Ave. (bet. Sackett & Union Sts.), Brooklyn, 718-857-1950; www.press195.com
☑ The "press trend" lives on at this "casual" Park Slope paninoteca proffering "a million" (ok, about 35) kinds of "interesting", "delicious" and "cheap" sandwiches; locals say "one of the great summertime pleasures" is lingering over "a glass of wine" in its "adorable garden."

Primavera ◑
23 | 22 | 23 | $65

1578 First Ave. (82nd St.), 212-861-8608; www.primaveranyc.com
■ "Like a fine wine", this "gracious" Upper East Side Italian "continues to age exceedingly well", remaining "on par" with the city's "finest" and attracting a crème de la crème clientele; owner Nicola Civetta ensures that the kitchen's "outstanding" handiwork and "charming" service are as "opulent" as the "dark-wood-paneled setting"; P.S. don't miss "truffle season."

Prime Grill
22 | 18 | 17 | $56

60 E. 49th St. (bet. Madison & Park Aves.), 212-692-9292; www.theprimegrill.com
■ This "sophisticated" Midtown steakhouse/sushi bar is about "as good as kosher's likely to get" thanks to "outstanding" beef and fish enjoyed in "vivacious" (read: "noisy") environs; it's "pricey" with sometimes "spotty" service, but most think it's "worth" it.

Primola ◑
23 | 15 | 20 | $57

1226 Second Ave. (bet. 64th & 65th Sts.), 212-758-1775
☑ "Celebs and heavy-hitters" are among the regulars enjoying "excellent" seafood and pastas at this East Side Italian; it's a "noisy", "convivial" scene that "never disappoints" – especially if "you're in the 'in' crowd" – but "hold on to your wallet" because it costs to dine with "Woody and company."

Provence ◑
22 | 21 | 20 | $50

38 MacDougal St. (Prince St.), 212-475-7500; www.provence-soho.com
■ Handsome, "flower"-filled, wood-paneled quarters with an "enclosed garden" at this SoHo French set the stage for a "perfect romantic evening" enhanced by "sumptuous" Provençal cuisine and "charming" service; if a few whisper that it's a "bit pricey" and "could use updating", most are glad it "never changes."

Provence en Boite
∇ 22 | 20 | 21 | $34

8303 Third Ave. (bet. 83rd & 84th Sts.), Brooklyn, 718-759-1515; www.provenceenboite.com
■ "French bistros don't get much more authentic" than this "quaint" Bay Ridge boîte where a "husband-and-wife team" supply "delicious"

Gallic classics and "attentive" service; but it's the "phenomenal desserts" from their on-site patisserie that really induce drools.

Prune
24 | 14 | 20 | $44

54 E. First St. (bet. 1st & 2nd Aves.), 212-677-6221

☑ Chef Gabrielle Hamilton "is a star" and her "hip" East Village New American "a true treasure" gush foodies wowed by her "simple" yet "surprising" combos of "under-used ingredients"; it's "tiny" and "always crowded", so be prepared to "play kneesies with the next table"; P.S. the "fantastic brunch" is worth getting up "early" for.

Public ◑
23 | 25 | 19 | $49

210 Elizabeth St. (bet. Prince & Spring Sts.), 212-343-7011; www.public-nyc.com

■ At this "happening" NoLita International with an Antipodean bent ("kangaroo", anyone?), the "very cool", "industrial-library" decor is a "stylish" foil for the kitchen's "sophisticated" creations; a "hot spot" by night, surveyors also tout it as a brunch place too.

Pump Energy Food
18 | 5 | 14 | $13

113 E. 31st St. (bet. Lexington Ave. & Park Ave. S.), 212-213-5733
31 E. 21st St. (bet. B'way & Park Ave.), 212-253-7676
40 W. 55th St. (bet. 5th & 6th Aves.), 212-246-6844
112 W. 38th St. (bet. B'way & 6th Ave.), 212-764-2100 ⊠
www.thepumpenergyfood.com

☑ "Healthy fast food" is not an oxymoron at these all-over-town stops where "high protein, low fat" is the mantra and "coupons for free stuff" pump up the value; doubters find it "a little bland", with a "gymnasium"-like vibe that encourages delivery or takeout.

Punch ◑
20 | 19 | 20 | $35

913 Broadway (bet. 20th & 21st Sts.), 212-673-6333; www.punch-nyc.com

☑ Decode the "clever descriptions" on its "lengthy menu" and you're in for a "novel" meal at this "friendly" Flatiron Eclectic with circus-themed decor; if some say it's "nothing to get too excited about", others opine it's "a sure bet" for a "relaxing", modestly priced repast.

Pure Food and Wine
– | – | – | E

(fka Verbena)

54 Irving Pl. (bet. 17th & 18th Sts.), 212-477-1010; www.purefoodandwine.com

Chef Matthew Kenney (ex Commune, Commissary) raises the profile of raw-vegan fare with this stylish Gramercy newcomer, the city's first upscale outpost of the California-born movement; look for creative cuisine cleverly cobbled from fresh fruits and veggies, with nothing heated above 118° F (to preserve the live enzymes).

Puttanesca
19 | 14 | 17 | $34

859 Ninth Ave. (56th St.), 212-581-4177; www.puttanesca.com

☑ Hoofing that extra "block" to Ninth Avenue nets show-goers a "lower-cost" but not lower-quality meal thanks to this "old-fashioned" Hell's Kitchen Italian that's "packed and loud" pre-curtain; its "fine assortment of pastas" and such are served with "no pretensions" and "no surprises", which suits some but has others yawning "ho-hum."

Pylos ◑
24 | 23 | 20 | $37

128 E. Seventh St. (bet. Ave. A & 1st Ave.), 212-473-0220; www.pylosrestaurant.com

■ "Finally, a hip place with delicious Greek food" cheer admirers of this new East Village "favorite" offering "upscale twists" on "rustic" classics in a "tasteful" space hung with "lovely clay pots"; since it's been discovered, "reservations are a must."

Q, a Thai Bistro

21 | 19 | 20 | $35

108-25 Ascan Ave. (bet. Austin & Burns Sts.), Queens, 718-261-6599

■ "Manhattan comes to Forest Hills" via this "sexy, spicy" Thai where "quality" dishes (both "traditional and nontraditional") arrive in "small", "SoHo"-style digs; admirers attest it's one of the area's more "highbrow" options.

Quartino

▽ 22 | 19 | 20 | $30

11 Bleecker St. (Elizabeth St.), 212-529-5133 ⊟
21-23 Peck Slip (Water St.), 212-349-4433

■ "Just like eating at nonna's house" – if she's "health-conscious" and "organic"-minded – this "rustic" South Street Seaport Ligurian pays "attention to the ingredients" in its "simple, delicious" preparations; N.B. a new, unrated NoHo branch offers vegetarian fare plus fish.

Quatorze Bis

22 | 19 | 20 | $52

323 E 79th St. (bet. 1st & 2nd Aves.), 212-535-1414

■ For a bit of "Paris on East 79th Street", try this "upscale" French bistro offering "better-than-average" cooking with a "hint of sophistication"; the "cheerful" service and "classy", "antique poster"–adorned room are two reasons why it's "always busy."

Queen

24 | 13 | 20 | $38

84 Court St. (bet. Livingston & Schermerhorn Sts.), Brooklyn, 718-596-5955;
www.queenrestaurant.com

■ This Brooklyn Heights "queen of Italians" has "still got it after all these years", producing "traditional yet not run-of-the-mill" dishes served by a staff that "makes you feel like family"; if it "doesn't look like much" despite a "redo" a couple of years back, no one minds much.

Quercy

▽ 23 | 17 | 20 | $39

242 Court St. (Baltic St.), Brooklyn, 718-243-2151

■ A "welcome respite" from the "too-hip" contenders on Smith Street, this Cobble Hill French bistro pleases with "excellent" classic dishes and "attentive" service; though it's a boon that "you can always get a table", supporters say it "deserves to be better known."

Quintessence

17 | 12 | 15 | $28

566 Amsterdam Ave. (bet. 87th & 88th Sts.), 212-501-9700
353 E. 78th St. (bet. 1st & 2nd Aves.), 212-734-0888
263 E. 10th St. (bet. Ave. A & 1st Ave.), 646-654-1823
www.raw-q.com

☑ "Live food" is the concept at this über-"healthy" trio where "adventurous" diners dig into the "extraordinarily creative" "all-raw, all-vegan" cuisine; though it's "not for the timid" (who find it "weird" and "tasteless"), fans "feel renewed after eating here."

Rachel's American Bistro

18 | 13 | 17 | $35

608 Ninth Ave. (bet. 43rd & 44th Sts.), 212-957-9050;
www.rachels9thavenue.com

■ Pre-theater, this "upbeat" Hell's Kitchen bistro is a "sardine factory" thanks to its "bargain-for-the-quality" New American fare and "quick", get-you-out-in-time service; however, nonfans of "noise" opt for post-curtain dining, when you can "sit and enjoy a long meal."

Radio Perfecto ◐

17 | 18 | 17 | $25

1187 Amsterdam Ave. (118th St.), 212-932-8555
190 Ave. B (bet. 11th & 12th Sts.), 212-477-3366

☑ "Always jumpin'", this "funky" East Village International (with a new Upper West Side outpost) broadcasts a "reasonable", "something-for-all" comfort-food roster amid a bevy of 1940's-era Bakelite radios; no wonder it's a hit with "student" types, who only wish the "imperfecto" staff would cut the "static."

Raga

▽ 23 | 18 | 21 | $35

433 E. Sixth St. (bet. Ave. A & 1st Ave.), 212-388-0957; www.raganyc.com
■ The fragrant "smell of spices" in the air hints at the "delicious" fusion "interpretations" of Indian dishes at this "tranquil" East Village standout, considered by some to be the "poor man's Tabla"; quite "affordable" prices and a "friendly" staff ice the cake.

Rain

21 | 20 | 18 | $39

1059 Third Ave. (bet. 62nd & 63rd Sts.), 212-223-3669
100 W. 82nd St. (bet. Amsterdam & Columbus Aves.), 212-501-0776
www.rainrestaurant.com
☑ Long a "favorite" for "exciting tastes" at "conservative" tabs, these crosstown "jungle"-themed Pan-Asians are "still packed" with "attractive" "young" things enjoying the lively scene; if a few find the fare "generic", most report that the "delightful drinks" will "put a smile on your face."

RAINBOW ROOM

19 | 27 | 21 | VE

GE Bldg., 30 Rockefeller Plaza, 65th fl. (bet. 49th & 50th Sts.), 212-632-5100;
www.rainbowroom.com
■ Yes, it's the "stunning" "bird's-eye view of the city" that really "makes" it, but at this "legendary" 65th-floor Rock Center "classic", the "glamorous" deco decor and "decent" Italian fare also "live up to the hype"; it "can't be beat" for "special occasions or for serious dancing", but sadly, since being acquired by the Ciprianis, it's only open on Friday and Saturday nights and for an "amazing" Sunday brunch (fortunately, the Rainbow Grill down the hall is open nightly).

Rao's ☒⇆

20 | 14 | 20 | $59

455 E. 114th St. (Pleasant Ave.), 212-722-6709; www.raos.com
■ "You've got to know someone who knows someone" to even think about getting a table at this "incredible" "old-school" Harlem Southern Italian, where the roster of celebrity guests provides better theater than on Broadway – and a recent "whacking" only turned up the "hype"; just keep in mind, if owner Frank Pellegrino takes your call or bartender "Nicky the Vest remembers your name, you've made it in NY."

Raoul's ◑

22 | 19 | 19 | $50

180 Prince St. (bet. Sullivan & Thompson Sts.), 212-966-3518;
www.raoulsrestaurant.com
■ 30 years old and still "retaining its swagger", this SoHo French bistro remains "dependable" for "fantastic" fare and a "happening", "artsy" scene presided over by an "engaging" staff; the "romantic" garden room is a favored "late-night" destination, particularly for "canoodlers."

Rare Bar & Grill

19 | 16 | 16 | $28

Shelburne Murray Hill Hotel, 303 Lexington Ave. (37th St.), 212-481-1999
☑ "Burgermeisters" make a beeline for this Murray Hill patty place that serves first-rate variations on the classic (Kobe beef, Roquefort, truffle, etc.) to an "attractive professional crowd"; while there are complaints about "clumsy" service, most consider it a "great idea, well done" and well-priced.

Rasputin

▽ 18 | 19 | 19 | $73

2670 Coney Island Ave. (Ave. X), Brooklyn, 718-332-8111;
www.rasputincabaret.com
☑ Visitors to this "over-the-top" Sheepshead Bay Russian cabaret should "drink heavily" in order to best enjoy the "flamboyant" floor

shows and dancing that it's famous for; there are also "decadent" delectables, but most "go for the party, not the food" – "na zdorovje!"

Raymond's Cafe
▽ | 21 | 17 | 21 | $33

88 Seventh Ave. (bet. 15th & 16th Sts.), 212-929-1778
■ "Gracious, low-priced meals" are increasingly hard to find in happening Chelsea, but this "comfortable" "neighborhood" standby comes across with reliable American fare and "charming" service; after 20 years on the scene, it's still a "favorite" of "local" folks.

Red Café
▽ | 21 | 19 | 21 | $28

78 Fifth Ave. (Prospect Pl.), Brooklyn, 718-789-1100
■ "Drop in anytime" at this "tiny", "no 'tude" Park Slope New American where "you can't go wrong" with any of the "hearty, delicious" dishes on its "small menu"; equally appealing are the very "good prices."

Red Cat
24 | 20 | 22 | $47

227 10th Ave. (bet. 23rd & 24th Sts.), 212-242-1122; www.theredcat.com
■ Way West Chelsea is home to this pricey, "full-of-energy" Med–New American that's considered "the cat's meow" thanks to its "imaginative, well-prepared" cuisine, "attentive" staff and "cool farmhouse" quarters; the "bustling" front bar also is a "favorite" for its "killer cocktails" and "can't-go-wrong" snacks.

Redeye Grill ●
21 | 19 | 19 | $50

890 Seventh Ave. (56th St.), 212-541-9000; www.redeyegrill.com
■ The signature "dancing shrimp" headline the menu at Shelly Fireman's "big, brash" New American that's not only "convenient to City Center and Carnegie Hall", but is also well located for "tourists" and area "business" lunchers; its "something-for-everyone" offerings and private spaces also make it a "great place to go with a large group" or to host a party, even though the tabs can pinch.

Red Garlic ●
19 | 12 | 16 | $28

916 Eighth Ave. (bet. 54th & 55th Sts.), 212-489-5237; www.redgarlicrestaurant.com
☑ Despite "dumpy", "no-atmosphere" digs, this Hell's Kitchen Thai still lures locals with an "imaginatively presented" menu that includes lots of "seafood specialties"; it may be a "little pricey" for the genre, but given what you get, most consider it a "bargain."

Regency
▽ | 19 | 20 | 22 | $64

Regency Hotel, 540 Park Ave. (61st St.), 212-339-4050; www.loewshotels.com
■ This Tisch-owned Upper East Side hotel offers two contiguous New American eateries, The Library and 540 Park; by day, the latter is famed for its see-and-be-seen power breakfast with great power people-watching (e.g. mayors, senators, corporate titans), but come nightfall it morphs into the cabaret fixture Feinstein's at the Regency.

Regional Thai
18 | 14 | 15 | $26

1479 First Ave. (77th St.), 212-744-6374
208 Seventh Ave. (22nd St.), 212-807-9872 ●
☑ "Comfortable neighborhood places" for food that's a "step above the ordinary", these Thai twins are "convenient" and "moderately priced"; nonetheless, an unimpressed contingent considers them "mediocre at best."

Relish ●
19 | 19 | 16 | $26

225 Wythe Ave. (bet. Metropolitan Ave. & N. 3rd St.), Brooklyn, 718-963-4546
■ Housed in a "beautifully" revamped stainless-steel diner, this "retro" magnet for Williamsburg "hipsters" offers "dressed-up" New

American comfort food served by the "cutest" (if sometimes "lackadaisical") staff; locals also relish the "excellent weekend brunch" and "cool" back garden.

Remi
22 | 22 | 20 | $54

145 W. 53rd St. (bet. 6th & 7th Aves.), 212-581-4242

■ It's "always a pleasure" to dine at this "well-honed" Midtown Venetian where the "beautiful" Adam Tihany–designed decor is as "decadent" as the "*squisito*" cuisine; it remains a favorite of the "power-lunch" set even "after all these years", but for those who are eating at their desks there's "terrific" takeout at the adjacent Remi To Go.

René Pujol
22 | 19 | 22 | $54

321 W. 51st St. (bet. 8th & 9th Aves.), 212-246-3023

■ "Everything old is new again" at this "charming", albeit pricey, Theater District French that's long been a "cozy" "standby" for pre-curtain dining with "first-rate" service; seekers of "serene" environs wait till the show-goers have left to better savor the "quiet" atmosphere and "inviting fireplace."

Republic
18 | 14 | 15 | $20

37 Union Sq. W. (bet. 16th & 17th Sts.), 212-627-7172;
www.thinknoodles.com

☑ The "communal benches" are always "packed" at this mod Pan-Asian noodle "warehouse" where the "roaring" din from the young customers means that "no one hears you slurping"; given its "one-for-every-mood" selection of "always-good" dishes, fans insist it's one of the "best bargains on Union Square."

Re Sette
22 | 19 | 19 | $49

7 W. 45th St. (bet. 5th & 6th Aves.), 212-221-7530;
www.resette.com

☑ You'll "dine like a king" at this Midtown Italian appointed in "medieval" splendor, where the "kitchen sings" with dishes from the Barese region, even if the staff sometimes "stumbles"; the upstairs private party room is "perfect for a large group", but bring your platinum card as all this royal treatment ain't cheap.

Rêve
– | – | – | M

1347 Second Ave. (71st St.), 212-288-5285

Helmed by Puffy Combs' former private chef, this East Side newcomer offers French cuisine rêvé up with some Asian accents; the dreamy interior features exposed brick, dark woods and red banquettes, all bathed in a romantic candlelit glow.

Revival
∇ 20 | 19 | 19 | $32

2367 Frederick Douglass Blvd. (127th St.), 212-222-8338;
www.harlemrevival.com

☑ "Dimly lit and romantic", this welcome addition to Harlem's dining scene offers a "perfect mood for seduction" abetted by really good French-Caribbean vittles; the only discordant note is "slow service" that's in "need of a bit more polish."

Rhône ●☒
17 | 20 | 15 | $43

63 Gansevoort St. (bet. Greenwich & Washington Sts.), 212-367-8440;
www.rhonenyc.com

☑ An "industrial", "high-tech" setting distinguishes this "dark" den from its Meatpacking District neighbors, though some wonder whether it's a "restaurant or a lounge"; most agree it's best employed as a "wine bar", but it does offer some "surprisingly good" (if "overpriced") Franco-Asian nibbles.

Rice ⇄
19 | 16 | 15 | $18

227 Mott St. (bet. Prince & Spring Sts.), 212-226-5775 ☾
81 Washington St. (bet. Front & York Sts.), Brooklyn, 718-222-9880
www.riceny.com
☑ "Funky, relaxed" respites for "zippy" light Eclectic meals, this NoLita-Dumbo duo has habitués saying it's "what fast food ought to be"; if a few feel "portions could be more generous", no one's complaining about "prices so low it's bewildering."

Rice 'n' Beans
19 | 6 | 15 | $21

744 Ninth Ave. (bet. 50th & 51st Sts.), 212-265-4444;
www.ricenbeansrestaurant.com
☑ "*Delicioso*" declare devotees of this "tiny", "humble" Theater District "hole-in-the-wall" where "plentiful portions" of "tasty, hearty" Brazilian food comes at "can't-be-beat" prices; claustrophobes who cringe at the "cramped quarters" say it's also "great for takeout."

Riingo
20 | 20 | 18 | $56

Alex Hotel, 205 E. 45th St. (bet. 2nd & 3rd Aves.), 212-867-4200; www.riingo.com
☑ "Star" chef Marcus Samuelsson (Aquavit) prepares an "innovative" modern Japanese menu made for sharing at this new Midtowner that evokes raves for its "stylish" decor and "elegant" following; however, "disappointed" diners describe a "mixed experience", citing "average-at-best" cooking, "disorganized" service and "obscene" prices.

Risotteria
20 | 11 | 16 | $21

270 Bleecker St. (Morton St.), 212-924-6664; www.risotteria.com
■ To "get your risotto fix", try out this "friendly", no-frills West Village Italian supplying "more varieties" of the dish "than you can imagine", plus panini and salads, all at a "modest price"; those who object to its "extremely small space" go the "take-out" route.

River
18 | 17 | 18 | $28

345 Amsterdam Ave. (bet. 76th & 77th Sts.), 212-579-1888
■ You can "satisfy that itch" for Vietnamese and Thai tastes "without having to travel Downtown" at this West Side "neighborhood standby"; the fare is reliably "fresh" and if the "bamboo"-heavy setting seems too "cheesy", there's also "super-fast delivery."

RIVER CAFE
25 | 28 | 25 | $76

1 Water St. (bet. Furman & Old Fulton Sts.), Brooklyn, 718-522-5200;
www.rivercafe.com
■ It's "the view, the view, the view" that keeps "romantics" swooning at Buzzy O'Keeffe's "swanky" New American (rated No. 1 for Decor in this *Survey*) tucked under the Brooklyn Bridge, though the "wonderful", "beautifully presented" cuisine and "stellar" service are just as "spectacular"; in short, it's "the best date [place] in the city", and while the prix fixe–only dining here is quite "expensive", the enamored enthuse it's "worth every penny."

Riverdale Garden
▽ 23 | 20 | 20 | $44

4576 Manhattan College Pkwy. (242nd St.), Bronx, 718-884-5232;
www.theriverdalegarden.com
■ "Upscale" dining comes to Riverdale via this "out-of-the-way" New American arrival offering "sophisticated" seasonal cuisine; a "lovely space", "wood-burning stove" and "gorgeous" garden offset pricing that "seems a little expensive for the neighborhood."

Riverview
▽ 18 | 18 | 17 | $46

2-01 50th Ave. (49th Ave.), Queens, 718-392-5000; www.riverviewny.com
■ This Long Island City newcomer has early visitors calling it a "triple threat", what with the "fabulous decor", "to-die-for" Manhattan

skyline views and an Eclectic menu that shows "big potential"; though the overall experience may be "surprisingly romantic", it's also "surprisingly pricey for Queens."

rm ☒

25 | 21 | 24 | $69

33 E. 60th St. (bet. Madison & Park Aves.), 212-319-3800; www.rmseafood.com

■ "Another triumph" for chef Rick Moonen, this "elegant" East Side seafooder is a showcase for "high-quality" ocean fare; a "smooth-as-silk" staff presides over its "relaxed, clubby" quarters, and though it's "expensive", most feel it offers true "value" since dining here "doesn't disappoint."

ROBERTO'S

26 | – | 22 | $44

603 Crescent Ave. (Hughes Ave.), Bronx, 718-733-9503

■ "Leave your choices to Roberto" and "prepare to enter heaven" at this just moved, "old world–style" Bronx Italian where the dishes are "mind-blowingly delicious" and served by an unfailingly "warm" staff; just "go early" or prepare for a "mythic wait", because it takes "no reservations" and is enormously "popular"; N.B. a move a block away outdates the Decor score.

Roc ◑

22 | 21 | 21 | $47

190-A Duane St. (Greenwich St.), 212-625-3333

■ A "small place with a big heart", this TriBeCa Italian attracts "cool cats" with its "casual-chic" setup and "delicious" albeit "pricey" cooking; thanks to a "friendly" ambiance and "gracious" service, it's a favorite of "locals", who "always feel at home" here.

Rocco

▽ 20 | 15 | 19 | $38

181 Thompson St. (bet. Bleecker & Houston Sts.), 212-677-0590; www.roccorestaurant.com

■ The "original Rocco" – around since 1922 – is a "tiny" Southern Italian that "never disappoints" thanks to its "reliable" "old-style" dishes and "welcoming" staff; no surprise it's often "packed", partly because it's "less expensive" than many of its West Village neighbors.

Rock Center Café

19 | 21 | 19 | $44

Rockefeller Ctr., 20 W. 50th St. (bet. 5th & 6th Aves.), 212-332-7620; www.restaurantassociates.com

☑ "Don't let the tourists have all the fun" at this handsome rinkside Rock Center American where you can "watch the skaters" in the winter or "sit outside" in summer; despite grumbles about "bland" grub and "sticker-shock" tabs, it's hard to beat for pure "NYC atmosphere."

Rocking Horse

22 | 17 | 17 | $35

182 Eighth Ave. (bet. 19th & 20th Sts.), 212-463-9511

■ A "chichi crowd", "cute Chelsea-boy staff" and moderate pricing keep this "trendy" fusion Mexican hopping, but the real "stars of the show" are the "delicious" eats and "knockout" margaritas; the space is "cool", though "crowded, noisy" conditions are "not so rockin.'"

Rolf's

17 | 20 | 15 | $35

281 Third Ave. (22nd St.), 212-477-4750

☑ A "Teutonic wonderland" in wintertime when it's gussied up in "zany" Christmas splendor, this "old-world" Gramercy German puts out "hearty", "authentic" grub all year long; it also "keeps the beers flowing" at the bar, which can get a "bit rowdy" on weekends.

Roppongi ◑

20 | 15 | 18 | $33

434 Amsterdam Ave. (81st St.), 212-362-8182; www.ropponginyc.com

■ "Upper Westsiders in the know" consider this "pleasant, relaxed" Japanese a local "favorite" for "fresh, inventive sushi";

what it "lacks in ambiance", it makes up for with "attentive service" and for being a "less-crowded alternative to Haru" across the street.

ROSA MEXICANO ●   23 | 21 | 20 | $47
61 Columbus Ave. (62nd St.), 212-977-7700
1063 First Ave. (58th St.), 212-753-7407   *vintage 2006*
www.rosamexicano.com
■ Considered by many to be the "gold standard" for "upscale", "modern" Mexican eating, these crosstown siblings draw "crowds" with their "outrageously good" food (notably the "heavenly" guacamole "made at your table") and "devilish" pomegranate margaritas; just "make sure you have reservations" and "hit the ATM twice" before you come.

Rose Water   24 | 19 | 22 | $39
787 Union St. (6th Ave.), Brooklyn, 718-783-3800
■ There's "love and care in every aspect" of this "excellent", "matchbox"-size Park Slope New American that's worth seeking out for its "intriguing seasonal" cuisine; for any doubters "farm-fresh" ingredients, an "eager" staff, "cozy" ambiance and "amazing values" seal the deal.

Rossini's ●   22 | 19 | 23 | $54
108 E. 38th St. (bet. Lexington & Park Aves.), 212-683-0135;
www.rossinisrestaurant.com
■ After more than 25 years, this "old-fashioned" Murray Hill Northern Italian remains "on the mark" thanks to "excellent" food and a "professional" staff that "smothers you with kindness"; on weekends, live opera performances enhance the ambiance.

Rothmann's   22 | 20 | 20 | $59
3 E. 54th St. (bet. 5th & Madison Aves.), 212-319-5500;
www.rothmannssteakhouse.com
☑ The "porterhouse is the way to go" at this "upscale" Midtown steakhouse that also supplies "delicious" seafood and "impressive" wines served by "doting" staffers; skeptics shrug it's "nothing special", but others insist you'll "feel like a king" – though you may have to "mortgage the castle" first.

Roth's Westside Steak   19 | 15 | 18 | $47
680 Columbus Ave. (93rd St.), 212-280-4103;
www.rothswestsidesteakhouse.com
☑ Beefeaters ballyhoo this "solid" steakhouse as a "godsend to the Upper West Side" given its first-rate meats and "pleasant" ambiance enlivened by live jazz, even if cynics sigh it's "mediocre" and "overpriced"; P.S. there are cheaper, Italian-accented options in its highly touted new Grill Room.

Route 66 Cafe ●   17 | 13 | 16 | $20
858 Ninth Ave. (bet. 55th & 56th Sts.), 212-977-7600
☑ "There's something for everyone" on the Eclectic-Southwestern menu at this "kitschy" Hell's Kitchen diner where "large portions" and "fair prices" keep regulars regular; indeed, its "worthwhile" Sunday brunch may be the "best-kept secret" in these parts.

Royal Siam   20 | 11 | 16 | $25
240 Eighth Ave. (bet. 22nd & 23rd Sts.), 212-741-1732
☑ It "might not be the prettiest" palace in Chelsea, but this "casual" neighborhood "standby" offers a "tempting range" of "delicious" Thai dishes at "bargain" tabs; "accommodating" service and a "relaxing" vibe trump the "dull" decor.

Roy's New York
25 | 20 | 21 | $49

Marriott Financial Ctr., 130 Washington St. (bet. Albany & Carlisle Sts.), 212-266-6262; www.roysrestaurant.com

■ While there are "no palm trees" at this Financial District link of chef Roy Yamaguchi's international chain, the "stellar" Hawaiian fusion fare and "dreamy" decor just might "transport you" to the "tropics"; sure, it's "out of the way" and a "bit pricey", but its "business"-oriented clientele doesn't seem to mind.

RUBY FOO'S ●
20 | 22 | 18 | $40

1626 Broadway (49th St.), 212-489-5600
2182 Broadway (77th St.), 212-724-6700
www.brguestrestaurants.com

■ One part Chinese "mah-jongg palace", one part "kitschy fun house", this Upper West Side–Times Square duo of "decorated-to-the-hilt" Pan-Asians is "jam-packed on any given night" with "young thirtysomethings and families" soaking up the "over-the-top" atmosphere; the food's "always good" too.

Rue 57 ●
18 | 19 | 17 | $43

60 W. 57th St. (6th Ave.), 212-307-5656

▲ Offering an "ambitious" assortment of "sushi, French cuisine and glitzy cocktails", this "lovely" Midtown brasserie is a "terrific" choice for breakfast, lunch or "pre–Carnegie Hall"; a few rue "deafening" noise levels, "haughty" service and "expensive" tabs, but most describe "delightful" dining.

Rughetta
22 | 16 | 22 | $42

347 E. 85th St. (bet. 1st & 2nd Aves.), 212-517-3118

■ Upper Eastsiders feel "lucky" to have this "welcoming treasure" offering "scrumptious", "moderately priced" Southern Italiana served by a "dedicated" staff; though it's decidedly "small", the "quaint" feel is "made for romance."

Russian Samovar ●
20 | 17 | 18 | $46

256 W. 52nd St. (bet. B'way & 8th Ave.), 212-757-0168; www.russiansamovar.com

■ "19th-century Russian decadence" lives on at this Theater District "destination" offering "wonderful", "straight-from-the-motherland" cuisine washed down with "killer" infused vodkas; the often "raucous" scene really gets going when the "impromptu performances" start round the piano.

Ruth's Chris Steak House
23 | 20 | 21 | $59

885 Second Ave. (bet. 47th & 48th Sts.), 212-759-9496
148 W. 51st St. (bet. 6th & 7th Aves.), 212-245-9600
www.ruthschris.com

▲ "It may be a formula, but it's a great one" say sybarites savoring the "super", "sizzling" steaks "bathed in butter" at these chophouse chain outposts; the service is "pampering" and the decor "pleasing", but some maintain the "local" competition is "far superior", especially given the serious price tags.

Sabor ●
19 | 17 | 17 | $35

462 Amsterdam Ave. (bet. 82nd & 83rd Sts.), 212-579-2929
1725-1727 Second Ave. (89th St.), 212-828-0003

▲ These crosstown Nuevo Latino "havens for lovers of caipirinhas" and "killer sangria" have plenty of avid adherents, but the consensus crumbles somewhat when it comes to the "creative tapas": friends say they're "addictive", but the less-addicted report that they offer "very little food for the $."

S'Agapo ●
∇ 22 | 12 | 17 | $34

34-21 34th Ave. (35th St.), Queens, 718-626-0303

☑ "No-nonsense Greek food at its finest" – especially "great grilled fish" – is on the plate at this "friendly" Astoria "trip to Crete"; while it's "strictly Formica" inside, the "outdoor patio is romantic", especially "on a sultry summer night."

Sahara ●
21 | 14 | 13 | $25

2337 Coney Island Ave. (bet. Aves. T & U), Brooklyn, 718-376-8594; www.saharapalace.com

☑ Brave the "bustling" atmosphere at this "noisy" Gravesend Middle Eastern and you'll be rewarded with a "gold mine" of "inexpensive" "Turkish delights"; there's also a "lovely outdoor garden" that makes you "forget you're in Brooklyn" even if the service reminds you.

SAIGON GRILL ●
23 | 9 | 16 | $20

620 Amsterdam Ave. (90th St.), 212-875-9072
1700 Second Ave. (88th St.), 212-996-4600
www.saigongrill.com

☑ "Prepare to stand in line" at these "no-frills" Vietnamese crosstown twins, local "favorites" for "superb" dishes priced "dirt cheap"; the West Side location was "recently expanded", yet it's still "always crowded", leading many to "get delivery instead."

Sala ●
19 | 19 | 18 | $35

344 Bowery (Great Jones St.), 212-979-6606

■ The "sangria flows freely" and the "flavorful" tapas "keep on comin'" at this "hip" NoHo Spaniard that's "ideal" for "groups and sharing" but also "sexy" enough "for a date"; don't miss the "cool" downstairs lounge, which hosts "live DJs" on weekends.

Salaam Bombay
22 | 17 | 17 | $34

317 Greenwich St. (bet. Duane & Reade Sts.), 212-226-9400; www.salaambombay.com

■ At this roomy TriBeCa Indian, you can "dine like a king" while a "sitar player" creates an "enchanted" mood – and distracts from service "needing improvement"; the real "hidden jewel" here is the buffet brunch that boosters call "the mother of all bargains."

Salam Cafe
∇ 19 | 20 | 16 | $32

104 W. 13th St. (bet. 6th & 7th Aves.), 212-741-0277

☑ "Transportingly" appointed in "lovely" "casbah" style, this North African–Mideastern "treasure" tucked away in the West Village has a "faithful" following for its "scrumptious" specialties and "warm" vibe; while service is "well meaning", the pace can be "lackadaisical" (expect "a long meal").

Sal Anthony's
17 | 16 | 17 | $36

168 First Ave. (bet. 10th & 11th Sts.), 212-674-7014
55 Irving Pl. (bet. 17th & 18th Sts.), 212-982-9030
133 Mulberry St. (bet. Grand & Hester Sts.), 212-925-3120
www.salanthonys.com

☑ "Go for the bargain prix fixe" deals at this "trusty" Italian trio advise locals who don't seem to mind if the "simple" fare's on the "mediocre" side and the digs are a little "tired"; P.S. the First Avenue branch ("formerly Lanza") dates back to 1904, and feels it.

Sala Thai ●
21 | 12 | 17 | $27

1718 Second Ave. (bet. 89th & 90th Sts.), 212-410-5557

☑ "Always a winner" say Upper Eastsiders who sala-vate over this Thai's "consistently high-quality" classics at what-a-"steal" prices; a local "old reliable", it's a "little rundown", but "one bite and you'll forget" the surroundings.

Salsa y Salsa
19 | 15 | 13 | $25

206 Seventh Ave. (bet. 21st & 22nd Sts.), 212-929-2678

■ At this "little Mexican joint" in Chelsea, the "standard" dishes are "tasty", tabs are "cheap" and the "dinerish" setup "kitschy and colorful"; "fabulous frozen cocktails" keep the party going strong, even when the staff's "professionalism" flags.

Salt ⊠
21 | 18 | 18 | $40

29A Clinton St. (bet. Houston & Stanton Sts.), 212-979-8471 ◗
58 MacDougal St. (bet. Houston & Prince Sts.), 212-674-4968

■ Something of an "insiders' neighborhood joint", this "unpretentious" SoHo New American delivers "delicious", "simple-yet-inventive" fare from a "shoebox" of a kitchen – and its "cozy", "communal table"–equipped room isn't much bigger; the Lower East Side offshoot is geared more toward drinking and snacking.

Salute!
18 | 18 | 18 | $40

270 Madison Ave. (39th St.), 212-213-3440

☑ Murray Hill denizens depend on the "fresh pastas" and other eats at this "convenient" Italian, which also boasts an "out-of-this-world antipasto table"; however, a few gripe about "noisy" acoustics and "uneven" food that's "a bit pricey"; P.S. for a "quick lunch", hit the adjacent take-out annex.

Sambuca
19 | 16 | 18 | $35

20 W. 72nd St. (bet. Columbus Ave. & CPW), 212-787-5656

■ "Bring your appetite" to this West Side "Carmine's wanna-be" (but "without the circuslike noise and waits"), where the "garlicky" Italian grub comes "family-style" in "overwhelming portions"; "romantic it's not", but it's ideal for "chowdowns" at "terrific value."

Sammy's ◗
18 | 8 | 13 | $19

301-303 Sixth Ave. (Carmine St.), 212-337-9888
453 Sixth Ave. (11th St.), 212-924-6688

☑ When "quick, cheap and delicious Chinese" is in order, Villagers turn to this "reliable" twosome, either overlooking the "functional" decor and "impersonal" service or opting for "ridiculously fast" delivery; N.B. Carmine Street has a sushi bar, while 11th Street features "filling" noodle soups.

Sammy's Roumanian
19 | 9 | 16 | $48

157 Chrystie St. (Delancey St.), 212-673-0330

☑ It's "a bar mitzvah every day" at this "unbelievably tacky" Lower East Side "basement" "institution", where "singing waiters" dish out "stick-to-your-arteries", "schmaltzy" (i.e. liquid chicken fat) Jewish cooking amid free-flowing "vodka bottles on ice"; just "bring dancing shoes", "Alka-Seltzer" and your gold card for this once in a lifetime experience.

Sam's Noodle Shop ◗
19 | 11 | 16 | $18

411 Third Ave. (29th St.), 212-213-2288

■ The "decor's so much better" since the (relatively) "snazzy" "recent renovations" at this no-frills Gramercy Chinese "favorite", while the food's as "tasty" and "cheap" as ever; "you can't beat" its "amazing noodle soups", which may actually "cure the common cold."

Sandobe ◗
20 | 13 | 15 | $23

167 First Ave. (bet. 10th & 11th Sts.), 212-505-3348

☑ Its move around the corner last year slightly "improved the decor" of this still-modest East Village Japanese, but the main attraction remains "inventive" fresh sushi; better still, "portions are amazing" and "fantastically cheap", though an unconvinced few whisper that quality is "not the greatest."

San Domenico
22 | 21 | 21 | $69

240 Central Park S. (bet. B'way & 7th Ave.), 212-265-5959; www.sandomenicony.com

☒ It's "everything that sophisticated dining should be" enthuse admirers of this recently redecorated "aristocratic Northern Italian" on Central Park South, where a "well-heeled" crowd collects for "perfectly nuanced" dishes via chef Odette Fada; despite a few grumbles about "high" tabs, it's right up there with the very best of NYC Italians and is a real bargain for a casual weekday lunch.

San Pietro ●☒
24 | 21 | 23 | $64

18 E. 54th St. (bet. 5th & Madison Aves.), 212-753-9015; www.sanpietro.net

■ "Power brokers" and weary shoppers rub elbows during "hopping lunch" hours at this "elegant", "clubby" Midtown Italian offering "heavenly" specialties from Campagna plus "formal but friendly" service by "gentlemanly" waiters; it's a taste of "la dolce vita", soured only by prices seemingly sent down by San Pietro himself.

Sant Ambroeus
∇ 22 | 20 | 19 | $42

259 W. Fourth St. (Perry St.), 212-604-9254

■ A "welcome addition" to the West Village, this "swank reincarnation" of the Upper East Side's erstwhile king of espresso and gelati has its faithful "Euro" crowd "traipsing down" for trademark panini and dolci; dinner features more serious (and seriously priced) Milanese cuisine.

Sapori d'Ischia
∇ 26 | 17 | 21 | $43

55-15 37th Ave. (56th St.), Queens, 718-446-1500

■ A real "find" ("if you can find it") on a "warehouse-lined street" in "industrial Woodside", this retail-store-by-day, restaurant-by-night serves "superb", "wonderfully authentic" Southern Italian cuisine; live music (including opera on Sunday nights) makes meals even more "special"; N.B. there's also a small wine bar.

Sapphire Indian
20 | 19 | 19 | $39

1845 Broadway (bet. 60th & 61st Sts.), 212-245-4444; www.sapphireny.com

■ For a "calm, reliable" meal in the "hectic" Lincoln Center area, try this Indian offering "savory", "exotic" dishes in "truly refined" environs; a few consider it "a bit pricey" for the genre, but that's not true of the $11.95 "bargain" lunch buffet.

Sapporo East ●
23 | 9 | 18 | $22

245 E. 10th St. (1st Ave.), 212-260-1330

☒ Thanks to "excellent" sushi, noodles and bento boxes at "best-deal-in-town" prices, this "no-frills" East Village Japanese is "a mob scene"; "long lines" and "cramped" digs don't deter Sapporo-ters on "student budgets" who find it particularly handy for "late-night" fueling.

Sarabeth's
21 | 17 | 17 | $30

423 Amsterdam Ave. (bet. 80th & 81st Sts.), 212-496-6280
Chelsea Mkt., 75 Ninth Ave. (bet. 15th & 16th Sts.), 212-989-2424
Hotel Wales, 1295 Madison Ave. (bet. 92nd & 93rd Sts.), 212-410-7335
Whitney Museum, 945 Madison Ave. (75th St.), 212-570-3670
www.sarabeth.com

☒ "Bring your Sunday paper" to while away the "long wait" that precedes one of "the best brunches around" at these "quaint country inn"–style Americans; they're a bit "twee" for some tastes, but there's nothing "precious" about the seriously "delicious" baked goods, jams and such; N.B. the Chelsea branch is mainly takeout.

Sardi's
15 | 22 | 18 | $50

234 W. 44th St. (bet. B'way & 8th Ave.), 212-221-8440; www.sardis.com
▣ This Theater District "institution" is "a must for Broadway buffs" and "out-of-towners", if just for its "classic" Great White Way ambiance – with any luck "you may see some stars" (at least among the "caricatures on the wall"); as for the Continental cuisine, it's no showstopper, even if the prices may be.

Sarge's Deli ◐
19 | 7 | 14 | $21

548 Third Ave. (bet. 36th & 37th Sts.), 212-679-0442; www.sargesdeli.com
▣ "One of NY's last true Jewish delis", this Murray Hill vet dispenses "wisecracks" along with "humongous" pastrami sandwiches, "delish knishes" and other classics 24/7; those who find the digs a little too "retro" "go for takeout" or delivery.

SAUL
27 | 20 | 24 | $47

140 Smith St. (bet. Bergen & Dean Sts.), Brooklyn, 718-935-9844
■ A "quiet storefront" in Boerum Hill hides what's resoundingly voted "one of the finer restaurants" in Brooklyn, thanks to namesake Saul Bolton's "subtle, sophisticated", "top-flight" New American cuisine served by an "outstanding" crew in "modern, simple" (some say "spartan") environs; the few who find it "too expensive for the neighborhood" should check out the $30 weeknight prix fixe "steal."

Savann
▽ 20 | 15 | 19 | $36

414 Amsterdam Ave. (bet. 79th & 80th Sts.), 212-580-0202; www.savannrestaurant.com
■ Those who've discovered this "inconspicuous" Upper West Side French-Med relish its "creative" cooking and "homey" quarters overseen by a pleasingly "low-key" staff; the "decent" weekend brunch and outdoor seating are other enticements that leave regulars wondering "why isn't it busier?"

Savoia
22 | 18 | 18 | $27

277 Smith St. (bet. DeGraw & Sackett Sts.), Brooklyn, 718-797-2727
■ You'll "feel like you're eating with the family" at this always-"packed" Carroll Gardens Southern Italian that's known for its "bravo" "brick-oven pizzas" but offers plenty of other reliable, "rustic" choices too; the "tiny" room is manned by a "warm, welcoming" staff and has "lots of character" (if not much elbow room).

Savoy
23 | 20 | 22 | $51

70 Prince St. (Crosby St.), 212-219-8570
■ At this SoHo Med–New American, it's "always a pleasure" to sample chef Peter Hoffman's "subtle", "creative" cuisine conjured from "seasonal" ingredients "foraged from the Greenmarket"; kudos also go to the "gracious" staff and "serene" upstairs space, but the "jury's still out" on the street-level bar area that was "updated" awhile back.

Sazerac House
18 | 14 | 20 | $28

533 Hudson St. (Charles St.), 212-989-0313; www.sazerachouse.com
▣ It was "Cajun before Cajun was cool" boast loyal patrons of this 40-year-old West Village standby set in a circa-1826 "landmark building"; though the general consensus on the food is "dependable" but only "decent", it's still a locus for "great N'Awlins fun" enhanced by a "campy, friendly" staff.

Scaletta
20 | 18 | 22 | $50

50 W. 77th St. (bet. Columbus Ave. & CPW), 212-769-9191; www.scalettaristorante.com
■ Amid the bustle of the Upper West Side, this "blessedly quiet", "unrushed and gracious" Northern Italian is "treasured" by mature

locals; perhaps the menu is "not very original", but the "civilized" air and "charming" service make it a "terrific place to take mom and dad."

Scalinatella ◐
24 | 18 | 21 | $66

201 E. 61st St. (3rd Ave.), 212-207-8280

☑ "Walk down the staircase and get a big surprise" at this East Side "below-ground grotto" where the "super-fresh", "lovingly prepared" Italian "classics" are "outstanding" and delivered by an "aim-to-please" staff; however, you might want to pre-qualify for "a home-equity loan before you go."

SCALINI FEDELI ⊠
27 | 26 | 25 | $76

165 Duane St. (bet. Greenwich & Hudson Sts.), 212-528-0400;
www.scalinifedeli.com

■ "Invent a special occasion if you have to" but by all means go to this "superlative" TriBeCa Northern Italian that's "in the middle of nowhere" but well "worth the trek"; its "divine" cuisine is matched by "romantic, gorgeous" barrel-vaulted quarters (Bouley's original home) and "impeccable" "formal" service, so no one's too surprised that tabs run usually "high."

Schiller's ◐
19 | 20 | 16 | $35

131 Rivington St. (Norfolk St.), 212-260-4555; www.schillersny.com

☑ "The budget choice for Keith McNally followers" is this "happening" Lower East Side "retro diner/bar" that's been "packed" from day one with a "vital" "post-hip" crowd; the drinks "can't be beat", the Eclectic eats are "darn good for the price" and if the service at times seems "disinterested" and the "decibel level" high, most are too caught up in the "buzzing vibe" to mind; P.S. "the bathrooms are a must-see."

Scopa
20 | 18 | 18 | $37

79 Madison Ave. (28th St.), 212-686-8787;
www.scoparestaurant.com

■ An oft-"overlooked gem" in an area desperate for decent restaurants, this "spacious", "pleasant" Gramercy Italian specializes in cicchetti (small plates) and "remarkably good" "thin-crust grilled pizzas"; there's also a "wonderful bar" and next-door take-out shop.

Scuba Sushi ⊠
– | – | – | M

(fka Mi)

66 Madison Ave. (bet. 27th & 28th Sts.), 212-252-8888

Set in a narrow Gramercy space, this trendy Asian fusion newcomer sports oddly memorable decor, particularly its mural of a swimming pool complete with scuba gear–clad mannequins suspended in front of it; regulars sip sake in the front lounge or perch on one of the drumlike seats at the sushi bar.

SEA
22 | 22 | 16 | $23

75 Second Ave. (bet. 4th & 5th Sts.), 212-228-5505
114 N. Sixth St. (Berry St.), Brooklyn, 718-384-8850 ◐

■ Williamsburg "hipsters" tout this "affordable" Thai "paradise" in "sleek, chic" "gargantuan" quarters "pulsing" with "dance-club" beats, where the fare is "fresh and highly flavored" but served by a staff that often "can't get it right"; decorwise the East Village original can't compete, though its "rock-bottom prices" are hard to beat.

Sea Grill ⊠
24 | 24 | 22 | $58

Rockefeller Ctr., 19 W. 49th St. (bet. 5th & 6th Aves.), 212-332-7610

■ You can count on "superb" seafood at this "wow destination", a "refined", "quiet escape amid the hubbub of Rockefeller Center"; insiders urge "ignore the tourists" and "expensive" tabs and focus instead on the "magical" rinkside view.

Second Avenue Deli ●
23 | 10 | 15 | $23

156 Second Ave. (10th St.), 212-677-0606; www.2ndavedeli.com
■ "God bless" this East Village Jewish deli, a "temple to corned beef, pastrami and chicken soup" where worshipers endure "crowded", "hectic" conditions, "waits for a table" and "old-time" "sassy" service to "stuff themselves to the gills"; it's "not for the cholesterol-conscious", but it's among the "best in NY – ergo, the world."

Seppi's ●
17 | 16 | 16 | $44

Le Parker Meridien, 123 W. 56th St. (bet. 6th & 7th Aves.), 212-708-7444;
www.seppisnewyork.com
☒ Its "late-night" hours and "convenient location" near Carnegie Hall and City Center may be its biggest virtues, but this Parker Meridien French bistro is also appreciated by many for its "decent" eats and "cozy", "dark" environs; still, vocal critics cite "painfully slow" service and consider it "expensive" for what it is.

Serafina ●
19 | 16 | 15 | $37

38 E. 58th St. (bet. Madison & Park Aves.), 212-832-8888 ☒
29 E. 61st St. (bet. Madison & Park Aves.), 212-702-9898
393 Lafayette St. (4th St.), 212-995-9595
1022 Madison Ave., 2nd fl. (79th St.), 212-734-2676
www.serafinarestaurant.com
☒ "Full of fashionistas" and "Euros" downing "fabulous" pizzas and pastas, this Uptown-Downtown Italian quartet is always good for some "boisterous fun"; "decent prices" and an ability to "accommodate large groups" help to explain why most surveyors are willing to overlook the "mediocre-at-best" service.

Serendipity 3 ●
20 | 21 | 16 | $26

225 E. 60th St. (bet. 2nd & 3rd Aves.), 212-838-3531;
www.serendipity3.com
■ To find "happiness in a dish", visit this "landmark" East Side cafe/toy store specializing in "heavenly desserts" that are guaranteed to "stop any diet in its tracks"; yes, the "lines are outrageous" and the space "crowded", but the "*Alice in Wonderland*" ambiance and that "damn addicting" frozen hot chocolate are "necessary for every child's development."

Sette
20 | 18 | 18 | $39

191 Seventh Ave. (bet. 21st & 22nd Sts.), 212-675-5935;
www.nycrg.com
☒ "Fresh, quality" fare, "unfailingly polite" service and a "stylish-without-attitude" atmosphere have some Chelsea dwellers calling this "mellow" new Italian "a welcome addition" to the neighborhood; however, some surveyors shrug "nothing earth-shattering."

Sette Mezzo ●⊟
23 | 13 | 19 | $56

969 Lexington Ave. (bet. 70th & 71st Sts.), 212-472-0400
■ The "see-and-be-seen" "power scene" at this "clubby" East Side Italian "never disappoints", nor does the "superb" cuisine; the same can't be said of the service, however, since regulars are treated "like family" but outsiders may find it "not so friendly"; P.S. bring lots of cash – they don't take plastic and it's "not cheap."

Seven ●
17 | 17 | 17 | $36

350 Seventh Ave. (bet. 29th & 30th Sts.), 212-967-1919
☒ "What a surprise" to find a "decent" New American option for "low-key dining" convenient to Penn Station and perfect "pre–Madison Square Garden"; even if "nothing special", it's a "much-needed" "oasis" amid the area's "desert of sports bars."

718

▽ 23 | 22 | 22 | $38

35-01 Ditmars Blvd. (35th St.), Queens, 718-204-5553

■ The "ambitious, delicious" French cuisine with Spanish accents at this newcomer "in the wilds of Astoria" has locals cheering "finally, a Queens restaurant with a creative palate"; expect "sensational tapas", "out-of-this-world" desserts and more served in "sexy", "romantic" digs by a "friendly" staff.

71 Clinton Fresh Food

24 | 17 | 21 | $54

71 Clinton St. (bet. Rivington & Stanton Sts.), 212-614-6960; www.71clintonfreshfood.com

■ Credit this "cool" New American Lower East Side pioneer with "proven staying power": since 1999 it's been "a foodie's heaven" turning out "some of the most delicious and imaginative" cuisine going, and it "hasn't lost its shine post-Wylie"; a "very hip" yet "friendly" staff helps compensate for the "crowded", "closet"-size quarters.

71 Irving Place

19 | 17 | 16 | $14

71 Irving Pl. (bet. 18th & 19th Sts.), 212-995-5252; www.irvingfarm.com

◪ "Some of the best darn coffee in the city, hands down" is poured at this "adorable" Gramercy coffeehouse with a "Parisian" vibe and a "mouthwatering" pastry case; the downside of being the "perfect" "neighborhood hangout" is that it's "cramped" and "always crowded."

Sevilla ◉

22 | 14 | 19 | $36

62 Charles St. (W. 4th St.), 212-929-3189; www.sevillarestaurantandbar.com

■ This circa-1941 Greenwich Village Spaniard "hasn't changed in years" – and "that's a good thing" according to aficionados who adore its "dated" decor as much as the delicious, "garlicky" standards downed with "sangria by the gallon"; also easy to love are the "cheap prices" and "very hearty portions."

Sezz Medi'

▽ 22 | 18 | 20 | $30

1260 Amsterdam Ave. (122nd St.), 212-932-2901; www.sezzmedi.com

■ "Wonderful" brick-oven pizzas and "excellent housemade pastas" have neighbors calling this "comfortable" new Morningside Heights Italian "an asset" for the area; factor in the "charming" staff and "warm atmosphere", and early visitors are pledging to be "customers for life."

Shaan

20 | 20 | 19 | $38

Rockefeller Ctr., 57 W. 48th St. (bet. 5th & 6th Aves.), 212-977-8400; www.shaanofindia.com

■ "You always end up overeating" at this "lovely", "refined" Rockefeller Center Indian where the offerings are "terrific, both in variety and in taste"; if that's not enough, "the price is right", especially if you go for the $13.95 AYCE "bargain lunch buffet" or prix fixe dinner.

Shabu-Shabu 70

19 | 12 | 18 | $34

314 E. 70th St. (bet. 1st & 2nd Aves.), 212-861-5635

◪ "A real sleeper" on the Upper East Side, this unpretentious, moderately priced Japanese presents a great "group activity": preparing your own hot-pot meals at the table; "for those who don't feel like cooking", sushi and prepared dishes are delivered by a "friendly" staff.

Shabu-Tatsu ◉

▽ 20 | 14 | 18 | $31

216 E. 10th St. (bet. 1st & 2nd Aves.), 212-477-2972

◪ For a "novel" evening with "a date" or "a group", try this casual, easily afforable East Village Japanese's "authentic" sukiyaki and shabu-shabu; everything's "deliciously fresh, simple" and sure to "warm your soul", especially "on a cold winter night."

Shaffer City Oyster Bar & Grill ⊠ | 23 | 17 | 21 | $47 |
5 W. 21st St. (bet. 5th & 6th Aves.), 212-255-9827
■ "Heaven for the oyster lover", this "friendly, unpretentious", albeit pricey, Flatiron seafood grill presents a "grand" raw bar as well as "creative fish dishes"; regulars say if "one-of-a-kind" chef-owner-host Jay Shaffer is on hand, you should prepare "to be pampered."

Shanghai Cuisine ⇨ | 20 | 13 | 13 | $22 |
89 Bayard St. (Mulberry St.), 212-732-8988
✍ "Knockout" soup dumplings are the main attraction at this "slightly Americanized" C-town "secret", though there are plenty of other Shanghai specialties available; its 1930s "movie poster"–adorned interior is basic yet "better than most of its neighbors'", and the cash-only policy is pretty painless given "modest prices."

Shanghai Pavilion | ▽ 22 | 19 | 19 | $32 |
1378 Third Ave. (bet. 78th & 79th Sts.), 212-585-3388
■ "Some of the best Shanghai cooking around" can be found at this "elegant" East Side newcomer; early visitors say "every dish shows care and attention" and the modern surroundings reflect real "class"; all in all it's a welcome "escape from the same old, same old" and not at all bad when it comes to paying the check.

Share | – | – | – | M |
406 E. Ninth St. (bet. Ave. A & 1st Ave.), 212-777-2425; www.sharenyc.com
The name spells out the agenda of this pocket-size, midpriced East Villager that's all about sharable portions of seasonal Americana; diners partake either at the slim, street-level counter or descend to a smartly designed, communal-tabled room.

Shark Bar | ▽ 21 | 16 | 18 | $36 |
307 Amsterdam Ave. (bet. 74th & 75th Sts.), 212-874-8500;
www.soulfoodconcepts.com
■ For "Southern cookin' with style", hit this "sophisticated" West Side soul fooder whose "reasonably priced" eats are "never disappointing", even if its "seen-and-be-seen" scene is "a little played out"; still, the fact that it's always "crowded" speaks for itself.

Sharz Cafe & Wine Bar | 19 | 13 | 18 | $37 |
435 E. 86th St. (bet. 1st & York Aves.), 212-876-7282
✍ Patrons of this "neighborhoody" Yorkville Med "pick the wine first, then an entree" given its "extensive and varied" list of vintages; there's "nothing chichi" about the "cramped quarters", but the $18.50 "bargain early-bird prix fixe" alone keeps 'em coming back.

Shelly's New York ◑ | 20 | 19 | 20 | $52 |
104 W. 57th St. (bet. 6th & 7th Aves.), 212-245-2422; www.shellysnewyork.com
■ Shelly Fireman's "brassy" Midtown "crowd-pleaser" offers Carnegie Hall–goers and others "consistently good" surf 'n' turf and two "noisy" "stories of fun", including a "tremendous" raw bar on the first level and "wonderful" live jazz on the second; "just be prepared to shell out the bucks."

Sherwood Cafe ◑⇨ | ▽ 18 | 23 | 15 | $23 |
(aka Robin des Bois)
195 Smith St. (bet. Baltic & Warren Sts.), Brooklyn, 718-596-1609;
www.sherwoodcafe.com
✍ With "more funk than Stevie Wonder", this "relaxed" (often "slow") Boerum Hill bistro/flea market allows diners to sample "basic" French fare while eyeing an "odd assortment of furniture" and tchotchkes for sale; P.S. there's also a highly-touted back garden.

Shopsin's

▽ | 20 | 14 | 15 | $23 |

54 Carmine St. (Bleecker St.), 212-924-5160; www.shopsins.com

◪ Now in bigger, tidier quarters, this "quirky-as-it-gets" Village "institution" is a "love or hate" affair; "unique" chef-owner Kenny Shopsin cooks a "huge" variety of Eclectic dishes, all served with a "side of psychodrama" and in accordance with "bizarre" house rules (e.g. no customer may order what someone else at the table is having); in sum, it's one of those "truly NY" experiences.

Shore

19 | 15 | 19 | $39 |

41 Murray St. (bet. Church St. & W. B'way), 212-962-3750

◪ New England transplants trek to this "old-fashioned seafood shack" near City Hall for "affordable", "above-average" shore-style stuffing in "pub"-like digs; however, critics say "slow" service and somewhat "disappointing" offerings keep it from being in the "same league as its sister", fresh.

Shula's Steak House

20 | 18 | 19 | $60 |

Westin NY Times Sq., 270 W. 43rd St. (bet. B'way. & 8th Ave.), 212-201-2776; www.donshula.com

◪ This "memorabilia"-laden Times Square link in the NFL "celebrity" coach's chophouse chain contains "lineman"-size appetites with "gargantuan" slabs of great red meat and a full line-up of standard steakhouse sides; still, some surveyors say it's "boring" and suggest leaving it for "tourists who don't know NY has better" options.

Shun Lee Cafe ●

21 | 16 | 18 | $37 |

43 W. 65th St. (bet. Columbus Ave. & CPW), 212-769-3888

◪ Westsiders devour "delightful dim sum" at this attractive black-and-white cafe, which offers a "dizzying choice of little bites" available "anytime"; sure, "Chinatown's cheaper", but this is cleaner and from here "you can get to Lincoln Center in a minute."

Shun Lee Palace ●

25 | 21 | 23 | $51 |

155 E. 55th St. (bet. Lexington & 3rd Aves.), 212-371-8844

■ "After all these years", Michael Tong's East Side Chinese "grande dame" is still "spoiling" patrons with "superb" "upscale" cuisine ("absolutely the best above Canal Street") and "gracious" service; a minority calls its "calm", "classy" setting "dated", but for most, experiences here are always a "treat."

Shun Lee West ●

23 | 21 | 22 | $48 |

43 W. 65th St. (bet. Columbus Ave. & CPW), 212-595-8895

■ "Flavors crackle" on the plate at this "bustling" Lincoln Center "gourmet" Chinese, whose "top-flight" fare and "glamorous" decor ensure it's "the only one" for Westsiders who snub other "neighborhood" Sino options; "efficient", "class-act" service also helps make it a "pre- and post-theater pleaser."

Siam Inn ●

21 | 14 | 19 | $29 |

854 Eighth Ave. (bet. 51st & 52nd Sts.), 212-757-4006; www.siaminn.com

◪ "Experimentation is recommended" at this "quiet", "reliable" Theater District Thai whose "friendly" staff serves up a lengthy roster of "very fine" dishes; its nothing-special interior may suggest "takeout", but it's a "terrific deal" no matter where you eat.

Sipan ●

20 | 18 | 17 | $39 |

702 Amsterdam Ave. (94th St.), 212-665-9929

◪ The seafood-heavy fare at this midpriced Upper West Side Peruvian "standout" is like taking a quick trip "below the equator" without the plane ride; the only problems are "half-hearted" service and a "noisy" crowd, but "after two pisco sours, you won't care."

Sip Sak ⏺⇄
928 Second Ave. (bet. 49th & 50th Sts.), 212-583-1900
Irrepressible restaurant guru Orhan Yegen's latest venture, this bustling Midtown Turk serves inexpensive, super-fresh dips and kebabs in a long, narrow space; its BYO and cash-only policies help keep costs even lower.

`— — — I`

Sirabella's
`23 14 21 $39`
72 East End Ave. (bet. 82nd & 83rd Sts.), 212-988-6557
■ "Were it located one block west, you couldn't get in" to this unsung Upper East Side Tuscan according to admirers who, given its "tiny" proportions, aim to keep it a "best-kept secret"; those who know its "affordably priced" fare and "hospitable" service say it's well "worth squeezing in."

Sistina ⏺
`▽ 24 18 22 $62`
1555 Second Ave. (bet. 80th & 81st Sts.), 212-861-7660
☑ The "regulars keep it busy" at this Upper East Side Northern Italian that's beloved for its "amazing food and wine" served with "old-world" aplomb; if an unimpressed few find the "sedate" surroundings just "so-so" and the tabs a bit too-too, for most surveyors it's a "perfect fit."

66 ⏺
`20 24 20 $57`
241 Church St. (Leonard St.), 212-925-0202; www.jean-georges.com
☑ "You feel cool just being" at this "sleek", "scene-y" TriBeCa Chinese, thanks to Richard Meier's "beautiful", "Zen"-like space populated by a "so-hip" crowd; however, opinions split over Jean-Georges Vongerichten's "modern" "twist" on Shanghai cuisine: his myriad fans call it "masterful", but a few foes find it "surprisingly average", especially given prices that are unprecedented for Chinese dining.

Slice of Harlem
`▽ 20 10 17 $11`
308 Lenox Ave. (bet. 125th & 126th Sts.), 212-426-7400
☑ "Dine in or take out" – either way you'll "get your fill" of "crispy-crust" brick-oven pizza at this Harlem pie palace; sure, the decor may "leave a bit to be desired", but who's noticing given the "monster" slices at indisputably "reasonable" prices?

Smith & Wollensky ⏺
`23 17 20 $60`
797 Third Ave. (49th St.), 212-753-1530; www.smithandwollensky.com
■ Make "no bones about it" – this "noisy", "male-oriented" Midtown "meat palace" is "top-cow" for carnivores, thanks to its "fantastic hunks o' beef" and "kick-ass wine list"; when it's not too crowded to see, it also has a handsome steakhouse look with theatrically gruff waiters to complete the scene.

Snack
`23 12 17 $24`
105 Thompson St. (bet. Prince & Spring Sts.), 212-925-1040
☑ "If you're lucky enough to get a seat" at this "minuscule" SoHo Greek, you'll "see why it's worth" squeezing in for "fresh", "heavenly", "affordable" Hellenic dishes of a caliber "few and far between" in these parts; "claustrophobes" note that, true to its name, its offerings also make "outstanding" "picnic" fare.

Snackbar ⏺
`18 17 16 $38`
111 W. 17th St. (bet. 6th & 7th Aves.), 212-627-3700; www.snackbarnyc.us
☑ Go with friends and "share small plates of New American eats" at this "low-key", "cool"-looking Chelsea "hipster" whose menu follows a "mix 'n' match philosophy"; however, critics conclude "creative in concept, underwhelming in execution" and consider it "overpriced for snack food."

Snack Taverna
22 | 18 | 18 | $38

63 Bedford St. (Morton St.), 212-929-3499

■It may look like an "ordinary storefront", but this larger, "more upscale" Village sibling of SoHo's Snack surprisingly spins some of the "most imaginative treatments of Greek food", backed by a "refreshing" all-Hellenic wine list; there are gripes that it can get "cramped" and "noisy", yet romeos say it's "perfect for a date."

Soba Nippon
∇ 21 | 16 | 19 | $36

19 W. 52nd St. (bet. 5th & 6th Aves.), 212-489-2525; www.sobanippon.com

■Immerse yourself in "glorious contemplation of the buckwheat noodle" at this "lively" midpriced Midtown slurp house specializing in "damn good" soba and udon soups; no question "lunch is a madhouse", but insiders say it's relatively "empty" at dinner.

Sobaya
23 | 17 | 19 | $27

229 E. Ninth St. (bet. 2nd & 3rd Aves.), 212-533-6966

■This East Village soup shop is "keeping it real" for "NYU students" and "slurpers" of every stripe who "pack the house" for its namesake noodles swimming in "blissful broths"; devotees declare they "taste like no other" and offer serious "bang for your buck" to boot.

Soho Cantina ●
– | – | – | E

199 Prince St. (bet. MacDougal & Sullivan Sts.), 212-598-0303

A hip crowd digs into south-of-the-border bites at this lively Prince Street cantina whose candlelit setting (and prices) are more SoHo than Mexico; whether you sit inside or on the tiny veranda, don't miss the burrito gringo, made with Kobe beef.

Soho Steak ⊅
19 | 16 | 17 | $37

90 Thompson St. (bet. Prince & Spring Sts.), 212-226-0602

☑An increasingly rare example of "affordability" in "busy SoHo", this "reliable bet" for "flavorful steak frites" and other bistro basics is particularly "inexpensive" during "early-bird" hours; if it's "a little shopworn by now", the prevailing "Gallic touch" "makes for a pleasant evening" all the same.

Solera ☒
21 | 20 | 20 | $51

216 E. 53rd St. (bet. 2nd & 3rd Aves.), 212-644-1166; www.soleranty.com

■It's "like being in Barcelona" enthuse boosters of this "elegant" Midtown "taste of Spain" that's home to "high-priced" but "standout" "classic" dishes; for a less "formal" experience, you can order the "delicious" tapas at the bar that go down well with vinos and sherries from the "wonderful cellar."

Solo
– | – | – | VE

Sony Plaza Atrium, 550 Madison Ave. (bet. 55th & 56th Sts.), 212-833-7800; www.solonyc.com

Haute Mediterranean cuisine that's glatt kosher is the concept at this ambitious new Midtowner from the owner of Prime Grill; offering artfully presented entrees, tasting menus and raw-fish selections in an upscale setting, it's already a hit with deep-pocketed machers who prefer to go in groups, i.e. not solo.

Son Cubano ●☒
20 | 22 | 16 | $41

405 W. 14th St. (bet. 9th Ave. & Washington St.), 212-366-1640; www.soncubanonyc.com

☑There's "never a dull moment" at this "nightclub"-like Meatpacking District Cuban known for its "happening" live music, "potent" cocktails, "delicious" tapas and bountiful "eye candy"; it's just "a shame about the attitude" and the frequent need for "earplugs" (the "acoustics are killa").

Sosa Borella

| 20 | 15 | 18 | $36 |

832 Eighth Ave. (50th St.), 212-262-7774 ●
460 Greenwich St. (bet. Desbrosses & Watts Sts.), 212-431-5093
www.sosaborella.com

☑ The bi-hemispheric menu is "terrific" at this "moderately priced" TriBeCa Argentine-Italian and its West 50s offshoot, and the "low-key" vibe makes for "satisfying", "easy meals"; the only nitpick is service that's "friendly" but "erratic."

Soup Kitchen International, Al's 🗷⇥

| 25 | 2 | 9 | $13 |

259 W. 55th St. (bet. B'way & 8th Ave.), 212-757-7730;
www.therealsoupman.com

☑ "Judging by the lines" of "giddy" groupies that wrap around its Midtown block even in the "freezing cold" and gladly submit to owner Al Yeganeh's infamous "kitchen rules", this seasonal counter "immortalized in *Seinfeld*" "lives up to its rep" for truly "amazing" soups; the only mystery is "where does Al go" from May to November?

SouthWest NY

| 13 | 18 | 14 | $31 |

2 World Financial Ctr. (Liberty St.), 212-945-0528;
www.southwestny.com

☑ "Get a seat by the water and you're all set" advise those who've dabbled in the "yuppie singles scene" at this Financial District Southwestern's patio overlooking the WFC marina; never mind that the food's just "adequate" and service "lackluster" – "you can't beat" the "knockout view."

SPARKS STEAK HOUSE 🗷

| 25 | 19 | 21 | $64 |

210 E. 46th St. (bet. 2nd & 3rd Aves.), 212-687-4855;
www.sparksnyc.com

■ Seasoned steer-aholics suggest you don "loose-fitting clothing" before a visit to this "quintessential" Midtown moohouse where a "skilled" staff ferries "huge portions of tender beef" and "superb wines" to tables of "heavy-hitters" "closing deals" and "expensing" away heifer-size tabs; just "don't expect quick seating unless you've recently signed with the Yankees."

Sparky's American Food ●⇥

| ▽ 20 | 8 | 14 | $9 |

135A N. Fifth St. (Bedford Ave.), Brooklyn, 718-302-5151

☑ Paying "awesome attention to the finer points of fast food", this Williamsburg "lil' snacky joint" dispenses "divine" organic beef and soy dogs, burgers and fries, best laced with "homemade ketchup"; it ain't "much to look at", but most "addicts" are too busy munching to notice.

Spice

| 20 | 15 | 15 | $22 |

199 Eighth Ave. (bet. 20th & 21st Sts.), 212-989-1116
1411 Second Ave. (bet. 73rd & 74th Sts.), 212-988-5348
60 University Pl. (10th St.), 212-982-3758
www.spicenyc.net

☑ They're "fast, cheap and good", so no wonder these "mod"-looking Thais are "popular" with "young", "trendy" types who don't mind "waiting for a table" or dining "elbow-to-elbow"; still, "spotty" service and "airport runway"–like noise levels have many "getting delivery."

SPICE MARKET ● Gev-05

| 23 | 27 | 20 | $54 |

403 W. 13th St. (9th Ave.), 212-675-2322

■ "Keep the new concepts coming" urge followers of star chef Jean-Georges Vongerichten, who's opened this "stunning" instant "hit" in the Meatpacking District; a "knockout for both the tongue and the eyes", it serves "fantastic", "glamorized" Thai-Malay "street food" in a "lavish" Jacques Garcia–designed duplex that's "chock-full of stars" and other "beautiful" types; it's a nonstop party with all sorts of special spaces that are conducive to private parties.

Spotted Pig ● 22 | 18 | 18 | $38
314 W. 11th St. (Greenwich St.), 212-620-0393; www.thespottedpig.com
■ "Go early, put your name on the list and enjoy drinks at the bar" advise regulars of this "tiny", "friendly" and "very happening" (read: "overcrowded") West Village newcomer, where Brit chef April Bloomfield spins "fresh" takes on "London gastro-pub" fare with a slight Italian accent; moderate prices are the crowning touch.

Spring Street Natural ● 17 | 13 | 14 | $26
62 Spring St. (Lafayette St.), 212-966-0290; www.springstreetnatural.com
☑ "Whole foods types" "smell Ithaca" in NoLita at this long-running organic "paradise" that's not above serving "a martini with your macro platter"; while the decor "could use some spritzing-up" and the staff a shot of wheatgrass, the vibe is "pleasant" and the tabs "reasonable."

Sqc 20 | 15 | 16 | $40
270 Columbus Ave. (bet. 72nd & 73rd Sts.), 212-579-0100; www.sqcnyc.com
☑ Chef Scott Q. Campbell "thinks outside the brunch box" and offers reliably pleasing midpriced meals at his West Side New American that's "always packed" for good reason; skeptics say they might not endure the "aloof" service and "uncomfortable" seats were they not "addicted" to the "amazing" "house hot chocolate."

Sripraphai ⊅ ∇ 27 | 5 | 16 | $17
64-13 39th Ave. (bet. 64th & 65th Sts.), Queens, 718-899-9599
☑ If this Woodside BYO Thai "ever opened a Manhattan branch, there'd be lines around the block" swear those who've made the "trek on the 7 train" to sample its "fiery", "lip-smacking" specialties; while the "ambiance is nil", the garden and "great prices" compensate.

Stage Deli ● 18 | 9 | 13 | $24
834 Seventh Ave. (bet. 53rd & 54th Sts.), 212-245-7850; www.stagedeli.com
☑ You must "unhinge your jaw" to eat the "mile-high" sandwiches and other Jewish deli staples served in "ridiculously large portions" at this Theater District "classic"; maybe it finishes "second" to the nearby Carnegie, but "if you can handle the crowds and tourists" you "can't go wrong."

Stamatis ● 23 | 12 | 18 | $29
31-14 Broadway (bet. 31st & 32nd Sts.), Queens, 718-204-8964
29-12 23rd Ave. (bet. 29th & 31st Sts.), Queens, 718-932-8596
■ Join a "regular crowd of Greek" patrons at these "family-oriented", separately owned Astoria tavernas offering "generous portions" of "quality, homestyle" cooking on the "cheap"; sure, the decor's "tacky", but focus on the food and you're beside the "Aegean."

St. Andrews ● 18 | 16 | 18 | $36
120 W. 44th St. (bet. B'way & 6th Ave.), 212-840-8413
☑ Though "bangers and mash and haggis aren't high on everyone's wish list", most find the more ordinary surf 'n' turf options at this "cheery" Midtown Scottish pub "consistently good"; "handy" before a show, it's equally enticing for those "cute men in kilts" pouring "brilliant" single-malts behind the bar.

Starbucks 12 | 11 | 12 | $9
13-25 Astor Pl. (Lafayette St.), 212-982-3563 ●
241 Canal St. (Centre St.), 212-219-2725

(continued)

(continued)
Starbucks
4 Columbus Circle (enter on 58th St., bet. 8th & 9th Aves.), 212-265-0658
152-154 Columbus Ave. (67th St.), 212-721-0470 ◐
682 Ninth Ave. (47th St.), 212-397-2288
141-143 Second Ave. (9th St.), 212-780-0024
1642 Third Ave. (92nd St.), 212-360-0425
140 Varick St. (Spring St.), 646-230-9816
77 W. 125th St. (Lenox Ave.), 917-492-2454
300 W. 23rd St. (enter on 8th Ave., bet. 22nd & 23rd Sts.), 646-638-1571
Additional locations throughout the NY area
www.starbucks.com
☑ Addicts abhor this "corporate" coffee "monster's" "confusing terminology" ("tall isn't small!"), "cocktail"-worthy prices and increasingly "sloppy" shops, but admit they "can't start the day without" its "strong" (some say "burnt") "cups o' joe"; defenders wager "anyone who complains about it forgets what life was like" before the "invasion" from Seattle.

Starwich
_ | _ | _ | I
525 W. 42nd St. (bet. 10th & 11th Aves.), 212-736-9170; www.starwich.com
Gourmet sandwiches made to order from a choice of over 100 ingredients is the gimmick at this Port Authority–area link of a national chain; the chrome-and-white, user-friendly space comes equipped with leather couches, original artwork and Wi-Fi access.

Steak Frites ◐
17 | 16 | 16 | $40
9 E. 16th St. (bet. 5th Ave. & Union Sq. W.), 212-463-7101
☑ Those nostalgic for Montparnasse sit beneath "paintings of Paris" at this "lively" Union Square "standby" and "stick to what it does well" – "decent" renditions of the namesake dish; "unoriginal" it may be, but it's not too pricey and "serves its purpose", "weak" service notwithstanding.

Steamers Landing
18 | 19 | 20 | $38
1 Esplanade Plaza (bet. Albany & Liberty Sts., Hudson River), 212-432-1451; www.steamerslanding.com
■ Boasting an "awe-inspiring view of Lady Liberty", this Financial District anchor offers "good", "well-priced" seafood that's best enjoyed on one of its two patios – unlike many other alfresco spaces, they're bathed in "Hudson breezes" rather than "car and bus" fumes.

Stella del Mare ☒
▽ 23 | 20 | 23 | $47
346 Lexington Ave. (bet. 39th & 40th Sts.), 212-687-4425; www.stelladelmareny.com
■ A "find" in Murray Hill's dining "wasteland", this seafood-oriented Northern Italian serves "high-quality" fare in quarters with an appealing "old-world feel"; its mature clientele appreciates that it's "quiet" enough to "hear your companion", despite the piano bar up front.

St. Michel
▽ 22 | 18 | 20 | $45
7518 Third Ave. (bet. Bay Ridge Pkwy. & 76th St.), Brooklyn, 718-748-4411; www.stmichelrestaurant.com
■ "As strange as it sounds", there's "solid" French food to be had in Bay Ridge courtesy of this family-owned bistro that stands out in "a sea" of "Italian joints"; the "pleasant, unassuming atmosphere" and "friendly" staff delight its "upscale, older crowd."

Strata ◐☒
_ | _ | _ | M
915 Broadway (21st St.), 212-505-2192; www.stratanyc.com
In the vast Flatiron space that once housed Metronome, this midnight blue–hued New American serves updated comfort classics that stand

in contrast to its nightclub-ish looks, with a prominent bar and a dining room that feels like a dance floor outfitted with tables; a DJ booth–equipped balcony is a prime perch for scoping out the scene.

Strip House ◐
25 | 23 | 22 | $63

13 E. 12th St. (bet. 5th Ave. & University Pl.), 212-328-0000; www.theglaziergroup.com
■ "Sexy" rather than "machismo" defines the vibe at Peter and Penny Glazier's "energetic" Village chophouse that's tricked out like a "politically correct bordello"; sure it's "pricey", but it's "one of the best" for beef and comes complete with "kinky" retro cheesecake; players claim "take a hot date here and you'll definitely score."

Suba
18 | 26 | 18 | $45

109 Ludlow St. (bet. Delancey & Rivington Sts.), 212-982-5714; www.subanyc.com
☑ "Request seats" in the "seductive", "moat"-girded grotto at this Lower East Side Spaniard where the "dreamy" ambiance "is unlike any other"; the tapas and other eats are "tasty" to come, too "complicated" and "expensive" to others, but young romantics agree it's a "great date place" – "if this doesn't work, nothing will"; N.B. chef Alex Ureña (ex Marseille) arrived post-*Survey*.

Sueños ◐
22 | 20 | 18 | $44

311 W. 17th St. (bet. 8th & 9th Aves.), 212-243-1333; www.suenosnyc.com
☑ A "Mexican fiesta" awaits in this "colorful" yearling "tucked away" in a Chelsea alley, where chef Sue Torres (Rocking Horse, Hell's Kitchen) renders "robust", "innovative" dishes that "dazzle"; still, it can get "a little pricey" and some say it's "not running on all cylinders yet", with service that can "slow to a crawl when busy."

Sugiyama ⌷
26 | 20 | 25 | $95

251 W. 55th St. (bet. B'way & 8th Ave.), 212-956-0670; www.sugiyama-nyc.com
■ Skip the "trip to Japan" and use the "airfare to pay for a top kaiseki experience" at this sleek little Midtowner where master Nao Sugiyama and team wow "true foodies" with "out-of-this-world" multicourse menus backed up by "amazing service"; a meal here can take "hours" but you'll "remember it for a long time" – ditto "the bill."

Sui ◐
▽ 19 | 21 | 18 | $49

54 Spring St. (Lafayette St.), 212-965-9838
☑ This SoHo newcomer earns "points for innovation", both in its Japanese cuisine "infused with eclectic touches" and decor dominated by tanks of "wildly colored fish"; some fault "inattentive" service and "expensive" tabs, but optimists assert "it started slow but is improving."

Sultan ◐
20 | 13 | 18 | $33

1435 Second Ave. (bet. 74th & 75th Sts.), 212-861-0200; www.sultan-nyc.com
☑ "Delicious", "authentic" Turkish eats and "reasonable prices" qualify as pleasant "surprises" for pasta-weary Upper Eastsiders; it can get "noisy" and the decor's a bit "tired", but regulars reason "if it looked any better it'd be impossible to get in."

Sumile
24 | 21 | 22 | $68

154 W. 13th St. (bet. 6th & 7th Aves.), 212-989-7699; www.sumile.com
☑ Fusion fans find chef Josh DeChellis' "mixture of flavors and textures" "absolutely stunning" at this sushi-free Village Japanese, where the "innovative" fare is complemented by a "sleek", "mod" space and "NYC-style friendly" service; however, bottom-line types say once you "do the math" all those small-plate portions "can add up to a very large bill."

Sunburnt Cow
▽ 19 | 16 | 19 | $31

137 Ave. C (bet. 8th & 9th Sts.), 212-529-0005;
www.thesunburntcow.com

■ "Ozzie" expats and "kangaroo-loving" Yanks indulge their culinary "adventurism" indoors or in the garden beneath a retractable roof at this "funky" little Australian "picnic in Alphabet City"; while snobs don't appreciate "the paper plates", modest prices and an "extremely friendly", "g'day mate" attitude keep it often "packed."

Superfine
19 | 19 | 16 | $28

126 Front St. (Pearl St.), Brooklyn, 718-243-9005

☑ "Share a drink" at the bar or dine "with a laid-back crowd" of "arty parents and hipsters" at this "cavernous", "very cool"–looking Dumbo Med; its "small but appealing" menu "changes daily", while Sunday brunch features "kickin' bands"; the upside to "slow" service is that "no one ever feels rushed."

Supper ●▽
23 | 18 | 16 | $31

156 E. Second St. (bet. Aves. A & B), 212-477-7600

☑ Admirers say "go for the 'priest stranglers'" or any of the other "sumptuous homemade pastas" at this "cozy", cash-only East Village Northern Italian, and "don't let the communal tables" or "long lines" deter you; maybe some prefer "its brother Frank", but "good prices" clearly run in the family.

Surya
23 | 18 | 20 | $37

302 Bleecker St. (bet. Grove St. & 7th Ave.), 212-807-7770;
www.suryany.com

■ "Now that the trendinistas are gone", this West Village Indian "has settled in" as a fine source of "chicken tikka masala like Aunt Aruna used to make" and other delights (including some vegetarian "knockouts"); added pluses include attractive digs, a "cute garden" and a weekend brunch buffet.

Sushi Ann ☒
▽ 25 | 17 | 21 | $60

38 E. 51st St. (bet. Madison & Park Aves.), 212-755-1780

☑ For "top-notch sushi and sashimi" plus other traditional dishes untainted by "Americanized seasoning", purists head to this "high-end" Midtown Japanese; aesthetes assert the ambiance falls "behind restaurants of similar caliber", but prices don't: "bring your rich uncle" or "expense it."

Sushiden
25 | 18 | 22 | $55

19 E. 49th St. (bet. 5th & Madison Aves.), 212-758-2700
123 W. 49th St. (bet. 6th & 7th Aves.), 212-398-2800 ☒
www.sushiden.com

■ East or West, this Midtown duo is "a sure bet" for "wonderfully fresh, authentic" (i.e. no "fusion") sushi – "look at the Japanese tourists and businessmen" partaking and you'll know it's "for real"; while the decor's a bit "stale", service is "quick", making it a "favorite for lunch", especially on an "expense account."

Sushi Hana ●
22 | 17 | 18 | $35

466 Amsterdam Ave. (bet. 82nd & 83rd Sts.), 212-874-0369
1501 Second Ave. (78th St.), 212-327-0582
www.sushihana.com

■ "Two thumbs up" declare devotees of these "neighborhood" sushi twins deemed "worth" the "crowds" and "waits" for "big cuts" of "can't-be-beat" fish, plus "great hot entrees", at "moderate prices"; the West Side branch is known for its "cool vibe", while East Side patrons can "sneak around the corner to a sexy sake bar."

SUSHI OF GARI

402 E. 78th St. (bet. 1st & York Aves.), 212-
■ "Omakase-lovers" "make a reservation" a[...] the East Side hinterlands" to let "genius" chef [...] buds" with his "creative", "truly amazing" sushi; s[...] to say about the "average"-at-best decor, and as for p[...] "lucky not to live closer" because they'd "be broke by [...]"

Sushi Rose
23 | 13 | 18 | [...]

248 E. 52nd St., 2nd fl. (bet. 2nd & 3rd Aves.), 212-813-1800
■ The "half-price Saturday" deal excites "even jaded sushi snobs" at this Midtown Japanese, whose "generic" setting belies its "fantastic, fresh, beautifully presented" fish; admirers call it a "hidden jewel" in an "area with limited choices."

SushiSamba ◐
22 | 21 | 17 | $46

245 Park Ave. S. (bet. 19th & 20th Sts.), 212-475-9377
87 Seventh Ave. S. (bet. Bleecker & W. 4th Sts.), 212-691-7885
www.sushisamba.com
☑ It feels like "South Beach" at this "vibrant" Village-Flatiron duo where "under-30" "trendoids" kick up a "loud", "hot scene" while nibbling "delicious" sushi, seviche and other results of a happy "collision" of Japanese and South American tastes; downing a few Latin-accented cocktails may "cushion" the blow "when the bill comes."

SUSHI SEKI ◐
26 | 13 | 21 | $56

1143 First Ave. (bet. 62nd & 63rd Sts.), 212-371-0238
■ "Let chef Seki be your guide" advise aficionados who've discovered "how creative sushi can be" at this "modestly" appointed East Side Japanese, which some whisper is "more comfortable than Gari"; though "the magic doesn't come cheap", you're paying the airfare for that "simply sublime", "flown-in-daily" fish.

Sushi Sen-nin
25 | 13 | 20 | $50

49 E. 34th St. (bet. Madison & Park Aves.), 212-889-2208
1420 Third Ave. (bet. 80th & 81st Sts.), 212-249-4992 ☒
www.sushisennin.com
■ Perhaps there's an ocean-sprung pipeline feeding this Murray Hill Japanese (with a new East Side sibling); the fish is so "fresh", "you'd think it swam to the sushi bar" and if it's "a bit overpriced", given the "no-frills" settings, it's also "much needed" in these parts.

Sushiya
▽ 23 | 15 | 17 | $35

28 W. 56th St. (bet. 5th & 6th Aves.), 212-247-5760
■ This "welcoming", "simply" decorated Midtown Japanese "stands out" in a "touristy" area for its "reliably good", "oh-so-cheap" sushi and cooked specialties; insiders report it's a "great place for lunch during the week", but "to avoid crowds go on a weekend."

SUSHI YASUDA ☒
28 | 23 | 24 | $72

204 E. 43rd St. (bet. 2nd & 3rd Aves.), 212-972-1001; www.sushiyasuda.com
■ "Sit at the sushi bar and tell them to bring whatever" pleases the chef and you'll be "blown away" by the "buttery", "right-off-the-boat" cuts at Naomichi Yasuda's East 40s "temple of piscatory worship", voted the No. 1 Japanese in this *Survey*; the "gracious, attentive" and "knowledgeable" staff and "crisp, clean", "tranquil" surroundings further enhance the "top-notch", top-dollar experience.

Sushi Zen ☒
25 | 20 | 22 | $54

108 W. 44th St. (bet. B'way & 6th Ave.), 212-302-0707; www.sushizen-ny.com
■ "Amazing attention to texture, taste and presentation" yields supremely "high-quality" sushi at this Theater District Japanese,

boasts a "friendly" staff and, yes, a "Zen"-like ambiance; "more expensive than others in the area", but show-goers worth it"; N.B. there's alfresco seating in warm weather.

nningsen's
▽ 18 | 13 | 16 | $36

Fifth Ave. (bet. 30th & 31st Sts.), 212-465-1888
"A bit of an anachronism", this "old-fashioned" seafooder in a culinary "no man's land" near the Empire State Building earns nods for its "good" food, "fair prices" and "family atmosphere" complete with a "pleasant" singer/pianist; however, some say the concept is "promising" but the kitchen and service can "miss the mark."

Swagat Indian Cuisine
▽ 23 | 13 | 20 | $25

411A Amsterdam Ave. (bet. 79th & 80th Sts.), 212-362-1400
☑ Lured in by the "warm curry smell from the kitchen", Upper Westsiders who've discovered this Indian newcomer declare it an "excellent addition" to the neighborhood; "very tasty" dishes, "friendly people" and "reasonable prices" compensate for the somewhat "small" space.

Sweet Melissa
23 | 17 | 17 | $16

276 Court St. (bet. Butler & Douglass Sts.), Brooklyn, 718-855-3410
■ Cobble Hill's "temptress in a teapot" is this "itsy-bitsy" bakery/*salon de thé*, where light bites and "delicious French-inspired" pastries are raised to "an art form" and taste even better in the "charming" back garden; sure, it's "pricey" for what it is, but you're "paying for quality."

Sweet-n-Tart Cafe ●⊄
19 | 11 | 13 | $17

76 Mott St. (Canal St.), 212-334-8088
136-11 38th Ave. (Main St.), Queens, 718-661-3380
www.sweetntart.com
■ Known for their "outrageous selection of unique drinks", medicinal *tong shui* "soupy desserts" and "diverse dim sum", these lively cafes are a hit with "teens and daters" who focus on the "can't-be-beat" tabs rather than making tart comments about "negligible" service and "cafeteria"-esque digs.

Sweet-n-Tart Restaurant ●
19 | 12 | 14 | $20

20 Mott St. (Chatham Sq.), 212-964-0380; www.sweetntart.com
■ "Patrons from all walks of life" pour over the "humongous" menu of "Hong Kong–style" "delicacies" at this "cheap, tacky", cart-free dim sum, noodle and "bubbly drink" specialist; connoisseurs consider it a "wonderful" example of "the new wave in Chinatown."

Swifty's ●
17 | 17 | 17 | $57

1007 Lexington Ave. (bet. 72nd & 73rd Sts.), 212-535-6000; www.swiftysny.com
☑ This air-kissing East Side American "maintains its place as home" to the "old Mortimer's crowd" (i.e. the "Social Register" set), who come back from the Hamptons for the "fawning" treatment and the "buzz" as much as for the reassuringly predictable bistro fare and warm environs; however, outsiders warn service is "not so swifty" unless you're "in the club."

Sylvia's
16 | 12 | 17 | $27

328 Lenox Ave. (bet. 126th & 127th Sts.), 212-996-0660;
www.sylviassoulfood.com
☑ Both New Yorkers and "tourists from every country" make a beeline for this low-budget "Harlem icon" to feast on "decadent" (i.e. artery-clogging) soul food, enjoy the jazz brunch and hopefully spy the "elegant Miss Sylvia" herself; still, a "disappointed" contingent complains of "uneven" food, rather "disinterested" service and a "too-commercialized" profile.

subscribe to zagat.com

Symposium
19 | 14 | 20 | $23

544 W. 113th St. (bet. Amsterdam Ave. & B'way), 212-865-1011
☑ "Budget-strapped students" sigh "thank goodness some things are still sacred", like this "old, old" never-changing "Hellenic holdout" near Columbia that "keeps 'em from starving"; expect "homey" classics chosen from a "cartoonish" menu and served by an "efficient", "incredibly hospitable" staff.

TABLA
26 | 26 | 25 | $61

11 Madison Ave. (25th St.), 212-889-0667; www.tablany.com
■ There's "not a dull note in a meal" at this "stroke of Danny Meyer genius" on Madison Square Park, where "inventive" chef Floyd Cardoz "never ceases to amaze" with his Indian-inflected New American creations; add in "beautiful" decor, an "attentive" staff and a bargain $25 prix fixe lunch, and you've got a "delightful" overall experience – even if you must climb a flight of stairs to get it.

Table d'Hôte
22 | 15 | 21 | $43

44 E. 92nd St. (bet. Madison & Park Aves.), 212-348-8125
■ Marrying "city sophistication with country charm", this "postage stamp–size" Carnegie Hill French bistro is so "cozy", it can "make mobility a problem"; the cuisine's "imaginative" and "competently served", and happily there's a $22.50 prix fixe to offset the "high" tabs.

Taboon
∇ 23 | 19 | 17 | $42

773 10th Ave. (52nd St.), 212-713-0271
■ Named for the clay oven in which its bread is baked, this Hell's Kitchen newcomer is "highly recommended" for its Med–Middle Eastern eats; it can get "noisy" and the staff still needs polishing, but few mind since it's a "sorely needed" addition to the area.

Takahachi
21 | 14 | 19 | $32

85 Ave. A (bet. 5th & 6th Sts.), 212-505-6524 ●
145 Duane St. (bet. Church St. & W. B'way), 212-571-1830
www.takahachi.com
■ The "chef's specials are the way to go" at this "affordable", typically understated Japanese duo, though really you "can't go wrong" with any of the regular sushi and hot menu items; "go before 7 PM for the early-bird special."

Taksim ●
∇ 21 | 15 | 17 | $16

1030 Second Ave. (bet. 54th & 55th Sts.), 212-421-3004
■ According to admirers, this "small" Midtown BYO Turk has improved under "new, friendlier ownership"; while insiders suggest its "appetizers are the best", "everything's wonderfully spiced" and "cheap" to boot, making it especially "rare in the area."

Talia's Steakhouse ●
∇ 20 | 16 | 15 | $42

668 Amsterdam Ave. (bet. 92nd & 93rd Sts.), 212-580-3770;
www.taliassteakhouse.com
☑ Kosher-keeping carnivores "welcome" this glatt steakhouse yearling to the Upper West Side declaring it "does a good job", "considering the limits of kashruth"; however, most agree the "service could use some work", as could the "unexciting" decor.

Tamarind ●
25 | 23 | 22 | $47

41-43 E. 22nd St. (bet. B'way & Park Ave. S.), 212-674-7400;
www.tamarinde22.com
■ Far from your "typical curry house", this "posh" Flatiron Indian makes for "highly memorable" meals thanks to its "fresh", "delicately spiced" cuisine, "serene", "impeccably decorated" quarters (try to "score one of the booths") and "cordial" service; it's also "a

...n cost, but its next-door Tea House offers "lighter" ...sive fare.

Tang Pavilion
22 | 16 | 20 | $34
65 W. 55th St. (bet. 5th & 6th Aves.), 212-956-6888
■ This Shanghai specialist is "more sophisticated" than most other Midtown Chinese options and still "half the price" of some high-profile rivals; the decor's "decent" enough, but many opt for delivery that's "so fast, you'd think they cooked it in your lobby."

Tanoreen
∇ 24 | 10 | 20 | $24
7704 Third Ave. (bet. 77th & 78th Sts.), Brooklyn, 718-748-5600
☑ "Don't shy from the adventure" of visiting this veggie-friendly Middle Eastern "find" in Bay Ridge; owner Rawia Bishara will treat you "like a guest in her home", serving "fresh, delicious" fare, notably "the best meze", at prices as "cheap" as the "storefront" space is unpretentious.

TAO ◐
22 | 27 | 19 | $52
42 E. 58th St. (bet. Madison & Park Aves.), 212-888-2288;
www.taorestaurant.com
☑ "Buddha's ready for the big screen" as are the beautiful people who congregate to "worship" his 16-ft. tall likeness at this movie theater–turned–Midtown mega "scene", where the Pan-Asian eats are "surprisingly good" but more than "overshadowed" by the "phenomenal" surroundings and "serious bar action"; high prices, "long waits", "rushed" service and "ungodly" noise can create some bad karma.

Taormina ◐
∇ 21 | 16 | 19 | $41
147 Mulberry St. (bet. Grand & Hester Sts.), 212-219-1007
■ "Classically Little Italy, from the decor to the food" sums up this "above-average" Italian veteran that offers "accommodating" service and old-school ambiance to boot; the sidewalk seats offer "great people-watching", but not as good as when one-time regular John Gotti was around.

Tartine ⊄
22 | 14 | 16 | $26
253 W. 11th St. (W. 4th St.), 212-229-2611
■ If "you can get a table" – quite a challenge, given the no reservations policy and "tiny" quarters – "you can't go wrong" at this "affordable" "slice of Paris" transported to the West Village; it's BYO, so "bring some wine" to wash down the "delicious" bistro basics, but arrive "early to avoid the lines."

Taste
20 | 16 | 18 | $46
Eli's Manhattan, 1413 Third Ave. (80th St.), 212-717-9798;
www.elizabar.com
☑ Upper Eastsiders say Eli Zabar's "not-too-chic, not-too-loud" bistro/wine bar can be "delightful" for dinner thanks to "high-quality" New American food and "unusual" wines (by day it serves cafeteria-style meals); still, some wish the prices were more "realistic", though there's always the $14 AYCE weekend brunch.

TASTING ROOM ▨
27 | 17 | 25 | $56
72 E. First St. (bet. 1st & 2nd Aves.), 212-358-7831
■ "Smart folks share" so they can "sample everything" on Colin Alevras' "magnificent" market-driven menu at this East Village New American whose "closet-size" quarters (just 25 seats) provide an excuse "to sit close" to your tasting partner; add a "tremendous" "all-American wine list" and "solicitous" service and it's clear why the cost is no object at this up-and-comer.

Taverna Kyclades ●
24 | 13 | 19 | $29

33-07 Ditmars Blvd. (bet. 33rd & 35th Sts.), Queens, 718-545-8666
☑ As "long lines attest", this "small, quaint" Astoria Greek is a "favorite" for "amazing meze" and "perfectly cooked" seafood at modest prices; maybe the decor's "nothing to write home about", but you'll "feel at home" thanks to the "friendly" staff, and there's outdoor seating in summer.

TAVERN ON THE GREEN
14 | 24 | 17 | $58

Central Park W. (bet. 66th & 67th Sts.), 212-873-3200;
www.tavernonthegreen.com
☑ The "quintessential place to celebrate" anything is this "over-the-top" Central Park American whose "fairyland" Crystal Room and huge garden area are the "must-see" backdrops for everything from "tourist"-jammed brunches to "surreal" holiday meals; sure, "you can find better food elsewhere", but few can conjure up the same "magic" or create a more festive party.

Tea & Sympathy
20 | 16 | 16 | $23

108 Greenwich Ave. (bet. 12th & 13th Sts.), 212-807-8329;
www.teaandsympathynewyork.com
☑ "Watch your elbows or you'll knock the teapots off the tables" at this "tiny" Village tea shop dispensing "English charm" and "comforting" British food to "expats and Anglophiles"; just follow owner Nicky's "rules" or you may "get no sympathy" from the staff.

Tea Box
∇ 22 | 21 | 18 | $31

Takashimaya, 693 Fifth Ave. (bet. 54th & 55th Sts.), 212-350-0180
■ A "civilized respite" in the basement of a Midtown department store, this "darling" tearoom is a "best-kept secret" for "resting weary shopping feet"; "light", "beautifully presented" Japanese-American fare makes it a "ladies' lunch" magnet, and it's also "perfect" for afternoon tea.

teany ●
20 | 15 | 15 | $15

90 Rivington St. (bet. Ludlow & Orchard Sts.), 212-475-9190;
www.teany.com
☑ "Adorable" is how Lower East Side alterna types describe musician Moby's vegan cafe that's, yes, "teeny", but boasts a "huge tea selection", as well as sandwiches, cakes and such; groupies shrug who cares if service is "spacey" – there's a chance the M-man might "pop in."

Tello's
17 | 16 | 19 | $33

263 W. 19th St. (bet. 7th & 8th Aves.), 212-691-8696; www.chelseadining.com
☑ "Frank and Tony are on the jukebox" at this "old-school" Chelsea Italian, an afforable "holdout in an area of up-and-comers"; it's a "reliable" bet for "red-sauce favorites" served by an "enthusiastic" staff, leading locals to say it's "not to be missed."

Telly's Taverna ●
22 | 14 | 19 | $31

28-13 23rd Ave. (bet. 28th & 29th Sts.), Queens, 718-728-9056
■ "There's no seaside" in view from this Astoria taverna, but some still "believe they're in Greece" thanks to "generous portions" of "very fresh fish"; if the setup is "simple", the vibe's "warm and caring", and the garden is "a must in summer."

Tenement
∇ 20 | 21 | 18 | $36

157 Ludlow St. (bet. Rivington & Stanton Sts.), 212-766-1270;
www.tenementlounge.com
☑ No, it's "not your tante Rivke's tenement", but this "reasonably priced" American "comfort" fooder serves as a "chill" hangout for

today's "trendy" Lower Eastsiders; while scenesters wonder if "the buzz is gone" already, most are just glad there's "rarely a wait" in the heart of a "rockin' neighborhood."

Tennessee Mountain
16 10 14 $29

143 Spring St. (Wooster St.), 212-431-3993; www.tnmountain.com
☑ Break out the "wet naps" and "Tums" at this "family-friendly" SoHo BBQ joint whose "messy ribs" promise its "college-type" clientele "sticky fingers" and a "full stomach"; if "slow" service and "tacky" digs detract, the Monday and Tuesday AYCE deal is hard to beat.

Teodora
20 16 19 $45

141 E. 57th St. (bet. Lexington & 3rd Aves.), 212-826-7101
■ An "incongruous" "neighborhood" "hideaway" in the midst of Midtown, this "non-Americanized" (except for the price) Northern Italian trattoria "tries very hard to please" with its "hearty" specialties and "warm" ambiance; downstairs the "sedate" quarters can be "tight", so regulars head for the "more appealing" upstairs.

Teresa's
17 10 13 $18

103 First Ave. (bet. 6th & 7th Sts.), 212-228-0604
80 Montague St. (Hicks St.), Brooklyn, 718-797-3996
☑ They'll "fill you up" without emptying your wallet at these East Village–Brooklyn Heights pierogi palaces that dole out "copious portions" of Polish "comfort food" with "no pretense"; critics cite "terse" service and "dinerish" decor, but given the "value", "what can you expect?"

Terra
▽ 17 15 20 $30

939 Eighth Ave. (bet. 55th & 56th Sts.), 212-262-5354; www.terranyc.com
☑ Though "not well known", this earthy West Side Italian wins "neighborhood" favor with its "varied menu" and "friendly service"; the brick-and-tile style is "nothing exceptional", but most maintain it's good enough at the price.

Terrace in the Sky
22 25 22 $62

400 W. 119th St. (bet. Amsterdam Ave. & Morningside Dr.), 212-666-9490
■ It's "high-level dining" – literally – at this "genteel" Morningside Heights penthouse boasting a "million-dollar" view and "civilized" French-Med fare to "please" "Columbia parents" or a special someone; the "traditionally romantic" experience includes "a harp playing in the background", as well as prices that are almost as "stunning" as the scenery.

Terra 47
▽ 21 16 16 $32

47 E. 12th St. (bet. B'way & University Pl.), 212-358-0103; www.terra47.com
■ So "satisfying" "you forget it's healthy" say admirers of this Village organic offering a "deliciously prepared" International menu ranging "from vegan to meat" in a "hip yet warm" space; it's terra firma for crunchy types, who hardly notice the "spacey" service.

Tevere
▽ 22 18 19 $50

155 E. 84th St. (bet. Lexington & 3rd Aves.), 212-744-0210
■ "Kosher never had it so good" as at this "amazing" Upper East Side Italian, an "old favorite" among the observant for "dependable" food that's "costly" "but worth it"; the "quality and service" are "better than most" of its rivals, so it's no wonder it's often "tightly packed."

Texas Smokehouse BBQ
— — — I

438 Second Ave. (25th St.), 212-725-9800
This new Gramercy barbecue joint vends low-cost, Lone Star–style smoked meats against a down-home backdrop of vintage photos and

battered metal signs; some 20 brands of bourbon and a twangy country soundtrack add additional authenticity.

THALASSA
24 | 26 | 23 | $57

179 Franklin St. (bet. Greenwich & Hudson Sts.), 212-941-7661; www.thalassanyc.com

■ "Move over, Milos" exult boosters of this "gourmet Greek" seafooder in TriBeCa, where "exquisite", "fresher-than-fresh" fish is served "as it's meant to be" in a "stylish" "open" space with "lovely" "nautical" flourishes; "solicitous" service leaves most equally "impressed", as do the "fat checks" produced by "per-pound" prices.

Thalia ◑
21 | 21 | 18 | $46

828 Eighth Ave. (50th St.), 212-399-4444; www.restaurantthalia.com

■ A "touch of class" where the Theater District "could use it", this New American draws a "non-touristy" crowd with "inventive cuisine" and a "soigné setting" featuring "high ceilings", broad windows and a "lively" lounge; "pleasant" service that "gets you out on time" makes it a "best bet" "before a show."

39 East
▽ 22 | 27 | 18 | $41

213-41 39th Ave. (Bell Blvd.), Queens, 718-229-1620; www.39-east.com

☑ "Finally" Baysiders detect a "Manhattan scene" on Bell Boulevard courtesy of this "upscale" new arrival, which serves "creative" Pan-Asian food amid "beautiful" dharma decor; while most "welcome" an instant "'it' spot", a few skeptics who find it on the pricey side opine "you're paying for atmosphere."

36 Bar and BBQ ◑
▽ 22 | 18 | 20 | $31

5 W. 36th St. (5th Ave.), 212-563-3737

■ Rising "above the horde" of Korean BBQ joints, this do-it-yourself Garment District standout goes "new wave" with a "hip", "futuristic" look and "surprisingly high-quality ingredients"; "no-attitude" service adds to the "enjoyment", but if the style's "not traditional", neither are the largish-for-the-genre tabs.

Thomas Beisl ◑
23 | 18 | 20 | $36

25 Lafayette Ave. (Ashland Pl.), Brooklyn, 718-222-5800

■ "If you can pronounce the names", the "*wünderbar*" "authentic Viennese" dishes at chef Thomas Ferlesch's "charming" Fort Greene Austrian are "worth traveling for"; its "comfortable" "bistro" feel recalls a "homey" "corner of old Europe", and the location and "personable" service are both "perfect" "for a BAM night."

Three of Cups ◑
18 | 17 | 17 | $24

83 First Ave. (5th St.), 212-388-0059; www.threeofcupsnyc.com

☑ East Villagers head for this "funky" Italian to refuel on its good brick-oven pizza and "red-sauce" pastas "without spending too much"; it's "great for groups", and the "hole-in-the-wall bar downstairs" is the place to find insolvent "rock 'n' roller wanna-bes" in their cups.

360 ⊭
24 | 14 | 17 | $36

360 Van Brunt St. (bet. Sullivan & Wolcott Sts.), Brooklyn, 718-246-0360

■ Though "remote", this "unassuming" "Red Hook outpost" is a "worthy destination" for a "terrific" (if "limited") New French lineup, including "reasonable" wines and a $25 prix fixe "bargain" that "can't be beat"; the "cozy", "casual" room is "always full" of "hip, arty" locals, so you'd better "make a reservation" before going.

Tierras Colombianas ⌘
21 | 11 | 17 | $20

33-01 Broadway (33rd St.), Queens, 718-956-3012
82-18 Roosevelt Ave. (82nd St.), Queens, 718-426-8868

☑ "Plan on fasting" before hitting this Queens duo for "overflowing plates" of "simple" but "irresistible" Colombian "home cooking" (think "mountains of meat") "at the right price"; never mind the "cafeterialike" digs, the "cholesterol" "high" is "worth cheating on your diet."

Time Cafe ●
15 | 14 | 14 | $28

2330 Broadway (85th St.), 212-579-5100
380 Lafayette St. (Great Jones St.), 212-533-7000
www.timecafenyc.com

☑ These roomy Uptown-Downtown Americans clock in as "ordinary", though the grub is "good enough" for partisans; equal time goes to those ticked off at "pedestrian" eats and "out-to-lunch" service, but the attached Moroccan bars are always pleasant for a drink.

Tio Pepe ●
▽ 18 | 15 | 18 | $32

168 W. Fourth St. (bet. 6th & 7th Aves.), 212-242-9338; www.tiopepenyc.com

☑ As an "ol' standby" in the Village, this "friendly" Spanish-Mexican "lives up to its rep" for "tasty" food made more "enjoyable" by fair prices and a "good drink list"; everyone's treated "like a regular" and there's a "cute" garden, so the majority shrug and say uncle.

TOCQUEVILLE
26 | 22 | 24 | $64

15 E. 15th St. (bet. 5th Ave. & Union Sq. W.), 212-647-1515

■ "An isle of civility" off Union Square, this French-American offers "superb" "adult dining", with "felicitous" cuisine from chef Marco Moreira's "expert kitchen" "beautifully served" in a "simple yet refined" setting; "it'll cost you", but cognoscenti say it's money "well spent" because this "standard-bearer", while "easily overlooked", "outdoes" many of the "big guys."

Tommaso's
▽ 21 | 17 | 19 | $40

1464 86th St. (bet. 14th & 15th Aves.), Brooklyn, 718-236-9883

■ "Food, wine and opera" are the muses at this "old-style" Bensonhurst Italian, where "bigger-than-life" owner Thomas Verdillo sometimes "sings for you", providing counterpoint to the "hearty" cooking and a "first-class" vino selection; "locals swear by it", recommending it as "worth checking out."

TOMOE SUSHI ⌧
26 | 7 | 15 | $38

172 Thompson St. (bet. Bleecker & Houston Sts.), 212-777-9346

☑ "Patience" is rewarded at this Village Japanese, where sushiphiles endure "heinous waits" in lines stretching nearly to Tokyo to savor "generously cut", "unbelievably fresh and succulent fish" at "rock-bottom prices"; maybe the "cramped quarters" offer "zero ambiance", but given the "commitment" to "hall-of-fame" quality, it's easy to "forget about everything else."

Tomo Sushi & Sake Bar ●
18 | 13 | 15 | $26

2850 Broadway (bet. 110th & 111th Sts.), 212-665-2916

☑ This Morningside Heights Japanese stays "busy" catering to "Columbia kids" "on the run" who appreciate a "reliable" source of "ok sushi" at a mo' "reasonable price"; but though it "serves a need", naysayers knock "generic" fish and "blasé service."

Tom's ⌧⌘
▽ 20 | 18 | 25 | $13

782 Washington Ave. (Sterling Pl.), Brooklyn, 718-636-9738

■ "Always a treat" for nostalgists, this '30s-era Prospect Heights coffee shop is still a "favorite" for "real" American "comfort" fare and "syrupy-sweet drinks" including nonpareil egg creams served by the "friendliest", "fastest" folks around; it's a "landmark" for all-day breakfasts – now "if only they'd stay open for dinner."

Tony's Di Napoli

19 | 14 | 18 | $32

1606 Second Ave. (83rd St.), 212-861-8686
147 W. 43rd St. (bet. B'way & 6th Ave.), 212-221-0100
www.tonysdinapoli.com

☑ "*Abbondanza*" rules at these "hectic" "stroller-derby" Italians known for "basic red-sauce" standards "on the cheap" dished out family-style in "bowls larger than many NYC apartments"; if a few cry "Carmine's clone", most find themselves in "garlic heaven."

Topaz Thai

20 | 11 | 16 | $26

127 W. 56th St. (bet. 6th & 7th Aves.), 212-957-8020

☑ "Lunchtime crowds" declare this Midtown "hole-in-the-wall" a "winner" for "pungent" "traditional" Thai, but count on "elbow-to-elbow" seating and "don't expect any decor"; "convenient to Carnegie Hall", it's also a "bargain" and "super fast."

Top of the Tower

▽ 14 | 26 | 17 | $53

Beekman Tower, 3 Mitchell Pl. (1st Ave. & 49th St.), 212-980-4796;
www.mesuite.com

☑ "Magnificent" views, art deco elegance and lilting piano music add up to "built-in romance" at this correctly named Midtown aerie, though the "average" American-Continental food may not be quite "worthy of" the extraordinary setting; you can always "just have cocktails" in the "piano bar" or give what is sure to be a spectacular private party.

Torre di Pisa ☒

▽ 19 | 22 | 19 | $50

19 W. 44th St. (bet. 5th & 6th Aves.), 212-398-4400; www.torredipisa.us

☑ Partisans praise David Rockwell's "delightful", richly colored Tower of Pisa–inspired design at this Midtown Northern Italian, even if the cuisine has less-"inventive" leanings; pluses include "solicitous service" and a favorable "pre-theater location", though some suggest that prices tilt toward "excessive."

Tossed

19 | 8 | 11 | $13

295 Park Ave. S. (bet. 22nd & 23rd Sts.), 212-674-6700
30 Rockefeller Plaza Concourse (bet. 49th & 50th Sts.), 212-218-2525 ☒
www.tossed.com

☑ You "design your own salad" at this "made-to-order" pair featuring a "variety" of toppings plus "creative" "new sandwiches in crêpes"; "custom" comes "pricey" though, so bring lotsa lettuce; N.B. the Flatiron outpost offers seating and dinnertime table service, but the Rock Center sibling is takeout only.

Totonno Pizzeria Napolitano

24 | 10 | 15 | $20

462 Second Ave. (26th St.), 212-213-8800
1544 Second Ave. (bet. 80th & 81st Sts.), 212-327-2800
1524 Neptune Ave. (bet. W. 15th & 16th Sts.), Brooklyn, 718-372-8606 ⇥
www.totonnos.com

■ Long hailed as a Coney Island "pizza nirvana" for its pies' "fresh, crispy" "perfection", the original location still "reeks" of "crotchety" "authenticity"; the full-menu Yorkville site is less legit but more convenient, while the Gramercy rookie "shows promise."

Tournesol ◑

23 | 16 | 22 | $37

50-12 Vernon Blvd. (bet. 50th & 51st Aves.), Queens, 718-472-4355;
www.tournesolnyc.com

■ "Left Bank" refugees "feel at home" with the "marvelous" Gallic food and "winning" service at this "quaint" Long Island City bistro, which maintains "high standards" despite "tight" digs; it's also a haven for "value" just a "subway stop away from Manhattan."

Town

25 | 26 | 23 | $73

Chambers Hotel, 15 W. 56th St. (bet. 5th & 6th Aves.), 212-582-4445; www.townnyc.com

■ Join the "'in' crowd" at this "tony" Midtown New American that routinely "dazzles" with its "swank", "dramatic space" and "artful" cuisine from chef Geoffrey Zakarian; "polished" service completes the "top-shelf" "experience", and "platinum-card" pricing is considered "well worth" it when it's time to "go to town."

Trata Estiatorio

22 | 16 | 18 | $50

1331 Second Ave. (bet. 70th & 71st Sts.), 212-535-3800; www.trata.com

☑ The seafood is so "fresh" you can taste "the Mediterranean" at this East Side Greek; "grilled to perfection" and "simply served" in a "neighborhood" setting, the "fabulous" fish's "per-pound" pricing can add up, but the early prix fixe is a "great deal" and the tab is more controllable if you stick to the appealing appetizers.

Trattoria Alba ●☒

19 | 16 | 20 | $37

233 E. 34th St. (bet. 2nd & 3rd Aves.), 212-689-3200

☑ This Murray Hill Northern Italian is a "low-key" "local" "staple" for "traditional" cooking that "fills you up" but "doesn't break the bank"; "grown-up" sorts in particular appreciate the "quiet" environs.

Trattoria Dell'Arte ●

22 | 20 | 20 | $51

900 Seventh Ave. (bet. 56th & 57th Sts.), 212-245-9800; www.trattoriadellarte.com

■ "On target" as ever, this "vibrant" Midtown Italian "stalwart" has "fine" food, including the "ultimate antipasti bar", and "lots of character", from the "entertaining" staff to the enormous "plaster body parts" adorning its walls; it perpetually "hops" with loyal "throngs" who agree it's a "great prelude" to nearby Carnegie Hall, or anything else.

Trattoria Dopo Teatro ●

16 | 16 | 15 | $39

125 W. 44th St. (bet. B'way & 6th Ave.), 212-869-2849; www.dopoteatro.com

☑ Show-goers say this "Theater District standby" "has its own charm" when "standard" Italian and "efficient", curtain-conscious service will suffice; others find the "assembly-line" performance "nothing to rave about", though the "garden room" is considered a "pretty" "secret."

TRATTORIA L'INCONTRO

27 | 18 | 23 | $43

21-76 31st St. (Ditmars Blvd.), Queens, 718-721-3532; www.trattorialincontro.com

■ "Reason enough to move to Astoria", this "incredible" Italian features chef Rocco Sacramone playing at the "top of his game" creating "exceptional" cuisine (with a "tremendous" list of daily specials) as a "personable staff" keeps the "hubbub" in control; it's "not fancy", but cooking "doesn't get much better" – especially for the price; N.B. an adjacent wine bar is in the works at press time.

Trattoria Pesce & Pasta

18 | 13 | 16 | $29

262 Bleecker St. (bet. 6th Ave. & 7th Ave. S.), 212-645-2993 ●
625 Columbus Ave. (bet. 90th & 91st Sts.), 212-579-7970
1079 First Ave. (59th St.), 212-888-7884 ●
1562 Third Ave. (bet. 87th & 88th Sts.), 212-987-4696 ●
www.pescepasta.com

☑ "Simple" but surprisingly good, this "hospitable" quartet supplies "hearty" "fixes" of "no-fuss Italian" cuisine with an "emphasis on the *pesce*"; they're "casual" enough to be labeled "no-frills", but given the "can't-be-beat value", they "get crowded fast" and stay that way.

Trattoria Romana 24 | 16 | 20 | $38

1476 Hylan Blvd. (Benton Ave.), Staten Island, 718-980-3113;
www.trattoriaromana.com

☑ Staten Islanders insist this "friendly" local "favorite" is "comparable to the best" for "classic old-style Italian"; though its popularity leads to inevitable "noise and crowds", few dispute "these people know how to cook" – now if only they'd "increase the space around the tables."

Tre Pomodori 19 | 12 | 17 | $25

210 E. 34th St. (bet. 2nd & 3rd Aves.), 212-545-7266
1742 Second Ave. (bet. 90th & 91st Sts.), 212-831-8167

☑ About the most "affordable" Italian "short of take-out pizza" is dished out at these modest Eastsiders that "efficiently" serve "hefty portions" of the "standards" at an "amazingly" "low cost"; never mind if the "cramped" digs "could use a makeover."

Triangolo ●⑦ 21 | 16 | 21 | $35

345 E. 83rd St. (bet. 1st & 2nd Aves.), 212-472-4488

■ A "neighborhood secret" "hidden away" in Yorkville, this "relaxed" "midlevel Italian" is a "reliable" source of "really good" pastas and such served in "quaint" digs; the "pleasant" style extends to "friendly pricing", though the "cash-only" rule can be less agreeable.

Tribeca Grill 21 | 19 | 20 | $53

375 Greenwich St. (Franklin St.), 212-941-3900;
www.myriadrestaurantgroup.com

☑ Drew Nieporent and Robert De Niro's "classy" New American "put TriBeCa on the map", and though a few critics say it "ain't what it used to be", it still satisfies with its reliably good food, vibrant mien, "excellent" wines and "professional" service; fortunately, it's also "easier to get into than their nearby Nobu."

Trinity ⑤ – | – | – | E

TriBeCa Grand Hotel, 2 Sixth Ave. (bet. Walker & White Sts.), 212-519-6678;
www.tribecagrand.com

Chef Franklin Becker (ex Local) has resurfaced at this trendy TriBeCa hotel venue that showcases creative, albeit pricey, global-accented fare in an intimate wedge of a setting; thankfully, a wall of banquettes mutes the roar from the adjacent Church Lounge.

Trio 23 | 20 | 22 | $42

167 E. 33rd St. (bet. Lexington & 3rd Aves.), 212-685-1001

■ An "unexpected delight" in an "obscure" Murray Hill locale, this "authentic" Med proffers "top-notch" Croatian food and wines served with "hospitable" brio, "just like in the old country"; a low-lit setting with a "pianist some evenings" enhances the chances it'll "win you over."

Triomphe 25 | 23 | 23 | $59

Iroquois Hotel, 49 W. 44th St. (bet. 5th & 6th Aves.), 212-453-4233;
www.triomphe-newyork.com

■ This "tiny" "Theater District gem" "shines bright" as a "hushed" "hideaway" for "soft conversation" over "fabulous" New French fare, making for a "romantic" overture to a show; "sweet, attentive" service rounds out an "elegant" but "unpretentious" "pleasure" that's a most "welcome change for the area."

Tropica ⑤ 22 | 19 | 19 | $49

MetLife Bldg., 200 Park Ave. (enter on 45th St., bet. Lexington & Park Aves.), 212-867-6767; www.restaurantassociates.com

■ "Convenience" and "delicious", "Caribbean-influenced" seafood attract "business" types to this Grand Central–area "sleeper", where the Key West–style setting is also "great for drinks"; "high" prices are no problem, at least "when it's on the company", but there's a "drawback – it's closed on weekends."

Tsampa ●
∇ 19 | 20 | 18 | $25

212 E. Ninth St. (bet. 2nd & 3rd Aves.), 212-614-3226

☑ "Calmness prevails" at this East Village Tibetan, a place to tsample "delicately" spiced food in "holistic" digs reminiscent of "an episode of *Kung Fu*"; it's "soothing" ("wish they had a spa") and "easy on the wallet", though unenlightened palates call it all "pretty bland."

Tse Yang
24 | 24 | 23 | $59

34 E. 51st St. (bet. Madison & Park Aves.), 212-688-5447

■ It "doesn't get any better" for "upscale Chinese" than this veteran Midtowner whose "top-shelf" offerings ("go for the Peking duck") and "impeccable service" are "fit for an emperor"; the "enchanting" "aquarium"-filled milieu is just as impressive, though of course all that "class" comes "extravagantly priced."

Tuk Tuk ∅
∇ 21 | 15 | 18 | $21

204 Smith St. (bet. Baltic & Butler Sts.), Brooklyn, 718-222-5598

☑ "Definitely not generic" say fans of this Cobble Hill Thai that lets you tuck into "spicy, expertly prepared" fare served by "friendly" folks at "great value" prices; "thankfully", the food "can stand on its own" since many "don't get" the weekend jazz bands and "drab" room.

Tupelo Grill ⊠
18 | 18 | 17 | $46

1 Penn Plaza (33rd St., bet. 7th & 8th Aves.), 212-760-2700; www.tupelogrill.com

☑ Given the dining "dearth" around MSG, this "decent" American is "a no-brainer" for a "meet-up pre- or post-" event; the food and "comfortable digs" may be "unremarkable" and it's not cheap, but "at least it gives you a choice" in the surrounding "abyss."

Turkish Kitchen
22 | 19 | 19 | $37

386 Third Ave. (bet. 27th & 28th Sts.), 212-679-6633; www.turkishkitchenny.com

■ "As good as any" "this side of the Bosphorus", this affordable Gramercy "Turkish delight" is a "crowd-pleaser" offering "abundant portions" of "delectable" meats and mezes; the "bi-level", "flame-red" interior and "killer drinks" induce "sensory intoxication", and the "deservedly busy" Sunday brunch is "not to be missed."

Turkuaz
20 | 21 | 18 | $34

2637 Broadway (100th St.), 212-665-9541; www.turkuazrestaurant.com

■ To "escape" the Upper West Side for a "bedouin experience", try out this "authentic" Turk, where a "billowing" "desert tent" interior sets the mood for "piquant" food and "1001 nights of fun"; the "seraglio" setup strikes most as "memorable", and "for better or worse there's belly dancing" Thursday–Saturday.

Turmeric
– | – | – | M

29 W. 21st St. (bet. 5th & 6th Aves.), 212-206-0056

Taking a page (and a chef) from nearby Tamarind, this new Flatiron Southern Indian stresses seafood, though traditional stalwarts like tandoori chicken and saag panir are also represented; lunch box specials ranging from $6.95 to $9.95 please penny-pinchers.

Tuscan
19 | 23 | 19 | $56

622 Third Ave. (40th St.), 212-404-1700; www.chinagrillmgt.com

☑ Known for "comfy" "contemporary" dining that's "rare in Midtown", this "impressive" Italian attracts the "corporate power" set with a "creative menu" built around meats and a "great-looking" space that also draws a decent "bar crowd"; still, a few grumble "portions are slight" and "overpriced", so "thank goodness for expense accounts."

Tuscan Square
17 18 15 $44

16 W. 51st St. (bet. 5th & 6th Aves.), 212-977-7777

🔲 The "large" scale squares well with "big Midtown suits" at this Rock Center Northern Italian, a supplier of "satisfying" fare in a cavernous, "rustic" space; maybe it's "pricey" and "service isn't fast", but it's popular as a "centrally located" fallback that also offers "takeout downstairs at lunchtime."

Tuscany Grill
24 18 21 $42

8620 Third Ave. (bet. 86th & 87th Sts.), Brooklyn, 718-921-5633

■ You "can't go wrong with any dish" on the "top-notch" menu at this "consistently" "enjoyable" Bay Ridge Northern Italian, where everyone is treated "like part of the family"; the "small, dim" setting makes it a "cute date place" for those "trying not to overimpress."

12th St. Bar & Grill
21 19 19 $34

1123 Eighth Ave. (bet. 11th & 12th Sts.), Brooklyn, 718-965-9526

■ This "tried-and-true" Park Sloper "makes you want to be a regular" given its "cheery" vibe, ok New American food and "Brooklyn prices"; an "attractive" locus for "local color", it "does a fine job" with "no big surprises", though a few say the staff "takes its time" about it.

21 CLUB ⊠
21 22 23 $63

21 W. 52nd St. (bet. 5th & 6th Aves.), 212-582-7200; www.21club.com

■ "Still vital" as Midtown's "power-rating barometer", this seriously pricey "jacket-and-tie" "icon" preserves its "old glory" thanks to a "rock-solid" American menu, which is matched by the "first-rate" staff's "professional aplomb"; as a "deal-making" locus dating back to "speakeasy times", its downstairs bar/dining room has "cachet" that "never fails to impress"; P.S. check out its many "classy" private party rooms, especially the "legendary wine cellar."

26 Seats
23 18 21 $34

168 Ave. B (bet. 10th & 11th Sts.), 212-677-4787; www.26seats.com

■ That's right, "literally 26" seats "fill up quickly" as patrons "squeeze" into this East Villager for "sinfully good" French fare served with a "personal" touch by folks who "clearly care"; it's an "affordable" "treat" with plenty of "charming" "candlelit" atmosphere – just "don't expect much leg room."

Two Boots
19 11 14 $14

42 Ave. A (3rd St.), 212-254-1919 ◐
37 Ave. A (bet. 2nd & 3rd Sts.), 212-505-2276
74 Bleecker St. (B'way), 212-777-1033 ◐
Grand Central, lower level (42nd St. & Lexington Ave.), 212-557-7992
30 Rockefeller Plaza, downstairs (bet. 49th & 50th Sts.), 212-332-8800 ⊠
201 W. 11th St. (7th Ave. S.), 212-633-9096 ◐
514 Second St. (bet. 7th & 8th Aves.), Brooklyn, 718-499-3253
www.twoboots.com

■ Taking pizza "beyond the normal slice", this "fun", "kitschy", kid-friendly chain gives its "crispy" pies a "zesty" Louisiana "spin" defined by "spicy" sauce, "funky toppings" and "campy" names; the separately managed Park Slope site offers a full menu of Cajun eats and all the appearances of a "suburban outing."

212 ◐
18 18 17 $42

133 E. 65th St. (bet. Lexington & Park Aves.), 212-249-6565;
www.212restaurant.com

🔲 A "hot" mix of "Euro-hip" and "twentysomething" "prep" types frequents this "noisy" East Side nexus, known for its lightish French-Italian bites and "great vodka list"; of course, "food isn't the real focus" for those who find it all "totally superficial" yet "quite the scene."

Typhoon 🗷
17 **17** **14** **$39**

22 E. 54th St. (bet. 5th & Madison Aves.), 212-754-9006

🗷 "When it hits", the Thai-fusion food at this Midtown eatery/ "brewhouse" can be "satisfying", though it hardly takes most by storm; the "loud" downstairs bar "can be off-putting", though it plainly "fills a need" for the local "professional singles crowd."

Ubol's Kitchen
▽ **25** **11** **21** **$21**

24-42 Steinway St. (bet. Astoria Blvd. & 25th Ave.), Queens, 718-545-2874

🗷 In an "exotic corner of Astoria", this "friendly" "little" Thai "excels" with "totally authentic" food that's "rich" and "spicy" enough to "clear up a cold instantaneously"; the decor may be "humorously cheesy", but with such "cheap and plentiful" chow, "who cares?"

Uguale ●
▽ **22** **19** **20** **$41**

396 West St. (W. 10th St.), 212-229-0606

■ "Beautiful summer sunsets" and "views across the Hudson" help keep this "serene" West Village Italian a "romantic" rendezvous for "pleasant" dining and "old-school" service; its location "off the beaten path" makes it a "great backup" since it's easy to "get a table."

UK New York
– **–** **–** **M**

22 Warren St. (bet. B'way & Church St.), 212-513-0111; www.uknewyork.com

Bringing a bit of the British Isles to the Big Apple, this TriBeCa English pub serves updated tavern classics washed down with premium Anglo ales; convenient to the courthouses, it's a natural for jury duty if you don't fall asleep after lunch.

Ulrika's
21 **16** **19** **$43**

115 E. 60th St. (bet. Lexington & Park Aves.), 212-355-7069; www.ulrikas.com

■ For a "change of pace" in East Midtown, try this "inviting" Scandinavian featuring "wonderful" "traditional" specialties, "understated" "Swedish farmhouse decor" and "attentive" service from "cute blondes"; fans say skol to Nordic "charm" that's particularly "winning" during the "winter holidays."

Umberto's Clam House ●
19 **13** **17** **$34**

178 Mulberry St. (Broome St.), 212-343-2053
2356 Arthur Ave. (186th St.), Bronx, 718-220-2526
www.umbertosclamhouse.com

🗷 A Little Italy "standby" since "the good old days", this durable, "open-late" Italian still serves "lots of" "nothing-fancy" pasta and seafood, often to "tourists" who expect "the *Sopranos* cast to arrive"; antis who argue it's "run-of-the-mill" and "resting on its laurels" may find a fresher scene at its new outpost on Arthur Avenue.

Uncle George's ●⇇
18 **8** **13** **$21**

33-19 Broadway (34th St.), Queens, 718-626-0593; www.unclegeorges.us

🗷 "You won't go hungry" at this "24-hour Greek fix", a "hectic" Astoria "greasy spoon" that's a "best buy" for "gigantic" helpings of "home-cooked" "peasant food"; "there's no decor" and "service ranges from stoic to surly", but the "large crowds" don't come here for "frills."

Uncle Jack's Steakhouse
22 **18** **21** **$61**

440 Ninth Ave. (bet. 34th & 35th Sts.), 212-244-0005 🗷
39-40 Bell Blvd. (40th Ave.), Queens, 718-229-1100
www.unclejacks.com

■ "Kobe beef in Queens" alone is enough to make this "traditional" Bayside steakhouse (with a West Side spin-off) a carnivore's choice for "mouthwatering" beef in "oversize" cuts with "price tags to match"; "sweet-talking" staffers, who keep it "on par" with the "high-end" joints, help "justify" spending all that jack.

Uncle Nick's

20 | 11 | 15 | $30

747 Ninth Ave. (bet. 50th & 51st Sts.), 212-245-7992

■ Always "a hoot", this "economical" Hell's Kitchen "fixture" "packs 'em in" for "flavorful" Greek "taverna" fare (the "flaming cheese is a must") in portions "fit for Hercules"; those who nix the "rough" service, "cramped seating" and frequently "frantic" feeling find refuge in the "Ouzaria next door."

UNION PACIFIC ⊠

24 | 25 | 23 | $69

111 E. 22nd St. (bet. Lexington Ave. & Park Ave. S.), 212-995-8500; www.unionpacificrestaurant.com

■ The Gramercy "flagship" of chef/"persona" Rocco DiSpirito "runs like clockwork", showing plenty of "sizzle" and "originality" in its "top-caliber" New American cuisine; "smooth" service and a "serene" "contemporary" backdrop set a "very adult" tone, and though it's all tailored to "big spenders", the lunchtime $20 prix fixe deal "can't be beat."

UNION SQUARE CAFE

27 | 23 | 26 | $61

21 E. 16th St. (bet. 5th Ave. & Union Sq. W.), 212-243-4020

■ An "enduring" "all-star", Danny Meyer's "benchmark" New American off Union Square "has the magic" to elicit "wall-to-wall smiles" – credit goes to chef Michael Romano's "exhilarating", "soul-satisfying" cuisine, "seamless service" from "the smartest staff" going and a "genteel" but "not-too-formal" ambiance; while you'll "thank your lucky stars" when you land a "coveted reservation", those who "can't wait" "can always sit at the bar" for a "primo" bite.

Uno Chicago Grill ●

15 | 13 | 14 | $21

432 Columbus Ave. (81st St.), 212-595-4700
220 E. 86th St. (bet. 2nd & 3rd Aves.), 212-472-5656
391 Sixth Ave. (bet. 8th St. & Waverly Pl.), 212-242-5230
South Street Seaport, 89 South St. (Pier 17), 212-791-7999
55 Third Ave. (bet. 10th & 11th Sts.), 212-995-9668
9201 Fourth Ave. (92nd St.), Brooklyn, 718-748-8667
39-02 Bell Blvd. (39th Ave.), Queens, 718-279-4900
107-16 70th Rd. (bet. Austin St. & Queens Blvd.), Queens, 718-793-6700
37-11 35th Ave. (38th St.), Queens, 718-706-8800
www.unos.com

◪ Most disregard the "name change" and "stick to" the "same old" "fattening" deep-dish pizzas doled out at this "serviceable" chain catering to "families" hungry "for a taste of the 'burbs"; but some Chicago chauvinists call the "cheesy" scene and "assembly-line" grub a "disservice" to the Midwest.

Üsküdar

21 | 11 | 18 | $30

1405 Second Ave. (bet. 73rd & 74th Sts.), 212-988-2641

■ This Upper Eastsider's "minuscule" size guarantees "very personal" attention to go with the "terrific Turkish food" and "value" that keep it "crowded with regulars"; most agree the struggle to "squeeze in" is "worth braving", though given the "lack of decor" takeout is a big plüs too.

Utsav

21 | 19 | 18 | $35

1185 Sixth Ave., 2nd fl. (enter on 46th or 47th Sts., bet. 6th & 7th Aves.), 212-575-2525

■ Adventurers say it's "worth the search" for this "upstairs" Midtown "secret" to try out "appealing" regional Indian dishes "you don't see

in most" outposts of the Raj; "spacious" digs and "unrushed" service
lend an "upscale" feel, and the $13.95 lunch buffet is always a "treat."

Va Bene ▽ 19 16 18 $43
1589 Second Ave. (bet. 82nd & 83rd Sts.), 212-517-4448
☑ "Kosher can indeed be *bene*" according to advocates of this
"solid" Upper East Side Italian, where the dairy Roman fare is so
"fresh" and "authentic" it's downright "surprising"; a few question
the cost, but alternatives being "hard to come by", most maintain
it's well "worth it."

Vago ☒ ▽ 18 17 18 $47
29 W. 56th St. (bet. 5th & 6th Aves.), 212-765-5155
■ Nothing flashy and "not too crowded", this Midtown Italian is
"comfortable" for a traditional bite away from the big-city bustle;
enterprising types go for the "good lunch deal" ($21.95 prix fixe), and
the pre-theater menu offers incentive to step out early.

V&T ◐ 20 9 13 $19
1024 Amsterdam Ave. (bet. 110th & 111th Sts.), 212-666-8051
☑ Scholars "swear by" the "greasy, saucy, cheesy" pizza at this "old-
school" Columbia-area Italian, a "longtime" "favorite" for pie-lovers
"not finicky about decor or service"; "chowdowns" for "cheap" make
it an undergrad "dream."

Vatan 22 23 22 $32
409 Third Ave. (29th St.), 212-689-5666
■ You can "indulge" "till you pop" and "never feel guilty" at this
Gramercy AYCE vegetarian, where $22.95 buys an "amazing" "never-
ending plate" served in a "Disney-like" Indian village; the "congenial"
staff "makes life easy": just "slip off your shoes" and "keep asking for
more" – until you can't anymore.

Va Tutto ▽ 19 18 17 $36
23 Cleveland Pl. (bet. Kenmare & Spring Sts.), 212-941-0286; www.vatutto.com
☑ "Rustic" right down to its "delightful" "back garden", this
NoLita Italian supplies the "reliable" pastas "every neighborhood
needs"; doubters say the menu's "ordinary" and the staff "can be
overwhelmed", but plenty of "warm" atmosphere more than "makes
up" for any lapses.

Vegetarian Paradise 20 10 16 $18
33-35 Mott St. (Canal St.), 212-406-6988
144 W. Fourth St. (bet. MacDougal St. & 6th Ave.), 212-260-7130
☑ The "scarily authentic" "pseudo-meat dishes" at these separately
owned Chinatown-Village Chinese vegetarians could fool "die-hard"
carnivores, prompting admirers to wonder "how they do it"; however,
doubters deem the "uneven" eats and "lousy decor" less than heavenly.

Vela ◐☒ ▽ 17 22 17 $51
55 W. 21st St. (bet. 5th & 6th Aves.), 212-675-8007; www.velarestaurant.com
■ "Trendy" on arrival, this Flatiron newcomer serves "interesting"
Japanese fare with a dash of "Brazilian flair" in "dark" Far East
environs decked with hanging lamps and bamboo; "upscale" prices
don't deter seekers of "cool atmosphere" that gets hotter as the late-
night "lounge scene" revs up.

Veniero's ◐ 23 13 13 $14
342 E. 11th St. (bet. 1st & 2nd Aves.), 212-674-7070; www.venierospastry.com
☑ "Willpower succumbs" at this East Village Italian "pastry mecca",
an 1894 "period" piece famed for "dreamy desserts" that "justify
putting any diet on hold"; critics cite "insane lines", "packed"

quarters and servers who should "sweeten their attitudes", but when the sugar "jones" strikes it's "sooo worth it."

Vento ⭘
∇ 21 | 21 | 21 | $45

675 Hudson St. (14th St.), 212-699-2400;
www.brguestrestaurants.com

■ Showing "lots of promise", Steve Hanson's "triangle-shaped" Meatpacking District Italian newcomer is already packing in a "cool crowd" thanks to "light", "well-prepared" food served with "friendly" "spunk"; look for a "noisy" multilevel setting lined with tall windows and "exposed brick" with the "added bonuses" of a "sexy" underground lounge and ample outdoor seating.

Vera Cruz ⭘
18 | 13 | 15 | $24

195 Bedford Ave. (bet. N. 6th & 7th Sts.), Brooklyn, 718-599-7914

◪ An "easy" "oldie" on the Williamsburg strip, this "*muy cheap*" Mexican is usually "hopping" with locals out for "quick", "home-cooked" meals ("gotta get their special corn") and "great margaritas"; if the indoors gets too "cozy", the "patio out back" is "always a treat."

VERITAS
27 | 22 | 25 | $79

43 E. 20th St. (bet. B'way & Park Ave. S.), 212-353-3700;
www.veritas-nyc.com

■ The truly "phenomenal" wine list ("as thick as *War and Peace*") at this "top-class" Flatiron New American meets its match in chef Scott Bryan's "sumptuous" prix fixe menu; at $68 it may seem "costly", but the "expert" service and "intimate", "understated" room help make every meal here truly a "special event."

Vermicelli
20 | 16 | 19 | $30

1492 Second Ave. (bet. 77th & 78th Sts.), 212-288-8868

■ Yes, the "Italian-sounding" "name is misleading", but the affordable Vietnamese fare at this Yorkville standby is honestly "first-rate" and arrives in "big portions"; extra incentives include "a steal" of a "box-lunch special" and "open-air" tables for summer.

Veronica ☒
∇ 21 | 3 | 14 | $16

240 W. 38th St. (bet. 7th & 8th Aves.), 212-764-4770

◪ Although it "doesn't look like much", this Garment District cafeteria's "generous" helpings of "real homestyle cooking" (amazing American for breakfast, *multo bene* Italian for lunch) are just "what fast food should be"; the weekdays-only "breadline" setup offers "no glitter", but it's the "ultimate" for a frugal feed.

Veselka ⭘
19 | 12 | 13 | $17

144 Second Ave. (9th St.), 212-228-9682; www.veselka.com

◪ "Insomniacs" seeking "cheap eats with oomph" turn to this 24/7 East Village Ukrainian "relic" offering a "huge" "comfort-food" menu in "hectic", "too-bright" digs; "grumpy service gives it character" claim the "quasi-hip" types for whom it's a "necessity."

Via Brasil
∇ 20 | 15 | 20 | $35

34 W. 46th St. (bet. 5th & 6th Aves.), 212-997-1158

■ "Forget about cholesterol and indulge" in the "delightful" Brazilian chow at this "laid-back" Midtowner, home to "huge servings of stews, grilled meat" and other "hearty", "good-value" fare; the staff aims "to please", and live *carioca* tunes are "a bonus" Wednesday-Saturday.

Via Emilia ☒⊟
21 | 13 | 17 | $30

240 Park Ave. S. (bet. 19th & 20th Sts.), 212-505-3072

■ "Fresh pasta" fans are "transported" to "tortelloni heaven" "for just a few bucks" at this "low-key" cash-only Flatiron trattoria; it's an "unexpected" "find" for "down-to-earth" Northern Italian, but since there are "no reservations" and it's "no longer a secret", you'd better expect "a wait."

Viand
16 | 7 | 15 | $18

2130 Broadway (75th St.), 212-877-2888 ●
300 E. 86th St. (2nd Ave.), 212-879-9425 ●
1011 Madison Ave. (78th St.), 212-249-8250
673 Madison Ave. (bet. 61st & 62nd Sts.), 212-751-6622 ⊄
◪ "Eat it and beat it" could be the motto at this "convenient" East Side coffee shop quartet, serving "the basics" to everyone from cops to ladies in fur; though "far from elegant", it "satisfies" with "decent grub", including a much praised turkey breast sandwich, and a "mock-abusive" staff working at peak "efficiency"; N.B. the separately owned East 80s outfit operates round the clock.

Via Oreto
20 | 15 | 19 | $43

1121-23 First Ave. (bet. 61st & 62nd Sts.), 212-308-0828
◼ Mama-and-son proprietors make everyone "so welcome" at this East Side "comfort" cucina where the repertoire of "home-cooked" Italian "standbys" draws "a hearty *buon appetito*" from the whole "neighborhood"; the "family feel" keeps it "very popular", and the Sunday meatballs alone "are worth the trip."

Via Quadronno
21 | 16 | 17 | $34

25 E. 73rd St. (bet. 5th & Madison Aves.), 212-650-9880;
www.viaquadronno.com
◼ The East Side meets "Milano" at this "happening", "Euro-filled" Italian cafe, where "beautiful" sorts squeeze into "tight", "placemat-size tables" for great panini and some of the "best cappuccino" in town; the prices may be high for such "simple" fare, but given the address, "what do you expect?"

ViceVersa ⧉
22 | 21 | 21 | $50

325 W. 51st St. (bet. 8th & 9th Aves.), 212-399-9291
◼ The "warmth" "really shows" at this "airy" modern Hell's Kitchen Northern Italian "oasis", where the "sedate vibe" and "attentive service" make the kitchen's "delightful" handiwork "taste that much better"; given its fine food and "upscale" but "relaxed" style, fans applaud it as "a perfect pre-theater stop"; P.S. check out the patio.

Vico ●⊄
21 | 15 | 20 | $49

1302 Madison Ave. (bet. 92nd & 93rd Sts.), 212-876-2222
◪ This Carnegie Hill "standby" "plays to the neighborhood crowd" with "first-rate" Italian fare and "sweet" service – for anyone in the "club"; outsiders may find the reception "a bit haughty" and the "no-credit-cards" dictum "a pain" in light of its top-of-the-line tabs.

Victor's Cafe ●
20 | 18 | 18 | $43

236 W. 52nd St. (bet. B'way & 8th Ave.), 212-586-7714; www.victorscafe.com
◼ Zip "to the tropics" by way of this Hell's Kitchen "taste of Cuba", the "real" thing for "stick-to-the-ribs" food and "lively surroundings" that encourage everyone to "feel right at home" (especially after "a mojito or three"); it's something "different" pre-theater, but beware of "upscale prices."

Villa Berulia
22 | 20 | 25 | $46

107 E. 34th St. (bet. Lexington & Park Aves.), 212-689-1970
◼ One visit and you're "part of the *famiglia*" at this "retro" Murray Hill vet, known for "classic" Northern Italian food and "hospitality" from a staff that "almost reads your mind"; though "a bit shopworn", it "definitely delivers" "leisurely" dining like it "used to be."

Village ◐
62 W. Ninth St. (bet. 5th & 6th Aves.), 212-505-3355;
www.villagerestaurant.com

20	20	20	$41

■ Counted as "an asset" for the Village, this "upscale" but "easygoing" "neighborhood bistro" offers "delicious" New American–French food in a "lovely wood-paneled room"; natives say its "accommodating" style "deserves to be discovered" beyond the area.

Villa Mosconi ⊠
69 MacDougal St. (bet. Bleecker & Houston Sts.), 212-673-0390;
www.villamosconi.com

▽ 21	14	20	$40

■ Followers "know just what to expect" at this "enduring and endearing" West Village Italian, i.e. very good "traditional" fare and "warm", "courteous" service at "fair prices"; it's "long-standing" and looks it, but "locals" hope the "old-world charm" "never changes."

Vince and Eddie's
70 W. 68th St. (bet. Columbus Ave. & CPW), 212-721-0068

18	16	17	$44

☑ Attendees at "nearby Lincoln Center" applaud this "congenial" "retreat" for "hearty" American grub in "small", "quaint" quarters outfitted with "intimate" fireplaces and a "hidden garden"; still, a few fret it's "too crowded for comfort" and so "homey" that it's hard to "rationalize its prices."

Vincent's ◐
119 Mott St. (Hester St.), 212-226-8133; www.originalvincents.com

21	13	17	$31

☑ "Their sauce is second to none" promise partisans of this Little Italy centenarian, where the affordable Southern Italian fare "brings tears to your eyes"; sure, it's "lacking" in looks and beset by the "map-and-camera crowd", but "if it weren't good it wouldn't still be there."

Vine ⊠
25 Broad St. (Exchange Pl.), 212-344-8463; www.vinefood.com

19	18	18	$51

☑ "Cozier than your typical Wall Streeter", this "innovative" New American gives its clientele a chance to talk business over "high-quality" cuisine; the downstairs room in a "former bank vault" is "perfect for a power lunch", but holdouts hedge on what they describe as "inconsistent" cooking and "steep" prices.

Vinnie's Pizza ◐
285 Amsterdam Ave. (bet. 73rd & 74th Sts.), 212-874-4382

21	8	13	$12

☑ "At least the pizza wasn't redesigned" at this Upper Westsider, now "glammed up" (relatively speaking) into an Italian eatery but still "memorable" mostly for its "fantastic", super-cheesy pies; yes, it's often "crowded – for good reason."

Virgil's Real BBQ
152 W. 44th St. (bet. B'way & 6th Ave.), 212-921-9494; www.virgilsbbq.com

21	14	17	$31

☑ "Serious eating" goes on at this "boisterous" Times Square "crowd-pleaser" that's best known for serving "obscene" portions of "hard-core", "fall-off-the-bone" BBQ ("consult your physician" first); despite "tourist hordes" and "tacky" surroundings, for most of our surveyors it's a "satisfying" "down-home fix."

Vittorio Cucina
308-310 Bleecker St. (bet. Grove St. & 7th Ave. S.), 212-463-0730;
www.vittoriocri.com

▽ 23	15	20	$37

■ This "quaint", "welcoming" Village "standby" "couldn't be more Italian" given its "region-of-the-month" menu and signature "cheese-wheel pasta" dish; regulars who like its "old-fashioned" ways head here "to be taken care of", often opting for the "comfortable back garden" in good weather.

Vivolo ◐
20 | 18 | 19 | $45

140 E. 74th St. (bet. Lexington & Park Aves.), 212-737-3533
■ A "mainstay" for "quieter" East Side dining, this bi-level brownstone provides "dependable Italian" and "pro service" in a "mature" ambiance; if some find it "a little dated", it's a "comfortable old friend" to "long-term patrons" who note that the "early-bird's a bargain."

Vong
24 | 24 | 23 | $60

200 E. 54th St. (3rd Ave.), 212-486-9592; www.jean-georges.com
■ Still "an experience to be savored", Jean-Georges Vongerichten's vaunted Midtown French-Thai "dazzles the tongue and eye" with "tantalizing" fusion fare and an "exotic", high-ceilinged space presided over by a "suave" staff; for those who "gong" the "undersized, overpriced" servings, there's always the "amazing value of the prix fixe pre-theater" deal.

Voyage
▽ 20 | 21 | 18 | $43

117 Perry St. (Greenwich St.), 212-255-9191
☑ West Village wayfarers consider this "cozy", travel-themed New American just the ticket for "top-level" cuisine with a "creative" Southern spin that ventures "all over the map"; critics claim "service can be spotty", but it's a "quiet" stopover that merits "more attention."

V Steakhouse
– | – | – | VE

Time Warner Ctr., 10 Columbus Circle, 4th fl. (60th St. at B'way), 212-823-9500
From über-toque Jean-Georges Vongerichten comes this new Time Warner Center high-end steakhouse where Niman Ranch beef is accompanied by a variety of inventive sauces and condiments; its rococo, Jacques Garcia–designed setting makes a witty nod to its Central Park view via gilded trees hung with crystal chandeliers.

Walker's ◐
17 | 14 | 16 | $27

16 N. Moore St. (Varick St.), 212-941-0142
■ An "everyday" "staple" in the "heart of TriBeCa", this "low-key" tavern plies "better-than-standard" "pub grub" and other "honest" eats in an "antique" setting dating to the 1890s; given that it's "relaxing" and "underpriced", habitués ask "what's not to love?"

WALLSÉ ◐
26 | 22 | 23 | $60

344 W. 11th St. (Washington St.), 212-352-2300; www.wallserestaurant.com
■ "Gemütlich" chef Kurt Gutenbrunner has epicures "in the know" waltzing into his West Village enclave of "Viennese charm" to relish "memorable" "modern" renderings of Austrian fare and a "terrific wine selection" in a setting that's "tasteful" and "intimate" "but not stuffy"; "pricey" it may be, but an "eager-to-please" staff is one more reason it's an all-around "special place."

Water Club
21 | 25 | 21 | $60

East River at 30th St. (enter on E. 23rd St.), 212-683-3333; www.thewaterclub.com
■ The "dazzling view" from this East River barge "heightens" the pleasure of downing the "delicious" American fare featuring seafood and an "amazing brunch"; "polished service" and a "streamlined" maritime setting make it a "romantic favorite" that's "worth the splurge" "at least once"; P.S. they'll go overboard to help you have a "great" "private party."

Water's Edge ⌧
23 | 25 | 24 | $59

44th Dr. & East River (Vernon Blvd.), Queens, 718-482-0033; www.watersedgenyc.com
■ With "magnificent views" to give it an edge, this Long Island City New American sets "high standards" for a "romantic" "occasion"

with a "wonderfully prepared" seafood-centric menu, "first-class" ambiance and even a "complimentary water taxi" from Midtown; "gold-card" pricing can pinch, but most people are too charmed "to look at the check."

WD-50
23 | 20 | 23 | $65

50 Clinton St. (bet. Rivington & Stanton Sts.), 212-477-2900; www.wd-50.com

☑ "Not for timid palates", this Lower East Side American-Eclectic is a showcase for "mad genius" chef Wylie Dufresne who ventures "totally outside the box" with "brilliant" "avant cuisine"; a "knowledgeable staff" helps diners "navigate" the "unexpected combinations", but skeptics say it "tries too hard", knocking "too-cute" dishes at "sky-high prices."

West Bank Cafe ●
19 | 15 | 18 | $39

Manhattan Plaza, 407 W. 42nd St. (bet. 9th & 10th Aves.), 212-695-6909

■ This "popular" Theater District New American generates a "good buzz" thanks to its "warm welcome" and "consistently pleasing" (if "predictable") menu; overall it's an "affordable", "unpretentious" performance, with "steady" staffers ensuring ticket-holders a "fast in and out, if needed."

Westville ●
21 | 13 | 18 | $22

328 E. 14th St. (bet. 1st & 2nd Aves.), 212-598-9998
210 W. 10th St. (bet. Bleecker & W. 4th Sts.), 212-741-7971

■ Producing New American "cheap eats" with "flair", this "neat" "beach shack"–esque West Villager (and its East Village clone) serve delicious food in a "casual" scrubbed-white "shoebox"; it's a "personable" pit stop, but "go at an off hour" or expect "killer" waits.

White Horse Tavern ●♿
12 | 14 | 13 | $18

567 Hudson St. (11th St.), 212-989-3956

☑ Toast "the ghost of Dylan Thomas" and "watch the West Villagers stroll by" from the "outside tables" at this (circa 1880) "landmark" saloon, where "long-lost fraternity brothers" horse around over American "munchies" and "cold beer"; though saddled with "run-of-the-mill" grub, it's still the stuff of "legends."

Whole Foods Café
19 | 12 | 11 | $16

Time Warner Ctr., 10 Columbus Circle, downstairs (B'way, bet. 58th & 60th Sts.), 212-823-9600; www.wholefoods.com

☑ Never mind the "celeb-chef" places upstairs – "the wonder of the Time Warner Center" for many is this "mammoth" supermarket with its self-serve cafe proffering a "gazillion" "fresh", "inviting" Eclectic choices, from salads to pizzas to sushi; but "whoa, is this place crowded" and per-pound prices can really take a toll.

'wichcraft
22 | 12 | 15 | $16

49 E. 19th St. (bet. B'way & Park Ave. S.), 212-780-0577; www.wichcraftnyc.com

■ "Sorry mom", but this Flatiron breakfast-and-lunch counter next to Tom Colicchio's Craft and Craftbar "raises sandwich-making to an art" with its "bewitching" array of "gourmet" "quick bites" and sweet "treats"; though "a little pricey" for "fast" fare, it's way "classier" than a deli; N.B. a TriBeCa twin is in the works at press time.

Wild Ginger ●
19 | 20 | 18 | $26

51 Grove St. (bet. Bleecker St. & 7th Ave. S.), 212-367-7200; www.wildginger-ny.com

■ More "calming" than wild, this West Village Thai offers "old favorites" with "a bit of a kick" in "low-lit", bamboo-trimmed environs that encourage "lingering"; "solicitous" service and "incredibly reasonable" prices help keep things "serene."

Willow
17 | 17 | 18 | $45

1022 Lexington Ave. (73rd St.), 212-717-0703

☑ It's "not hip", but locals applaud this Upper Eastsider's "pleasant" French-American meals and the fact "you can hear" across the tables when dining at this "understated" two-story townhouse; the "close quarters" are hardly a nuisance since it's "never very crowded."

Wo Hop ◑⇗
20 | 5 | 14 | $16

17 Mott St. (Canal St.), 212-267-2536

☑ A bona fide Chinatown "dive", this hoppin' 24-hour "perennial" provides "really good", "greasy" Chinese and "fast, rude service" "for a pittance"; since this place is about "the best you can do at 4 AM", you won't hear many complaints about the woeful, low-budget quarters.

Wolfgang's Steakhouse ⊠
24 | 24 | 20 | $65

4 Park Ave. (33rd St.), 212-889-3369; www.wolfgangssteakhouse.com

■ This Murray Hill spot stays true to "top-line steakhouse" protocol with "superb" beef ("like butter") and "excellent service" (natch) in an "impressive" space notable for its "vaulted tile ceiling" and "high noise level"; though "Luger's this ain't", it's "already a success" as a go-to for well-heeled carnivores who want to stay in the 212.

Wollensky's Grill ◑
23 | 15 | 19 | $45

201 E. 49th St. (3rd Ave.), 212-753-0444; www.smithandwollensky.com

■ Boasting the "same quality" as its upstairs brother Smith & Wollensky, this Midtown pub/grill allows customers to "save a few bucks" on "high-class burgers" and steaks while avoiding any fuss and clamor; the "advertising and/or media" types say this is where to find "everyone" in the biz.

Wondee Siam
23 | 9 | 16 | $19

792 Ninth Ave. (bet. 52nd & 53rd Sts.), 212-459-9057 ⇗
813 Ninth Ave. (bet. 53rd & 54th Sts.), 917-286-1726

☑ They look "unassuming", but these Hell's Kitchen holes-in-the-wall are "authentic" wonders for "awesome" Thai on the "cheap"; the northerly locale is preferable but still "lame" atmosphere-wise, so "close your eyes and enjoy" or opt for "quick" takeout and delivery.

Won Jo ◑
21 | 12 | 15 | $29

23 W. 32nd St. (bet. B'way & 5th Ave.), 212-695-5815

☑ You will "smell like a wood fire, but eat like a king" at this 24/7 Garment District Korean, a "pretty authentic" option for BBQ "grilling at the table"; even with a sushi sideline it's "one of the cheaper" of the breed, though that's reflected in its "typical" downscale digs.

Woo Lae Oak
23 | 24 | 20 | $47

148 Mercer St. (bet. Houston & Prince Sts.), 212-925-8200;
www.woolaeoaksoho.com

■ As "fashionable" as "Seoul food" gets, this "sizzling" SoHo Korean's "main attraction" of "cook-your-own" BBQ is a "mouthwatering" way to entertain a "big group" of friends; the "chic", "minimalist" room is definitely "not your traditional" setup, but even with "upscale" prices it's a "welcome change" from K-town.

World Yacht
∇ 14 | 24 | 18 | $72

Pier 81, W. 41st St. & Hudson River (12th Ave.), 212-630-8100;
www.worldyacht.com

☑ "Lovely" views of the skyline, plus music and dancing are "what you're paying for" on this boat cruise, since the New American "hotel food" is almost incidental; still, for a "romantic interlude", albeit one that's "not for the fast crowd", you can hardly do better.

Wu Liang Ye
| 22 | 12 | 16 | $27 |

215 E. 86th St. (bet. 2nd & 3rd Aves.), 212-534-8899
338 Lexington Ave. (bet. 39th & 40th Sts.), 212-370-9648
36 W. 48th St. (bet. 5th & 6th Aves.), 212-398-2308

■ "Bring on the heat" is the rallying cry at this "genuine" Szechuan trio that "doesn't pull any punches" "if you ask for it spicy"; "adventurous diners" say its "variety" of "distinctive" dishes makes others "pale in comparison", and if the backdrop is "blah", at least it won't cost "all your yuan."

X.O. ⊘
| 19 | 11 | 12 | $17 |

148 Hester St. (bet. Bowery & Elizabeth St.), 212-965-8645
96 Walker St. (bet. Centre & Lafayette Sts.), 212-343-8339

☑ Daring types tout the "huge selection" of unusual Hong Kong–style options at these "bustling" low-budget Chinatown Chinese; regrettably, the kinda "tacky" decor and "haphazard" service aren't so unique.

Xunta
| 20 | 13 | 13 | $26 |

174 First Ave. (bet. 10th & 11th Sts.), 212-614-0620;
www.xuntatapas.com

■ Purveying "tasty" tapas to East Villagers "on a budget", this "lively" Spaniard is apt to be "packed" with "sangria-fueled" twentysomethings who detect "no frills, but no need for them"; despite "long waits" and small, "not very comfy" digs, the majority emerges "full and happy."

YAMA
| 25 | 12 | 16 | $36 |

38-40 Carmine St. (bet. Bedford & Bleecker Sts.), 212-989-9330
122 E. 17th St. (Irving Pl.), 212-475-0969 ⊠
92 W. Houston St. (bet. La Guardia Pl. & Thompson St.), 212-674-0935
www.yamarestaurant.com

☑ Until they "can afford Nobu", sushiphiles go for "orca"-size "slabs" of "super-fresh", "melt-in-your-mouth" fish at this Japanese trio; there's "not much glamour" or service, but "top quality" and "gentle prices" lead to "tough" waits and crowding "to the gills"; N.B. the Carmine Street branch takes reservations.

Ye Waverly Inn
| 16 | 22 | 19 | $39 |

16 Bank St. (Waverly Pl.), 212-929-4377

☑ "What the Village is all about", this "olde-style" survivor is a haven "for all seasons" with a "quaint" interior, "soothing" cobbled garden and "lovely fireplaces"; if the "decent but unexciting" American-Continental menu "doesn't measure up", for "charm alone" it's "hard to beat."

York Grill
| 23 | 20 | 22 | $44 |

1690 York Ave. (bet. 88th & 89th Sts.), 212-772-0261

■ Denizens of Yorkville's "culinary desert" are "very pleased" with this "upscale" "oasis" and its "appealing menu" of "consistently excellent" American dishes; factor in "warm", "professional service" and a mature yet "relaxed vibe", and there's little wonder that it's a "neighborhood favorite."

Yuca Bar ◗
| ∇ 21 | 19 | 22 | $29 |

111 Ave. A (7th St.), 212-982-9533; www.yucabarrestaurant.com

■ "On the up and up" with Pan-Latin fans, this welcome new East Villager serves a peripatetic menu (plus brunch with a salsified "twist") to a gaucho soundtrack in candlelit digs; sidewalk tables and open floor-to-ceiling doors add to the "airy", easygoing feel, as do the "fabulous" mojitos.

Yujin
20 | 22 | 19 | $51

24 E. 12th St. (bet. 5th Ave. & University Pl.), 212-924-4283; www.yujinnyc.com

☑ Huge in "nontraditional" ambition, this "nouvelle Japanese" Villager does "vibrant" meals (including "creative sushi") in "funky" "modernist" environs; it's "interesting" and "atmospheric" enough to make some "wonder where the people are", though its "pricey" tabs may provide a clue.

Yuka
22 | 10 | 17 | $25

1557 Second Ave. (bet. 80th & 81st Sts.), 212-772-9675

☑ "How do they do it?" is the mystery at this Upper East Side Japanese whose $18 AYCE sushi binge "doesn't skimp on the fish" and "actually tastes good"; maybe the place is "not much to look at" and "long lines" are routine, but big eaters "can't go wrong" here.

Yuki Sushi ◐
21 | 15 | 20 | $28

656 Amsterdam Ave. (92nd St.), 212-787-8200

■ Upper Westsiders "say *hai* to excellent sushi" at this "very popular" Japanese eatery, an "agreeable" source of "big", "artful rolls" and "efficient" service "at a decent price"; as an "appetizing respite" in a dining-deficient area, it "thrives" in spite of the "bad choice of name."

Yura & Co.
20 | 12 | 15 | $22

1292 Madison Ave. (92nd St.), 212-860-8060
1645 Third Ave. (92nd St.), 212-860-8060
1659 Third Ave. (93rd St.), 212-860-8060

☑ "Mainstays" for "informal", "budget" snacking, these Carnegie Hill American bakery/cafes attract "Pashmina-clad" moms and "Spence girls" willing to "break the bathing-suit diet"; despite "spartan" settings, "limited seating" and "erratic service", they're "always jammed" with regulars who "crave" their "simple delights."

Zabar's Cafe ⌷
20 | 5 | 10 | $15

2245 Broadway (80th St.), 212-787-2000; www.zabars.com

■ You "eat and run" at this "no-frills" white formica Upper Westsider where the "first-rate" "finger food" comes courtesy of the grocery "institution" next door; those "lucky enough to get a stool" nosh at a "cramped" countertop, while reading their morning papers; more patient sorts just "take it home."

Zarela
21 | 16 | 18 | $41

953 Second Ave. (bet. 50th & 51st Sts.), 212-644-6740; www.zarela.com

■ "Hold on to your sombrero" because it's always a "fiesta" at this East Side Mexican that's usually "packed like a piñata" with "noisy" fans of its "*muy bueno*" cuisine and "lethal" margaritas; the "accommodating" staff is led by Zarela Martinez, who's on hand to ensure "everybody feels good" especially on the calmer second floor.

Zaytoons
22 | 13 | 17 | $16

472 Myrtle Ave. (bet. Hall St. & Washington Ave.), Brooklyn, 718-623-5522
283 Smith St. (Sackett St.), Brooklyn, 718-875-1880

☑ Locals zay "you'll be glad you stumbled on" these Smith Street–Fort Greene BYO "canteens" serving "delicious" Mideastern fare at "bargain-basement prices"; though they're bare-bones and "undermanned", multitudes tune in for "solid" taste and "value."

Zebú Grill
∇ 22 | 18 | 23 | $36

305 E. 92nd St. (bet. 1st & 2nd Aves.), 212-426-7500

■ "They should patent their feijoada" say enthusiasts of this "funky" "little" Upper East Side Brazilian, where the menu highlighting grilled meats is "limited" but "rich in flavor"; with a genial "Rio" vibe and "great service", it's a place that "deserves more attention."

Zen Palate

19 17 17 $26

2170 Broadway (bet. 76th & 77th Sts.), 212-501-7768
663 Ninth Ave. (46th St.), 212-582-1669
34 Union Sq. E. (16th St.), 212-614-9291
www.zenpalate.com

☑ "Get your gluten on" at these "ingenious" mock-meat vegetarian "sanctuaries" offering meals that appeal to the "mind, body and wallet" (they're even "surprisingly bearable" for carnivores); the "spare, peaceful" settings work "better than Xanax", though not for those few who find them "bland" and "off-putting."

Zerza ●

▽ 21 21 20 $31

304 E. Sixth St. (bet. 1st & 2nd Aves.), 212-529-8250; www.zerzabar.com

■ Though "out of place amid" the Curry Row Indian cadre, this East Village Med-Moroccan is "a find" for "terrific" tagines and other "flavorful" dishes in "intimate" duplex digs; given the "exotic setting" (complete with "sexy" downstairs lounge), "inventive" cocktails and "decent prices", it's "great for dates."

Zeytin

▽ 20 17 20 $37

519 Columbus Ave. (85th St.), 212-579-1145

■ Take the "shortcut to Ankara" via this Upper West Side Turkish newcomer, a subdued hideaway whose "delicious, aromatic" specialties and "caring" staff make it a most "welcome addition" in an area "lacking" interesting options; "so far, so good" report locals.

Zeytuna

19 15 14 $17

161 Maiden Ln. (Front St.), 212-514-5858
59 Maiden Ln. (William St.), 212-742-2436

■ "So many decisions" is the refrain at these "cafeteria-style" Financial District cafes adjacent to "gourmet" agoras, where an Eclectic "cornucopia of delights" awaits; the "food court–type" indoor/outdoor seating is "handy" and priced right for the Wall Street lunch "masses."

Zipi Zape

– – – I

152 Metropolitan Ave. (Berry St.), Brooklyn, 718-599-3027

Spain lands in Williamsburg at this festive tapas specialist, named for the Iberian cartoon characters portrayed in comic strips on its walls; in addition to Galician hot and cold bites – fried béchamel croquettes, anyone? – there are also *bocadillos* (little sandwiches) and a full bar.

Zitoune

18 19 18 $41

46 Gansevoort St. (Greenwich St.), 212-675-5224

☑ "Hard to find but easy to like", this "rockin'" Moroccan brings a "relaxed" vibe to the Meatpacking District with its "memorable" food, "personable service" and "authentic" Casablanca charm; still, critics say it's "a little pricey" for "average" eats.

Zócalo

20 16 16 $35

174 E. 82nd St. (bet. Lexington & 3rd Aves.), 212-717-7772
Grand Central, lower level (42nd St. & Vanderbilt Ave.), 212-687-5666
www.zocalo.us

■ This "convivial" Upper Eastsider is favored for its "creative", "truly Mexican menu" and "potent" margaritas, but remember to take "earplugs" since the bar's "throngs" are "still going strong"; in addition, the "convenient" Grand Central spin-off makes a "surprisingly pleasant" commuter cantina.

Zoë

21 19 19 $45

90 Prince St. (bet. B'way & Mercer St.), 212-966-6722

■ SoHo shoppers "count on" this "smart", "popular" New American for "delish" dishes prepared with "imagination" in a "cute open kitchen" and served by a "polite staff"; though it can be "clamorous" and is definitely not cheap, it's considered a "safe" bet, especially during brunch when it really "sparkles."

Zona Rosa ⌧

▽ 20 | 18 | 20 | $42

40 W. 56th St. (bet. 5th & 6th Aves.), 212-247-2800; www.zonarosarestaurant.com

■ Venture "beyond the traditional taco" at this "charming" new Midtowner, where the "nuevo" "twist" on Mexican "tastes amazing" and the bi-level, retro-"fashionable" space aims for the "trendy" zone; with "gracious service" and "excellent specialty drinks", it shows "high potential – as it should "at these prices."

Zum Schneider ⇗

18 | 16 | 15 | $23

107 Ave. C (7th St.), 212-598-1098; www.zumschneider.com

☑ "Grab a stein" at this East Village "*brauhaus*", the "closest thing to Bavaria" around with "predictable" German grub chased by nonstop "liters of beer"; there's an "open-air setup" for summer, but unless "liquid" meals count, some feel "food is not the focus."

Zum Stammtisch

23 | 19 | 19 | $34

69-46 Myrtle Ave. (bet. 69th Pl. & 70th St.), Queens, 718-386-3014; www.zumstammtisch.com

■ The "overflowing plates" have "lederhosen" popping at this Glendale German stalwart that's a "schnitzel heaven" thanks to "classic" dishes "done right", "quaint" "Alpine-like" digs and "real" "Bavarian" service; it's "*gemütlich*" for the "whole family."

Zuni ◐

17 | 12 | 17 | $32

598 Ninth Ave. (43rd St.), 212-765-7626

☑ Partisans pitch this "small", "casual" Hell's Kitchen "hangout" as an "alternative" for "home-cooked" New American "with a Southwest touch"; "service is relaxed" and there's "not much decor", but it makes sense as an "affordable", "theater-handy" "standby."

Zutto

23 | 18 | 20 | $36

62 Greenwich Ave. (bet. 7th Ave. S. & W. 11th St.), 212-367-7204
77 Hudson St. (Harrison St.), 212-233-3287
www.sushizutto.com

■ "Where the locals go for sushi", this TriBeCa-Village Japanese duo boasts "phenomenally fresh" fish and other "irresistible" food served with "no attitude" in an "inviting" "oasis of calm"; it can "be counted on for quality" at a "reasonable price", leading admirers to ask "why wait weeks" for Nobu?

Indexes

CUISINES
LOCATIONS
SPECIAL FEATURES

CUISINES

(Restaurant Names, Food ratings and neighborhoods)

Afghan

Afghan Kebab/18/multi. loc.
Pamir/20/E 70s

African

Les Enfants Terribles/21/Low E Side

American (New)

Abigael's/20/Garment
Above/19/W 40s
Aesop's Tables/21/Staten Is.
Alias/22/Low E Side
Amuse/20/Chelsea
Angus McIndoe/19/W 40s
Annisa/27/G Vil.
Aureole/27/E 60s
Battery Gardens/–/Fin. District
Beacon/23/W 50s
Biltmore Room/25/Chelsea
Bistro Ten 18/21/W 100s
Black Duck/20/Gramercy
Blue Hill/26/G Vil.
Blue Mill/–/G Vil.
Blue Ribbon/25/multi. loc.
Blue Ribbon Bakery/23/G Vil.
Blue Star/20/Cobble Hill
Blue Water/24/Union Sq.
Boat House/17/E 70s
Bridge Cafe/21/Fin. District
Bull Run/20/Fin. District
Butter/20/G Vil.
Café Botanica/21/W 50s
Cafe S.F.A./17/E 40s
Café St. Bart's/18/E 50s
Candela/18/Union Sq.
Carriage House/17/Chelsea
Caviar Russe/25/E 50s
Chestnut/22/Carroll Gdns.
Chop't Salad/20/Union Sq.
Cibo/20/E 40s
Cocotte/22/Park Slope
Compass/21/W 70s
Cornelia St. Cafe/18/G Vil.
Craft/26/Flatiron
Craftbar/23/Flatiron
Cub Room/19/SoHo
Cup/–/Astoria
Dano/19/Gramercy
davidburke/donatella/25/E 60s
Deborah/22/G Vil.
Dish/18/Low E Side
District/20/W 40s
Downtown Atlantic/21/Boerum Hill
Druids/19/W 50s
Duane Park Cafe/23/TriBeCa
DuMont/21/Williamsburg

Eatery/18/W 50s
Eleven Madison/26/Gramercy
elmo/15/Chelsea
Essex/18/Low E Side
Etats-Unis/25/E 80s
Fifty Seven 57/23/E 50s
Five Front/21/Dumbo
Five Points/22/NoHo
Fives/24/W 50s
44/20/W 40s
44 & X/21/W 40s
Fraunces Tavern/16/Fin. District
Fred's at Barneys/18/E 60s
Garden Cafe/27/Prospect Heights
Giorgio's Gramercy/23/Flatiron
good/21/G Vil.
Gotham B&G/27/G Vil.
Grace/17/TriBeCa
Gramercy Tavern/28/Flatiron
Grocery/26/Carroll Gdns.
Guastavino's/18/E 50s
Halcyon/20/W 50s
Harbour Lights/17/Seaport
Harrison/24/TriBeCa
Hearth/24/E Vil.
Heights Cafe/17/Bklyn Hts.
Henry's/17/W 100s
Henry's End/25/Bklyn Hts.
HK/20/Garment
Hope & Anchor/20/Red Hook
Ian/22/E 80s
Ida Mae/22/Garment
industry (food)/19/E Vil.
Inside/20/G Vil.
Isabella's/19/W 70s
Jane/21/G Vil.
Jasper/–/G Vil.
Jefferson/24/G Vil.
Jerry's/17/SoHo
Josephina/19/W 60s
Josephs/–/W 40s
Kitchen 22/82/21/multi. loc.
Knickerbocker/19/G Vil.
Lenox Room/19/E 70s
Levana/19/W 60s
Lever House/23/E 50s
Louie's Westside/16/W 80s
Lunchbox Food/19/G Vil.
Magnolia/21/Park Slope
March/27/E 50s
Mark's/23/E 70s
Mas/28/G Vil.
Mercer Kitchen/22/SoHo
Merchants, N.Y./15/multi. loc.
Mix in NY/18/W 50s

Mojo/*22/E Vil.*
Monkey Bar/*18/E 50s*
Morrells/*20/multi. loc.*
My Most Favorite/*18/W 40s*
New Leaf/*19/Wash. Hts. & Up*
NoHo Star/*17/NoHo*
Norma's/*25/W 50s*
North Sq./*24/G Vil.*
Oceana/*26/E 50s*
Océo/*22/W 40s*
One/*18/Meatpacking*
One C.P.S./*21/W 50s*
One if by Land/*25/G Vil.*
101/*21/Bay Ridge*
Ouest/*25/W 80s*
Parish & Co./*21/Chelsea*
Park Avalon/*20/Flatiron*
Park Ave Cafe/*24/E 60s*
Patroon/*21/E 40s*
Pearl Room/*24/Bay Ridge*
per se/*29/W 60s*
Philip Marie/*21/G Vil.*
Picket Fence/*–/Midwood*
Place/*22/G Vil.*
Pop/*18/G Vil.*
Pop Burger/*19/Meatpacking*
Porters/*17/Chelsea*
Prune/*24/E Vil.*
Rachel's American/*18/W 40s*
Red Café/*21/Park Slope*
Red Cat/*24/Chelsea*
Redeye Grill/*21/W 50s*
Regency/*19/E 60s*
Relish/*19/Williamsburg*
River Cafe/*25/Dumbo*
Riverdale Garden/*23/Bronx*
Rose Water/*24/Park Slope*
Salt/*21/multi. loc.*
Saul/*27/Boerum Hill*
Savoy/*23/SoHo*
Seven/*17/Chelsea*
71 Clinton/*24/Low E Side*
Share/*–/E Vil.*
Snackbar/*18/Chelsea*
SQC/*20/W 70s*
Strata/*–/Flatiron*
Tabla/*26/Gramercy*
Taste/*20/E 80s*
Tasting Room/*27/E Vil.*
Tea Box/*22/E 50s*
Thalia/*21/W 50s*
Time Cafe/*15/multi. loc.*
Tocqueville/*26/Union Sq.*
Town/*25/W 50s*
Tribeca Grill/*21/TriBeCa*
12th St. Bar/Grill/*21/Park Slope*
21 Club/*21/W 50s*
Union Pacific/*24/Gramercy*
Union Sq. Cafe/*27/Union Sq.*
Veritas/*27/Flatiron*

Village/*20/G Vil.*
Vine/*19/Fin. District*
Voyage/*20/G Vil.*
Water's Edge/*23/LIC*
WD-50/*23/Low E Side*
West Bank Cafe/*19/W 40s*
Westville/*21/E Vil.*
'wichcraft/*22/Flatiron*
Willow/*17/E 70s*
World Yacht/*14/W 40s*
York Grill/*23/E 80s*
Zoë/*21/SoHo*
Zuni/*17/W 40s*

American (Traditional)

Algonquin Hotel/*15/W 40s*
Alias/*22/Low E Side*
America/*14/Flatiron*
American Grill/*19/Staten Is.*
Annie's/*17/E 70s*
Barking Dog/*16/multi. loc.*
Bayard's/*23/Fin. District*
Boat Basin Cafe/*11/W 70s*
Brennan & Carr/*21/Sheepshead Bay*
Brooklyn Diner/*16/W 50s*
Bryant Park Cafe/Grill/*16/W 40s*
Bubba Gump/*15/W 40s*
Bubby's/*18/multi. loc.*
Cafe Nosidam/*19/E 60s*
Cafeteria/*18/Chelsea*
Chelsea Grill/*17/Chelsea*
City Bakery/*22/Flatiron*
City Grill/*16/W 70s*
City Hall/*21/TriBeCa*
Coffee Shop/*16/Union Sq.*
Comfort Diner/*16/multi. loc.*
Corner Bistro/*23/G Vil.*
Cupping Room/*18/SoHo*
Diner/*21/Williamsburg*
Diner 24/*–/Chelsea*
E.A.T./*18/E 80s*
Edward's/*17/TriBeCa*
EJ's Luncheonette/*16/multi. loc.*
Elaine's/*13/E 80s*
Elephant & Castle/*17/G Vil.*
Empire Diner/*15/Chelsea*
ESPN Zone/*13/W 40s*
Fairway Cafe/*19/W 70s*
Fanelli's Cafe/*15/SoHo*
Fred's/*17/W 80s*
Friend of a Farmer/*17/Gramercy*
Good Enough to Eat/*20/W 80s*
Grilled Cheese/*20/Low E Side*
Hard Rock Cafe/*12/W 50s*
Heartland Brew./*14/multi. loc.*
Home/*21/G Vil.*
Houston's/*20/multi. loc.*
Hudson Cafeteria/*18/W 50s*
Jackson Hole/*17/multi. loc.*
Jekyll & Hyde/*10/W 50s*

J.G. Melon/*21/E 70s*
Joe Allen/*16/W 40s*
Johnny Rockets/*14/G Vil.*
Luke's Bar/Grill/*17/E 70s*
Mama's Food /*22/multi. loc.*
Marion's/*16/NoHo*
Mars 2112/*9/W 50s*
Mayrose/*15/Flatiron*
McHales/*20/W 40s*
MetroCafe/Wine/*19/Flatiron*
Metropolitan Cafe/*16/E 50s*
Michael Jordan's/*20/E 40s*
Mickey Mantle's/*13/W 50s*
MJ Grill/*20/Fin. District*
Neary's/*16/E 50s*
92/*15/E 90s*
Odeon/*19/TriBeCa*
Once Upon a Tart/*21/SoHo*
O'Neals'/*17/W 60s*
Parsonage/*22/Staten Is.*
Penelope/*21/Murray Hill*
Pershing Square/*15/E 40s*
Pete's Tavern/*13/Gramercy*
Picket Fence/*–/Midwood*
P.J. Clarke's/*16/E 50s*
Popover Cafe/*18/W 80s*
Raymond's Cafe/*21/Chelsea*
Rock Center Café/*19/W 50s*
Sarabeth's/*21/multi. loc.*
Sazerac House/*18/G Vil.*
Serendipity 3/*20/E 60s*
Sparky's/*20/Williamsburg*
Swifty's/*17/E 70s*
Tavern on Green/*14/W 60s*
Tenement/*20/Low E Side*
Tom's/*20/Prospect Heights*
Top of the Tower/*14/E 40s*
Tupelo Grill/*18/Garment*
21 Club/*21/W 50s*
Uno Chicago Grill/*15/multi. loc.*
Vince & Eddie's/*18/W 60s*
Walker's/*17/TriBeCa*
Water Club/*21/Murray Hill*
Westville/*21/multi. loc.*
White Horse Tav./*12/G Vil.*
Wollensky's Grill/*23/E 40s*
Ye Waverly Inn/*16/G Vil.*
Yura & Co./*20/E 90s*

Argentinean

Azul Bistro/*22/Low E Side*
Chimichurri Grill/*23/W 40s*
Hacienda Argentina/*20/E 70s*
Novecento/*21/SoHo*
Pampa/*21/W 90s*
Sosa Borella/*20/multi. loc.*

Asian

Aja/*–/E 50s*
Asia de Cuba/*24/Murray Hill*

bluechili/*21/W 50s*
Bright Food Shop/*19/Chelsea*
Cafe Asean/*22/G Vil.*
China Grill/*23/W 50s*
Chow Bar/*21/G Vil.*
Citrus Bar & Grill/*19/W 70s*
Daily Chow/*17/E Vil.*
Faan/*18/multi. loc.*
Gobo/*24/G Vil.*
Haikara Grill/*20/E 50s*
Hakata Grill/*20/W 40s*
Hispaniola/*20/Wash. Hts. & Up*
Lotus/*16/Meatpacking*
Nana/*22/Park Slope*
O.G./*22/E Vil.*
Pacific Grill/*–/Seaport*
Rain/*21/multi. loc.*
Rêve/*–/E 70s*
Rhône/*17/Meatpacking*
Roy's NY/*25/Fin. District*
Ruby Foo's/*20/multi. loc.*
Sammy's/*18/G Vil.*
Scuba Sushi/*–/Gramercy*
Tao/*22/E 50s*
39 East/*22/Bayside*

Australian

Eight Mile Creek/*20/Little Italy*
Sunburnt Cow/*19/E Vil.*

Austrian

Café Sabarsky/*22/E 80s*
Cafe Steinhof/*18/Park Slope*
Danube/*27/TriBeCa*
Thomas Beisl/*23/Ft. Greene*
Wallsé/*26/G Vil.*

Bakeries

Amy's Bread/*23/multi. loc.*
Au Bon Pain/*14/multi. loc.*
Chez Laurence/*19/Murray Hill*
City Bakery/*22/Flatiron*
Columbus Bakery/*19/multi. loc.*
La Bergamote/*26/Chelsea*
Le Pain Quotidien/*20/multi. loc.*
Yura & Co./*20/E 90s*

Barbecue

Biscuit/*18/Prospect Heights*
Blue Smoke/*20/Gramercy*
Brother Jimmy's BBQ/*17/multi. loc.*
Cho Dang Gol/*23/Garment*
Daisy May's BBQ/*23/W 40s*
Dallas BBQ/*15/multi. loc.*
Do Hwa/*21/G Vil.*
Hog Pit BBQ/*17/Meatpacking*
Lucy /*18/Flatiron*
Pearson's BBQ/*17/multi. loc.*
Tennessee Mtn./*16/SoHo*
Texas Smokehouse/*–/Gramercy*

36 Bar & BBQ/*22/Garment*
Virgil's BBQ/*21/W 40s*

Belgian

Café de Bruxelles/*21/G Vil.*
Le Pain Quotidien/*20/multi. loc.*
Markt/*19/Meatpacking*
Petite Abeille/*19/multi. loc.*

Brazilian

Casa/*21/G Vil.*
Churrascaria Plata./*22/multi. loc.*
Circus/*19/E 60s*
Coffee Shop/*16/Union Sq.*
Green Field/*18/Corona*
Malagueta/*25/Astoria*
Rice 'n' Beans/*19/W 50s*
SushiSamba/*22/Flatiron*
Via Brasil/*20/W 40s*
Zebú Grill/*22/E 90s*

Burmese

Mingala Burmese/*18/multi. loc.*

Cajun

Acme B&G/*17/NoHo*
Bayou/*20/Harlem*
Bourbon St. Cafe/*17/Bayside*
Cooking with Jazz/*25/Whitestone*
Delta Grill/*20/W 40s*
Great Jones Cafe/*23/NoHo*
Jacques-Imo's/*20/W 70s*
Mara's Homemade/*21/E Vil.*
Mardi Gras/*18/Forest Hills*
Natchez/*22/E Vil.*
107 West/*17/multi. loc.*
Sazerac House/*18/G Vil.*
Two Boots/*19/Park Slope*

Californian

Michael's/*21/W 50s*

Caribbean

A/*22/W 100s*
Black Cat/*–/E Vil.*
Brawta Caribbean/*22/Boerum Hill*
Don Pedro's/*20/E 90s*
Ideya/*20/SoHo*
Ivo & Lulu/*23/SoHo*
Justin's/*15/Flatiron*
Liquors/*19/Ft. Greene*
Negril/*20/multi. loc.*
Plantain/*22/Garment*
Revival/*20/Harlem*
Tropica/*22/E 40s*

Cheese Steaks

BB Sandwich/*19/G Vil.*
Carl's Steaks/*22/Murray Hill*
Hope & Anchor/*20/Red Hook*

Chinese

(* dim sum specialist)
Au Mandarin/*20/Fin. District*
Café Evergreen*/*20/E 60s*
Chiam*/*22/E 40s*
China Fun*/*16/multi. loc.*
Chin Chin/*23/E 40s*
Dim Sum Go Go*/*19/Ctown*
East Lake*/*21/Flushing*
Evergreen Shanghai*/*17/multi. loc.*
Excellent Dumpling/*20/Ctown*
Friendhouse/*18/E Vil.*
Fuleen Seafood/*23/Ctown*
Golden Unicorn*/*20/Ctown*
Grand Sichuan/*22/multi. loc.*
Jing Fong*/*19/Ctown*
Joe's Shanghai/*21/multi. loc.*
Lili's Noodle/*17/multi. loc.*
Mandarin Court*/*19/Ctown*
Mee Noodle Shop/*17/multi. loc.*
Mr. Chow/*24/E 50s*
Mr. K's/*24/E 50s*
New Green Bo/*23/Ctown*
Nice*/*19/Ctown*
NoHo Star/*17/NoHo*
No. 1 Chinese/*16/E Vil.*
Ocean Palace*/*20/Ocean Parkway*
Ollie's/*16/multi. loc.*
Oriental Garden*/*25/Ctown*
Our Place*/*20/multi. loc.*
Peking Duck*/*22/multi. loc.*
Phoenix Garden/*23/E 40s*
Pig Heaven/*19/E 80s*
Ping's Seafood*/*21/multi. loc.*
Sam's Noodle Shop/*19/Gramercy*
Shanghai Cuisine/*20/Ctown*
Shanghai Pavilion/*22/E 70s*
Shun Lee Cafe*/*21/W 60s*
Shun Lee Palace/*25/E 50s*
Shun Lee West/*23/W 60s*
66*/*20/TriBeCa*
Sweet-n-Tart Cafe*/*19/multi. loc.*
Sweet-n-Tart Rest.*/*19/Ctown*
Tang Pavilion/*22/W 50s*
Tse Yang/*24/E 50s*
Veg. Paradise*/*20/multi. loc.*
Wo Hop/*20/Ctown*
Wu Liang Ye/*22/multi. loc.*
X.O.*/*19/Ctown*

Coffeehouses

Cafe Lalo/*19/W 80s*
Caffe Reggio/*17/G Vil.*
DT.UT/*16/multi. loc.*
Edgar's Cafe/*19/W 80s*
Ferrara/*22/Little Italy*
French Roast/*15/multi. loc.*
Grey Dog's Coffee/*22/G Vil.*
Le Pain Quotidien/*20/multi. loc.*

Omonia Cafe/18/multi. loc.
Once Upon a Tart/21/SoHo
71 Irving Place/19/Gramercy
Starbucks/12/multi. loc.

Coffee Shops/Diners

Burger Heaven/16/multi. loc.
Chat 'n Chew/17/Union Sq.
Comfort Diner/16/multi. loc.
Cup/–/Astoria
Diner/21/Williamsburg
Diner 24/–/Chelsea
EJ's Luncheonette/16/multi. loc.
Empire Diner/15/Chelsea
Florent/19/Meatpacking
Googie's/15/E 70s
Mayrose/15/Flatiron
Moonstruck/14/multi. loc.
Tom's/20/Prospect Heights
Veselka/19/E Vil.
Viand/16/multi. loc.

Colombian

Tierras Colomb./21/multi. loc.

Continental

Café Pierre/23/E 60s
Four Seasons/26/E 50s
Kings' Carriage/21/E 80s
Murals on 54/–/W 50s
Palm Court/19/W 50s
Park Place/23/Bronx
Parsonage/22/Staten Is.
Petrossian/24/W 50s
Piccola Venezia/25/Astoria
Sardi's/15/W 40s
Top of the Tower/14/E 40s
Ye Waverly Inn/16/G Vil.

Creole

Bayou/20/Harlem
Delta Grill/20/W 40s
Jacques-Imo's/20/W 70s
Mara's Homemade/21/E Vil.
Mardi Gras/18/Forest Hills
Natchez/22/E Vil.
Revival/20/Harlem
Two Boots/19/Park Slope

Cuban

Asia de Cuba/24/Murray Hill
Cafe Con Leche/17/multi. loc.
Café Habana/22/NoLita
Calle Ocho/22/W 80s
Cuba/–/G Vil.
Cuba Libre/18/Chelsea
Havana Central/17/Union Sq.
Havana Chelsea/20/Chelsea
Son Cubano/20/Meatpacking
Victor's Cafe/20/W 50s

Delis

Artie's Deli/17/W 80s
Barney Greengrass/23/W 80s
Ben's Kosher Deli/17/multi. loc.
Carnegie Deli/20/W 50s
Ess-a-Bagel/23/multi. loc.
Katz's Deli/22/Low E Side
Mill Basin Deli/20/Mill Basin
Pastrami Queen/18/E 80s
Sarge's Deli/19/Murray Hill
Second Ave Deli/23/E Vil.
Stage Deli/18/W 50s
Zabar's Cafe/20/W 80s

Dessert

Amy's Bread/23/multi. loc.
Cafe Lalo/19/W 80s
Café Sabarsky/22/E 80s
Caffe Rafaella/17/G Vil.
Caffe Reggio/17/G Vil.
ChikaLicious/25/E Vil.
City Bakery/22/Flatiron
Edgar's Cafe/19/W 80s
Ferrara/22/Little Italy
Junior's/18/multi. loc.
Krispy Kreme/22/multi. loc.
La Bergamote/26/Chelsea
Lady Mendl's/21/Gramercy
My Most Favorite/18/W 40s
Omonia Cafe/18/multi. loc.
Once Upon a Tart/21/SoHo
Park Ave Cafe/24/E 60s
Payard Bistro/24/E 70s
Provence en Boite/22/Bay Ridge
Serendipity 3/20/E 60s
Sweet Melissa/23/Cobble Hill
Veniero's/23/E Vil.

Dominican

Bohio/21/Wash. Hts. & Up
Cafe Con Leche/17/multi. loc.
El Malecon/20/multi. loc.

Eastern European

Kiev/15/E Vil.
Sammy's Roumanian/19/Low E Side

Eclectic

aka Cafe/19/Low E Side
Alice's Tea Cup/19/W 70s
Biltmore Room/25/Chelsea
B. Smith's/18/W 40s
Cal. Pizza Kitchen/15/E 60s
Carol's Cafe/24/Staten Is.
Chance/–/Boerum Hill
Chubo/23/Low E Side
Delegates Din. Rm./17/E 40s
Dishes/21/E 40s
East of Eighth/16/Chelsea
5 Ninth/–/Meatpacking

Hudson Cafeteria/18/W 50s
Josephina/19/W 60s
Josie's/20/W 70s
Mix It/–/NoLita
NoHo Star/17/NoHo
Océo/22/W 40s
Public/23/NoLita
Pump Energy Food/18/multi. loc.
Punch/20/Flatiron
Radio Perfecto/17/multi. loc.
Rice/19/multi. loc.
Riverview/18/LIC
Route 66 Cafe/17/W 50s
Schiller's/19/Low E Side
Shopsin's/20/G Vil.
Terra 47/21/G Vil.
Trinity/–/TriBeCa
WD-50/23/Low E Side
Whole Foods Café/19/W 50s
World Yacht/14/W 40s
Zeytuna/19/Fin. District

Egyptian

Casa La Femme/17/E 50s

English

(See also Fish and Chips)
Spotted Pig/22/G Vil.
Tea & Sympathy/20/G Vil.
UK New York/–/TriBeCa

Ethiopian

Ethiopian/20/E 80s
Ghenet/21/NoLita
Meskerem/20/multi. loc.

European

August/23/G Vil.

Filipino

Cendrillon/22/SoHo
Kuma Inn/24/Low E Side

Fish and Chips

A Salt & Battery/19/multi. loc.
Chip/CurryShop/18/Park Slope

French

A.O.C. Bedford/23/G Vil.
Bambou/21/E Vil.
Barbès/22/Murray Hill
Bayard's/23/Fin. District
Bistro Le Steak/18/E 70s
Black Cat/–/E Vil.
Bouterin/21/E 50s
Café Boulud/27/E 70s
Café des Artistes/22/W 60s
Cafe Gitane/20/NoLita
Café Pierre/23/E 60s
Cocotte/22/Park Slope
Darna/20/W 80s

Django/20/E 40s
Fives/24/W 50s
Fleur de Sel/25/Flatiron
44/20/W 40s
Gavroche/–/G Vil.
Indochine/21/G Vil.
Ivo & Lulu/23/SoHo
Jack's Luxury/24/E Vil.
Kitchen Club/22/Little Italy
La Baraka/20/Little Neck
La Bergamote/26/Chelsea
La Boîte en Bois/22/W 60s
La Metairie/23/G Vil.
Landmarc/24/TriBeCa
Le Bernardin/28/W 50s
Le Colonial/21/E 50s
Les Enfants Terribles/21/Low E Side
L'Orange Blouc/17/So/lo
Loulou/22/Ft. Greene
Mark's/23/E 70s
Mercer Kitchen/22/SoHo
Mix in NY/18/W 50s
Montrachet/25/TriBeCa
Once Upon a Tart/21/SoHo
per se/29/W 60s
René Pujol/22/W 50s
Rêve/–/E 70s
Revival/20/Harlem
Rhône/17/Meatpacking
718/23/Astoria
Sherwood Cafe/18/Boerum Hill
Soho Steak/19/SoHo
Terrace in Sky/22/W 100s
26 Seats/23/E Vil.
Uguale/22/G Vil.
Vong/24/E 50s
Willow/17/E 70s

French (Bistro)

A/22/W 100s
Alouette/20/W 90s
A.O.C./18/G Vil.
À Table/19/Ft. Greene
Bacchus/20/Boerum Hill
Banania Cafe/21/Cobble Hill
BarTabac/17/Boerum Hill
Belleville/21/Park Slope
Bistro Cassis/22/Chelsea
Bistro du Nord/18/E 90s
Bistro Les Amis/21/SoHo
Bistro St. Mark's/21/Park Slope
Bistrot Margot/17/NoLita
Brasserie Julien/18/E 80s
Cafe Joul/20/E 50s
Cafe Loup/18/G Vil.
Cafe Luluc/20/Cobble Hill
Cafe Luxembourg/20/W 70s
Cafe Un Deux/15/W 40s
CamaJe/21/G Vil.

French (Brasserie)

French (New)

14 Wall Street/*19/Fin. District*
Jean Georges/*27/W 60s*
Le Cirque 2000/*25/E 50s*
Métisse/*21/W 100s*
Pascalou/*21/E 90s*
Petrossian/*24/W 50s*
Picholine/*26/W 60s*
Savann/*20/W 70s*
360/*24/Red Hook*
Tocqueville/*26/Union Sq.*
Triomphe/*25/W 40s*
212/*18/E 60s*
Village/*20/G Vil.*

German

Hallo Berlin/*19/multi. loc.*
Heidelberg/*17/E 80s*
Killmeyer's/*17/Staten Is*
Rolf's/*17/Gramercy*
Zum Schneider/*18/E Vil.*
Zum Stammtisch/*23/Glendale*

Greek

Avra Estiatorio/*23/E 40s*
Cávo/*20/Astoria*
Christos Hasapo/*21/Astoria*
Eliá/*26/Bay Ridge*
Elias Corner/*23/Astoria*
Esperides/*24/Astoria*
Ethos/*21/Murray Hill*
Gus' Place/*20/G Vil.*
Ithaka/*19/E 80s*
Karyatis/*20/Astoria*
Kyma/*19/W 40s*
Meltemi/*20/E 50s*
Metsovo/*17/W 70s*
Milos/*25/W 50s*
Molyvos/*23/W 50s*
Niko's Med. Grill/*18/W 70s*
Omonia Cafe/*18/multi. loc.*
Periyali/*25/Flatiron*
Pylos/*24/E Vil.*
S'Agapo/*22/Astoria*
Snack/*23/SoHo*
Snack Taverna/*22/G Vil.*
Stamatis/*23/Astoria*
Symposium/*19/W 100s*
Taverna Kyclades/*24/Astoria*
Telly's Taverna/*22/Astoria*
Thalassa/*24/TriBeCa*
Trata Estiatorio/*22/E 70s*
Uncle George's/*18/Astoria*
Uncle Nick's/*20/W 50s*

Haitian

Kombit/*–/Prospect Heights*

Hamburgers

Better Burger/*15/multi. loc.*
Big Nick's Burger/*17/W 70s*

Blue 9 Burger/*19/E Vil.*
Boat Basin Cafe/*11/W 70s*
Burger Heaven/*16/multi. loc.*
burger joint/*24/W 50s*
Chelsea Grill/*17/Chelsea*
Cité Grill/*20/W 50s*
Corner Bistro/*23/G Vil.*
Cozy Soup/Burger/*18/G Vil.*
db Bistro Moderne/*25/W 40s*
DuMont/*21/Williamsburg*
Fanelli's Cafe/*15/SoHo*
Hard Rock Cafe/*12/W 50s*
Houston's/*20/Gramercy*
Island Burgers/*23/W 50s*
Jackson Hole/*17/multi. loc.*
J.G. Melon/*21/E 70s*
Johnny Rockets/*14/G Vil.*
Luke's Bar/Grill/*17/E 70s*
Mama's Food /*22/G Vil.*
McHales/*20/W 40s*
New York Burger/*–/Flatiron*
P.J. Clarke's/*16/E 50s*
Pop Burger/*19/Meatpacking*
Rare B&G/*19/Murray Hill*
Sparky's/*20/Williamsburg*
White Horse Tav./*12/G Vil.*
Wollensky's Grill/*23/E 40s*

Hawaiian

Roy's NY/*25/Fin. District*

Hot Dogs

F & B/*19/multi. loc.*
Gray's Papaya/*20/multi. loc.*
Papaya King/*21/multi. loc.*
Sparky's/*20/Williamsburg*

Hungarian

Mocca/*19/E 80s*

Ice Cream Parlor

Emack & Bolio's/*23/multi. loc.*
L & B Spumoni/*23/Bensonhurst*
Serendipity 3/*20/E 60s*

Indian

Adä/*23/E 50s*
Amma/*23/E 50s*
Baluchi's/*18/multi. loc.*
Banjara/*24/E Vil.*
Bay Leaf/*19/W 50s*
Bombay Palace/*18/W 50s*
Bread Bar at Tabla/*24/Gramercy*
Brick Lane Curry/*20/E Vil.*
Bukhara Grill/*21/E 40s*
Cafe Spice/*19/multi. loc.*
Cardamomm/*19/Gramercy*
Chennai Garden/*22/Gramercy*
Chip/CurryShop/*18/Park Slope*
Chola/*24/E 50s*

Curry Leaf/20/multi. loc.
Dakshin Indian/18/multi. loc.
Darbar/–/E 40s
Dawat/23/E 50s
Delhi Palace/22/Jackson Hts.
Diwan/22/E 40s
Hampton Chutney/22/SoHo
Haveli/21/E Vil.
Indus Valley/23/W 100s
Jackson Diner/23/Jackson Hts.
Jewel of India/20/W 40s
Kalustyan's/–/Gramercy
Mirchi/21/G Vil.
Mitali/19/E Vil.
Mughlai/19/W 70s
Pongal/22/Gramercy
Raga/23/E Vil.
Salaam Bombay/22/TriBeCa
Sapphire Indian/20/W 60s
Shaan/20/W 40s
Spice Market/23/Meatpacking
Surya/23/G Vil.
Swagat Indian/23/W 70s
Tabla/26/Gramercy
Tamarind/25/Flatiron
Turmeric/–/Flatiron
Utsav/21/W 40s
Vatan/22/Gramercy

Irish

Neary's/16/E 50s

Israeli

Azuri Cafe/24/W 50s

Italian

(N=Northern; S=Southern)
Acappella (N)/24/TriBeCa
Acqua (S)/17/W 90s
Acqua Pazza/22/W 50s
Al Di La (N)/25/Park Slope
Aleo (N)/20/Flatiron
Alfredo of Rome (S)/17/W 40s
Aliseo Osteria/23/Prospect Heights
Amarone/18/W 40s
Amici Amore I/19/Astoria
Angelina's (S)/22/Staten Is.
Angelo's/Mulb. (S)/22/Little Italy
ápizz/23/Low E Side
Areo/24/Bay Ridge
Arezzo (N)/22/Flatiron
Arqua (N)/23/TriBeCa
Arté (N)/18/G Vil.
Arturo's Pizzeria/21/G Vil.
Assaggio (N)/19/W 80s
Azalea (N)/20/W 50s
Babbo/27/G Vil.
Baci/21/Bay Ridge
Baldoria/19/W 40s

Baldo Vino (N)/19/E Vil.
Bamonte's/21/Williamsburg
Baraonda (N)/18/E 70s
Barbalùc/20/E 60s
Barbetta (N)/20/W 40s
Barbuto/20/G Vil.
Barolo (N)/17/SoHo
Bar Pitti (N)/21/G Vil.
Bar Tonno/–/NoLita
Basso Est/22/Low E Side
Basta Pasta/19/Flatiron
Becco (N)/21/W 40s
Bella Blu (N)/19/E 70s
Bella Donna/17/E 70s
Bella Luna (N)/16/W 80s
Bella Via/20/LIC
Bellini/22/E 50s
Bello (N)/19/W 50s
Belluno (N)/21/Murray Hill
Beppe (N)/22/Flatiron
Bettola/–/W 70s
Bianca (N)/22/NoHo
Bice (N)/20/E 50s
Biricchino (N)/20/Chelsea
Bivio (N)/21/G Vil.
Borgo Antico/18/G Vil.
Bottino (N)/18/Chelsea
Bravo Gianni/21/E 60s
Bread Tribeca (N)/19/TriBeCa
Bricco (S)/18/W 50s
Brick Cafe (N)/23/Astoria
Brio/19/E 60s
Bruculino (S)/17/W 70s
Bruno/21/E 50s
Cacio e Pepe (S)/–/E Vil.
Cafe Nosidam/19/E 60s
Cafe Trevi (N)/21/E 80s
Caffe Buon Gusto/18/multi. loc.
Caffe Cielo (N)/19/W 50s
Caffe Grazie/18/E 80s
Caffe Linda/19/E 40s
Caffé/Green (N)/20/Bayside
Caffe Rafaella (N)/17/G Vil.
Caffe Reggio/17/G Vil.
Campagnola (S)/24/E 70s
Canaletto (N)/21/E 60s
Cantinella/23/E Vil.
Cara Mia/21/W 40s
Carino (S)/18/E 80s
Carmine's (S)/20/multi. loc.
Casa Mia/20/Gramercy
Cascina/19/W 40s
Caserta Vecc. (S)/21/Carroll Gdns.
Celeste (S)/24/W 80s
Cellini (N)/23/E 50s
Centolire (N)/20/E 80s
'Cesca (S)/24/W 70s
Chelsea Ristorante (N)/20/Chelsea
Chianti/22/Bay Ridge

Cuisine Index

Scopa (N)/*20/Gramercy*
Serafina (S)/*19/multi. loc.*
Sette/*20/Chelsea*
Sette Mezzo/*23/E 70s*
Sirabella's (N)/*23/E 80s*
Sistina (N)/*24/E 80s*
Sosa Borella/*20/multi. loc.*
Spotted Pig/*22/G Vil.*
Stella del Mare (N)/*23/Murray Hill*
Supper (N)/*23/E Vil.*
Taormina/*21/Little Italy*
Tello's/*17/Chelsea*
Teodora (N)/*20/E 50s*
Terra/*17/W 50s*
Tevere/*22/E 80s*
Three of Cups (S)/*18/E Vil.*
Tommaso's/*21/Bensonhurst*
Tony's Di Napoli (S)/*19/multi. loc.*
Torre di Pisa (N)/*19/W 40s*
Totonno Pizzeria/*24/multi. loc.*
Trattoria Alba (N)/*19/Murray Hill*
Trattoria Dell'Arte/*22/W 50s*
Trattoria Dopo/*16/W 40s*
Trattoria L'incontro/*27/Astoria*
Trattoria Pesce/*18/multi. loc.*
Trattoria Romana/*24/Staten Is.*
Tre Pomodori (N)/*19/multi. loc.*
Triangolo/*21/E 80s*
Tuscan (N)/*19/E 40s*
Tuscan Square (N)/*17/W 50s*
Tuscany Grill (N)/*24/Bay Ridge*
Two Boots/*19/E Vil.*
212/*18/E 60s*
Uguale/*22/G Vil.*
Umberto's Clam/*19/multi. loc.*
Va Bene/*19/E 80s*
Vago/*18/W 50s*
V&T/*20/W 100s*
Va Tutto (N)/*19/NoLita*
Veniero's/*23/E Vil.*
Vento/*21/Meatpacking*
Veronica/*21/Garment*
Via Emilia (N)/*21/Flatiron*
Via Oreto (S)/*20/E 60s*
Via Quadronno (N)/*21/E 70s*
ViceVersa (N)/*22/W 50s*
Vico/*21/E 90s*
Villa Berulia (N)/*22/Murray Hill*
Villa Mosconi (N)/*21/G Vil.*
Vincent's (S)/*21/Little Italy*
Vinnie's Pizza/*21/W 70s*
Vittorio Cucina/*23/G Vil.*
Vivolo/*20/E 70s*

Jamaican

Aki/*26/G Vil.*
Bambou/*21/E Vil.*
Maroons/*21/Chelsea*
Mo-Bay/*22/multi. loc.*

Japanese

(* sushi specialist)
Aki/*26/G Vil.*
Aki Sushi/*18/multi. loc.*
Angura/*–/E Vil.*
Asiate/*22/W 60s*
Avenue A Sushi/*17/E Vil.*
Bar Masa/*22/W 60s*
Benihana*/*16/multi. loc.*
Blue Ribbon Sushi*/*26/multi. loc.*
Bond Street*/*25/NoHo*
Choshi/*18/Gramercy*
Cube 63/*23/Low E Side*
Dojo/*14/multi. loc.*
Donguri/*28/E 80s*
East*/*16/multi. loc.*
Fujiyama Mama*/*19/W 80s*
Geisha/*22/E 60s*
Haru*/*22/multi. loc.*
Hasaki/*24/E Vil.*
Honmura An/*26/SoHo*
Ichiro*/*–/E 80s*
Inagiku/*23/E 40s*
Iron Sushi*/*19/Murray Hill*
Ivy's Cafe/*18/W 70s*
Japonica/*22/G Vil.*
Jewel Bako*/*27/E Vil.*
Kai/*27/E 60s*
Katsu-Hama*/*22/E 40s*
Kitchen Club/*22/Little Italy*
Kodama*/*19/W 40s*
Koi/*25/E Vil.*
Ko Sushi/*19/multi. loc.*
Kuruma Zushi*/*26/E 40s*
Lan*/*22/E Vil.*
Masa*/*28/W 60s*
Matsuri/*23/Chelsea*
Megu/*23/TriBeCa*
Menchanko-tei/*19/multi. loc.*
Minado/*19/Murray Hill*
Mishima*/*23/Murray Hill*
Mizu Sushi*/*24/Flatiron*
Monster Sushi*/*18/multi. loc.*
Nëo Sushi*/*23/W 80s*
Nippon*/*22/E 50s*
Nobu*/*28/TriBeCa*
Nobu Next Door*/*28/TriBeCa*
Omen/*24/SoHo*
Ony*/*18/multi. loc.*
Osaka/*23/Cobble Hill*
Ota-Ya/*22/E 80s*
Planet Thailand/*21/Williamsburg*
Poke*/*26/E 80s*
Prime Grill*/*22/E 40s*
Riingo*/*20/E 40s*
Roppongi*/*20/W 80s*
Sandobe*/*20/E Vil.*
Sapporo East*/*23/E Vil.*

Nick and Toni's/18/W 60s
Niko's Med. Grill/18/W 70s
Nisos/17/Chelsea
Olives/23/Union Sq.
Oznot's Dish/19/Williamsburg
Park/16/Chelsea
Picholine/26/W 60s
Place/22/G Vil.
Porters/17/Chelsea
Provence/22/SoHo
Provence en Boite/22/Bay Ridge
Red Cat/24/Chelsea
Savann/20/W 70s
Savoy/23/SoHo
Sezz Medi'/22/W 100s
Sharz Cafe/19/E 80s
Solera/21/E 50s
Solo/ /E 50s
Superfine/19/Dumbo
Taboon/23/W 50s
Terrace in Sky/22/W 100s
Trio/23/Murray Hill
Uncle Nick's/20/W 50s
Zerza/21/E Vil.

Mexican

Alma/22/Carroll Gdns.
Blockhead Burrito/17/multi. loc.
Bonita/22/Williamsburg
Bright Food Shop/19/Chelsea
Café Frida/19/W 70s
Café Habana/22/NoLita
Chango/16/Flatiron
Chipotle/20/multi. loc.
Cosmic Cantina/17/E Vil.
Dos Caminos/21/multi. loc.
El Parador Cafe/22/Murray Hill
El Paso Taqueria/22/E 90s
Gabriela's/17/multi. loc.
Hell's Kitchen/23/W 40s
Itzocan/25/multi. loc.
Ixta/–/Gramercy
La Palapa/21/multi. loc.
Lucy /18/Flatiron
Mamá Mexico/19/multi. loc.
Maya/24/E 60s
Maz Mezcal/20/E 80s
Mex. Mama/26/G Vil.
Mexican Radio/20/NoLita
Mexican Sandwich/20/Park Slope
Mi Cocina/23/G Vil.
Pacifico/19/Boerum Hill
Pampano/25/E 40s
Rocking Horse/22/Chelsea
Rosa Mexicano/23/multi. loc.
Salsa y Salsa/19/Chelsea
Soho Cantina/–/SoHo
Sueños/22/Chelsea
Tio Pepe/18/G Vil.

Vera Cruz/18/Williamsburg
Zarela/21/E 50s
Zócalo/20/multi. loc.
Zona Rosa/20/W 50s

Middle Eastern

Layla/18/TriBeCa
Mamlouk/24/E Vil.
Moustache/22/multi. loc.
Olive Vine Cafe/18/Park Slope
Oznot's Dish/19/Williamsburg
Sahara/21/Gravesend
Salam Cafe/19/G Vil.
Taboon/23/W 50s
Tanoreen/24/Bay Ridge
Zaytoons/22/multi. loc.

Moroccan

Barbès/22/Murray Hill
Bleu Evolution/17/Wash. Hts. & Up
Cafe Gitane/20/NoLita
Cafe Mogador/22/E Vil.
Chez Es Saada/17/E Vil.
Country Café/21/SoHo
Darna/20/W 80s
Le Souk/16/E Vil.
Medina/–/Chelsea
Salam Cafe/19/G Vil.
Zerza/21/E Vil.
Zitoune/18/Meatpacking

New England

Mary's Fish Camp/24/G Vil.
Pearl Oyster/27/G Vil.
Shore/19/TriBeCa

Noodle Shops

Bao Noodles/20/Gramercy
Big Wong/22/Ctown
Great NY Noodle/23/Ctown
Honmura An/26/SoHo
Kelley & Ping/18/SoHo
Lili's Noodle/17/multi. loc.
Mee Noodle Shop/17/multi. loc.
Menchanko-tei/19/multi. loc.
New Bo-Ky/21/Ctown
Ollie's/16/multi. loc.
Ony/18/multi. loc.
Pho Bang/20/multi. loc.
Pho Viet Huong/20/Ctown
Republic/18/Union Sq.
Sam's Noodle Shop/19/Gramercy
Soba Nippon/21/W 50s
Sobaya/23/E Vil.
Sweet-n-Tart Cafe/19/multi. loc.
Sweet-n-Tart Rest./19/Ctown

Nuevo Latino

Beso/22/Park Slope
Cabana/21/multi. loc.

Calle Ocho/*22/W 80s*
Citrus Bar & Grill/*19/W 70s*
Cuba Libre/*18/Chelsea*
DR-K/*22/Wash. Hts. & Up*
Esperanto/*20/E Vil.*
Hispaniola/*20/Wash. Hts. & Up*
Mojo/*22/E Vil.*
OLA/*22/E 40s*
Paladar/*18/Low E Side*
Patria/*23/Flatiron*
Sabor/*19/multi. loc.*

Pan-Latin
Yuca Bar/*21/E Vil.*

Persian/Iranian
Persepolis/*20/E 70s*

Peruvian
Cholita/*18/Boerum Hill*
Coco Roco/*20/Park Slope*
Flor de Mayo/*20/multi. loc.*
Lima's Taste/*18/E Vil.*
Mancora/*20/multi. loc.*
Sipan/*20/W 90s*
SushiSamba/*22/Flatiron*

Pizza
Al Forno Pizza/*22/E 70s*
Angelo's Pizza/*20/multi. loc.*
ápizz/*23/Low E Side*
Arturo's Pizzeria/*21/G Vil.*
Bella Blu/*19/E 70s*
Cal. Pizza Kitchen/*15/E 60s*
Cascina/*19/W 40s*
Caserta Vecchia/*21/Carroll Gdns.*
Dee's Pizza/*23/Forest Hills*
Denino's/*24/Staten Is.*
Di Fara/*27/Midwood*
Don Giovanni/*18/multi. loc.*
Franny's/*–/Prospect Heights*
Gonzo/*22/G Vil.*
Grimaldi's/*26/Dumbo*
Joe's Pizza/*24/multi. loc.*
John's Pizzeria/*22/multi. loc.*
La Bottega/*18/Chelsea*
L & B Spumoni/*23/Bensonhurst*
La Pizza Fresca/*20/Flatiron*
L'Asso/*–/NoLita*
La Villa Pizzeria/*20/multi. loc.*
Lento's/*21/multi. loc.*
Lil' Frankie's Pizza/*23/E Vil.*
Little Italy Pizza/*22/multi. loc.*
Lombardi's/*26/NoLita*
Mediterraneo/*19/E 60s*
Mezzaluna/*19/E 70s*
Naples 45/*18/E 40s*
Nick's/*23/multi. loc.*
Otto/*21/G Vil.*
Patsy's Pizzeria/*21/multi. loc.*

Pie/*17/E Vil.*
Pinch, Pizza/*21/Gramercy*
Pintaile's Pizza/*19/multi. loc.*
Pizza 33/*22/multi. loc.*
Savoia/*22/Carroll Gdns.*
Sezz Medi'/*22/W 100s*
Slice of Harlem/*20/Harlem*
Three of Cups/*18/E Vil.*
Totonno Pizzeria/*24/multi. loc.*
Two Boots/*19/multi. loc.*
Uno Chicago Grill/*15/multi. loc.*
V&T/*20/W 100s*
Vinnie's Pizza/*21/W 70s*

Polish
Teresa's/*17/multi. loc.*

Portuguese
Alfama/*22/G Vil.*
Alphabet Kitchen/*19/E Vil.*
Carvao/*18/E 70s*
Pão!/*22/SoHo*

Puerto Rican
La Taza de Oro/*19/Chelsea*

Russian
Caviarteria/*23/E 50s*
FireBird/*22/W 40s*
Rasputin/*18/Sheepshead Bay*
Russian Samovar/*20/W 50s*

Sandwiches
Amy's Bread/*23/multi. loc.*
Artie's Deli/*17/W 80s*
Barney Greengrass/*23/W 80s*
BB Sandwich/*23/W 40s*
Ben's Kosher Deli/*17/multi. loc.*
Bread Tribeca/*19/NoLita*
Brennan & Carr/*21/Sheepshead Bay*
Carl's Steaks/*22/Murray Hill*
Carnegie Deli/*20/W 50s*
Cosí/*17/multi. loc.*
Dishes/*21/E 40s*
E.A.T./*18/E 80s*
Ess-a-Bagel/*23/multi. loc.*
Grey Dog's Coffee/*22/G Vil.*
Grilled Cheese/*20/Low E Side*
Hale & Hearty/*19/multi. loc.*
Katz's Deli/*22/Low E Side*
Panino'teca 275/*22/Carroll Gdns.*
Pastrami Queen/*18/E 80s*
Peanut Butter/Co./*19/G Vil.*
Press 195/*20/Park Slope*
Sarge's Deli/*19/Murray Hill*
Second Ave Deli/*23/E Vil.*
71 Irving Place/*19/Gramercy*
Stage Deli/*18/W 50s*
Starwich/*–/W 40s*
Sweet Melissa/*23/Cobble Hill*

'wichcraft/*22/Flatiron*
Zabar's Cafe/*20/W 80s*

Scandinavian
AQ Cafe/*20/Murray Hill*
Aquavit/*26/W 50s*
Ulrika's/*21/E 60s*

Seafood
Acqua Pazza/*22/W 50s*
Aquagrill/*27/SoHo*
Atlantic Grill/*23/E 70s*
Avra Estiatorio/*23/E 40s*
Bar Tonno/–/*NoLita*
Black Duck/*20/Gramercy*
Blue Fin/*22/W 40s*
Blue Water/*24/Union Sq.*
Bubba Gump/*15/W 40s*
City Crab/*18/Flatiron*
City Hall/*21/TriBeCa*
City Lobster/*19/W 40s*
Docks Oyster Bar/*19/multi. loc.*
Dolphins/*17/E Vil.*
East West/–/*Park Slope*
Elias Corner/*23/Astoria*
Esca/*24/W 40s*
Fish/*20/G Vil.*
Foley's Fish/*20/W 40s*
Francisco's Centro/*21/Chelsea*
fresh./*23/TriBeCa*
Frutti di Mare/*17/E Vil.*
Fuleen Seafood/*23/Ctown*
Jack's Luxury/*24/E Vil.*
Josephs/–/*W 40s*
Jubilee/*22/E 50s*
Kam Chueh/*23/Ctown*
Lake Club/*20/Staten Is.*
Le Bernardin/*28/W 50s*
Le Pescadou/*20/SoHo*
Lobster Box/*16/Bronx*
London Lennie's/*20/Rego Park*
Lundy Bros./*15/Sheepshead Bay*
Manhattan Ocean/*24/W 50s*
Marina Cafe/*17/Staten Is.*
Mary's Fish Camp/*24/G Vil.*
McCormick & Schmick's/–/*W 50s*
Meltemi/*20/E 50s*
Mermaid Inn/*23/E Vil.*
Metro Fish/*19/Murray Hill*
Milos/*25/W 50s*
Minado/*19/Murray Hill*
Minnow/*22/Park Slope*
Moran's Chelsea/*19/Chelsea*
Morton's Steak/*23/E 40s*
Neptune Room/–/*W 80s*
Novecento/*21/SoHo*
Oak Room/*18/W 50s*
Oceana/*26/E 50s*
Ocean Grill/*22/W 70s*
Oriental Garden/*25/Ctown*

Oyster Bar/*21/E 40s*
Oyster Bar/Plaza/*19/W 50s*
Pacific Grill/–/*Seaport*
Pampano/*25/E 40s*
Pão!/*22/SoHo*
Pearl Oyster/*27/G Vil.*
Pearl Room/*24/Bay Ridge*
Pescatore/*18/E 50s*
Ping's Seafood/*21/multi. loc.*
Red Garlic/*19/W 50s*
rm/*25/E 60s*
Roy's NY/*25/Fin. District*
Sea Grill/*24/W 40s*
Shaffer City/*23/Flatiron*
Shelly's NY/*20/W 50s*
Shore/*19/TriBeCa*
St. Andrews/*18/W 40s*
Steamers/*18/Fin. District*
Stella del Mare/*23/Murray Hill*
Svenningsen's/*18/Garment*
Taverna Kyclades/*24/Astoria*
Telly's Taverna/*22/Astoria*
Thalassa/*24/TriBeCa*
Trata Estiatorio/*22/E 70s*
Tropica/*22/E 40s*
Umberto's Clam/*19/Little Italy*
Water's Edge/*23/LIC*

Small Plates
Alta/*21/G Vil.*
Bar Tonno/–/*NoLita*
Bello Sguardo/*22/W 70s*
Bread Bar at Tabla/*24/Gramercy*
Craftbar/*23/Flatiron*
Cru/–/*G Vil.*
Dish/*18/Low E Side*
Gonzo/*22/G Vil.*
Grace/*17/TriBeCa*
Kittichai/–/*SoHo*
La Table O & Co./*18/SoHo*
Le Zoccole/*20/E Vil.*
OLA/*22/E 40s*
One/*18/Meatpacking*
Perbacco/*23/E Vil.*
Plantain/*22/Garment*
Rocking Horse/*22/Chelsea*
Scopa/*20/Gramercy*
Share/–/*E Vil.*
Sumile/*24/G Vil.*
Taste/*20/E 80s*
Tasting Room/*27/E Vil.*

Soul Food
Amy Ruth's/*21/Harlem*
Brother Jimmy's BBQ/*17/multi. loc.*
Charles' Southern/*21/Harlem*
Duke's/*17/Gramercy*
Kitchenette/*19/multi. loc.*
Miss Mamie's/*22/Harlem*
Mo-Bay/*22/multi. loc.*

Old Devil Moon/20/E Vil.
Pink Tea Cup/20/G Vil.
Shark Bar/21/W 70s
Sylvia's/16/Harlem

Soup
Hale & Hearty/19/multi. loc.
Soup Kitchen Int'l/25/W 50s

South African
Madiba/20/Ft. Greene

South American
Boca Chica/21/E Vil.
Cafe Ronda/20/W 70s
Don Pedro's/20/E 90s
Paladar/18/Low E Side
Patria/23/Flatiron
Sabor/19/multi. loc.
SushiSamba/22/G Vil.

Southern
Amy Ruth's/21/Harlem
Biscuit/18/Prospect Heights
Bourbon St. Cafe/17/Bayside
Brother Jimmy's BBQ/17/multi. loc.
B. Smith's/18/W 40s
Charles' Southern/21/Harlem
Chat 'n Chew/17/multi. loc.
Duke's/17/Gramercy
Earl's/16/Murray Hill
Ida Mae/22/Garment
Jack's Luxury/24/E Vil.
Jezebel/19/W 40s
Justin's/15/Flatiron
Kitchenette/19/multi. loc.
Liquors/19/Ft. Greene
Londel's/21/Harlem
Maroons/21/Chelsea
Miss Mamie's/22/Harlem
Natchez/22/E Vil.
Old Devil Moon/20/E Vil.
Pink Tea Cup/20/G Vil.
Sylvia's/16/Harlem

Southwestern
Agave/19/G Vil.
Canyon Road/20/E 70s
Cilantro/17/multi. loc.
Cowgirl/16/G Vil.
Los Dos Molinos/19/Gramercy
Mesa Grill/23/Flatiron
Miracle Grill/20/multi. loc.
Route 66 Cafe/17/W 50s
SouthWest NY/13/Fin. District

Spanish
(* tapas specialist)
Allioli*/22/Williamsburg
Alphabet Kitchen/19/E Vil.
Azafran*/22/TriBeCa
Bolo*/23/Flatiron
Cafe Español/20/G Vil.
Casa Mono*/24/Gramercy
El Charro Español/21/G Vil.
El Cid*/22/Chelsea
El Faro/22/G Vil.
El Pote/20/Murray Hill
El Quijote/18/Chelsea
Euzkadi/18/E Vil.
Flor de Sol/20/TriBeCa
Francisco's Centro/21/Chelsea
La Paella*/21/E Vil.
Marichu*/21/E 40s
Ñ*/20/SoHo
Oliva/21/Low E Side
Pipa*/20/Flatiron
Sala/19/NoHo
718/23/Astoria
Sevilla/22/G Vil.
Solera*/21/E 50s
Suba*/18/Low E Side
Tio Pepe/18/G Vil.
Xunta*/20/E Vil.
Zipi Zape*/–/Williamsburg

Steakhouses
Angelo & Maxie's/21/Flatiron
Ben Benson's/22/W 50s
Benihana/16/multi. loc.
Bistro Le Steak/18/E 70s
BLT Steak/24/E 50s
Bobby Van's/23/multi. loc.
Bull & Bear/20/E 40s
Capital Grille/–/E 40s
Carne/17/W 100s
Chadwick's/22/Bay Ridge
Christos Hasapo/21/Astoria
Churrascaria Plata./22/multi. loc.
Cité/22/W 50s
Cité Grill/20/W 50s
City Hall/21/TriBeCa
Del Frisco's/24/W 40s
Delmonico's/21/Fin. District
Dylan Prime/23/TriBeCa
Embers/22/Bay Ridge
Fairway Cafe/19/W 70s
Frankie & Johnnie/22/multi. loc.
Frank's/20/Meatpacking
Gallagher's Steak/19/W 50s
Green Field/18/Corona
Hacienda Argentina/20/E 70s
Keens Steak/23/Garment
Knickerbocker/19/G Vil.
Le Marais/21/W 40s
Les Halles/20/multi. loc.
Macelleria/21/Meatpacking
Maloney & Porcelli/23/E 50s
Manhattan Grille/20/E 60s

MarkJoseph Steak/25/Fin. District
Michael Jordan's/20/E 40s
Monkey Bar/18/E 50s
Moran's Chelsea/19/Chelsea
Morton's Steak/23/E 40s
Napa/Son. Steak/19/Whitestone
Nebraska Steak/24/multi. loc.
Nick & Stef's Steak/20/Garment
Oak Room/18/W 50s
Old Homestead/23/Meatpacking
Outback Steak/15/multi. loc.
Palm/24/multi. loc.
Patroon/21/E 40s
Peter Luger/27/Williamsburg
Pietro's/22/E 40s
Post House/24/E 60s
Prime Grill/22/E 40s
Rothmann's/22/E 50s
Roth's Steak/19/W 90s
Ruth's Chris/23/multi. loc.
Shelly's NY/20/W 50s
Shula's Steak/20/W 40s
Smith & Wollensky/23/E 40s
Soho Steak/19/SoHo
Sparks Steak/25/E 40s
St. Andrews/18/W 40s
Steak Frites/17/Union Sq.
Strip House/25/G Vil.
Talia's Steak/20/W 90s
Tupelo Grill/18/Garment
Tuscan/19/E 40s
Uncle Jack's/22/multi. loc.
V Steakhouse/–/W 60s
Wolfgang's Steak/24/Murray Hill
Wollensky's Grill/23/E 40s

Tex-Mex

Burritoville/17/multi. loc.
Cowgirl/16/G Vil.
Mary Ann's/16/multi. loc.
107 West/17/multi. loc.

Thai

Bann Thai/21/Forest Hills
Basil/20/Chelsea
Chanpen Thai/19/W 50s
Elephant/22/E Vil.
Erawan/25/Bayside
Highline/–/Meatpacking
Holy Basil/23/E Vil.
Jaiya Thai/22/Gramercy
Jasmine/20/E 80s
Joya/23/Cobble Hill
Kin Khao/23/SoHo
Kittichai/–/SoHo
Kuma Inn/24/Low E Side
Lemongrass Grill/17/multi. loc.
Long Tan/19/Park Slope
Pad Thai/16/Chelsea

Pam Real Thai/22/W 40s
Peep/21/SoHo
Planet Thailand/21/Williamsburg
Pongsri Thai/19/multi. loc.
Q, a Thai Bistro/21/Forest Hills
Red Garlic/19/W 50s
Regional Thai/18/multi. loc.
River/18/W 70s
Royal Siam/20/Chelsea
Sala Thai/21/E 80s
SEA/22/multi. loc.
Siam Inn/21/W 50s
Spice/20/multi. loc.
Spice Market/23/Meatpacking
Sripraphai/27/Woodside
Topaz Thai/20/W 50s
Tuk Tuk/21/Cobble Hill
Typhoon/17/E 50s
Ubol's Kitchen/25/Astoria
Vong/24/E 50s
Wild Ginger/19/G Vil.
Wondee Siam/23/W 50s

Tibetan

Tsampa/19/E Vil.

Tunisian

Epices du Traiteur/21/W 70s

Turkish

Akdeniz/–/W 40s
Bereket/20/Low E Side
Beyoglu/20/E 80s
Dervish Turkish/19/W 40s
Divane/20/W 50s
Hemsin/21/Sunnyside
Kapadokya/20/Bklyn Hts.
Maia/–/E Vil.
Pasha/21/W 70s
Sip Sak/–/E 40s
Sultan/20/E 70s
Taksim/21/E 50s
Turkish Kitchen/22/Gramercy
Turkuaz/20/W 100s
Üsküdar/21/E 70s
Zeytin/20/W 80s

Vegetarian

(* vegan)
Angelica Kitchen*/20/E Vil.
Candle Cafe/79*/22/E 70s
Chennai Garden/22/Gramercy
Chop't Salad/20/Union Sq.
Counter/23/E Vil.
East West/–/Park Slope
Franchia/23/Murray Hill
Gobo*/24/G Vil.
Hangawi*/23/Murray Hill
Pongal/22/Gramercy
Pure Food*/–/Gramercy

Quartino/*22/NoHo*
Quintessence*/*17/multi. loc.*
Spring St. Natural/*17/NoLita*
Tanoreen/*24/Bay Ridge*
teany*/*20/Low E Side*
Terra 47/*21/G Vil.*
Tossed/*19/multi. loc.*
Tsampa/*19/E Vil.*
Vatan/*22/Gramercy*
Veg. Paradise/*20/multi. loc.*
Zen Palate/*19/multi. loc.*

Venezuelan

Caracas Arepa Bar/*21/E Vil.*
Flor's Kitchen/*20/multi. loc.*

Vietnamese

Anh/*19/Gramercy*
Bao Noodles/*20/Gramercy*
Bao 111/*23/E Vil.*
Boi/*23/E 40s*
Cyclo/*19/E Vil.*
Hue/*19/G Vil.*
Indochine/*21/G Vil.*
L'Annam/*18/multi. loc.*
Le Colonial/*21/E 50s*
MeKong/*18/multi. loc.*
Miss Saigon/*18/E 80s*
Monsoon/*19/W 80s*
Nam/*24/TriBeCa*
New Pasteur/*21/Ctown*
Nha Trang/*22/Ctown*
O Mai/*23/Chelsea*
Pho Bang/*20/multi. loc.*
Pho Viet Huong/*20/Ctown*
River/*18/W 70s*
Saigon Grill/*23/multi. loc.*
Vermicelli/*20/E 70s*

Manhattan

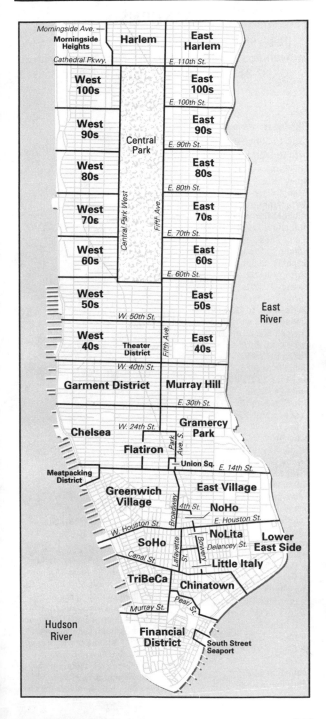

LOCATIONS

(Restaurant name followed by its street location.
A=Avenue, s=Street, e.g. 1A/116s=First Ave. at 116th St.;
3A/82-3s=Third Ave. between 82nd & 83rd Sts.)

MANHATTAN

Chelsea

(24th to 30th Sts., west of 5th;
14th to 24th Sts., west of 6th)

Amuse *18s/6-7A*
Amy's Bread *9A/15-6s*
Basil *23s/7-8A*
Better Burger *8A/19s*
Biltmore Room *8A/24-5s*
Biricchino *29s/8A*
Bistro Cassis *14s/7-8A*
Bottino *10A/24-5s*
Bright Food Shop *8A/21s*
Burritoville *23s/7-8A*
Cafeteria *7A/17s*
Carriage House *18s/6-7A*
Chelsea Bistro *23s/8-9A*
Chelsea Grill *8A/16-7s*
Chelsea Ristorante *8A/15-6s*
Cuba Libre *8A/18-9s*
Dallas BBQ *8A/23s*
Daniella *8A/26s*
Da Umberto *17s/6-7A*
Diner 24 *8A/15s*
Don Giovanni *10A/22-3s*
East of Eighth *23s/7-8A*
El Cid *15s/8-9A*
elmo *7A/19-20s*
El Quijote *23s/7-8A*
Empire Diner *10A/22s*
F & B *23s/7-8A*
Francisco's Centro *23s/6-7A*
Gascogne *8A/17-8s*
Grand Sichuan *9A/24s*
Hale & Hearty *9A/15-6s*
Havana Chelsea *8A/19-20s*
Intermezzo *8A/20-1s*
Krispy Kreme *23s/7-8A*
La Belle Vie *8A/19-20s*
La Bergamote *9A/20s*
La Bottega *9A/17s*
La Lunchonette *10A/18s*
La Taza de Oro *8A/14-5s*
Le Gamin *9A/21s*
Le Madri *18s/7A*
Le Singe Vert *7A/19-20s*
Le Zie 2000 *7A/20-1s*
Magnifico *9A/22s*
Maroons *16s/7-8A*

Mary Ann's *8A/16s*
Matsuri *16s/9A*
Medina *10A/28-9s*
Merchants, N.Y. *7A/16-7s*
Monster Sushi *23s/6-7A*
Moonstruck *23s/9A*
Moran's Chelsea *10A/19s*
Negril *23s/8-9A*
Nisos *8A/19s*
O Mai *9A/19-20s*
Pad Thai *8A/15-6s*
Parish & Co. *9A/22s*
Park *10A/17-8s*
Patsy's Pizzeria *23s/8-9A*
Pepe ... To Go *10A/24-5s*
Petite Abeille *18s/6-7A*
Pizza 33 *23s/8A*
Porters *7A/22-3s*
Raymond's Cafe *7A/15-6s*
Red Cat *10A/23-4s*
Regional Thai *7A/22s*
Rocking Horse *8A/19-20s*
Royal Siam *8A/22-3s*
Salsa y Salsa *7A/21-2s*
Sarabeth's *9A/15-6s*
Sette *7A/21-2s*
Seven *7A/29-30s*
Snackbar *17s/6-7A*
Spice *8A/20-1s*
Starbucks *8A/22-3s*
Sueños *17s/8-9A*
Tello's *19s/7-8A*

Chinatown

(Bet. Hester & Pearl Sts.,
bet. Bowery & Bway)

Big Wong *Mott/Bayard-Canal*
Canton *Division/Bowery-Market*
Dim Sum Go Go *Bway/Chatham*
Evergreen Shan. *Mott/Bayard-Canal*
Excellent Dumpling *Lafayette/Canal*
Fuleen Sea. *Division/Bowery-E. Bway*
Golden Unicorn *E. Bway/Catherine*
Grand Sichuan *Canal/Bowery*
Great NY Noodle *Bowery/Bayard*
HSF *Bowery/Bayard-Canal*
Jing Fong *Elizabeth/Bayard-Canal*
Joe's Shanghai *multi. loc.*
Kam Chueh *Bowery/Bayard-Canal*

Cafe Trevi *1A/81-2s*
Caffe Grazie *84s/5A-Mad*
Carino *2A/88-9s*
Centolire *Mad/85-6s*
Chef Ho's *2A/89-90s*
Cilantro *2A/88-9s*
Dakshin Indian *1A/88-9s*
Divino *2A/80-1s*
Donguri *83s/1-2A*
DT.UT *2A/84-5s*
E.A.T. *Mad/80-1s*
Elaine's *2A/88-9s*
Elio's *2A/84-5s*
Erminia *83s/2-3A*
Etats-Unis *81s/2-3A*
Ethiopian *York/83-4s*
Firenze *2A/82-3s*
Giovanni 25 *83s/5A-Mad*
Girasole *82s/Lex-3A*
Heidelberg *2A/85-6s*
Ian *86s/1-2s*
Ichiro *2A/87-8s*
Ithaka *86s/1-2A*
Jackson Hole *2A/83-4s*
Jacques Brasserie *85s/2-3A*
Jasmine *2A/84s*
Kings' Carriage *82s/2-3A*
Ko Sushi *York/85s*
Krispy Kreme *3A/84-5s*
Le Boeuf/Mode *81s/E. End-York*
Lentini *2A/81s*
Le Pain Quotidien *Mad/84-5s*
Le Refuge *82s/Lex-3A*
Lili's Noodle *3A/84-5s*
Luca *1A/88-9s*
Mangiarini *2A/82-3s*
Maz Mezcal *86s/1-2A*
Miss Saigon *3A/80-1s*
Mocca *2A/82-3s*
Nicola's *84s/Lex*
Ota-Ya *2A/81-2s*
Our Place *3A/82s*
Paola's *84s/2-3A*
Papaya King *86s/3A*
Pastrami Queen *Lex/85-6s*
Pearson's BBQ *81s/Lex-3A*
Penang *2A/83s*
Pig Heaven *2A/80-1s*
Pintaile's Pizza *York/83-4s*
Poke *85s/1-2A*
Primavera *1A/82s*
Rughetta *85s/1-2A*
Sabor *2A/89s*
Saigon Grill *2A/88s*
Sala Thai *2A/89-90s*
Sharz Cafe *86s/1A-York*
Sirabella's *East End A/82-3s*
Sistina *2A/80-1s*
Sushi Sen-nin *3A/80-1s*

Taste *3A/80s*
Tevere *84s/Lex-3A*
Tony's Di Napoli *2A/83s*
Totonno Pizzeria *2A/80-1s*
Trattoria Pesce *3A/87-8s*
Triangolo *83s/1-2A*
Uno Chicago Grill *86s/2-3A*
Va Bene *2A/82-3s*
Viand *86s/2A*
Wu Liang Ye *86s/2-3A*
York Grill *York/88-9s*
Yuka *2A/80-1s*
Zócalo *82s/Lex-3A*

East 90s & 100s
(Bet. 90th & 110th Sts.)

Barking Dog *3A/94s*
Bistro du Nord *Mad/93s*
Brother Jimmy's BBQ *3A/93s*
Don Pedro's *2A/96s*
El Paso Taqueria *multi loc.*
Itzocan *Lex/101s*
Jackson Hole *Mad/91s*
Joanna's *92s/5A-Mad*
Mary Ann's *2A/93s*
Nick's *2A/93-4s*
92 *92s/Mad*
Osso Buco *3A/93s*
Pascalou *Mad/92-3s*
Pinocchio *1A/90-1s*
Pintaile's Pizza *91s/5A-Mad*
Sarabeth's *Mad/92-3s*
Starbucks *3A/92s*
Table d'Hôte *92s/Mad-Park*
Tre Pomodori *2A/90-1s*
Vico *Mad/92-3s*
Yura & Co. *multi. loc.*
Zebú Grill *92s/1-2A*

Financial District
(South of Murray St.)

Au Bon Pain *multi. loc.*
Au Mandarin *Vesey/Bway*
Battery Gardens *Battery Park*
Bayard's *Hanover/Pearl*
Bridge Cafe *Water/Dover*
Bull Run *William/Pine*
Burritoville *Water/Broad*
Chipotle *Bway/Whitehall*
Cosí *Vesey/W. Side Hwy.*
Delmonico's *Beaver/William*
Fino *Wall/Pearl*
14 Wall Street *Wall/Broad-Bway*
Fraunces Tavern *Pearl/Broad*
Gigino/Wagner Pk *Battery/West*
Hale & Hearty *Broad/Beaver*
Joseph's *Hanover/Pearl*
Lemongrass Grill *William/Maiden*
Les Halles *John/Bway-Nassau*

subscribe to zagat.com

Ess-a-Bagel *1A/21s*
Friend of a Farmer *Irving/18-9s*
Houston's *Park S./27s*
I Trulli *27s/Lex-Park S.*
Ixta *29s/Mad-Park*
Jaiya Thai *3A/28s*
Kalustyan's *Lex/28s*
Lady Mendl's *Irving Pl./17-8s*
Lamarca *22s/3A*
L'Annam *3A/28s*
La Petite Auberge *Lex/27-8s*
Les Halles *Park S./28-9s*
Los Dos Molinos *18s/Irving-Park S.*
Novitá *22s/Lex-Park S.*
Park Bistro *Park S./28-9s*
Paul & Jimmy's *18s/Irving-Park S.*
Pete's Tavern *18s/Irving*
Pinch, Pizza *Park S./28-9s*
Pongal *Lex/27-8s*
Pongsri Thai *2A/18s*
Pure Food *Irving/17-8s*
Rolf's *3A/22s*
Sal Anthony's *Irving/17-8s*
Sam's Noodle Shop *3A/29s*
Scopa *Mad/28s*
Scuba Sushi *Mad/27-8s*
71 Irving Place *Irving/18-9s*
Tabla *Mad/25s*
Texas Smokehouse *2A/25s*
Totonno Pizzeria *2A/26s*
Turkish Kitchen *3A/27-8s*
Union Pacific *22s/Lex-Park S.*
Vatan *3A/29s*
Yama *17s/Irving*

Greenwich Village

(Houston to 14th Sts., west of
Bway, excluding NoHo and
Meatpacking District)
Agave *7A S./Charles-W. 10s*
Aki *4s/Barrow-Jones*
Alfama *Hudson/Perry*
Alta *W. 10s/5-6A*
Annisa *Barrow/7A S.-W. 4s*
A.O.C. *Bleecker/Grove*
A.O.C. Bedford *Bedford/Downing*
Arté *9s/5A-University*
Arturo's Pizzeria *Houston/Thompson*
A Salt & Battery *Greenwich A/12-3s*
Au Bon Pain *8s/Mercer*
August *Bleecker-Charles-W. 10s*
Babbo *Waverly/MacDougal-6A*
Baluchi's *6A/Washington*
Barbuto *Washington/Jane-W. 12s*
Bar Pitti *6A/Bleecker-Houston*
BB Sandwich *3s/MacDougal-6A*
Bivio *Hudson/Horatio*
Blue Hill *Washingtion Pl./Wash. Sq.*
Blue Mill *Commerce/Barrow*
Blue Ribbon Bak. *Downing/Bedford*

Borgo Antico *13s/5A-University*
Burritoville *Bleecker/7A S.*
Butter *Lafayette/Astor Pl.-4s*
Cafe Asean *10s/Greenwich-6A*
Café de Bruxelles *Greenwich A/13s*
Cafe Español *multi. loc.*
Cafe Loup *13s/6-7A*
Cafe Spice *University/10-1s*
Caffe Rafaella *7A S./Charles-W. 10s*
Caffe Reggio *MacDougal/Bleecker*
CamaJe *MacDougal/Bl.-Houston*
Casa *Bedford/Commerce*
Chat 'n Chew *16s/A/11-2s*
Chez Brigitte *Greenwich A/Bank-7A*
Chez Jacqueline *MacDougal/Blckr*
Chez Michallet *Bedford/Grove*
Chow Bar *4s/W. 10s*
Cornelia St. Cafe *Cornelia/Bloocker*
Corner Bistro *W. 4s/Jane*
Cosí *multi. loc.*
Cowgirl *Hudson/W. 10s*
Cozy Soup/Burger *Bway/Astor*
Crispo *14s/7-8A*
Cru *5A/9s*
Cuba *Thompson/Bleecker*
Da Andrea *Hudson/Perry-W. 11s*
Dallas BBQ *University/8s*
Da Silvano *6A/Bleecker-Houston*
Deborah *Carmine/Bedford-Bleecker*
Do Hwa *Carmine/Bedford-7A S.*
EJ's Luncheonette *6A/9-10s*
El Charro Español *Charles/7A S.*
Elephant & Castle *Greenwich A/6-7s*
El Faro *Greenwich s/Horatio*
Emack & Bolio's *7A/13-4s*
Empire Szechuan *multi. loc.*
Evergreen Shanghai *Bway/10s*
Extra Virgin *W/ 4s/Charles-Perry*
Faan *6A/8s*
50 Carmine *Carm./Bedford-Bleeck.*
Fish *Bleecker/Jones*
Flor's Kitchen *Waverly/6-7A*
French Roast *6A/11s*
Gavroche *14s/7-8A*
Gobo *6A/8s-Waverly Pl.*
Gonzo *13s/6-7A*
good *Greenwich A/Bank-W. 12s*
Gotham B&G *12s/5A-University*
Gradisca *13s/6-7A*
Gray's Papaya *6A/8s*
Grey Dog's Coffee *Carmine/Bedford*
Gus' Place *Waverly Pl./6-7A*
Home *Cornelia/Bleecker-W. 4s*
Hue *Charles/Bleecker*
Il Cantinori *10s/Bway-University*
Il Mulino *3s/Sullivan-Thompson*
Indochine *Lafayette/Astor-4s*
'ino *Bedford/Downing-6A*
Inside *Jones/Bleecker-W. 4s*
I Tre Merli *W. 10s/7A*

Harlem/East Harlem

(East of Morningside Ave.,
bet. 110th & 157th Sts.)

Little Italy

(Bet. Canal & Delancey Sts.,
& Bowery & Lafayette)

Eight Mile Creek *Mulberry/Prince*
Ferrara *Grand/Mott-Mulberry*
Grotta Azzurra *Broome/Mulberry*
Il Cortile *Mulberry/Canal-Hester*
Il Fornaio *Mulberry/Grand-Hester*
Il Palazzo *Mulberry/Grand-Hester*
Kitchen Club *Prince/Mott*
La Mela *Mulberry/Broome-Grand*
Li Hua *Grand/Baxter*
Nyonya *Grand/Mott-Mulberry*
Pellegrino's *Mulberry/Grand-Hester*
Pho Bang *Mott/Broome-Grand*
Positano *Mulberry/Canal-Hester*
Sal Anthony's *Mulberry/Grand*
Taormina *Mulberry/Grand-Hester*
Umberto's Clam *Mulberry/Broome*
Vincent's *Mott/Hester*

Lower East Side
(Houston to Canal Sts.,
east of Bowery)
aka Cafe *Clinton/Rivington-Stanton*
Alias *Clinton/Rivington*
ápizz *Eldridge/Rivington-Stanton*
Azul Bistro *Stanton/Suffolk*
Basso Est *Orchard/Stanton*
Bereket *Houston/Orchard*
Chubo *Clinton/Houston-Stanton*
Cube 63 *Clinton/Rivington-Stanton*
Dish *Allen/Rivington-Stanton*
Epicerie *Orchard/Rivington-Stanton*
Essex *Essex/Rivington*
Grilled Cheese *Ludlow/Houston*
'inoteca *Rivington/Ludlow*
Katz's Deli *Houston/Ludlow*
Kuma Inn *Ludlow/Delancey-Riv.*
Le Père Pinard *Ludlow/Houston*
Les Enfants Terribles *Canal/Ludlow*
Oliva *Houston/Allen*
Paladar *Ludlow/Houston-Stanton*
Petrosino *Norfolk/Houston*
Salt *Clinton/Houston-Stanton*
Sammy's Roum. *Chrystie/Delancey*
Schiller's *Rivington/Norfolk*
71 Clinton *Clinton/Rivington-Stanton*
Suba *Ludlow/Delancey-Rivington*
teany *Rivington/Ludlow-Orchard*
Tenement *Ludlow/Rivington-Stanton*
WD-50 *Clinton/Rivington-Stanton*

Meatpacking District
(Gansevoort to 15th Sts.,
west of 9th Ave.)
5 Ninth *9A/Gansevoort*
Florent *Gansevoort/Greenwich-Wash.*
Frank's *10A/15s*
Highline *Washington/Little W. 12s*
Hog Pit BBQ *9A/13s*
Lotus *14s/9A-Washington*

Macelleria *Gansevoort/Greenwich s*
Markt *14s/9A*
Meet *Gansevoort/Washington*
Old Homestead *9A/14-5s*
One *Little W. 12s/Hudson-9A*
Paradou *Little W. 12s/Greenwich s*
Pastis *9A/Little W. 12s*
Pop Burger *9A/14-5s*
Rhône *Gansevoort/Greenwich-Wash.*
Son Cubano *14s/9A-Washington*
Spice Market *13s/9s*
Vento *Hudson/14s*
Zitoune *Gansevoort/Greenwich s*

Murray Hill
(30th to 40th Sts., east of 5th)
AQ Cafe *Park/37-8s*
Artisanal *32s/Mad-Park*
Asia de Cuba *Mad/37-8s*
Barbès *36s/5A-Mad*
Barking Dog *34s/Lex-3A*
Belluno *Lex/39-40s*
Better Burger *3A/37s*
Blockhead Burrito *3A/33-4s*
Carl's Steaks *3A/34s*
Chez Laurence *Mad/38s*
Cinque Terre *38s/Mad-Park*
Cosette *33s/Lex-3A*
Da Ciro *Lex/33-4s*
Earl's *3A/37s*
El Parador Cafe *34s/1-2A*
El Pote *2A/38-9s*
Ethos *3A/33-4s*
Evergreen Shanghai *38s/5A-Mad*
Fino *36s/5A-Mad*
Franchia *Park/34-5s*
Frère Jacques *37s/5A-Mad*
Grand Sichuan *Lex/33-4s*
Hangawi *32s/5A-Mad*
Iron Sushi *3A/30-1s*
Jackson Hole *3A/35s*
Josie's *3A/37s*
La Giara *3A/33-4s*
Lemongrass Grill *34s/Lex-3A*
Madison Bistro *Mad/37-8s*
Marchi's *31s/2-3A*
Mee Noodle Shop *2A/30-31s*
Metro Fish *36s/5A-Mad*
Minado *32s/5A-Mad*
Mishima *Lex/30-1s*
Moonstruck *multi. loc.*
Notaro *2A/34-5s*
Patsy's Pizzeria *3A/34-5s*
Penelope *Lex/30s*
Pizza 33 *3A/33s*
Pump Energy Food *31s/Lex-Park S.*
Rare B&G *Lex/37s*
Rossini's *38s/Lex-Park*
Salute! *Mad/39s*

West 50s

Carne *Bway/105s*
Empire Szechuan *Bway/100s*
Flor de Mayo *Bway/101s*
Henry's *Bway/105s*
Indus Valley *Bway/100s*
Kitchenette *Amst./122-23s*
Mamá Mexico *Bway/101-2s*
Max *Amst./123s*
Métisse *105s/Amst.-Bway*
Ollie's *Bway/116s*

107 West *Bway/107-8s*
Pisticci *La Salle/Bway*
Radio Perfecto *Amst./118s*
Sezz Medi' *Amst./122s*
Symposium *113s/Amst.-Bway*
Terrace in Sky *119s/Amst.-Morn.*
Tomo Sushi *Bway/110-11s*
Turkuaz *Bway/100s*
V&T *Amst./110-11s*

BRONX

Dominick's *Arthur/Crescent-E. 187s*
El Malecon *Bway/231s*
Enzo's *Williamsbridge/Neill*
F & J Pine *Bronxdale/White Plains*
Lobster Box *City Island/Belden*
Madison's *Riverdale/258s*

Mario's *Arthur/184-86s*
Nebraska Steak *187/Hoffman*
Park Place *Mosholu/Bway*
Riverdale Garden *Manh. Coll./242s*
Roberto's *Crescent/Hughes*
Umberto's Clam *Arthur/186s*

BROOKLYN

Bay Ridge

Areo *3A/84-5s*
Baci *3A/71s*
Chadwick's *3A/89s*
Chianti *3A/86s*
Eliá *3A/86-7s*
Embers *3A/95-6s*
Lento's *3A/Ovington*
Omonia Cafe *3A/76-7s*
101 *4A/100-1s*
Pearl Room *3A/82s*
Provence en Boite *3A/83-4s*
St. Michel *3A/Bay Ridge-76s*
Tanoreen *3A/77-8s*
Tuscany Grill *3A/86-7s*
Uno Chicago Grill *4A/92s*

Bensonhurst

L & B Spumoni *86s/W.10-11s*
Tommaso's *86s/14-5A*

Boerum Hill

Bacchus *Atlantic/Bond*
BarTabac *Smith/Dean*
Brawta Caribbean *Atlantic/Hoyt*
Chance *Smith/Butler*
Cholita *Smith/Bergen-Dean*
Downtown Atlantic *Atlantic/Bond*
Pacifico *Pacific/Smith*
Saul *Smith/Bergen-Dean*
Sherwood Cafe *Smith/Baltic*

Brooklyn Heights

Caffe Buon Gusto *Montague/Henry*
Chipotle *Montague/Court*
Curry Leaf *Remsen/Clinton-Court*
Fatoosh *Hicks/Atlantic*
Hale & Hearty *Court/Remsen*
Heights Cafe *Montague/Hicks*
Henry's End *Henry/Cranberry*

Kapadokya *Montague/Clinton-Henry*
Noodle Pudding *Henry/Cranberry*
Queen *Court/Livingston*
Teresa's *Montague/Hicks*

Carroll Gardens

Alma *Columbia/DeGraw*
Caserta Vecchia *Smith/Baltic-Butler*
Chestnut *Smith/DeGraw-Sackett*
Ferdinando's *Union/Columbia-Hicks*
Fragole *Court/Carroll-1 Pl.*
Grocery *Smith/Sackett-Union*
Marco Polo *Court/Union*
Panino'teca 275 *Smith/DeGraw*
Patois *Smith/DeGraw-Douglass*
Savoia *Smith/DeGraw-Sackett*
Zaytoons *Smith/Sackett*

Clinton Hill

Locanda Vini *Gates/Cambridge*

Cobble Hill

Banania Cafe *Smith/Douglass*
Blue Star *Court/DeGraw-Kane*
Cafe Luluc *Smith/Baltic*
Faan *Smith/Baltic*
Joya *Court/Warren*
Lemongrass Grill *Court/Dean-Pac.*
Mancora *Smith/Warren-Wyckoff*
Osaka *Court/DeGraw-Kane*
Quercy *Court/Baltic*
Sweet Melissa *Court/Butler*
Tuk Tuk *Smith/Baltic-Butler*

Coney Island

Gargiulo's *15s/Mermaid-Surf*
Totonno Pizzeria *Neptune/W. 15-6s*

Downtown

Junior's *Flatbush/DeKalb*

. **FEATURES**

each category. Multi-location
es may vary by branch.)

(See also ~~...~~)
A Salt & Battery
Balthazar
Barney Greengrass
Bayard's
Brasserie
Bubby's
Cafe Con Leche
Cafe Luxembourg
Cafe Mogador
Carnegie Deli
City Bakery
City Hall
Cup
Cupping Room
Delmonico's
Diner 24
E.A.T.
Edward's
Florent
14 Wall Street
Good Enough to Eat
Googie's
Havana Central
HK
Home
Katz's Deli
Kitchenette
La Table O & Co.
Mayrose
Michael's
Mix It
Nice Matin
NoHo Star
Norma's
Otto
Pastis
Payard Bistro
Penelope
Pershing Square
Rue 57
Schiller's
Second Ave Deli
SQC
Tartine
Taste
Teresa's
Veronica
Whole Foods Café

Brunch
Aix
America
Aquagrill
Aquavit
Artisanal
Balthazar
Bistro St. Mark's
Blue Water
Bubby's
Café de Bruxelles
Café des Artistes
Cafe Luxembourg
Capsouto Frères
Celeste
Chez Oskar
Cornelia St. Cafe
Danal
davidburke/donatella
Eleven Madison
Fifty Seven 57
Five Points
Gascogne
Halcyon
Isabella's
Le Gigot
L'Orange Bleue
Manhattan Grille
Mark's
Metropolitan Cafe
Odeon
Ouest
Palm Court
Patois
Petrossian
Pipa
Provence
Prune
Public
River Cafe
Rocking Horse
Sarabeth's
718
Spotted Pig
Spring St. Natural
Sueños
Sylvia's
Tartine
Taste
Tavern on Green
Tribeca Grill
Wallsé
Water Club

Cal. Pizza Kitchen
Dojo
elmo
ESPN Zone
French Roast
Googie's
Hard Rock Cafe
Jekyll & Hyde
Johnny Rockets
Lundy Bros.
Mars 2112
Mayrose
Mickey Mantle's
92
Pete's Tavern
Sardi's
Tavern on Green

Dancing

Lotus
Rainbow Room
Rasputin
Tavern on Green
World Yacht

Entertainment

(Call for days and times of
performances)
Alfama (fado/jazz)
Allioli (flamenco)
Blue Fin (jazz)
Blue Smoke (jazz)
Blue Water (jazz)
Café Pierre (piano player/singer)
Chez Josephine (jazz/piano)
Cooking with Jazz (blues/jazz)
Delta Grill (blues/jazz/zydeco)
FireBird (harp/piano)
Flor de Sol (flamenco)
Ideya (salsa)
Knickerbocker (jazz)
Layla (belly dancing)
Londel's (jazz)
Madiba (South African bands)
Marion's (burlesque)
Ñ (flamenco)
Nino's (piano)
Oliva (Latin jazz)
Rainbow Room (orchestra)
Rasputin (cabaret)
River Cafe (piano)
Russian Samovar (guitar/vocals)
Son Cubano (Cuban bands)
Svenningsen's (jazz vocals)
Sylvia's (blues/gospel/jazz)
Tavern on Green (DJ/piano)
39 East (jazz)
Tommaso's (opera/piano/singers)
Walker's (jazz)

Fireplaces

Adä
Bayard's
Caffé/Green
Chelsea Bistro
Cornelia St. Cafe
I Trulli
Keens Steak
La Lanterna
Loulou
Lumi
March
Metsovo
Moran's Chelsea
One if by Land
Patois
per se
Piccola Venezia
Place
Portofino Grille
René Pujol
Savoy
Uguale
Vince & Eddie's
Vivolo
Water's Edge
Ye Waverly Inn

Game in Season

Aesop's Tables
Al Di La
Aquavit
Babbo
Bayard's
Beacon
Beppe
Café des Artistes
Craft
Daniel
Eight Mile Creek
Felidia
Fiamma Osteria
Four Seasons
Gascogne
Henry's End
Il Mulino
I Trulli
Jean Georges
La Grenouille
Landmarc
Levana
Madiba
Ouest
Peasant
Piccola Venezia
Picholine
River Cafe
Saul
Tocqueville

Gracious Hosts

Canton, *Eileen Leong*
Chanterelle, *Karen Waltuck*
Chez Josephine, *J.C. Baker*
Chin Chin, *James Chin*
davidburke, *Donatella Arpaia*
Fresco by Scotto, *Marion Scotto*
Gus' Place, *Gus Theodoro*
Kitchen Club, *Marja Samsom*
La Grenouille, *Charles Masson*
La Mirabelle, *Annick Le Douaron*
Lenox Room, *Tony Fortuna*
Neary's, *Jimmy Neary*
Nino's, *Nino Selimaj*
Paola's, *Paola Marracino*
Primavera, *Nicola Civetta*
Rao's, *Frank Pellegrino*
San Domenico, *Tony May*
Tasting Room, *Renée Alevras*
Tocqueville, *Jo-Ann Makovitzky*
Tommaso's, *Thomas Verdillo*

Historic Places

(Year opened; * building)

1763 Fraunces Tavern
1794 Bridge Cafe*
1826 Sazerac House*
1851 Bayard's*
1864 Pete's Tavern
1868 Old Homestead
1880 White Horse Tav.
1884 P.J. Clarke's
1885 Keens Steak
1887 Peter Luger
1888 Katz's Deli
1889 Amuse*
1890 Walker's*
1892 Ferrara
1894 Veniero's
1896 Rao's
1900 Bamonte's
1902 Algonquin Hotel
1902 Angelo's/Mulberry
1904 Ferdinando's
1904 Vincent's
1906 Barbetta
1907 Gargiulo's*
1907 Oak Room
1907 Palm Court
1908 Barney Greengrass
1908 Grotta Azzurra
1908 John's 12th Street
1909 Guastavino's*
1913 Oyster Bar
1917 Café des Artistes
1919 Mario's
1920 Blue Mill*
1920 Ye Waverly Inn
1921 Sardi's

1922 Fanelli's Cafe
1922 Rocco
1925 El Charro Español
1926 Palm
1927 Caffe Reggio
1927 El Faro
1927 Gallagher's Steak
1929 21 Club
1930 El Quijote
1930 Marchi's
1931 Café Pierre
1932 Pietro's
1934 Rainbow Room
1936 Tom's
1937 Carnegie Deli
1937 Denino's
1937 Le Veau d'Or
1937 Minetta Tavern
1937 Stage Deli
1938 Brennan & Carr
1938 Heidelberg
1938 Wo Hop
1941 Sevilla
1944 Patsy's
1945 Gino
1945 V&T
1946 Lobster Box
1947 Delegates Din. Rm.
1949 L & B Spumoni
1950 Junior's
1950 Marion's
1950 Pierre au Tunnel
1953 McHales
1954 Pink Tea Cup
1954 Second Ave Deli
1954 Serendipity 3
1954 Veselka

Holiday Meals

Beacon
Bellini
Café Botanica
Café des Artistes
Café Pierre
Chelsea Bistro
Chez Michallet
Duane Park Cafe
FireBird
Four Seasons
Fresco by Scotto
Gotham B&G
Gramercy Tavern
Halcyon
Molyvos
One C.P.S.
One if by Land
Ouest
Park Ave Cafe
Provence
River Cafe

Sea Grill
Tavern on Green
Terrace in Sky
Water Club
Water's Edge
Ye Waverly Inn

Hotel Dining

(Best of many)
Alex/Riingo
Algonquin/Algonquin
Carlyle/Dumonet
Chambers/Town
City Club/db Bistro Moderne
Elysée/Monkey Bar
Essex Hse.
    Alain Ducasse
    Café Botanica
Four Seasons/Fifty Seven 57
Hudson/Hudson Caf
Le Parker Meridien
    burger joint
    Norma's
    Seppi's
Lowell/Post House
Mandarin Oriental/Asiate
Maritime Hotel
    La Bottega
    Matsuri
Mark/Mark's
Marriott Financial/Roy's NY
Mercer/Mercer Kitchen
Morgans/Asia de Cuba
Peninsula/Fives
Pierre/Café Pierre
Plaza
    Oak Room
    One C.P.S.
    Oyster Bar/Plaza
    Palm Court
Regency/Regency
Ritz-Carlton CPS/Atelier
Royalton/44
Sherry Netherland
    Harry Cipriani
60 Thompson/Kittichai
Surrey/Café Boulud
Time/Océo
Trump Int'l/Jean Georges
Waldorf-Astoria
    Bull & Bear
    Inagiku
W Times Sq./Blue Fin
W Union Sq./Olives

Jacket Required

(* Tie also required)
Alain Ducasse*
Atelier

Aureole
Café Pierre
Daniel
Delegates Din. Rm.
Dumonet
Four Seasons
Gramercy Tavern
Harry Cipriani
Jean Georges
La Grenouille*
Le Bernardin
Le Cirque 2000
Picholine
Rainbow Room*
River Cafe
San Domenico
21 Club*
World Yacht

Jury Duty

(Near Foley Sq.)
Arqua
Big Wong
Bread Tribeca
City Hall
Da Nico
Ecco
Great NY Noodle
HSF
Il Cortile
Il Fornaio
Le Zinc
New Bo-Ky
New Green Bo
New Pasteur
Nha Trang
Odeon
Oriental Garden
Pho Viet Huong
Pongsri Thai
Taormina
UK New York
Wo Hop

Late Dining

(Besides most diners and
delis; weekday closing hour)
Angura (2 AM)
Arturo's Pizzeria (1 AM)
Avenue A Sushi (2 AM)
Balthazar (1 AM)
Bao 111 (2 AM)
Baraonda (1 AM)
BarTabac (1 AM)
Bar Tonno (3 AM)
Bereket (24 hrs.)
Big Nick's Burger (24 hrs.)
Blue Ribbon (2 AM)
Blue Ribbon Sushi (2 AM)

Brennan & Carr (1 AM)
Bubba Gump (1 AM)
Cafe Lalo (2 AM)
Cafeteria (24 hrs.)
Caffe Reggio (2 AM)
Carnegie Deli (4 AM)
Carriage House (1 AM)
Casa Mono (24 hrs.)
Cávo (2 AM)
Chez Josephine (1 AM)
Coffee Shop (5:30 AM)
Corner Bistro (3:30 AM)
Cosmic Cantina (5 AM)
Cozy Soup/Burger (24 hrs.)
Cup (24 hrs.)
Diner 24 (24 hrs.)
East Lake (2 AM)
Edgar's Cafe (1 AM)
Eight Mile Creek (1 AM)
Elaine's (2 AM)
elmo (1 AM)
Empire Diner (24 hrs.)
Fanelli's Cafe (1 AM)
Fiorello's Cafe (2 AM)
Florent (5 AM)
Frank (1 AM)
French Roast (24 hrs.)
Fuleen Seafood (4 AM)
Gam Mee Ok (24 hrs.)
Grace (4 AM)
Gray's Papaya (24 hrs.)
Great NY Noodle (3:30 AM)
HK (1 AM)
'ino (2 AM)
'inoteca (3 AM)
Jasper (2 AM)
J.G. Melon (2:30 AM)
Kam Chueh (3:30 AM)
Kang Suh (24 hrs.)
Kiev (24 hrs.)
Kum Gang San (24 hrs.)
La Bottega (1 AM)
La Lanterna (3 AM)
La Mela (2 AM)
Landmarc (2 AM)
Le Souk (2 AM)
L'Express (24 hrs.)
Lil' Frankie's Pizza (2 AM)
Lucky Strike (2 AM)
Luke's Bar/Grill (2 AM)
Marion's (2 AM)
Merchants, N.Y. (2 AM)
Ñ (2 AM)
Neary's (1 AM)
No. 1 Chinese (2 AM)
Odeon (2 AM)
Omen (1 AM)
Omonia Cafe (2 AM)
One (1 AM)

Park (1 AM)
Pastis (1 AM)
Perbacco (1 AM)
Pigalle (24 hrs.)
P.J. Clarke's (3 AM)
Planet Thailand (1 AM)
Pop Burger (4 AM)
Raoul's (2 AM)
Sahara (5 AM)
Sandobe (1:30 AM)
Sarge's Deli (24 hrs.)
Seppi's (2 AM)
Spotted Pig (2 AM)
SushiSamba (1 AM)
Sushi Seki (3 AM)
Three of Cups (1 AM)
Tio Pepe (1 AM)
212 (1 AM)
Uncle George's (4 AM)
Veselka (24 hrs.)
Vincent's (2 AM)
Walker's (1 AM)
West Bank Cafe (1 AM)
White Horse Tav. (2 AM)
Wo Hop (24 hrs.)
Wollensky's Grill (2 AM)
Won Jo (24 hrs.)

Meet for a Drink

(Most top hotels, bars and
the following standouts)
Amuse
Artisanal
Balthazar
Barbalùc
Biltmore Room
Blue Fin
Boat Basin Cafe
Boat House
Bond Street
Brick Cafe
Bryant Park Cafe/Grill
Cafe Luxembourg
City Hall
Dos Caminos
Eight Mile Creek
Four Seasons
Geisha
Gotham B&G
Grace
Guastavino's
HK
Keens Steak
La Bottega
Le Colonial
Lenox Room
L'Impero
Maloney & Porcelli
Mark's

Pylos, *Greek*
Red Café, *American*
Rêve, *French/Asian fusion*
Rickshaw Dumpling*, *Chinese*
Riingo, *American/Sushi*
Riverdale Garden, *American*
Riverview, *Eclectic*
Roe*, *Asian fusion*
R.U.B.*, *Barbecue*
Sachi's/25 Clinton*, *Japanese*
Sant Ambroeus, *Italian*
Sapa*, *French/Vietnamese*
Saravanaas*, *Indian*
Scottadito*, *Italian*
Scuba Sushi, *Asian fusion*
Seafood Factory*, *Seafood*
Sette, *Italian*
718, *French*
Shanghai Pavilion, *Chinese*
Silverleaf Tavern*, *American*
Sip Sak, *Turkish*
Soho Cantina, *Mexican*
Solo, *Kosher Mediterranean*
Spice Market, *SE Asian*
Spotted Pig, *Gastropub*
Stanton Social*, *Small Plates*
Starwich, *Sandwiches*
Strata, *American*
Sui, *Japanese fusion*
Sumile, *Japanese*
Sunburnt Cow, *Australian*
Swagat Indian, *Indian*
Taboon, *Mideastern/Med.*
Taksim, *Turkish*
Tempo*, *Mediterranean*
Texas Smokehouse, *barbecue*
39 East, *Asian fusion*
Trinity, *American*
Turmeric, *Indian*
UK New York, *British*
Uno Pizza Napoletana*, *Pizza*
Vela, *Japanese*
Vento, *Italian*
Viet Cafe*, *Vietnamese*
V, *Steakhouse*
Wakiya*, *Chinese*
Waldy's*, *Pizza*
Whole Foods, *Eclectic*
Wolfgang's, *Steakhouse*
Yuca Bar, *Pan-Latin*
Zeytin, *Turkish*
Zipi Zape, *Spanish*
Zona Rosa, *Mexican*

Outdoor Dining

(G=garden; P=patio;
S=sidewalk; T=terrace)
Aesop's Tables (G)
Allioli (G)

Alma (T)
A.O.C. (G)
Aquagrill (T)
Azalea (S)
Barbetta (G)
Barolo (G)
Bar Pitti (S)
Battery Gardens (P, T)
Blue Hill (G, P)
Blue Water (T)
Boat Basin Cafe (P)
Boat House (T)
Bottino (G)
Bryant Park (G, P, S)
Bubby's (S)
Cafe Centro (S)
Café St. Bart's (T)
Caffe Rafaella (S)
Cávo (G, P)
Chestnut (G)
Convivium Osteria (G)
Da Silvano (S)
Dolphins (G)
East of Eighth (G)
Esca (P)
Fiorello's Cafe (S)
Gascogne (G)
Gavroche (G)
Gigino/Wagner Pk (P)
Grocery (G)
Harbour Lights (T)
I Coppi (G)
Il Palazzo (G, S)
Isabella's (S)
I Trulli (G)
La Bottega (T)
Lattanzi (G)
Le Refuge (G)
L'Impero (P)
Long Tan (G)
Loulou (G)
March (T)
Marichu (P)
Markt (S, T)
Metropolitan Cafe (G)
New Leaf (P)
Ocean Grill (S)
Pace (T)
Pampano (T)
Panino'teca 275 (G)
Paradou (G)
Park (G)
Pastis (T)
Patois (G)
Pete's Tavern (S)
Pure Food (G)
River Cafe (G)
Riverview (P, T)
Sahara (G)

Sea Grill (G)
Sherwood Cafe (G)
SouthWest NY (T)
Steamers (T)
Surya (G)
Tartine (S)
Tavern on Green (G)
Terrace in Sky (T)
Top of the Tower (T)
Va Tutto (G)
Vento (S)
Vera Cruz (G)
ViceVersa (G)
Vittorio Cucina (G)
Water Club (P)
Water's Edge (P)
Zum Schneider (G, S)

People-Watching

Angus McIndoe
Asia de Cuba
Babbo
Balthazar
Barbuto
Bar Pitti
Bice
Blue Water
Da Silvano
Elio's
Fresco by Scotto
Il Cantinori
Indochine
Joe Allen
La Grenouille
Le Cirque 2000
Matsuri
Mr. Chow
Nobu
Pastis
Sardi's
Schiller's
Spice Market
Town
212

Power Scenes

Bayard's
Ben Benson's
City Hall
Coco Pazzo
Daniel
Delmonico's
Elio's
44
Four Seasons
Fresco by Scotto
Gabriel's
Gallagher's Steak
Gotham B&G
Harry Cipriani

Jean Georges
Keens Steak
La Grenouille
Le Bernardin
Le Cirque 2000
Michael's
Nobu
Peter Luger
Rao's
Regency
Smith & Wollensky
Sparks Steak
21 Club

Private Rooms/Parties

(Call for capacity)

Amuse
Barbetta
Battery Gardens
Bayard's
Blue Hill
Blue Water
Capital Grille
Cellini
Centolire
City Hall
Compass
Daniel
Del Frisco's
Delmonico's
Eleven Madison
ESPN Zone
Fiamma Osteria
F.illi Ponte
FireBird
Four Seasons
Fresco by Scotto
Gramercy Tavern
Guastavino's
Harbour Lights
Il Buco
Il Cortile
Jean Georges
Jezebel
Josephs
Keens Steak
La Grenouille
Le Bernardin
Lever House
L'Impero
Maloney & Porcelli
March
Megu
Michael's
Mi Cocina
Milos
Moran's Chelsea
Morton's Steak
Mr. Chow

Mr. K's
Oceana
One C.P.S.
Park
Park Ave Cafe
Patroon
Periyali
per se
Picholine
Redeye Grill
Remi
Re Sette
River Cafe
Rock Center Café
Sardi's
Scopa
Shelly's NY
Solo
Sparks Steak
Strata
Tao
Tavern on Green
Terrace in Sky
Thalassa
Trattoria Dopo
Tribeca Grill
Tuscan
21 Club
212
Vento
Vine
Water Club
Water's Edge

Pubs/Microbreweries

(See Zagat *NYC Nightlife*)
Angus McIndoe
Corner Bistro
Druids
Fanelli's Cafe
Gramercy Tavern
Heartland Brew.
J.G. Melon
Joe Allen
Keens Steak
Knickerbocker
Luke's Bar/Grill
Markt
McHales
Moran's Chelsea
Neary's
Pete's Tavern
P.J. Clarke's
Spotted Pig
St. Andrews
Typhoon
Walker's
White Horse Tav.
Wollensky's Grill

Quick Bites

Amy's Bread
A Salt & Battery
Azuri Cafe
BB Sandwich
Bereket
Brennan & Carr
Burritoville
Carl's Steaks
China Fun
Chip/CurryShop
City Bakery
Columbus Bakery
Cosí
Cosmic Cantina
Daisy May's BBQ
F & B
Fresco on the Go
Gray's Papaya
Grilled Cheese
Hale & Hearty
Hampton Chutney
'ino
Joe's Pizza
Papaya King
Press 195
Pump Energy Food
Quintessence
Rice 'n' Beans
Risotteria
Whole Foods Café
'wichcraft
Zabar's Cafe

Quiet Conversation

Asiate
Atelier
Bouterin
Café Botanica
Café Pierre
Chanterelle
Dumonet
Honmura An
Jean Georges
Kai
Kings' Carriage
La Grenouille
Le Bernardin
Le Madri
March
Mark's
Masa
Mr. K's
Petrossian
Picholine
rm
Terrace in Sky
Tocqueville
Tsampa

Sleepers
(Good to excellent
food, but little known)
Caviar Russe
Donguri
Eliá
Fives
Ivo & Lulu
Kam Chueh
Kuruma Zushi
La Cantina
Marinella
Mo-Bay
Nebraska Steak
Nippon
Pão!
Petrosino
Pisticci
Rocco
Sapori d'Ischia
Soba Nippon
Tevere
Veronica

Sunday Best Bets
(See also Hotel Dining)
America
Aquagrill
Artisanal
Balthazar
Blue Ribbon
Blue Water
Café de Bruxelles
Café des Artistes
Chez Michallet
Coco Pazzo
Five Points
La Mediterranée
Lupa
Mesa Grill
Mi Cocina
Moran's Chelsea
Odeon
Ouest
Park
Peter Luger
Prune
River Cafe
66
Tavern on Green
Trattoria Dell'Arte
Union Sq. Cafe
Water Club
Zoë

Tasting Menus
($ minimum)
Aix (92)
Alain Ducasse (150)

Annisa (68)
Asiate (85)
Atelier (128)
Aureole (89)
Babbo (59)
Blue Hill (65)
Bouley (75)
Café Boulud (105)
Chanterelle (105)
Cru (72)
Daniel (120)
Danube (75)
davidburke/donatella (75)
Eleven Madison (65)
Esca (65)
Fleur de Sel (75)
Four Seasons (120)
Gramercy Tavern (95)
Grocery (65)
Hearth (58)
Il Buco (65)
Jean Georges (118)
Jewel Bako (75)
Kai (110)
La Grenouille (115)
Le Bernardin (100)
Le Cirque 2000 (105)
Le Perigord (85)
L'Impero (85)
March (72)
Mark's (62)
Marseille (65)
Mas (68)
Masa (300)
Michael's (90)
Montrachet (79)
Oceana (110)
One if by Land (79)
Osteria del Circo (65)
Patria (79)
Payard Bistro (62)
per se (150)
Picholine (125)
River Cafe (90)
rm (100)
San Domenico (70)
Scalini Fedeli (85)
66 (66)
Solo (85)
Tabla (75)
Terrace in Sky (90)
Tocqueville (75)
Triomphe (75)
21 Club (70)
Union Pacific (85)
Vong (68)
Wallsé (85)
WD-50 (95)

Tea Service
Alice's Tea Cup
Café Pierre
Cafe S.F.A.
Danal
Franchia
Kai
Kings' Carriage
Lady Mendl's
Limoncello
Mark's
North Sq.
Palm Court
Payard Bistro
Sarabeth's
Sweet Melissa
Tea & Sympathy
Tea Box
teany

Theme Restaurants
Brooklyn Diner
Bubba Gump
ESPN Zone
Hard Rock Cafe
Jekyll & Hyde
Johnny Rockets
Mars 2112
Mickey Mantle's
Shula's Steak

Transporting Experience
Asiate
Bayard's
Boat House
Café des Artistes
Chez Josephine
FireBird
Il Buco
Jezebel
Keens Steak
Le Colonial
Masa
Matsuri
Megu
One if by Land
per se
Rainbow Room
Vatan
Water's Edge

Trendy
Balthazar
Biltmore Room
Casa Mono
'Cesca
Craft
davidburke/donatella
5 Ninth

Geisha
Hearth
'inoteca
Jewel Bako
Landmarc
L'Impero
Matsuri
Megu
Pastis
Schiller's
Spice Market
Spotted Pig

Views
Alma
Asiate
Battery Gardens
Boat Basin Cafe
Boat House
Bryant Park Cafe/Grill
Café Gray
Cafe S.F.A.
Caffé/Green
Cipriani Dolci
Delegates Din. Rm.
Five Front
Foley's Fish
Gigino/Wagner Pk
Harbour Lights
Heights Cafe
Hispaniola
Lake Club
Lobster Box
Marina Cafe
Michael Jordan's
per se
Pete's Downtown
Rainbow Room
River Cafe
Riverdale Garden
Riverview
Sea Grill
SouthWest NY
Steamers
Tavern on Green
Terrace in Sky
Top of the Tower
V Steakhouse
Water Club
Water's Edge
World Yacht

Visitors on Expense Account
Alain Ducasse
Bouley
Chanterelle
Craft
Daniel

Del Frisco's
Four Seasons
Il Mulino
Jean Georges
Kuruma Zushi
Lever House
Masa
Megu
Milos
per se
Petrossian
Primavera
Scalinatella
Scalini Fedeli

Waterside

Alma
Battery Gardens
Boat House
Caffé/Green
Grimaldi's
Harbour Lights
Lake Club
Lobster Box
Marina Cafe
River Cafe
Riverview
SouthWest NY
Steamers
Water Club
Water's Edge
World Yacht

Winning Wine Lists

Alain Ducasse
Atelier
Aureole
Babbo
Barbetta
Bayard's
Bouley
Chanterelle
Cité
Craft
Cru

Daniel
Danube
Del Frisco's
Dumonet
Eleven Madison
Felidia
Four Seasons
Gotham B&G
Gramercy Tavern
'inoteca
I Trulli
Jean Georges
La Grenouille
Landmarc
Le Bernardin
Le Cirque 2000
Le Perigord
L'Impero
Maloney & Porcelli
Manhattan Ocean
March
Michael's
Montrachet
Morrells
Oceana
Oyster Bar
Patria
per se
Piccola Venezia
Picholine
Post House
Remi
River Cafe
Scalini Fedeli
Smith & Wollensky
Sparks Steak
Tasting Room
Tavern on Green
Tocqueville
Tommaso's
21 Club
Union Sq. Cafe
Veritas
Water Club

Vintage Chart

...rt is designed to help you select wine to go with ...eal. It is based on the same 0 to 30 scale used ...ghout this *Survey*. The ratings (prepared by our ...nd **Howard Stravitz**, a law professor at the University ...South Carolina) reflect both the quality of the vintage ...nd the wine's readiness for present consumption. Thus, if a wine is not fully mature or is over the hill, its rating has been reduced. We do not include 1987, 1991–1993 vintages because they are not especially recommended for most areas. A dash indicates that a wine is either past its peak or too young to rate.

	'85	'86	'88	'89	'90	'94	'95	'96	'97	'98	'99	'00	'01	'02	'03
WHITES															
French:															
Alsace	24	–	22	28	28	27	26	25	25	26	25	26	27	25	–
Burgundy	26	25	–	24	22	–	28	29	24	23	26	25	23	27	24
Loire Valley	–	–	–	–	24	–	20	23	22	–	24	25	23	27	26
Champagne	28	25	24	26	29	–	26	27	24	24	25	25	26	–	–
Sauternes	21	28	29	25	27	–	21	23	26	24	24	24	28	25	26
Germany	25	–	25	26	27	25	24	27	24	23	25	24	29	27	–
California (Napa, Sonoma, Mendocino):															
Chardonnay	–	–	–	–	–	–	–	24	26	25	25	24	27	29	–
Sauvignon Blanc/Semillon	–	–	–	–	–	–	–	–	–	25	25	23	27	28	26
REDS															
French:															
Bordeaux	24	25	24	26	29	22	26	25	23	25	24	28	26	23	24
Burgundy	23	–	21	24	26	–	26	28	25	22	28	22	24	27	–
Rhône	25	19	27	29	29	24	25	23	24	28	27	27	26	–	25
Beaujolais	–	–	–	–	–	–	–	–	–	–	23	24	–	25	28
California (Napa, Sonoma, Mendocino):															
Cab./Merlot	27	26	–	21	28	29	27	25	28	23	26	23	27	25	–
Pinot Noir	–	–	–	–	–	–	–	–	24	24	25	24	26	29	–
Zinfandel	–	–	–	–	–	–	–	–	–	–	–	–	26	26	–
Italian:															
Tuscany	–	–	–	–	25	22	25	20	29	24	28	26	25	–	–
Piedmont	–	–	–	27	28	–	23	27	27	25	25	28	23	–	–